deus ex machina (DAY-us ex MAH-kin-ah):
Literally, "god from the machine." A person or force that arrives to provide an improbable solution to an impossible situation, named after the mechanical device used by Greek dramatists to lower actors playing deities onto the stage.

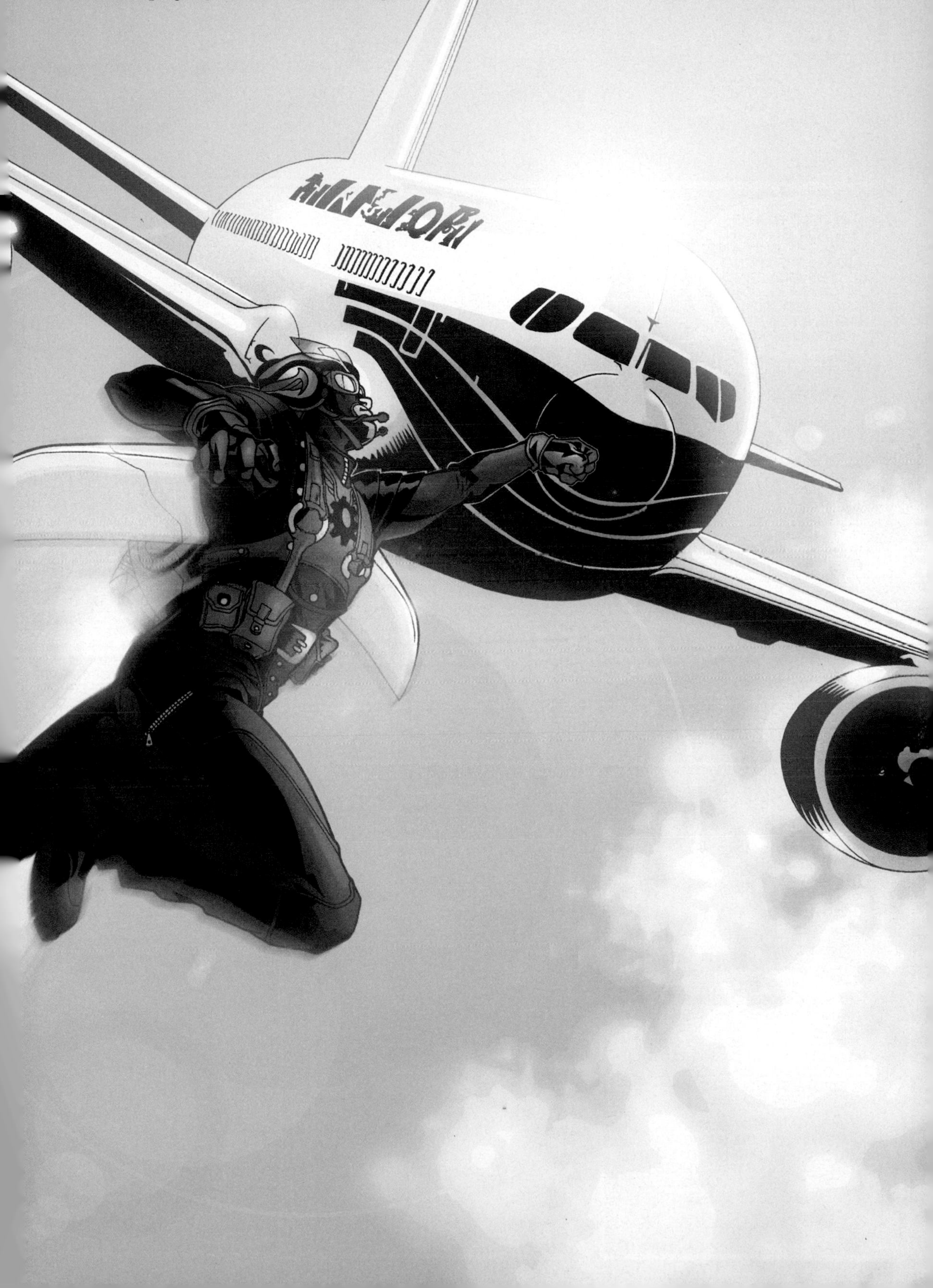

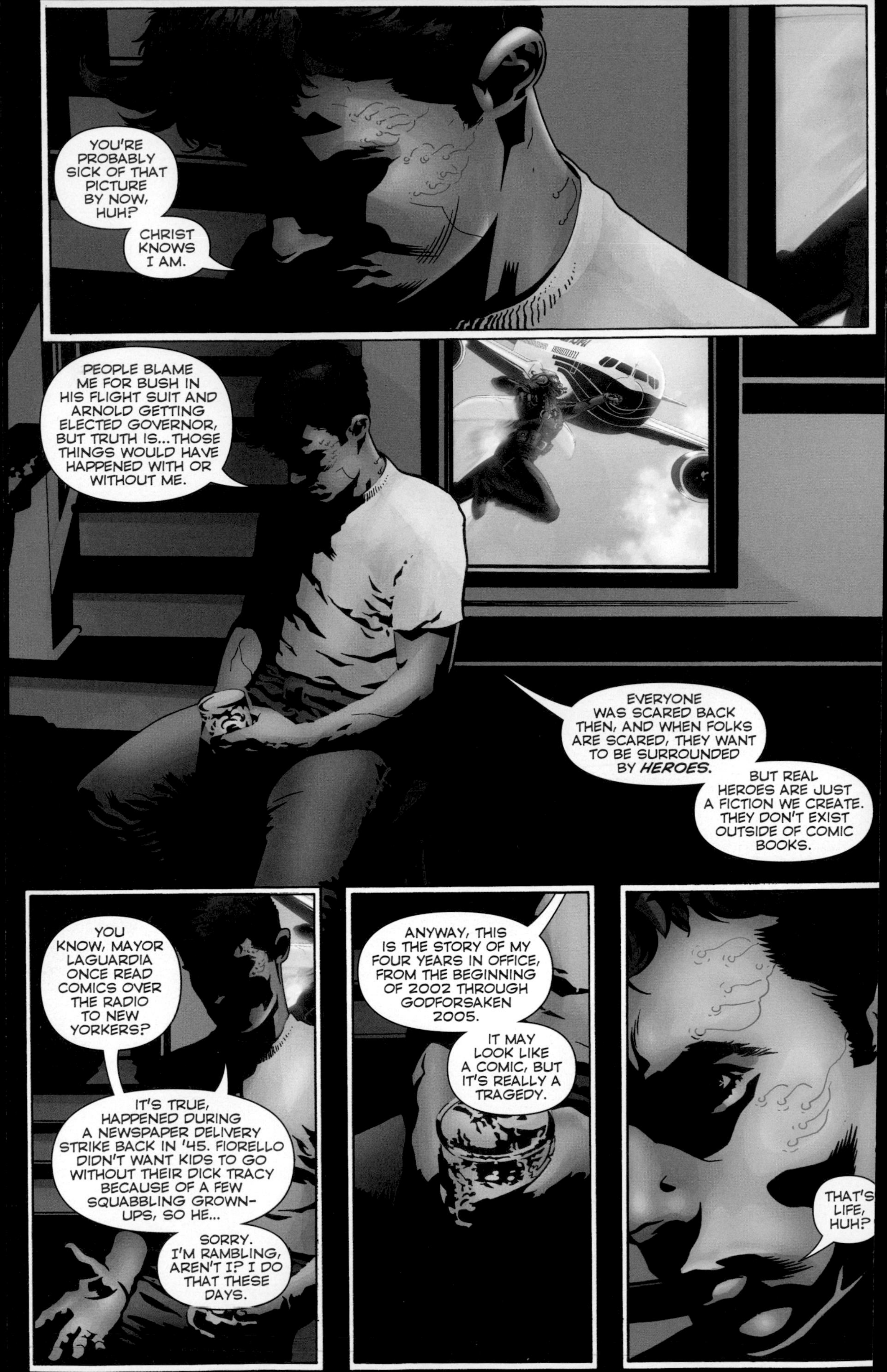
YOU'RE PROBABLY SICK OF THAT PICTURE BY NOW, HUH?
CHRIST KNOWS I AM.
PEOPLE BLAME ME FOR BUSH IN HIS FLIGHT SUIT AND ARNOLD GETTING ELECTED GOVERNOR, BUT TRUTH IS...THOSE THINGS WOULD HAVE HAPPENED WITH OR WITHOUT ME.
EVERYONE WAS SCARED BACK THEN, AND WHEN FOLKS ARE SCARED, THEY WANT TO BE SURROUNDED BY HEROES.
BUT REAL HEROES ARE JUST A FICTION WE CREATE. THEY DON'T EXIST OUTSIDE OF COMIC BOOKS.
YOU KNOW, MAYOR LAGUARDIA ONCE READ COMICS OVER THE RADIO TO NEW YORKERS?
IT'S TRUE, HAPPENED DURING A NEWSPAPER DELIVERY STRIKE BACK IN '45. FIORELLO DIDN'T WANT KIDS TO GO WITHOUT THEIR DICK TRACY BECAUSE OF A FEW SQUABBLING GROWN-UPS, SO HE...
SORRY. I'M RAMBLING, AREN'T I? I DO THAT THESE DAYS.
ANYWAY, THIS IS THE STORY OF MY FOUR YEARS IN OFFICE, FROM THE BEGINNING OF 2002 THROUGH GODFORSAKEN 2005.
IT MAY LOOK LIKE A COMIC, BUT IT'S REALLY A TRAGEDY.
THAT'S LIFE, HUH?

EX MACHINA

BOOK 1:
THE FIRST HUNDRED DAYS

Brian K. Vaughan: Writer

Tony Harris: Pencils & Covers

Tom Feister: Inks

JD Mettler: Colors

Jared K. Fletcher: Letters

Larry Berry: Design

Ex Machina created by Vaughan and Harris

Ben Abernathy, Editor–Original Series **Kristy Quinn,** Assistant Editor–Original Series **Alex Sinclair,** Editor
Bob Harras, Group Editor–Collected Editions **Robbin Brosterman,** Design Director–Books **Larry Berry,** Art Director

Diane Nelson, President **Dan DiDio and Jim Lee,** Co-Publishers
Geoff Johns, Chief Creative Officer **John Rood,** Executive Vice President–Sales, Marketing and Business Development
Patrick Caldon, Executive Vice President–Finance and Administration **Karen Berger,** Senior VP–Executive Editor, Vertigo
Amy Genkins, Senior VP–Business and Legal Affairs **Steve Rotterdam,** Senior VP–Sales and Marketing
John Cunningham, VP–Marketing **Terri Cunningham,** VP–Managing Editor **Alison Gill,** VP–Manufacturing
David Hyde, VP–Publicity **Sue Pohja,** VP–Book Trade Sales **Alysse Soll,** VP–Advertising and Custom Publishing
Bob Wayne, VP–Sales **Mark Chiarello,** Art Director

ISBN: 978-1-4012-0612-3

EX MACHINA: THE FIRST HUNDRED DAYS. Published by DC Comics, 1700 Broadway, New York, NY 10019. Cover, compilation copyright © 2005 Brian K. Vaughan and Tony Harris. All Rights Reserved. EX MACHINA is ™ Brian K. Vaughan and Tony Harris. **Originally published** by WildStorm in single magazine form as EX MACHINA #1-5 © 2004 Brian K. Vaughan and Tony Harris.

Vertigo and logo are ™ ... are entirely fictional. Printed on recyclable paper. Vertigo ... Printed in the United States. 12/08/2010. Fourth Pri...

DC Comics, a Warner B...

60000 0000 46384

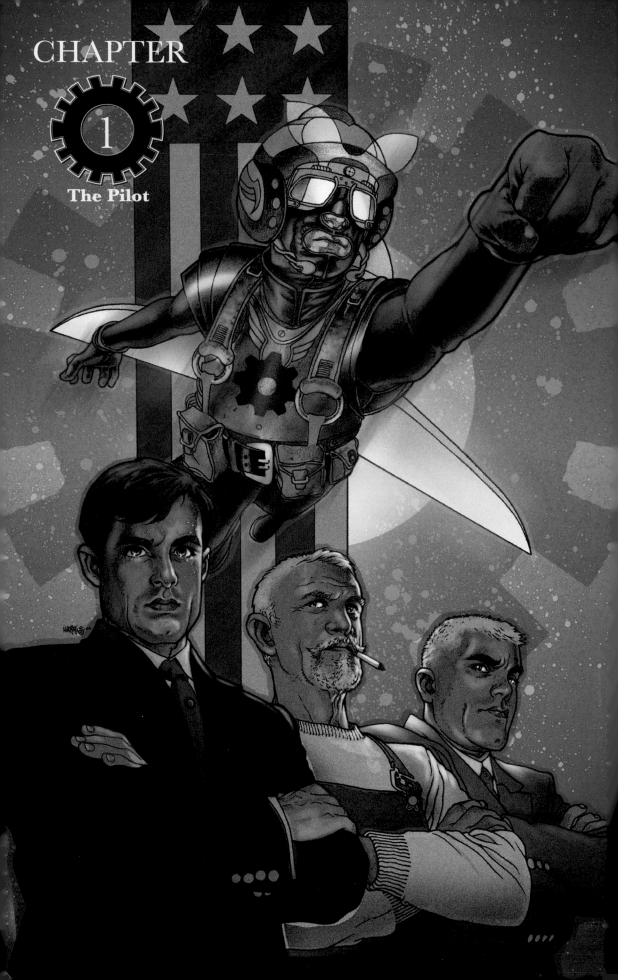

CHAPTER

1

The Pilot

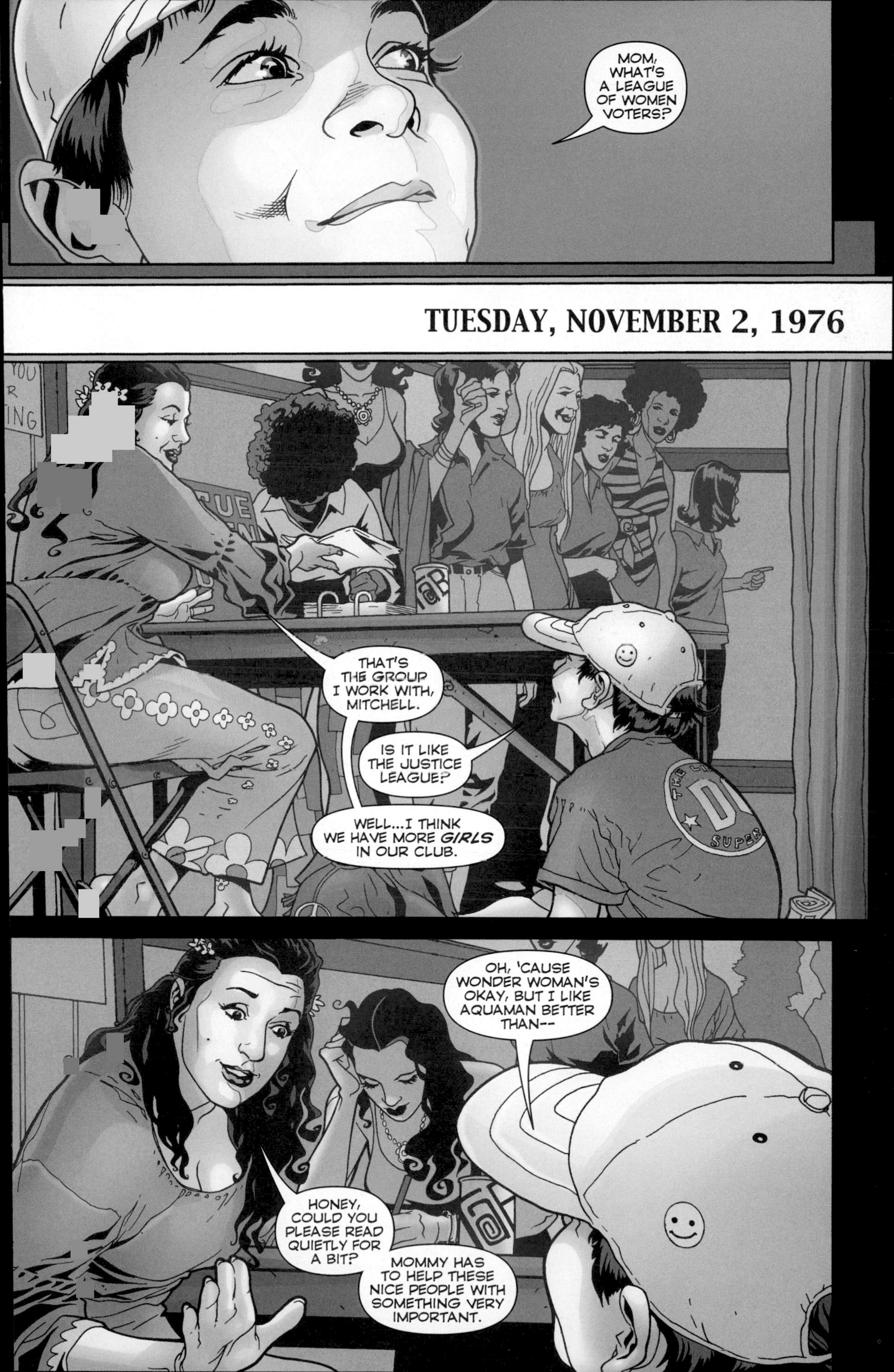
MOM, WHAT'S A LEAGUE OF WOMEN VOTERS?
TUESDAY, NOVEMBER 2, 1976
THAT'S THE GROUP I WORK WITH, MITCHELL.
IS IT LIKE THE JUSTICE LEAGUE?
WELL...I THINK WE HAVE MORE *GIRLS* IN OUR CLUB.
OH, 'CAUSE WONDER WOMAN'S OKAY, BUT I LIKE AQUAMAN BETTER THAN--
HONEY, COULD YOU PLEASE READ QUIETLY FOR A BIT?
MOMMY HAS TO HELP THESE NICE PEOPLE WITH SOMETHING VERY IMPORTANT.

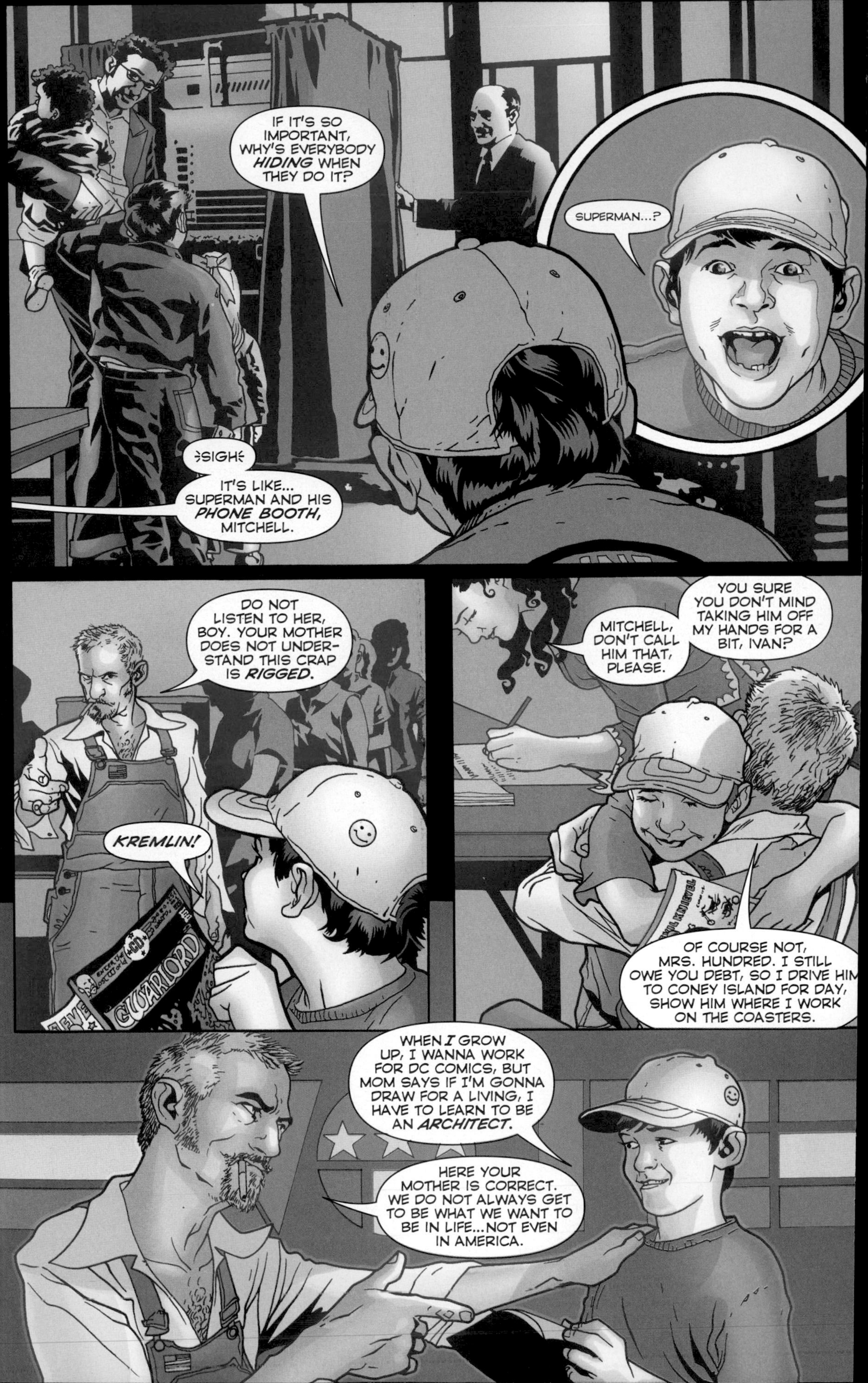
IF IT'S SO IMPORTANT, WHY'S EVERYBODY *HIDING* WHEN THEY DO IT?
SIGH
IT'S LIKE... SUPERMAN AND HIS *PHONE BOOTH,* MITCHELL.
SUPERMAN...?
DO NOT LISTEN TO HER, BOY. YOUR MOTHER DOES NOT UNDER-STAND THIS CRAP IS *RIGGED*.
KREMLIN!
MITCHELL, DON'T CALL HIM THAT, PLEASE.
YOU SURE YOU DON'T MIND TAKING HIM OFF MY HANDS FOR A BIT, IVAN?
OF COURSE NOT, MRS. HUNDRED. I STILL OWE YOU DEBT, SO I DRIVE HIM TO CONEY ISLAND FOR DAY, SHOW HIM WHERE I WORK ON THE COASTERS.
WHEN *I* GROW UP, I WANNA WORK FOR DC COMICS, BUT MOM SAYS IF I'M GONNA DRAW FOR A LIVING, I HAVE TO LEARN TO BE AN *ARCHITECT*.
HERE YOUR MOTHER IS CORRECT. WE DO NOT ALWAYS GET TO BE WHAT WE WANT TO BE IN LIFE...NOT EVEN IN AMERICA.

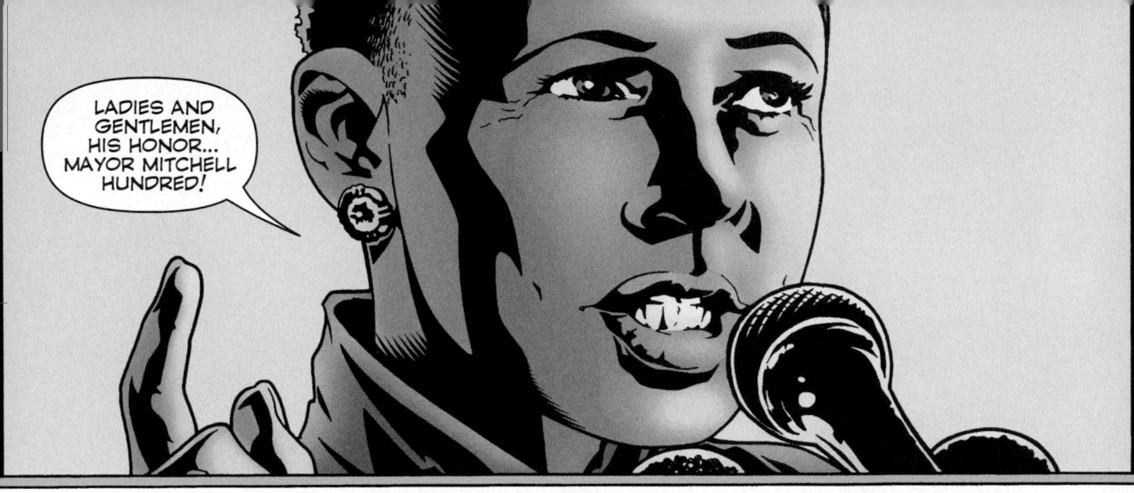
LADIES AND GENTLEMEN, HIS HONOR... MAYOR MITCHELL HUNDRED!

WEDNESDAY, JANUARY 9, 2002

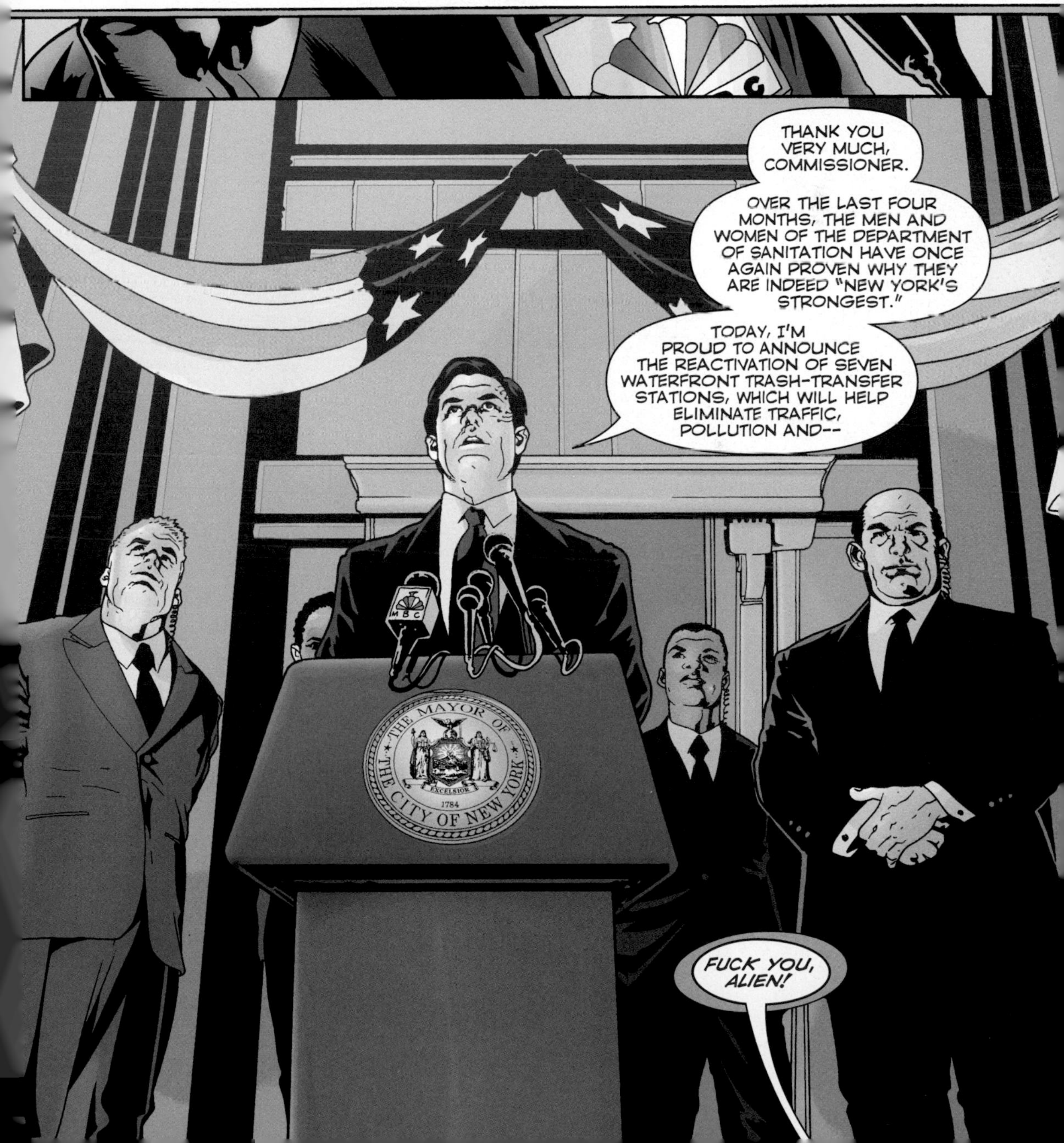
THANK YOU VERY MUCH, COMMISSIONER.
OVER THE LAST FOUR MONTHS, THE MEN AND WOMEN OF THE DEPARTMENT OF SANITATION HAVE ONCE AGAIN PROVEN WHY THEY ARE INDEED "NEW YORK'S STRONGEST."
TODAY, I'M PROUD TO ANNOUNCE THE REACTIVATION OF SEVEN WATERFRONT TRASH-TRANSFER STATIONS, WHICH WILL HELP ELIMINATE TRAFFIC, POLLUTION AND--
THE MAYOR OF THE CITY OF NEW YORK
EXCELSIOR
1784
FUCK YOU, ALIEN!

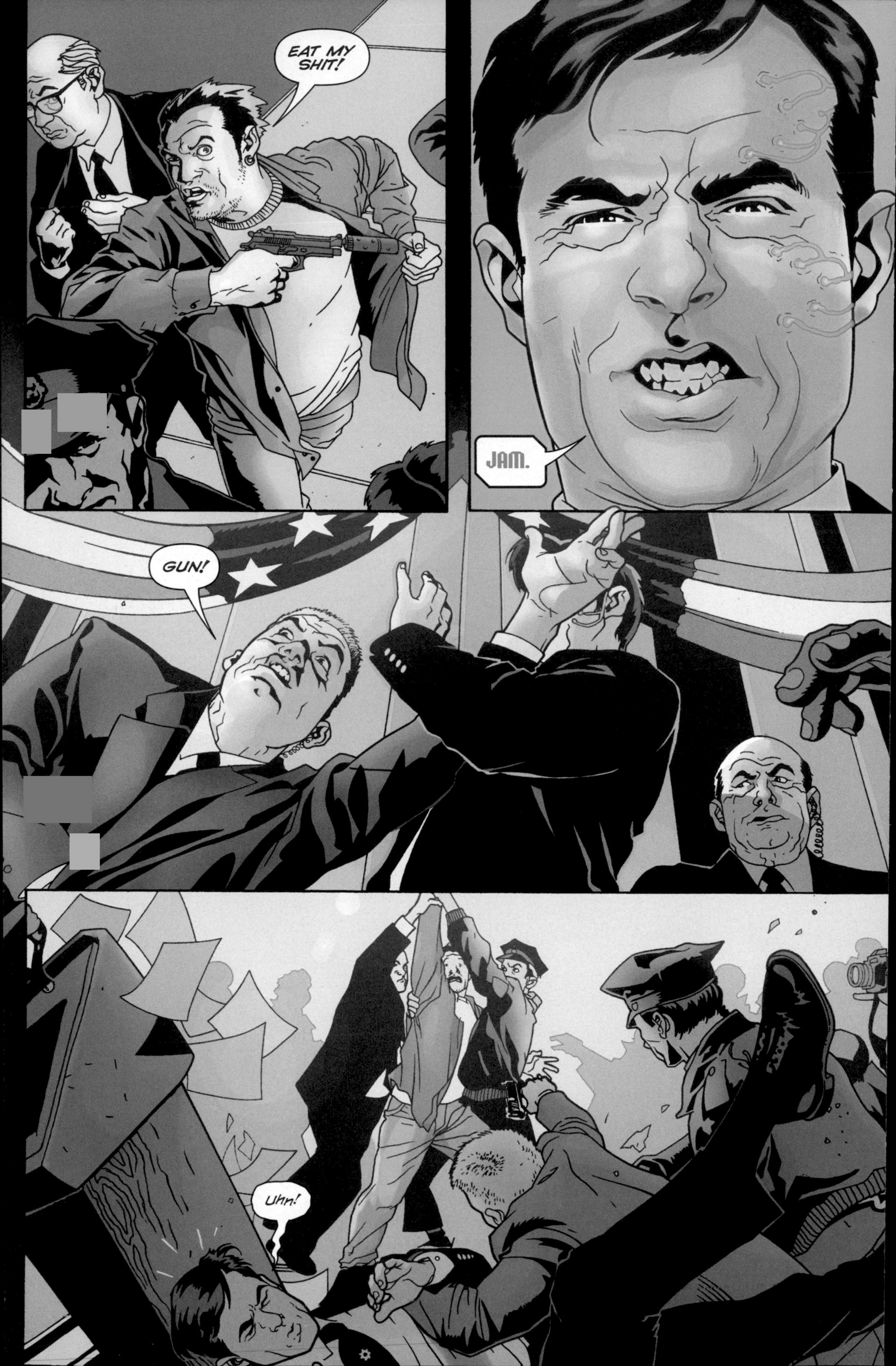
EAT MY SHIT!
JAM.
GUN!
Uhn!

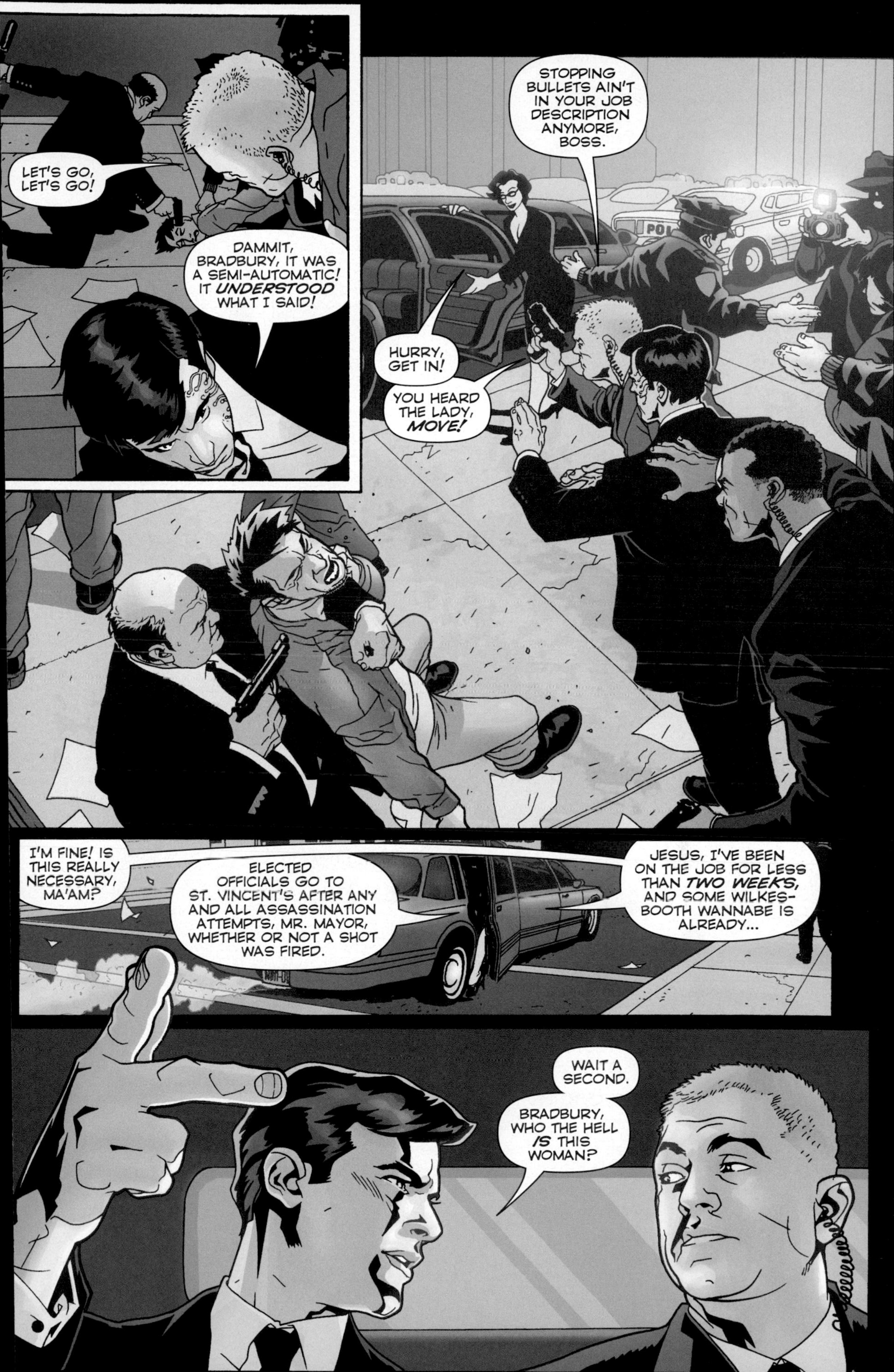
LET'S GO, LET'S GO!
DAMMIT, BRADBURY, IT WAS A SEMI-AUTOMATIC! IT *UNDERSTOOD* WHAT I SAID!
STOPPING BULLETS AIN'T IN YOUR JOB DESCRIPTION ANYMORE, BOSS.
HURRY, GET IN!
YOU HEARD THE LADY, *MOVE!*
I'M FINE! IS THIS REALLY NECESSARY, MA'AM?
ELECTED OFFICIALS GO TO ST. VINCENT'S AFTER ANY AND ALL ASSASSINATION ATTEMPTS, MR. MAYOR, WHETHER OR NOT A SHOT WAS FIRED.
JESUS, I'VE BEEN ON THE JOB FOR LESS THAN *TWO WEEKS*, AND SOME WILKES-BOOTH WANNABE IS ALREADY...
WAIT A SECOND.
BRADBURY, WHO THE HELL *IS* THIS WOMAN?

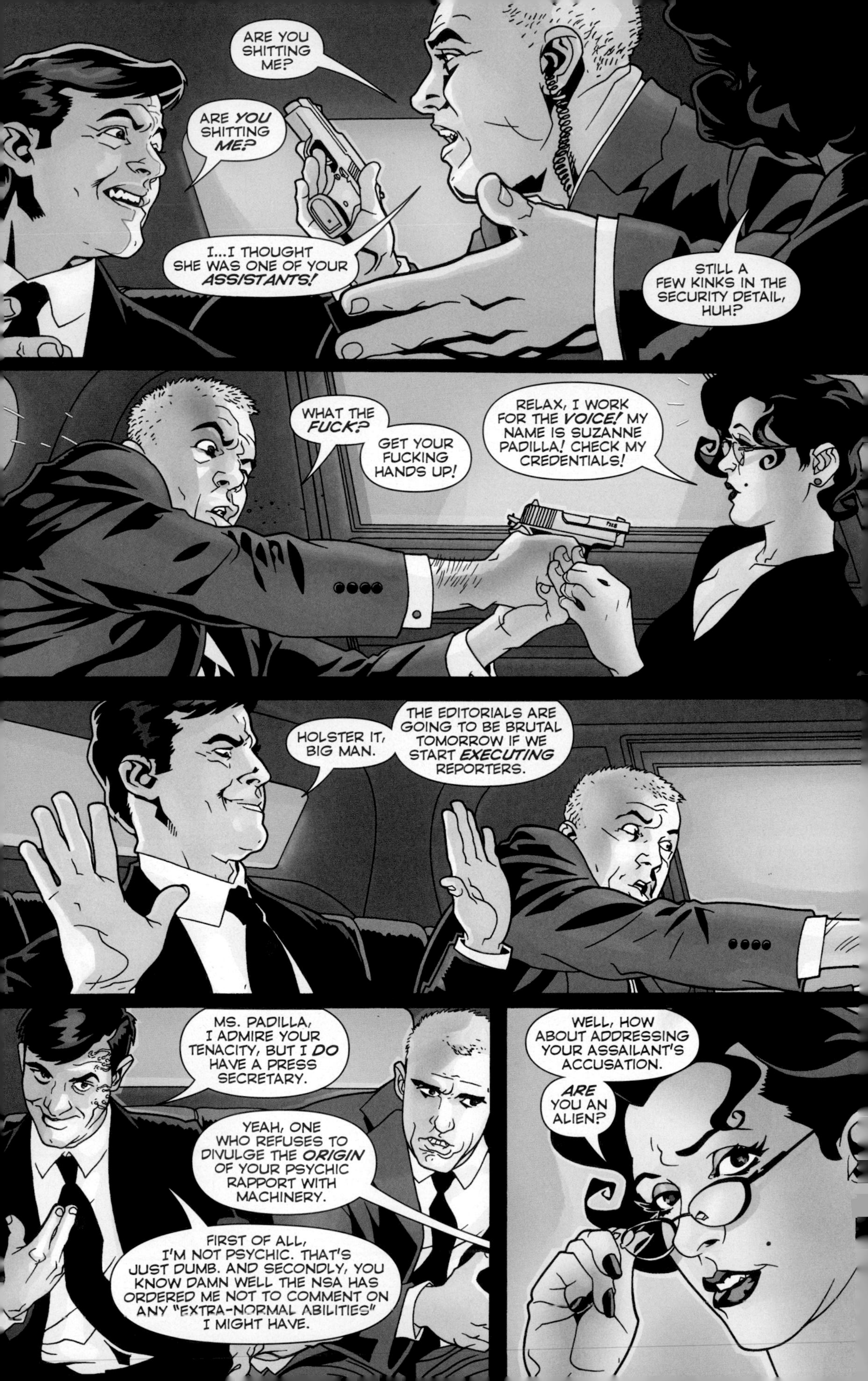
ARE YOU SHITTING ME?
ARE YOU SHITTING ME?
I...I THOUGHT SHE WAS ONE OF YOUR ASSISTANTS!
STILL A FEW KINKS IN THE SECURITY DETAIL, HUH?
WHAT THE FUCK?
GET YOUR FUCKING HANDS UP!
RELAX, I WORK FOR THE VOICE! MY NAME IS SUZANNE PADILLA! CHECK MY CREDENTIALS!
HOLSTER IT, BIG MAN.
THE EDITORIALS ARE GOING TO BE BRUTAL TOMORROW IF WE START EXECUTING REPORTERS.
MS. PADILLA, I ADMIRE YOUR TENACITY, BUT I DO HAVE A PRESS SECRETARY.
YEAH, ONE WHO REFUSES TO DIVULGE THE ORIGIN OF YOUR PSYCHIC RAPPORT WITH MACHINERY.
FIRST OF ALL, I'M NOT PSYCHIC. THAT'S JUST DUMB. AND SECONDLY, YOU KNOW DAMN WELL THE NSA HAS ORDERED ME NOT TO COMMENT ON ANY "EXTRA-NORMAL ABILITIES" I MIGHT HAVE.
WELL, HOW ABOUT ADDRESSING YOUR ASSAILANT'S ACCUSATION.
ARE YOU AN ALIEN?

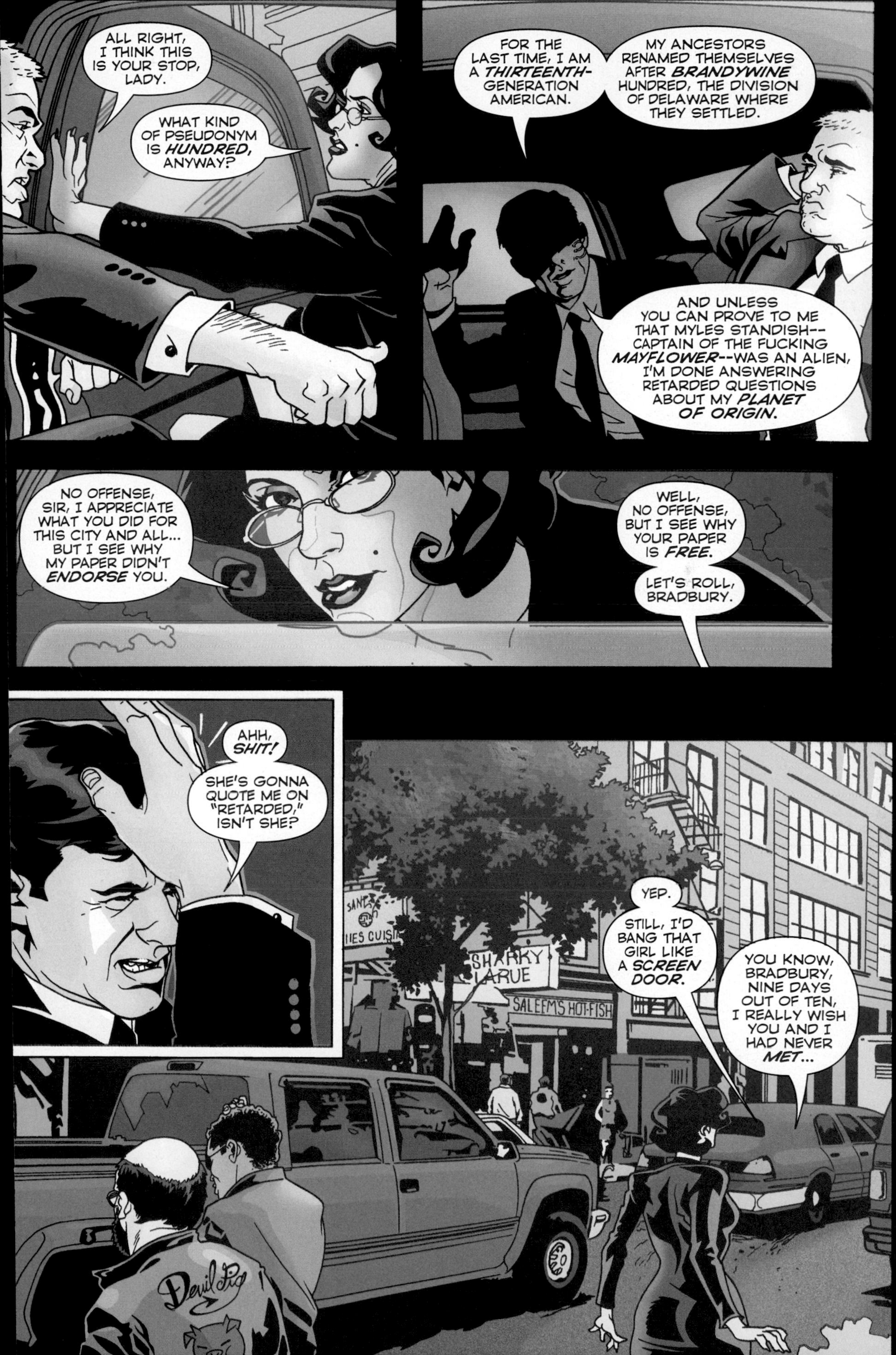
ALL RIGHT, I THINK THIS IS YOUR STOP, LADY.
WHAT KIND OF PSEUDONYM IS HUNDRED, ANYWAY?
FOR THE LAST TIME, I AM A THIRTEENTH-GENERATION AMERICAN.
MY ANCESTORS RENAMED THEMSELVES AFTER BRANDYWINE HUNDRED, THE DIVISION OF DELAWARE WHERE THEY SETTLED.
AND UNLESS YOU CAN PROVE TO ME THAT MYLES STANDISH--CAPTAIN OF THE FUCKING MAYFLOWER--WAS AN ALIEN, I'M DONE ANSWERING RETARDED QUESTIONS ABOUT MY PLANET OF ORIGIN.
NO OFFENSE, SIR, I APPRECIATE WHAT YOU DID FOR THIS CITY AND ALL... BUT I SEE WHY MY PAPER DIDN'T ENDORSE YOU.
WELL, NO OFFENSE, BUT I SEE WHY YOUR PAPER IS FREE.
LET'S ROLL, BRADBURY.
AHH, SHIT!
SHE'S GONNA QUOTE ME ON "RETARDED," ISN'T SHE?
YEP.
STILL, I'D BANG THAT GIRL LIKE A SCREEN DOOR.
YOU KNOW, BRADBURY, NINE DAYS OUT OF TEN, I REALLY WISH YOU AND I HAD NEVER MET...
SHARKY LARUE
SALEEM'S HOT-FISH
Devil Pig

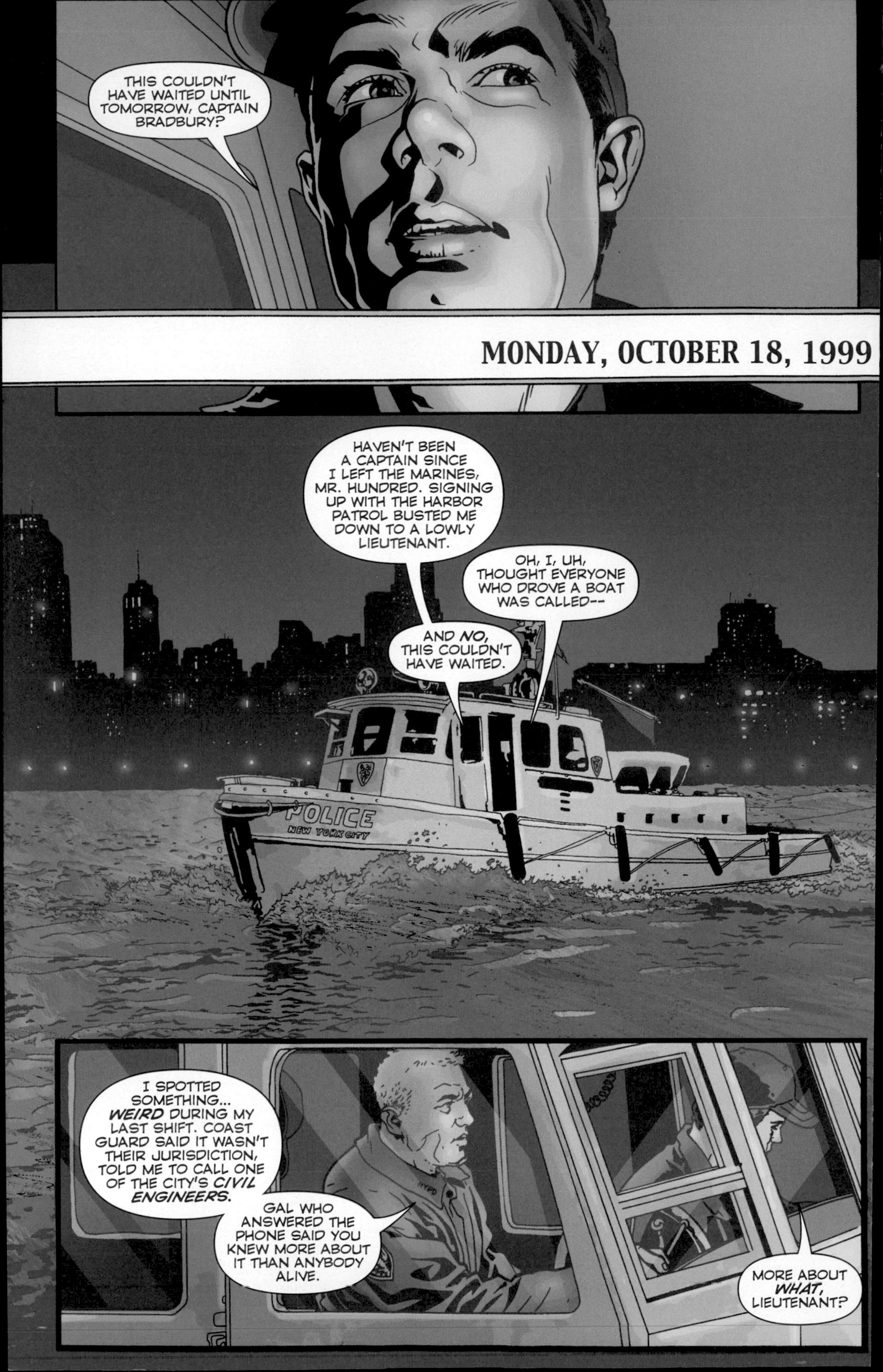

THIS COULDN'T HAVE WAITED UNTIL TOMORROW, CAPTAIN BRADBURY?
MONDAY, OCTOBER 18, 1999
HAVEN'T BEEN A CAPTAIN SINCE I LEFT THE MARINES, MR. HUNDRED. SIGNING UP WITH THE HARBOR PATROL BUSTED ME DOWN TO A LOWLY LIEUTENANT.
OH, I, UH, THOUGHT EVERYONE WHO DROVE A BOAT WAS CALLED--
AND *NO,* THIS COULDN'T HAVE WAITED.
POLICE
NEW YORK CITY
I SPOTTED SOMETHING... ***WEIRD*** DURING MY LAST SHIFT. COAST GUARD SAID IT WASN'T THEIR JURISDICTION, TOLD ME TO CALL ONE OF THE CITY'S ***CIVIL ENGINEERS.***
GAL WHO ANSWERED THE PHONE SAID YOU KNEW MORE ABOUT IT THAN ANYBODY ALIVE.
MORE ABOUT ***WHAT,*** LIEUTENANT?

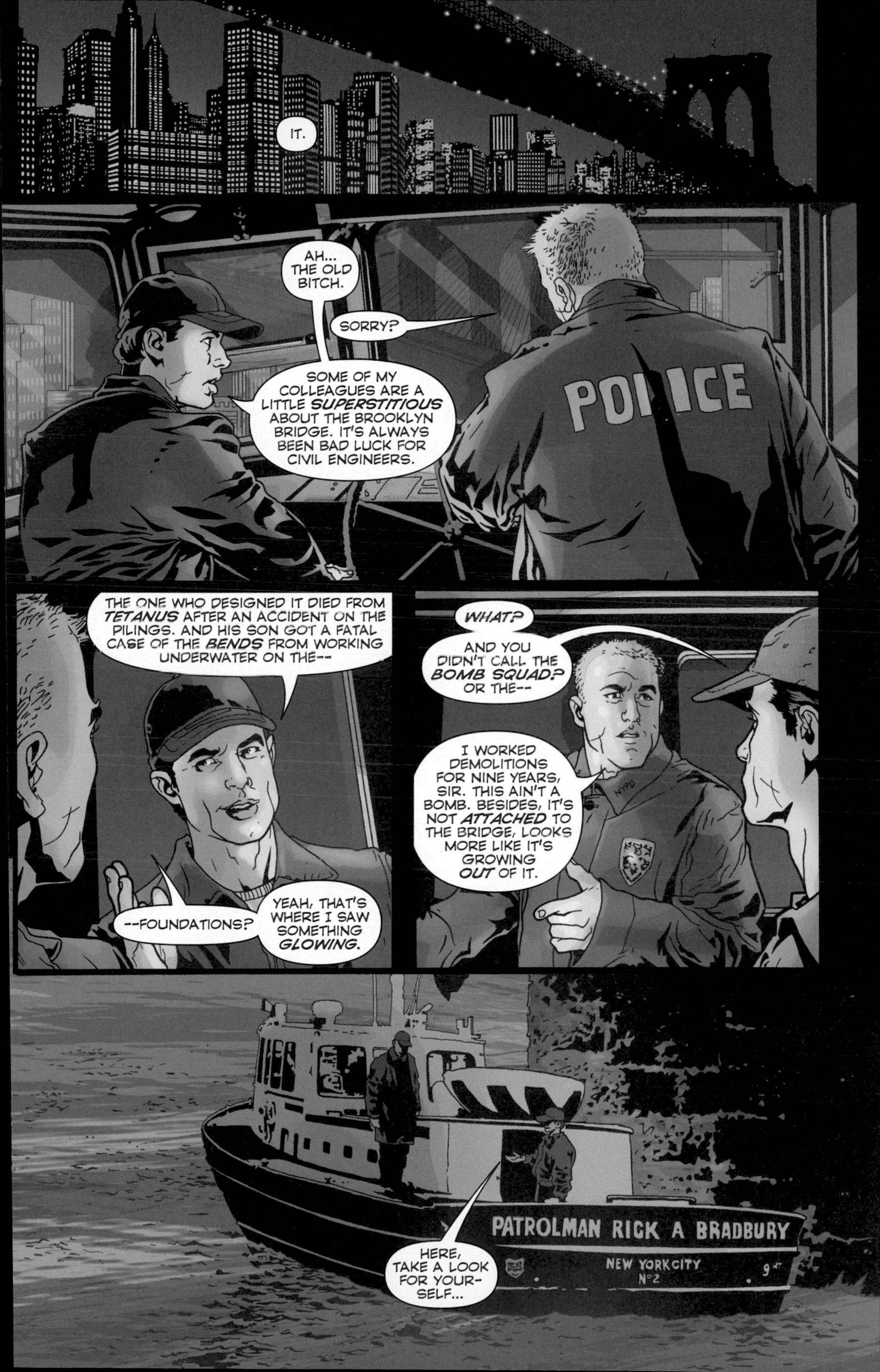
IT.
AH... THE OLD BITCH.
SORRY?
SOME OF MY COLLEAGUES ARE A LITTLE SUPERSTITIOUS ABOUT THE BROOKLYN BRIDGE. IT'S ALWAYS BEEN BAD LUCK FOR CIVIL ENGINEERS.
THE ONE WHO DESIGNED IT DIED FROM TETANUS AFTER AN ACCIDENT ON THE PILINGS. AND HIS SON GOT A FATAL CASE OF THE BENDS FROM WORKING UNDERWATER ON THE--
--FOUNDATIONS?
YEAH, THAT'S WHERE I SAW SOMETHING GLOWING.
WHAT?
AND YOU DIDN'T CALL THE BOMB SQUAD? OR THE--
I WORKED DEMOLITIONS FOR NINE YEARS, SIR. THIS AIN'T A BOMB. BESIDES, IT'S NOT ATTACHED TO THE BRIDGE, LOOKS MORE LIKE IT'S GROWING OUT OF IT.
POLICE
NYPD
PATROLMAN RICK A BRADBURY
NEW YORK CITY
N°2
HERE, TAKE A LOOK FOR YOURSELF...

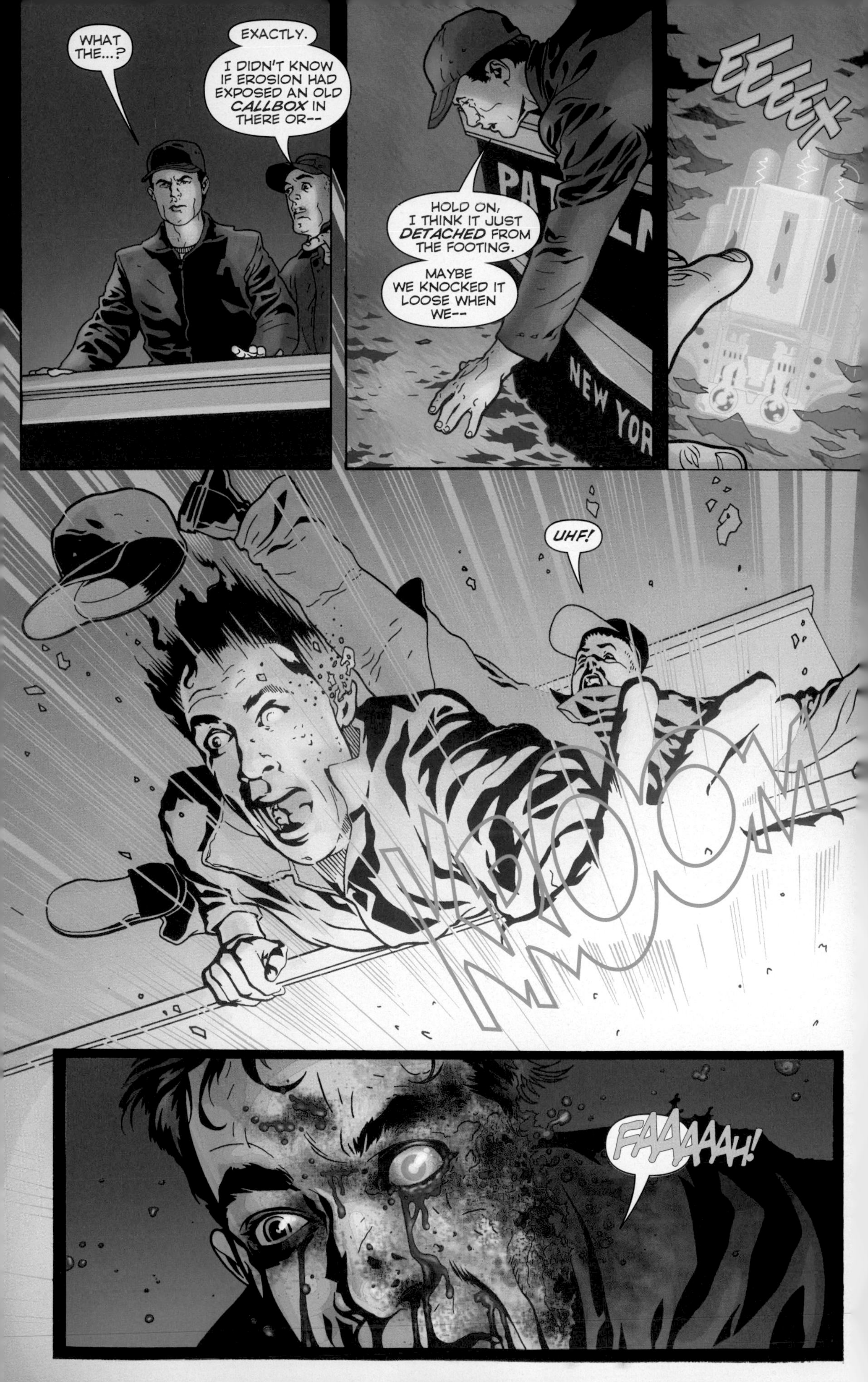
WHAT THE...?
EXACTLY.
I DIDN'T KNOW IF EROSION HAD EXPOSED AN OLD *CALLBOX* IN THERE OR--
PAT
NEW YOR
HOLD ON, I THINK IT JUST *DETACHED* FROM THE FOOTING.
MAYBE WE KNOCKED IT LOOSE WHEN WE--
EEEEEX
UHF!
WHOOOM
FAAAAAAH!

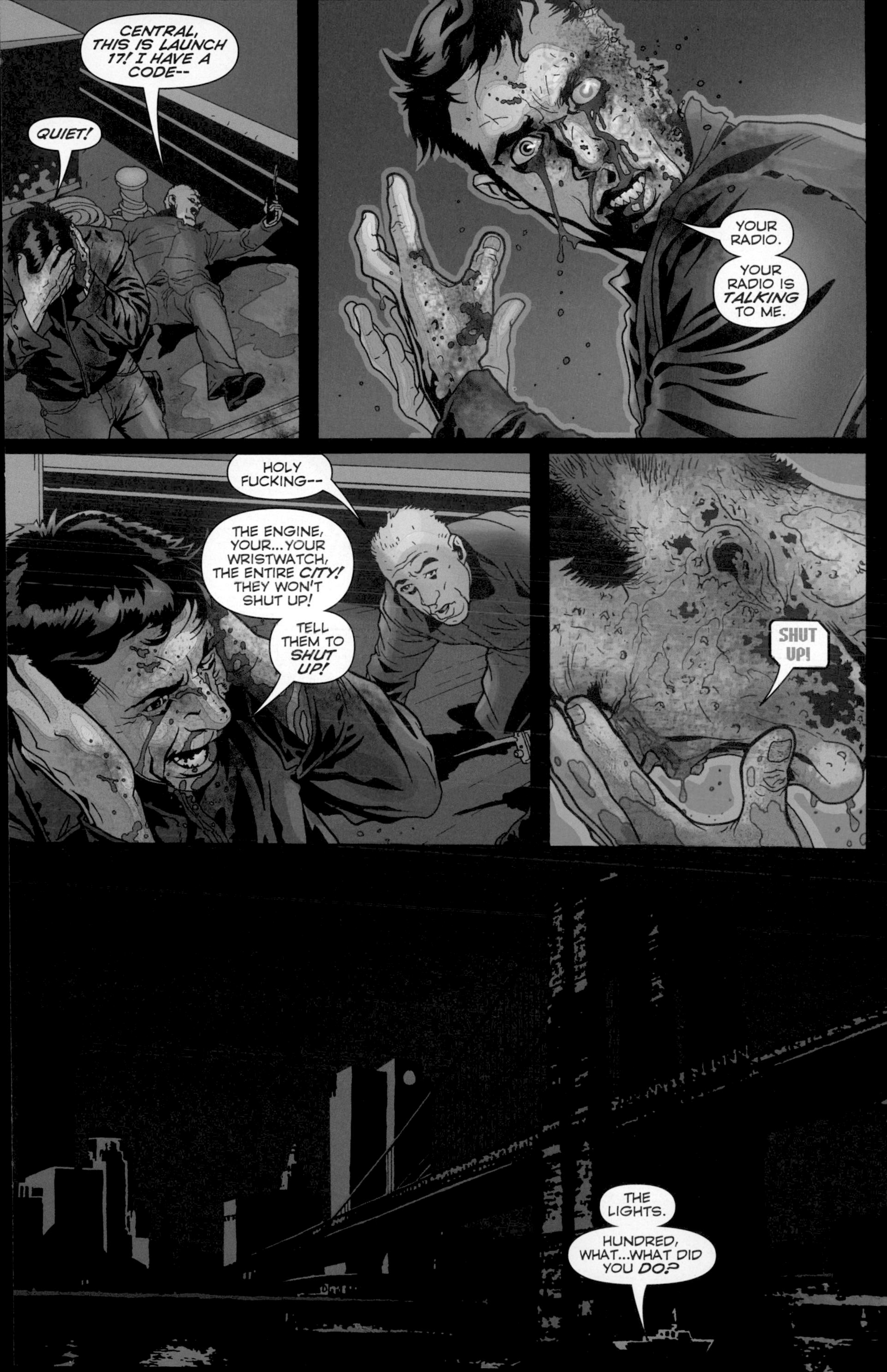
CENTRAL, THIS IS LAUNCH 17! I HAVE A CODE--
QUIET!
YOUR RADIO.
YOUR RADIO IS *TALKING* TO ME.
HOLY FUCKING--
THE ENGINE, YOUR...YOUR WRISTWATCH, THE ENTIRE *CITY!* THEY WON'T SHUT UP!
TELL THEM TO *SHUT UP!*
SHUT UP!
THE LIGHTS.
HUNDRED, WHAT...WHAT DID YOU *DO?*

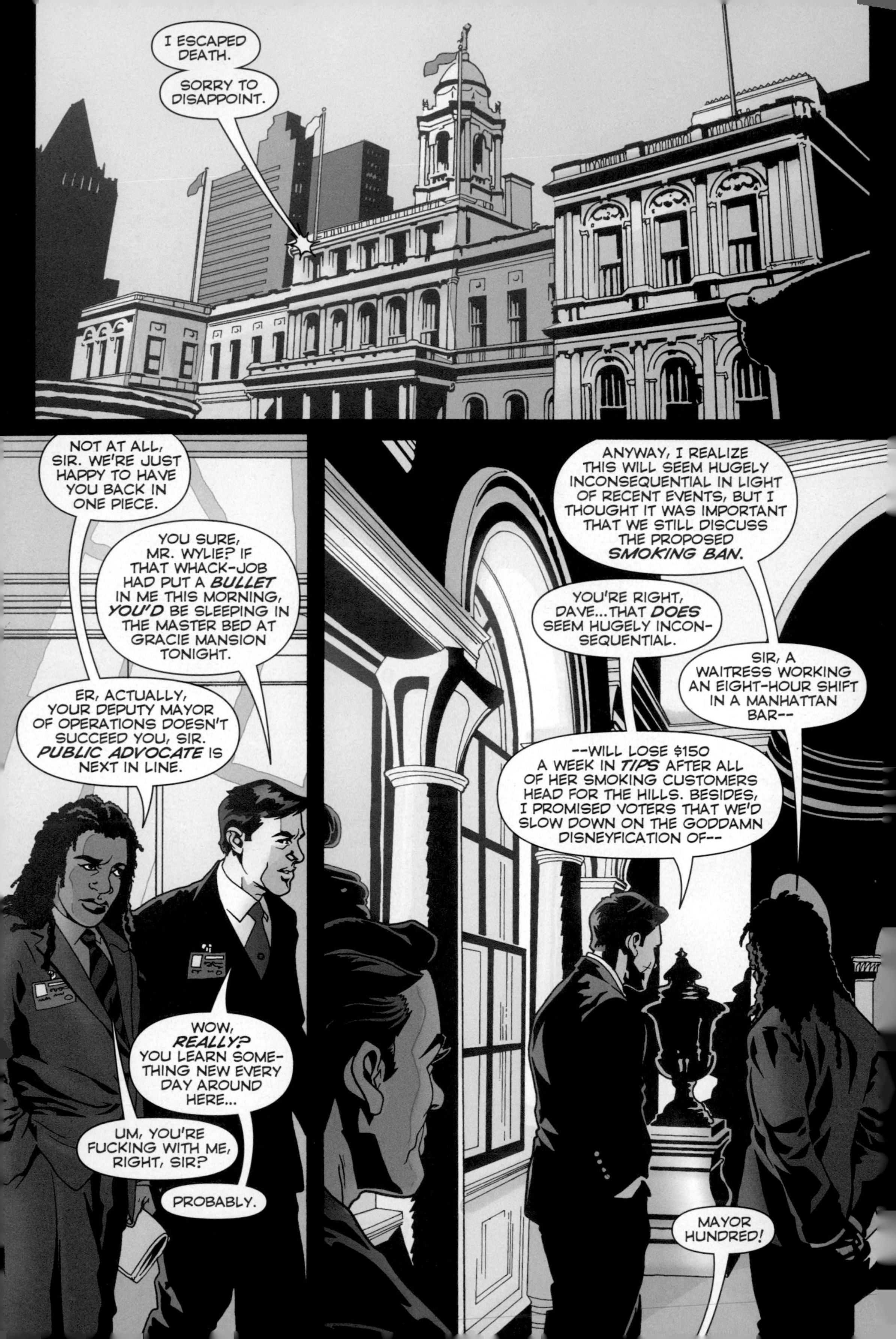
I ESCAPED DEATH.
SORRY TO DISAPPOINT.
NOT AT ALL, SIR. WE'RE JUST HAPPY TO HAVE YOU BACK IN ONE PIECE.
YOU SURE, MR. WYLIE? IF THAT WHACK-JOB HAD PUT A *BULLET* IN ME THIS MORNING, *YOU'D* BE SLEEPING IN THE MASTER BED AT GRACIE MANSION TONIGHT.
ER, ACTUALLY, YOUR DEPUTY MAYOR OF OPERATIONS DOESN'T SUCCEED YOU, SIR. *PUBLIC ADVOCATE* IS NEXT IN LINE.
WOW, *REALLY?* YOU LEARN SOME-THING NEW EVERY DAY AROUND HERE...
UM, YOU'RE FUCKING WITH ME, RIGHT, SIR?
PROBABLY.
ANYWAY, I REALIZE THIS WILL SEEM HUGELY INCONSEQUENTIAL IN LIGHT OF RECENT EVENTS, BUT I THOUGHT IT WAS IMPORTANT THAT WE STILL DISCUSS THE PROPOSED *SMOKING BAN*.
YOU'RE RIGHT, DAVE...THAT *DOES* SEEM HUGELY INCON-SEQUENTIAL.
SIR, A WAITRESS WORKING AN EIGHT-HOUR SHIFT IN A MANHATTAN BAR--
--WILL LOSE $150 A WEEK IN *TIPS* AFTER ALL OF HER SMOKING CUSTOMERS HEAD FOR THE HILLS. BESIDES, I PROMISED VOTERS THAT WE'D SLOW DOWN ON THE GODDAMN DISNEYFICATION OF--
MAYOR HUNDRED!

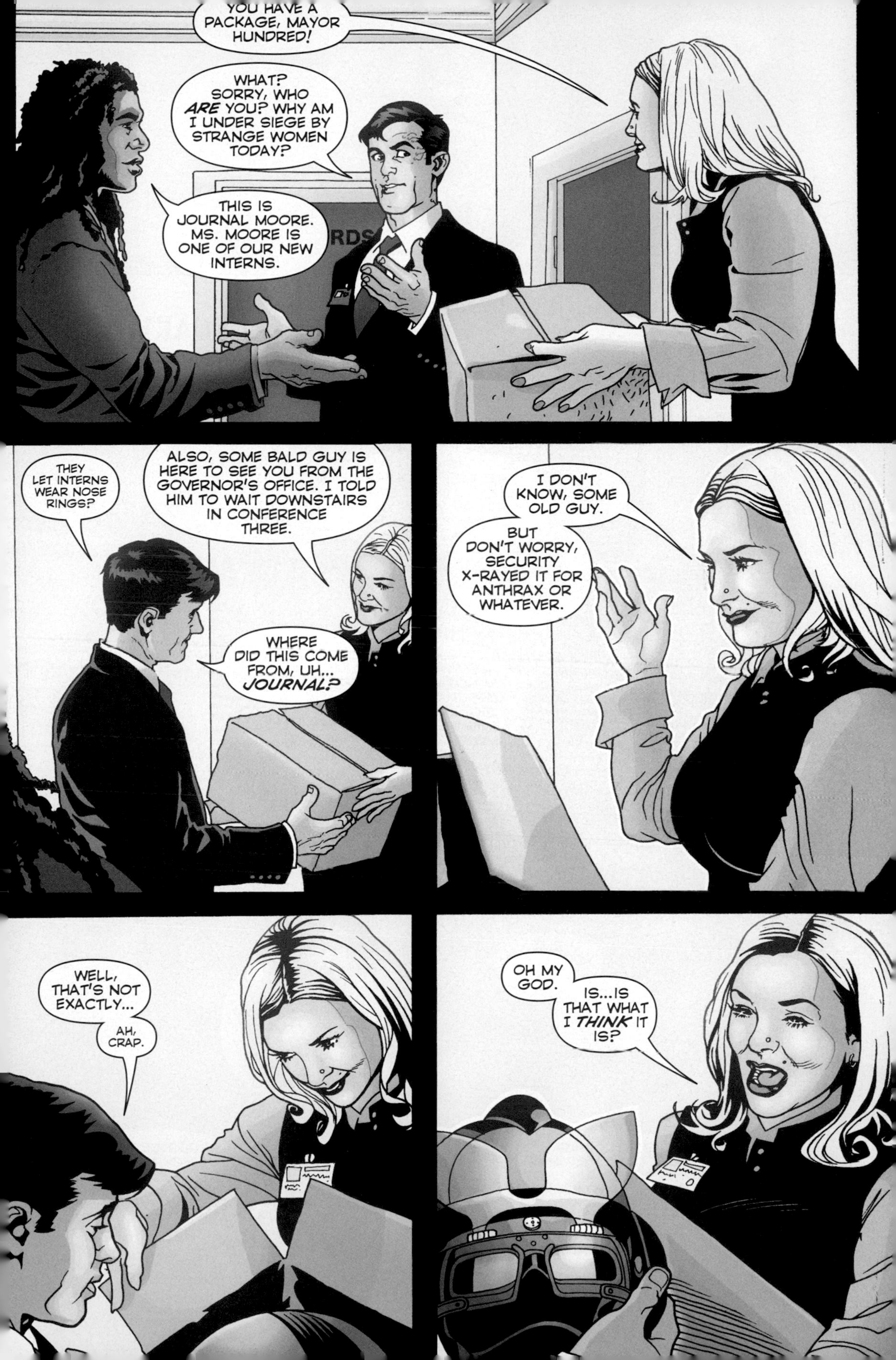
YOU HAVE A PACKAGE, MAYOR HUNDRED!
WHAT? SORRY, WHO *ARE* YOU? WHY AM I UNDER SIEGE BY STRANGE WOMEN TODAY?
THIS IS JOURNAL MOORE. MS. MOORE IS ONE OF OUR NEW INTERNS.
RDS
THEY LET INTERNS WEAR NOSE RINGS?
ALSO, SOME BALD GUY IS HERE TO SEE YOU FROM THE GOVERNOR'S OFFICE. I TOLD HIM TO WAIT DOWNSTAIRS IN CONFERENCE THREE.
WHERE DID THIS COME FROM, UH... *JOURNAL?*
I DON'T KNOW, SOME OLD GUY.
BUT DON'T WORRY, SECURITY X-RAYED IT FOR ANTHRAX OR WHATEVER.
WELL, THAT'S NOT EXACTLY...
AH, CRAP.
OH MY GOD.
IS...IS THAT WHAT I *THINK* IT IS?

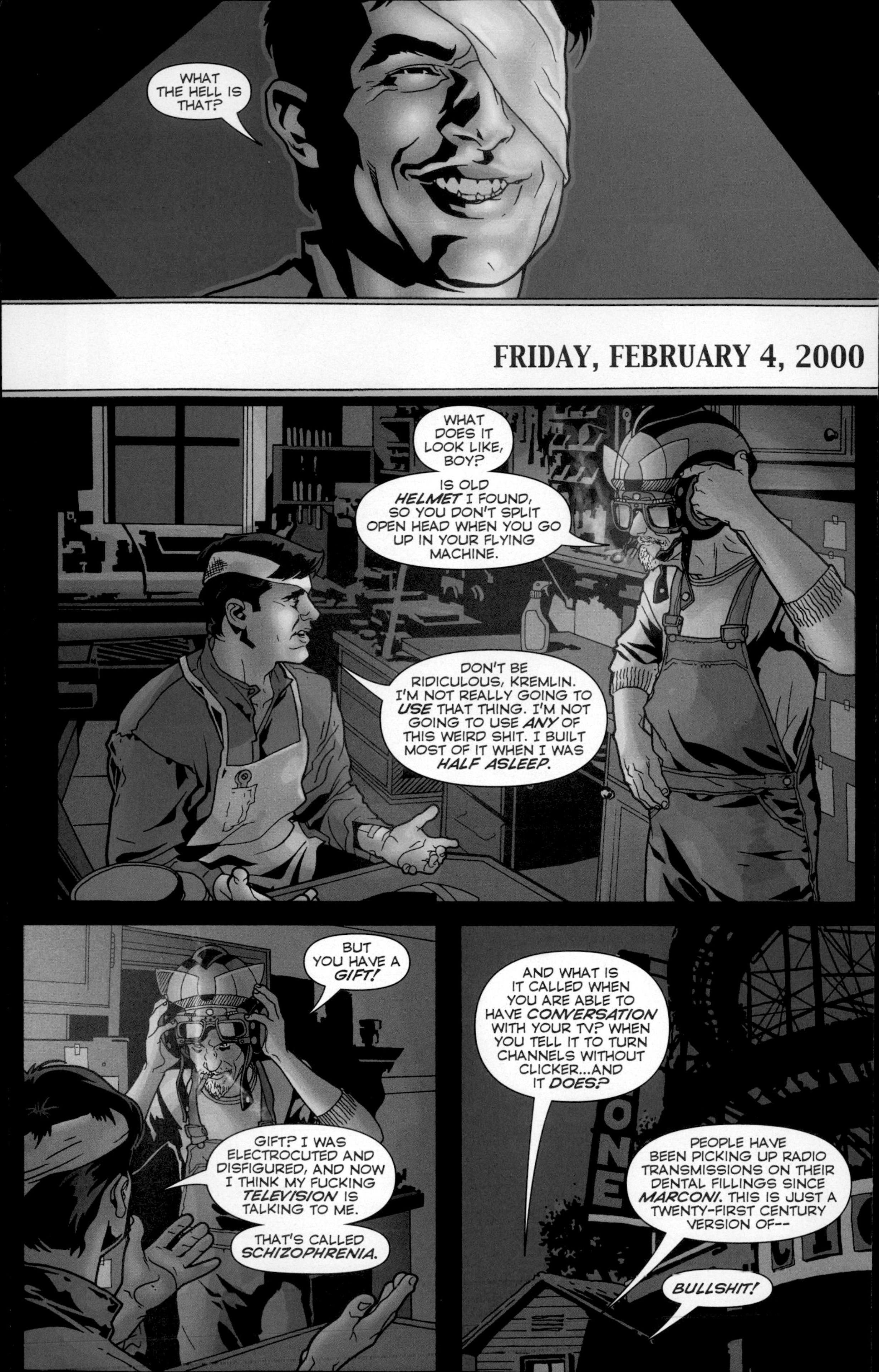
WHAT THE HELL IS THAT?
FRIDAY, FEBRUARY 4, 2000
WHAT DOES IT LOOK LIKE, BOY?
IS OLD HELMET I FOUND, SO YOU DON'T SPLIT OPEN HEAD WHEN YOU GO UP IN YOUR FLYING MACHINE.
DON'T BE RIDICULOUS, KREMLIN. I'M NOT REALLY GOING TO USE THAT THING. I'M NOT GOING TO USE ANY OF THIS WEIRD SHIT. I BUILT MOST OF IT WHEN I WAS HALF ASLEEP.
BUT YOU HAVE A GIFT!
GIFT? I WAS ELECTROCUTED AND DISFIGURED, AND NOW I THINK MY FUCKING TELEVISION IS TALKING TO ME.
THAT'S CALLED SCHIZOPHRENIA.
AND WHAT IS IT CALLED WHEN YOU ARE ABLE TO HAVE CONVERSATION WITH YOUR TV? WHEN YOU TELL IT TO TURN CHANNELS WITHOUT CLICKER...AND IT DOES?
PEOPLE HAVE BEEN PICKING UP RADIO TRANSMISSIONS ON THEIR DENTAL FILLINGS SINCE MARCONI. THIS IS JUST A TWENTY-FIRST CENTURY VERSION OF--
BULLSHIT!

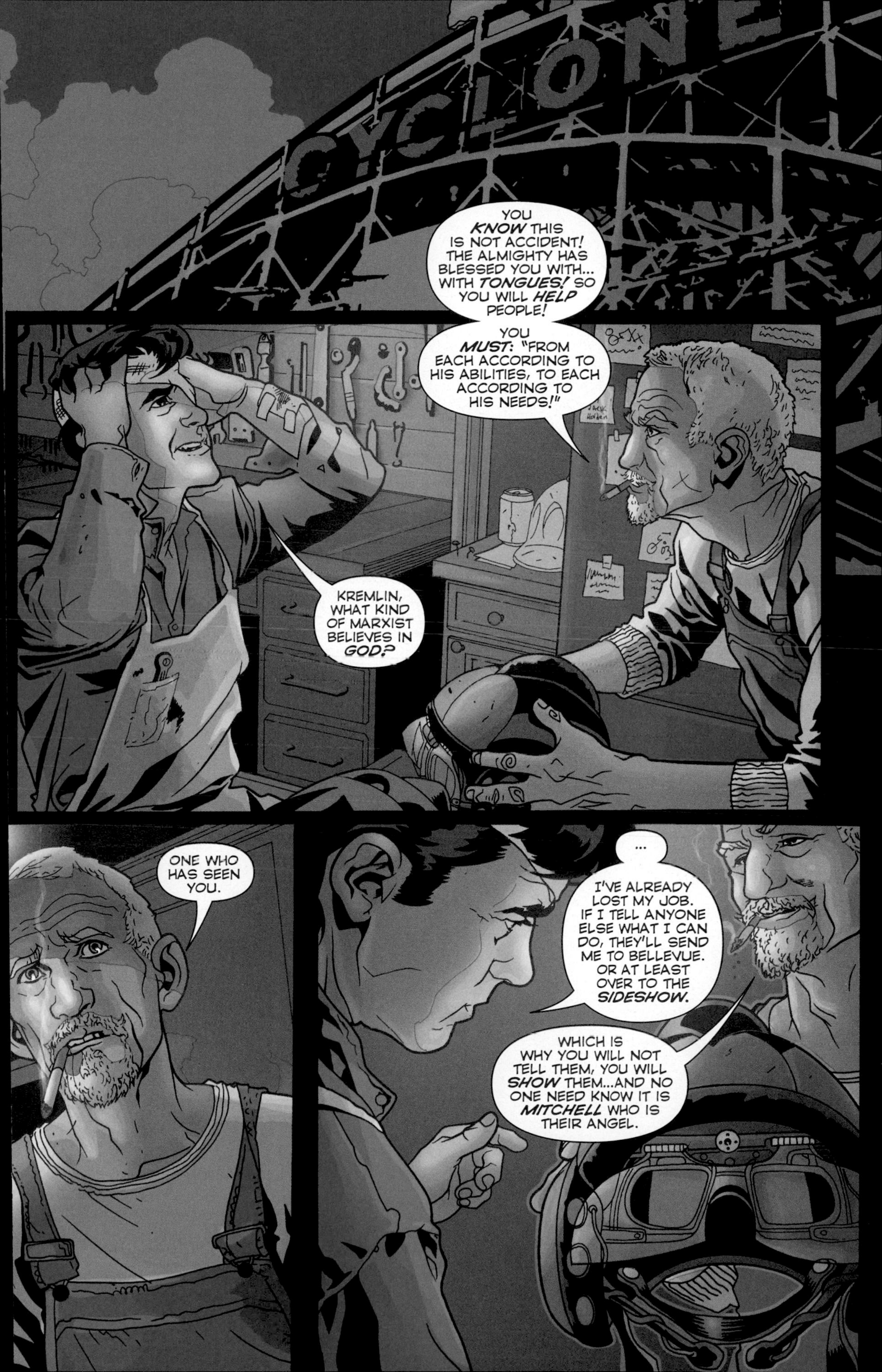
CYCLONE
YOU KNOW THIS IS NOT ACCIDENT! THE ALMIGHTY HAS BLESSED YOU WITH... WITH TONGUES! SO YOU WILL HELP PEOPLE!
YOU MUST: "FROM EACH ACCORDING TO HIS ABILITIES, TO EACH ACCORDING TO HIS NEEDS!"
KREMLIN, WHAT KIND OF MARXIST BELIEVES IN GOD?
ONE WHO HAS SEEN YOU.
...
I'VE ALREADY LOST MY JOB. IF I TELL ANYONE ELSE WHAT I CAN DO, THEY'LL SEND ME TO BELLEVUE. OR AT LEAST OVER TO THE SIDESHOW.
WHICH IS WHY YOU WILL NOT TELL THEM, YOU WILL SHOW THEM...AND NO ONE NEED KNOW IT IS MITCHELL WHO IS THEIR ANGEL.

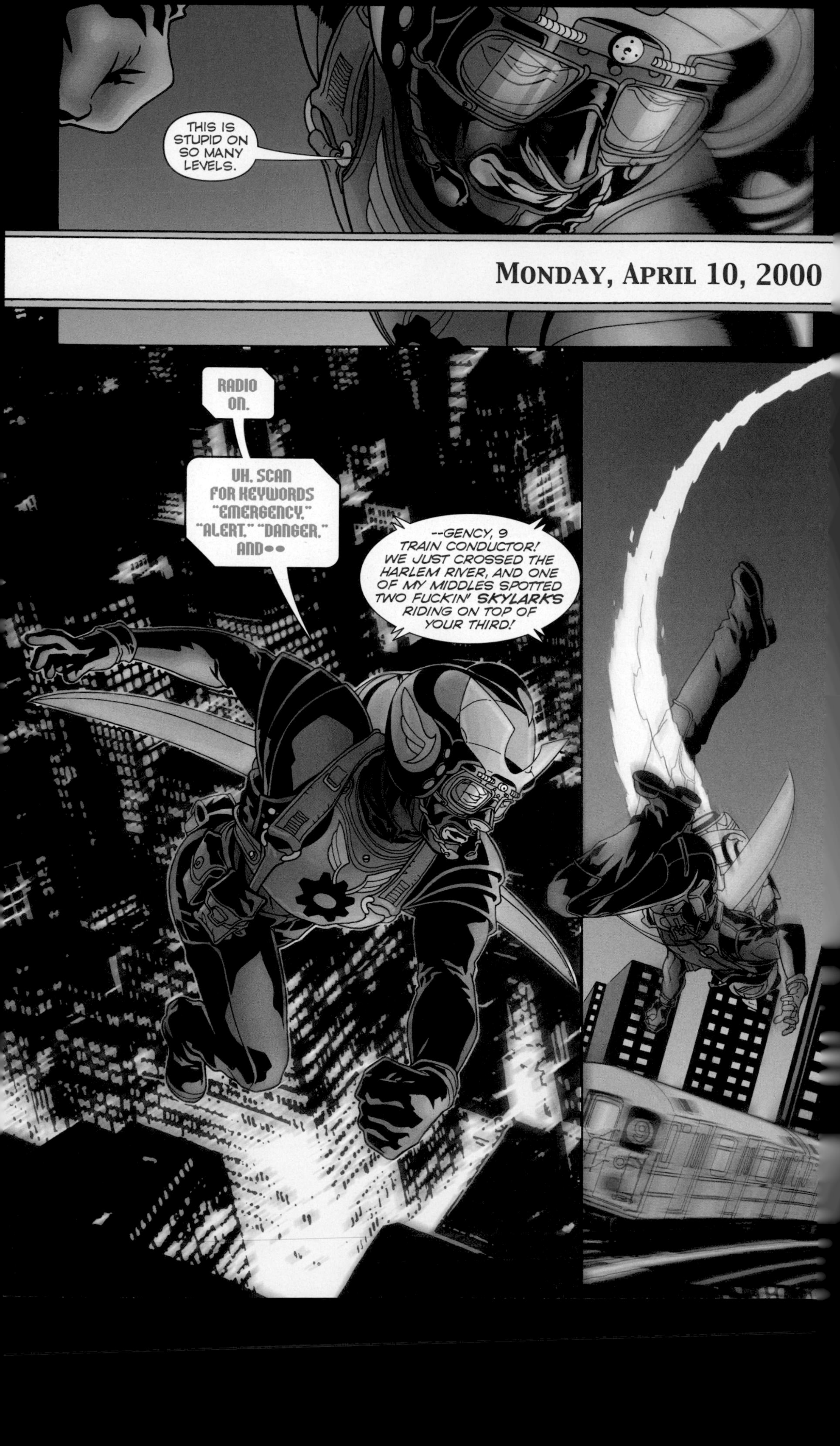
THIS IS STUPID ON SO MANY LEVELS.
MONDAY, APRIL 10, 2000
RADIO ON.
UH. SCAN FOR KEYWORDS "EMERGENCY." "ALERT." "DANGER." AND••
--GENCY, 9 TRAIN CONDUCTOR! WE JUST CROSSED THE HARLEM RIVER, AND ONE OF MY MIDDLES SPOTTED TWO FUCKIN' SKYLARKS RIDING ON TOP OF YOUR THIRD!

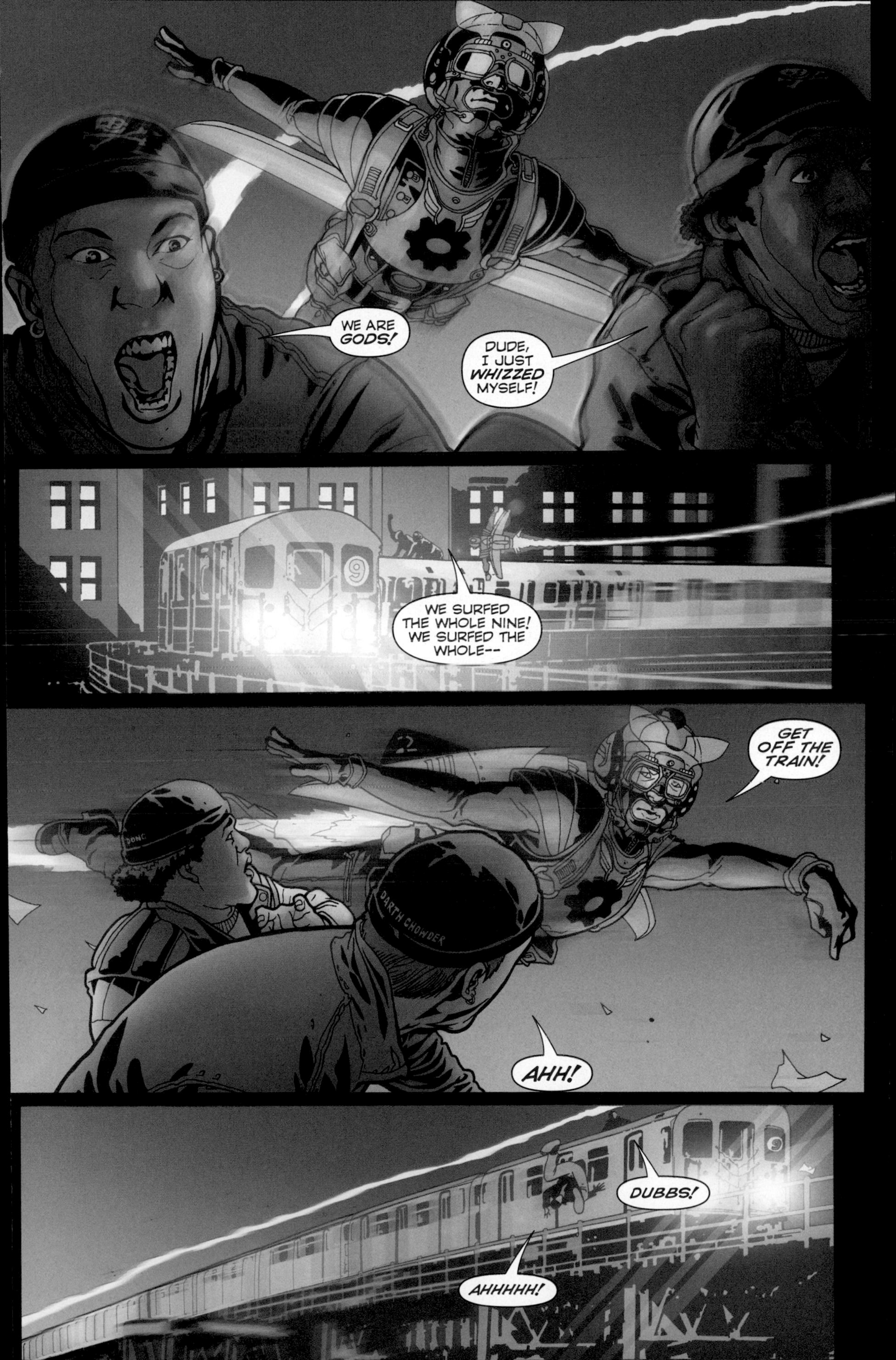
WE ARE GODS!
DUDE, I JUST WHIZZED MYSELF!
WE SURFED THE WHOLE NINE! WE SURFED THE WHOLE--
GET OFF THE TRAIN!
AHH!
DUBBS!
AHHHHH!

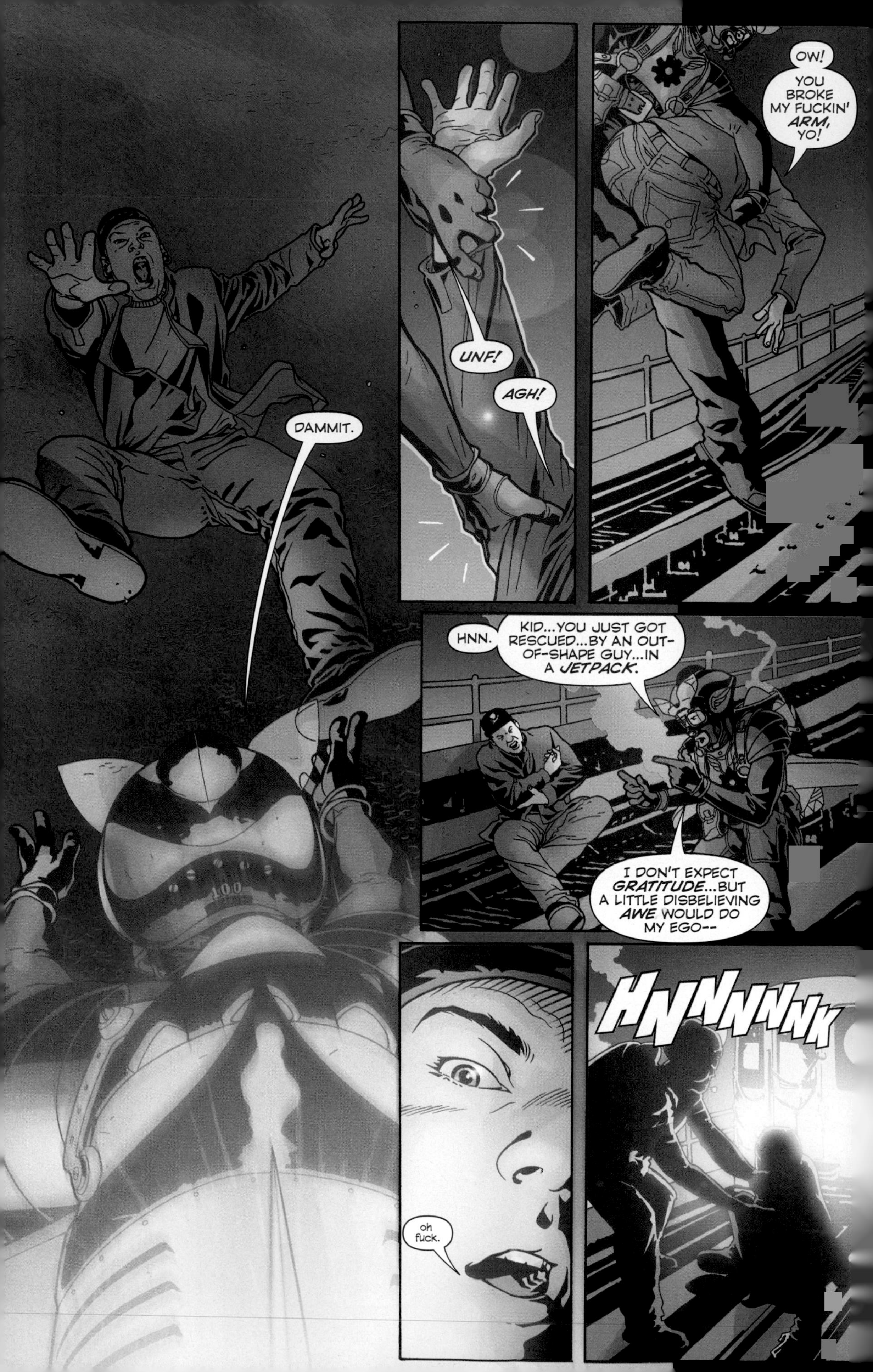
DAMMIT.
UNF!
AGH!
OW!
YOU BROKE MY FUCKIN' *ARM*, YO!
HNN.
KID...YOU JUST GOT RESCUED...BY AN OUT-OF-SHAPE GUY...IN A *JETPACK*.
I DON'T EXPECT *GRATITUDE*...BUT A LITTLE DISBELIEVING *AWE* WOULD DO MY EGO--
oh fuck.
HNNNNNNK

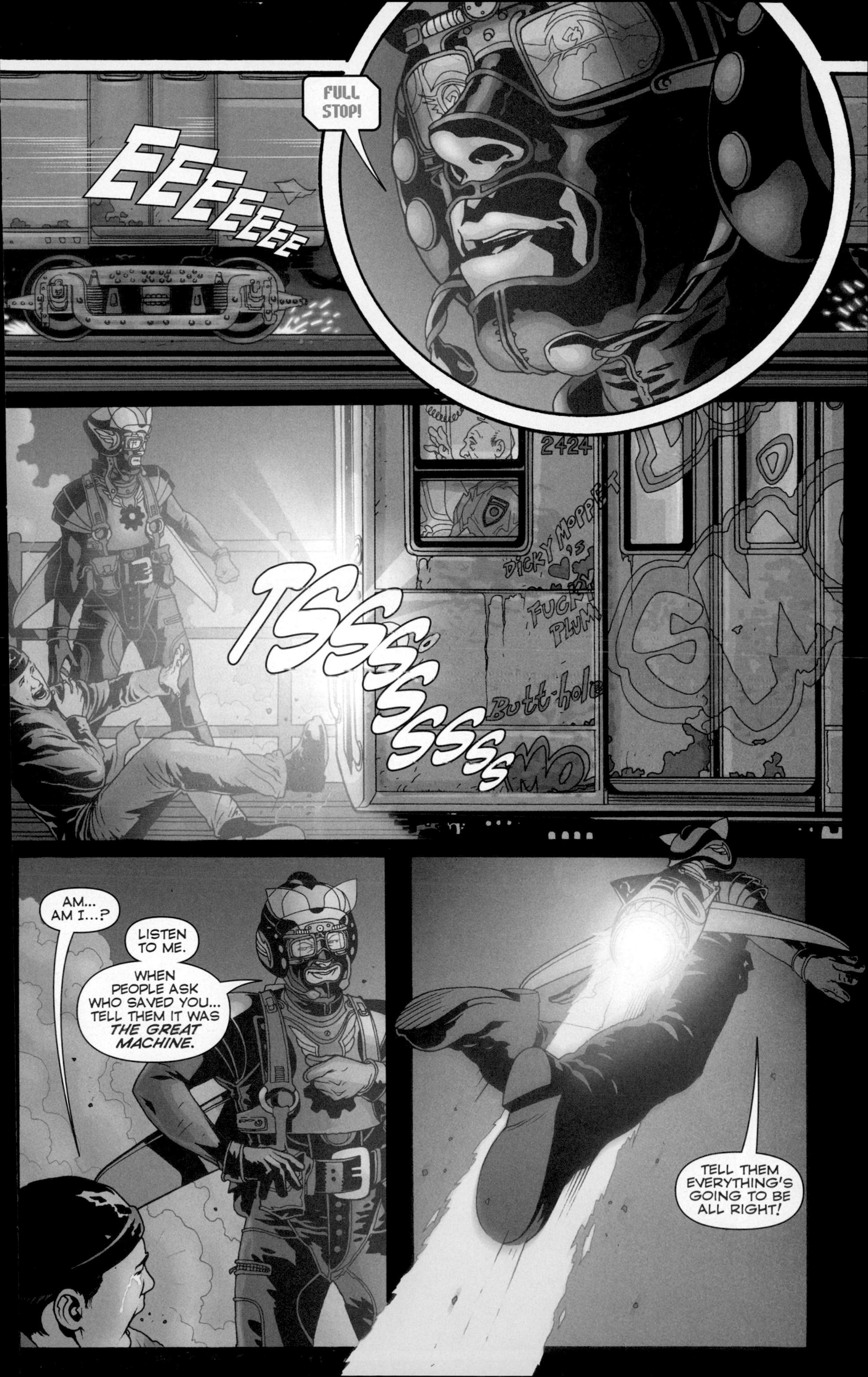
EEEEEEEE
FULL STOP!
2424
DICKY MOPPET 's
FUCK PLUM
Butt-hole
TSSSSSSSS
AM... AM I...?
LISTEN TO ME.
WHEN PEOPLE ASK WHO SAVED YOU... TELL THEM IT WAS *THE GREAT MACHINE*.
TELL THEM EVERYTHING'S GOING TO BE ALL RIGHT!

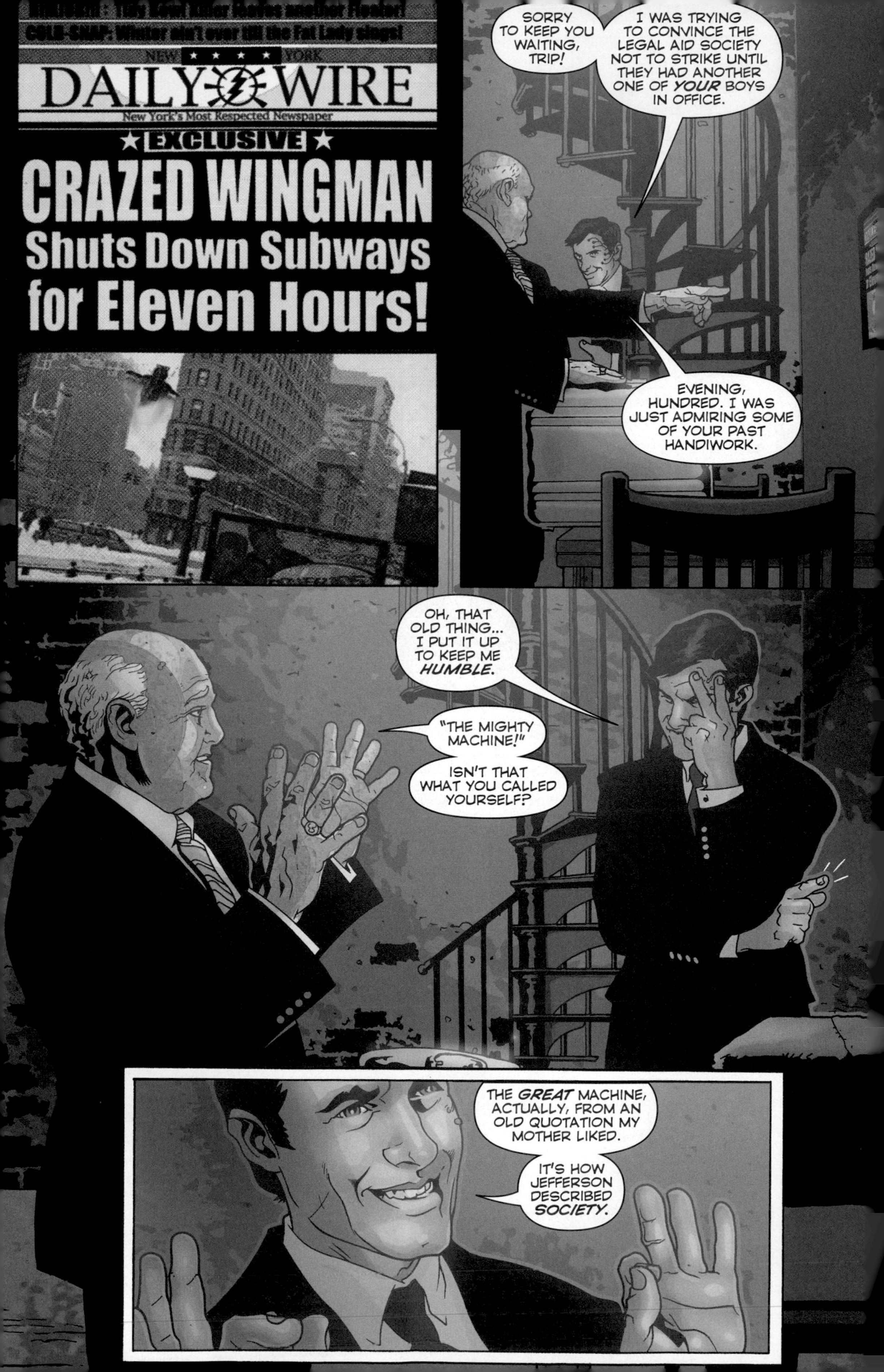
COLD-SNAP: Winter ain't over till the Fat Lady sings!
NEW ★ ★ ★ ★ YORK
DAILY WIRE
New York's Most Respected Newspaper
★ EXCLUSIVE ★
CRAZED WINGMAN
Shuts Down Subways for Eleven Hours!
SORRY TO KEEP YOU WAITING, TRIP!
I WAS TRYING TO CONVINCE THE LEGAL AID SOCIETY NOT TO STRIKE UNTIL THEY HAD ANOTHER ONE OF YOUR BOYS IN OFFICE.
EVENING, HUNDRED. I WAS JUST ADMIRING SOME OF YOUR PAST HANDIWORK.
OH, THAT OLD THING... I PUT IT UP TO KEEP ME HUMBLE.
"THE MIGHTY MACHINE!"
ISN'T THAT WHAT YOU CALLED YOURSELF?
THE GREAT MACHINE, ACTUALLY, FROM AN OLD QUOTATION MY MOTHER LIKED.
IT'S HOW JEFFERSON DESCRIBED SOCIETY.

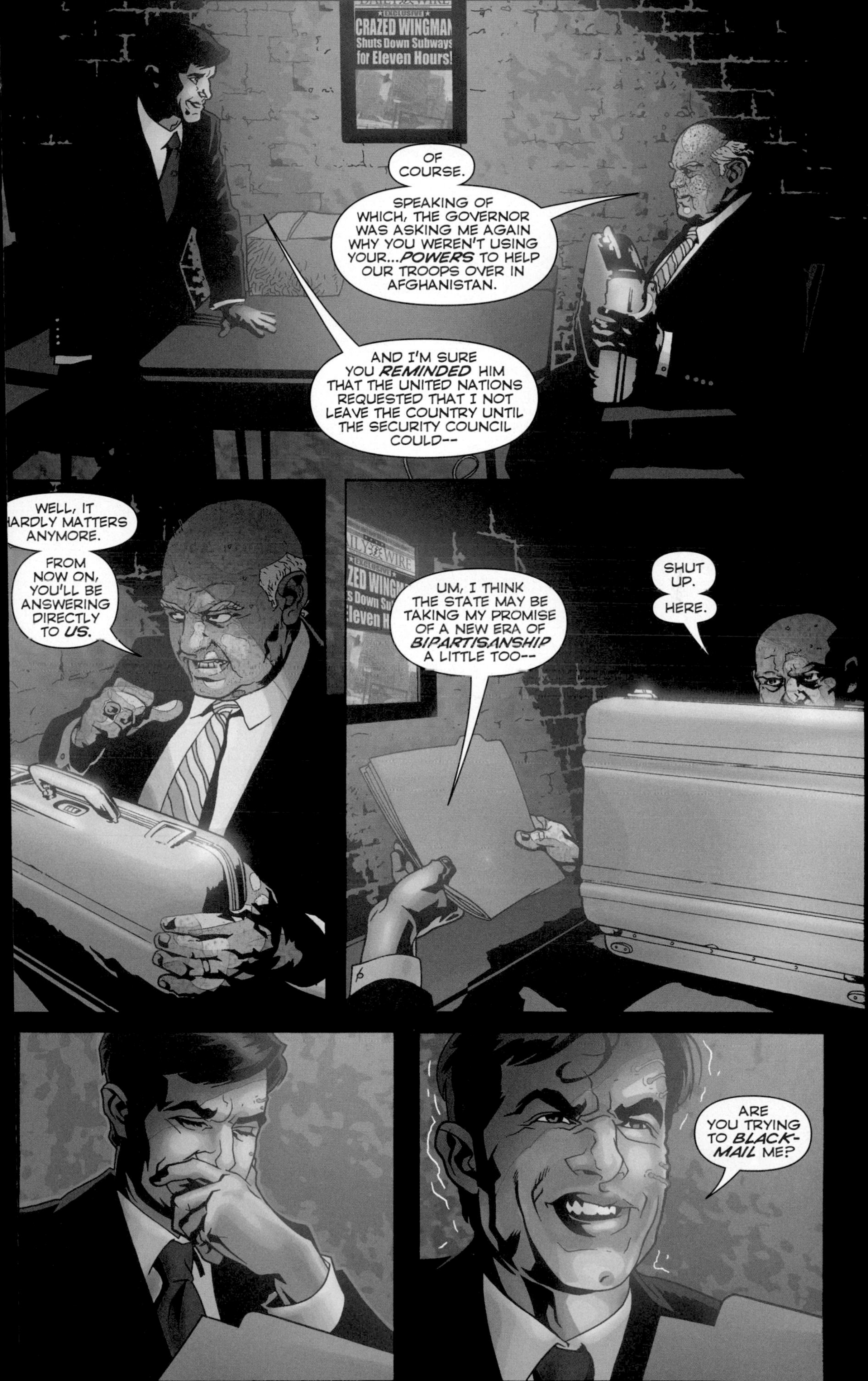

DAILY WIRE
EXCLUSIVE
CRAZED WINGMAN Shuts Down Subways for Eleven Hours!
OF COURSE.
SPEAKING OF WHICH, THE GOVERNOR WAS ASKING ME AGAIN WHY YOU WEREN'T USING YOUR...POWERS TO HELP OUR TROOPS OVER IN AFGHANISTAN.
AND I'M SURE YOU REMINDED HIM THAT THE UNITED NATIONS REQUESTED THAT I NOT LEAVE THE COUNTRY UNTIL THE SECURITY COUNCIL COULD--
WELL, IT HARDLY MATTERS ANYMORE.
FROM NOW ON, YOU'LL BE ANSWERING DIRECTLY TO US.
UM, I THINK THE STATE MAY BE TAKING MY PROMISE OF A NEW ERA OF BIPARTISANSHIP A LITTLE TOO--
SHUT UP.
HERE.
ARE YOU TRYING TO BLACK-MAIL ME?

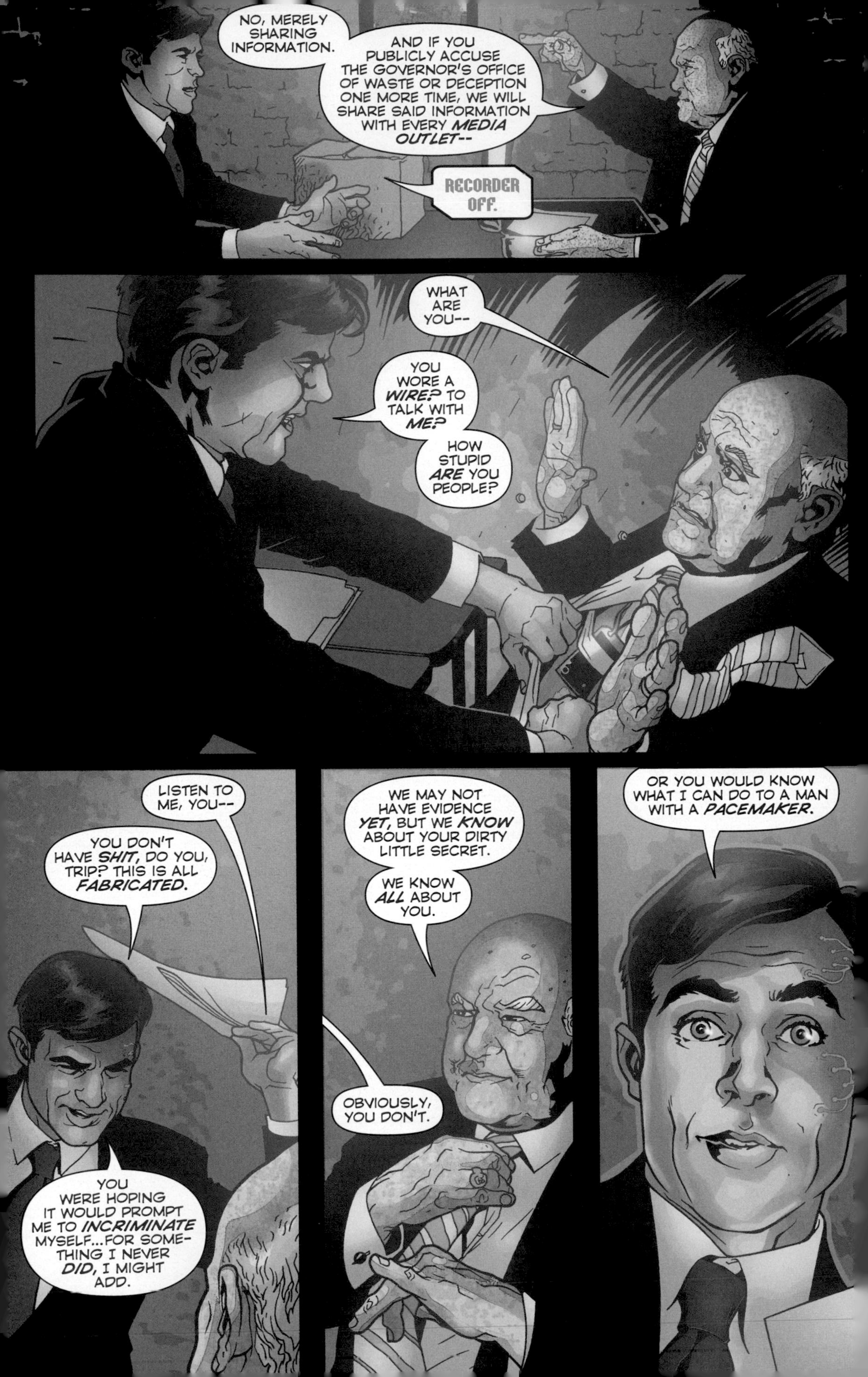
NO, MERELY SHARING INFORMATION.
AND IF YOU PUBLICLY ACCUSE THE GOVERNOR'S OFFICE OF WASTE OR DECEPTION ONE MORE TIME, WE WILL SHARE SAID INFORMATION WITH EVERY MEDIA OUTLET--
RECORDER OFF.
WHAT ARE YOU--
YOU WORE A WIRE? TO TALK WITH ME?
HOW STUPID ARE YOU PEOPLE?
LISTEN TO ME, YOU--
YOU DON'T HAVE SHIT, DO YOU, TRIP? THIS IS ALL FABRICATED.
YOU WERE HOPING IT WOULD PROMPT ME TO INCRIMINATE MYSELF...FOR SOMETHING I NEVER DID, I MIGHT ADD.
WE MAY NOT HAVE EVIDENCE YET, BUT WE KNOW ABOUT YOUR DIRTY LITTLE SECRET.
WE KNOW ALL ABOUT YOU.
OBVIOUSLY, YOU DON'T.
OR YOU WOULD KNOW WHAT I CAN DO TO A MAN WITH A PACEMAKER.

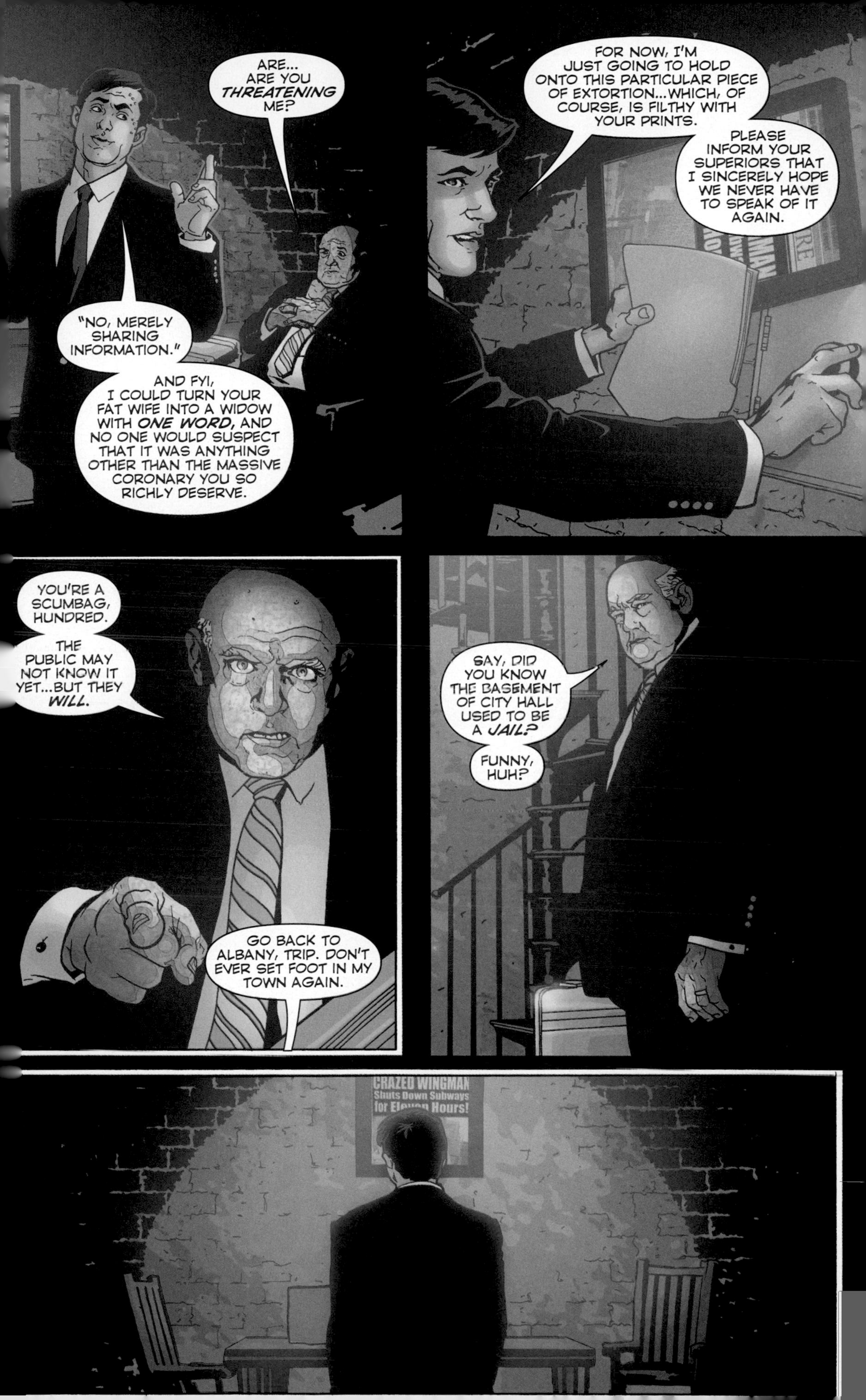

ARE... ARE YOU *THREATENING* ME?
"NO, MERELY SHARING INFORMATION."
AND FYI, I COULD TURN YOUR FAT WIFE INTO A WIDOW WITH *ONE WORD,* AND NO ONE WOULD SUSPECT THAT IT WAS ANYTHING OTHER THAN THE MASSIVE CORONARY YOU SO RICHLY DESERVE.
FOR NOW, I'M JUST GOING TO HOLD ONTO THIS PARTICULAR PIECE OF EXTORTION...WHICH, OF COURSE, IS FILTHY WITH YOUR PRINTS.
PLEASE INFORM YOUR SUPERIORS THAT I SINCERELY HOPE WE NEVER HAVE TO SPEAK OF IT AGAIN.
YOU'RE A SCUMBAG, HUNDRED.
THE PUBLIC MAY NOT KNOW IT YET...BUT THEY *WILL.*
GO BACK TO ALBANY, TRIP. DON'T EVER SET FOOT IN MY TOWN AGAIN.
SAY, DID YOU KNOW THE BASEMENT OF CITY HALL USED TO BE A *JAIL?*
FUNNY, HUH?
CRAZED WINGMAN
Shuts Down Subways
for Eleven Hours!

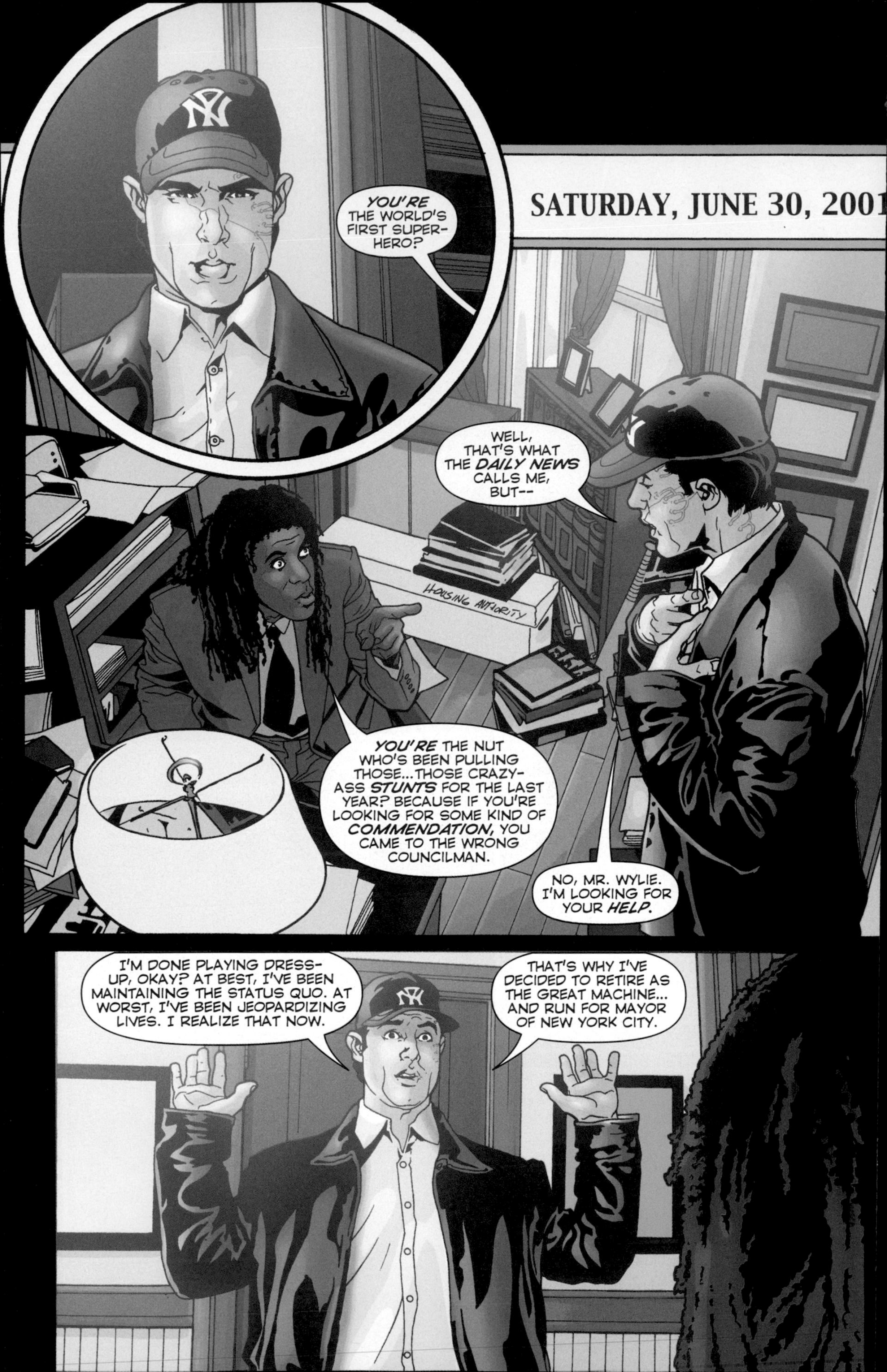
SATURDAY, JUNE 30, 2001
YOU'RE THE WORLD'S FIRST SUPER-HERO?
WELL, THAT'S WHAT THE DAILY NEWS CALLS ME, BUT--
HOUSING AUTHORITY
YOU'RE THE NUT WHO'S BEEN PULLING THOSE...THOSE CRAZY-ASS STUNTS FOR THE LAST YEAR? BECAUSE IF YOU'RE LOOKING FOR SOME KIND OF COMMENDATION, YOU CAME TO THE WRONG COUNCILMAN.
NO, MR. WYLIE. I'M LOOKING FOR YOUR HELP.
I'M DONE PLAYING DRESS-UP, OKAY? AT BEST, I'VE BEEN MAINTAINING THE STATUS QUO. AT WORST, I'VE BEEN JEOPARDIZING LIVES. I REALIZE THAT NOW.
THAT'S WHY I'VE DECIDED TO RETIRE AS THE GREAT MACHINE... AND RUN FOR MAYOR OF NEW YORK CITY.

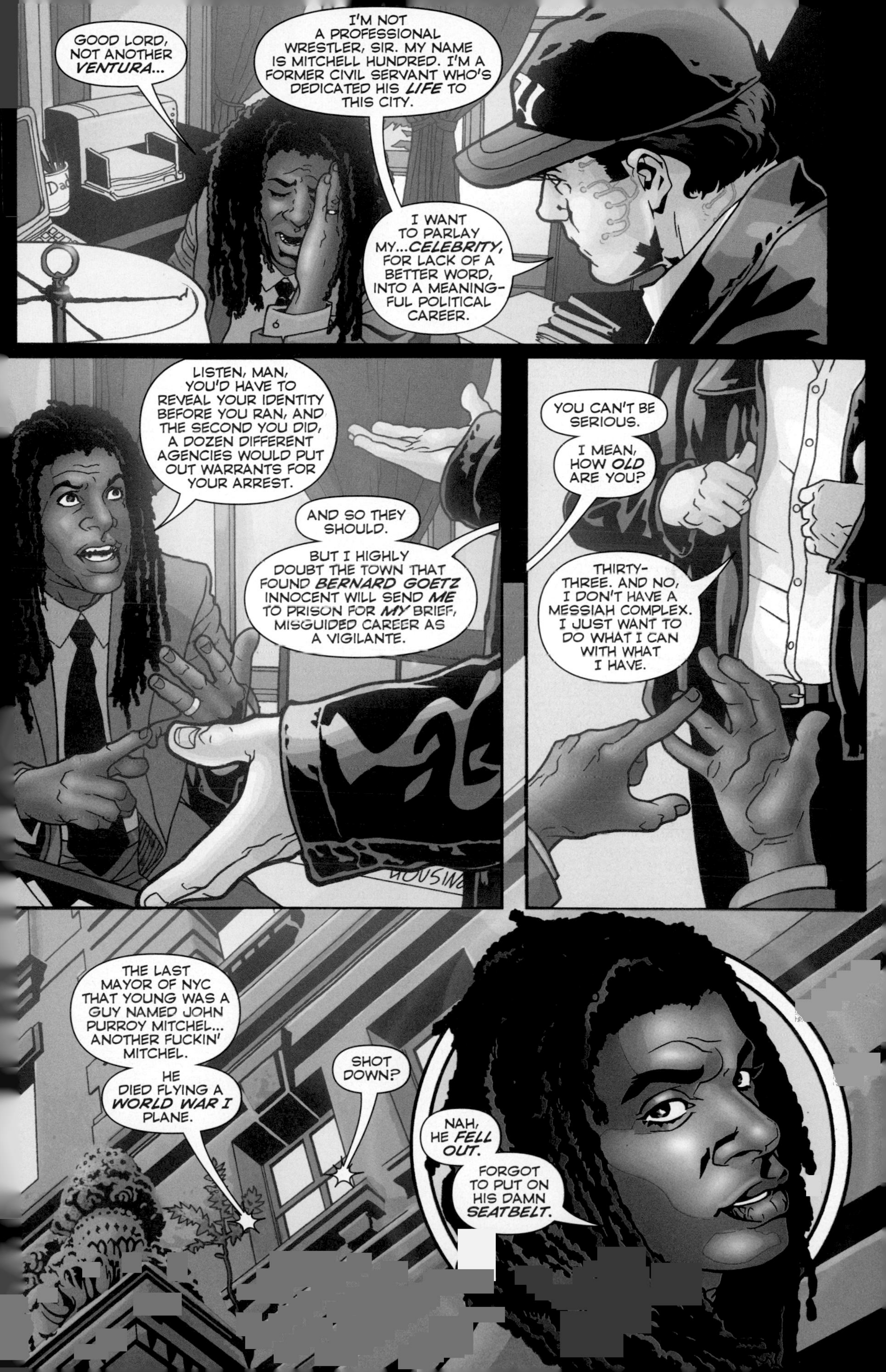
GOOD LORD, NOT ANOTHER VENTURA...
I'M NOT A PROFESSIONAL WRESTLER, SIR. MY NAME IS MITCHELL HUNDRED. I'M A FORMER CIVIL SERVANT WHO'S DEDICATED HIS LIFE TO THIS CITY.
I WANT TO PARLAY MY...CELEBRITY, FOR LACK OF A BETTER WORD, INTO A MEANINGFUL POLITICAL CAREER.
LISTEN, MAN, YOU'D HAVE TO REVEAL YOUR IDENTITY BEFORE YOU RAN, AND THE SECOND YOU DID, A DOZEN DIFFERENT AGENCIES WOULD PUT OUT WARRANTS FOR YOUR ARREST.
AND SO THEY SHOULD.
BUT I HIGHLY DOUBT THE TOWN THAT FOUND BERNARD GOETZ INNOCENT WILL SEND ME TO PRISON FOR MY BRIEF, MISGUIDED CAREER AS A VIGILANTE.
YOU CAN'T BE SERIOUS.
I MEAN, HOW OLD ARE YOU?
THIRTY-THREE. AND NO, I DON'T HAVE A MESSIAH COMPLEX. I JUST WANT TO DO WHAT I CAN WITH WHAT I HAVE.
THE LAST MAYOR OF NYC THAT YOUNG WAS A GUY NAMED JOHN PURROY MITCHEL... ANOTHER FUCKIN' MITCHEL.
HE DIED FLYING A WORLD WAR I PLANE.
SHOT DOWN?
NAH, HE FELL OUT.
FORGOT TO PUT ON HIS DAMN SEATBELT.

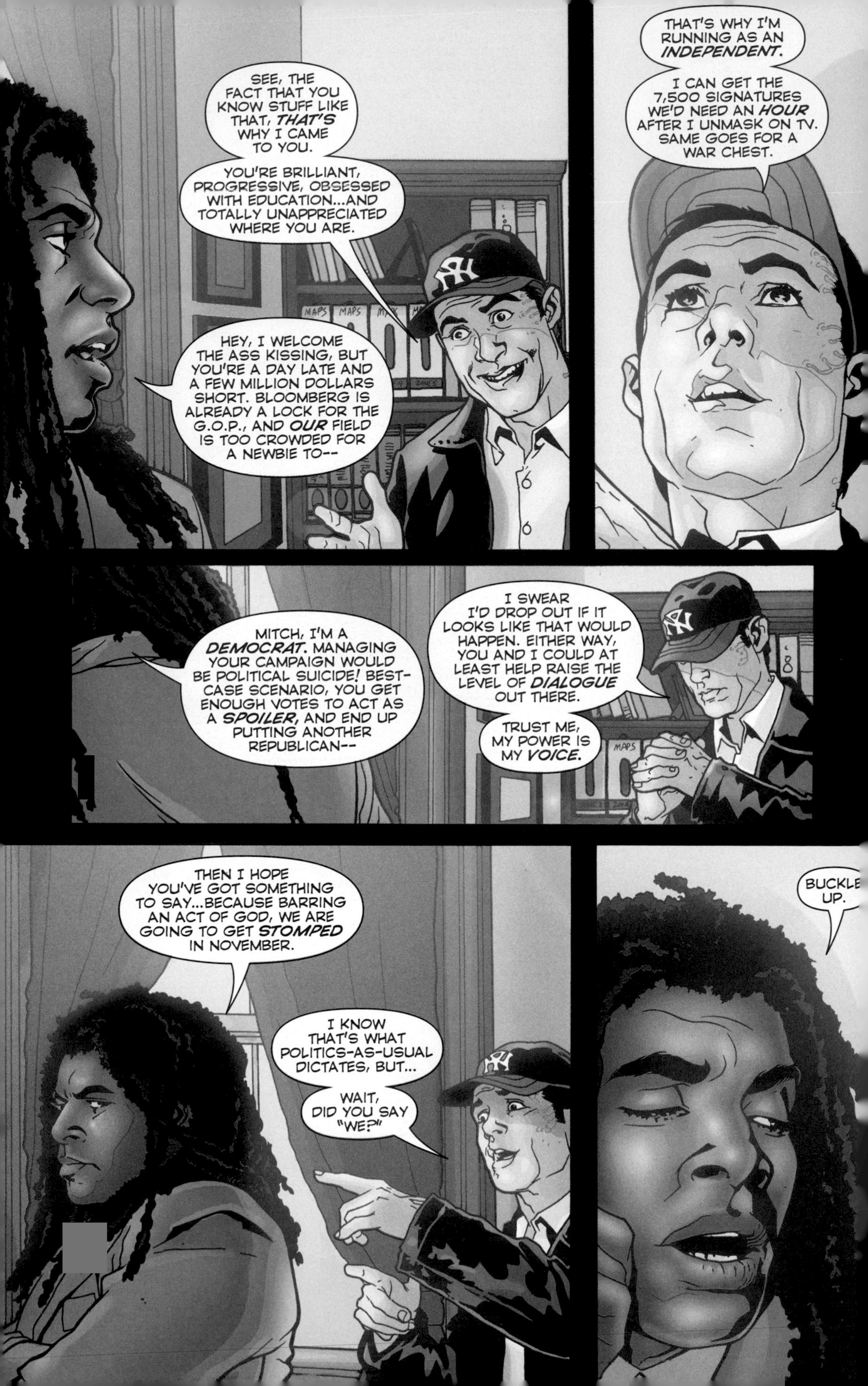
SEE, THE FACT THAT YOU KNOW STUFF LIKE THAT, *THAT'S* WHY I CAME TO YOU.
YOU'RE BRILLIANT, PROGRESSIVE, OBSESSED WITH EDUCATION...AND TOTALLY UNAPPRECIATED WHERE YOU ARE.
HEY, I WELCOME THE ASS KISSING, BUT YOU'RE A DAY LATE AND A FEW MILLION DOLLARS SHORT. BLOOMBERG IS ALREADY A LOCK FOR THE G.O.P., AND *OUR* FIELD IS TOO CROWDED FOR A NEWBIE TO--
THAT'S WHY I'M RUNNING AS AN *INDEPENDENT*.
I CAN GET THE 7,500 SIGNATURES WE'D NEED AN *HOUR* AFTER I UNMASK ON TV. SAME GOES FOR A WAR CHEST.
MITCH, I'M A *DEMOCRAT*. MANAGING YOUR CAMPAIGN WOULD BE POLITICAL SUICIDE! BEST-CASE SCENARIO, YOU GET ENOUGH VOTES TO ACT AS A *SPOILER,* AND END UP PUTTING ANOTHER REPUBLICAN--
I SWEAR I'D DROP OUT IF IT LOOKS LIKE THAT WOULD HAPPEN. EITHER WAY, YOU AND I COULD AT LEAST HELP RAISE THE LEVEL OF *DIALOGUE* OUT THERE.
TRUST ME, MY POWER IS MY *VOICE.*
THEN I HOPE YOU'VE GOT SOMETHING TO SAY...BECAUSE BARRING AN ACT OF GOD, WE ARE GOING TO GET *STOMPED* IN NOVEMBER.
I KNOW THAT'S WHAT POLITICS-AS-USUAL DICTATES, BUT...
WAIT, DID YOU SAY "WE?"
BUCKLE UP.

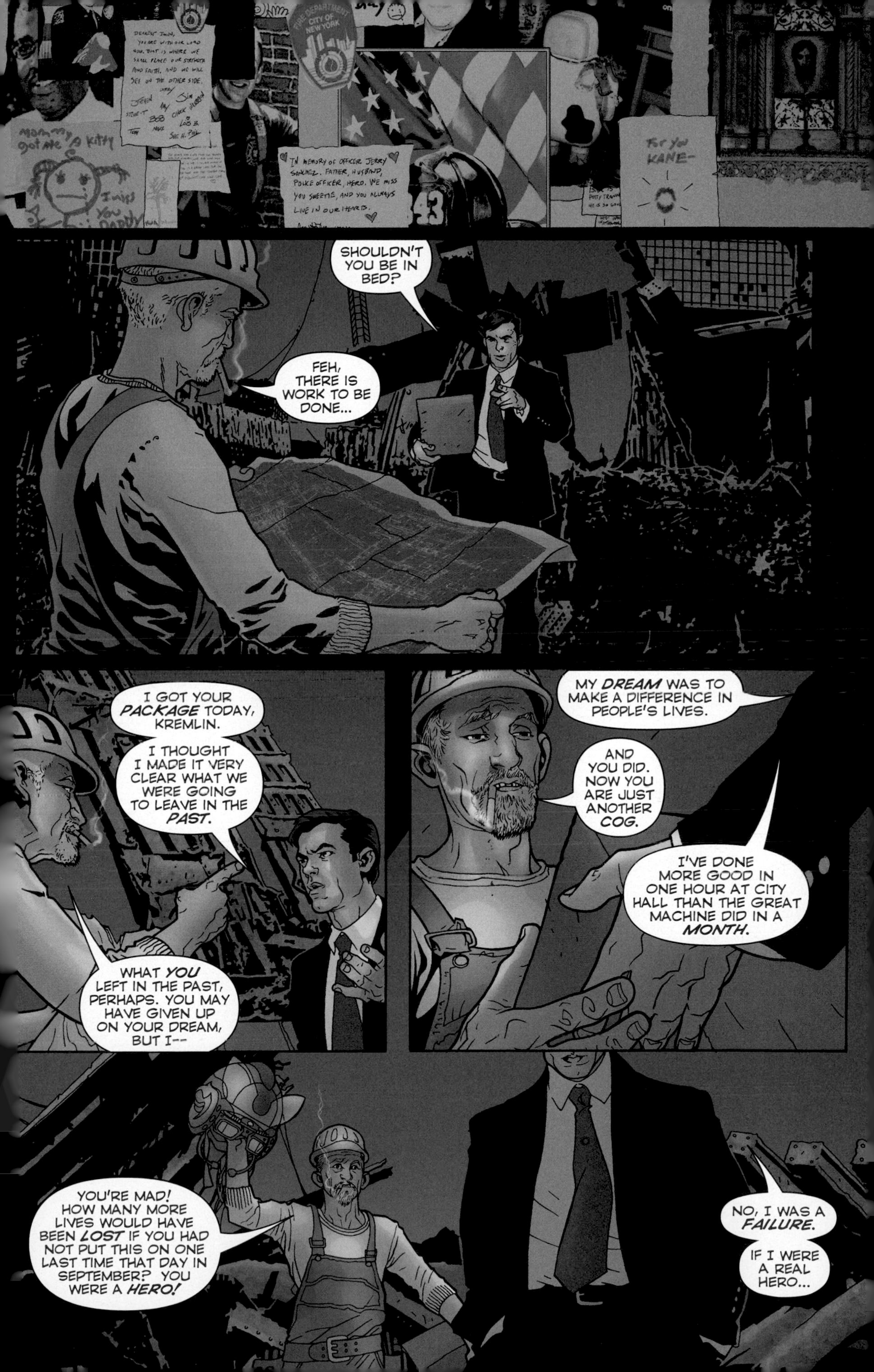
FIRE DEPARTMENT
CITY OF NEW YORK
DEAREST JOHN, YOU ARE WITH OUR LORD NOW. THAT IS WHERE WE SHALL PLACE OUR STRENGTH AND FAITH, AND WE WILL SEE ON THE OTHER SIDE.
MOMMY GOT ME A KITTY
I MISS YOU DADDY
IN MEMORY OF OFFICER JERRY SANCHEZ. FATHER, HUSBAND, POLICE OFFICER, HERO. WE MISS YOU SWEETIE, AND YOU ALWAYS LIVE IN OUR HEARTS.
43
FOR YOU KANE-
SHOULDN'T YOU BE IN BED?
FEH, THERE IS WORK TO BE DONE...
I GOT YOUR PACKAGE TODAY, KREMLIN.
I THOUGHT I MADE IT VERY CLEAR WHAT WE WERE GOING TO LEAVE IN THE PAST.
WHAT YOU LEFT IN THE PAST, PERHAPS. YOU MAY HAVE GIVEN UP ON YOUR DREAM, BUT I--
MY DREAM WAS TO MAKE A DIFFERENCE IN PEOPLE'S LIVES.
AND YOU DID. NOW YOU ARE JUST ANOTHER COG.
I'VE DONE MORE GOOD IN ONE HOUR AT CITY HALL THAN THE GREAT MACHINE DID IN A MONTH.
YOU'RE MAD! HOW MANY MORE LIVES WOULD HAVE BEEN LOST IF YOU HAD NOT PUT THIS ON ONE LAST TIME THAT DAY IN SEPTEMBER? YOU WERE A HERO!
NO, I WAS A FAILURE.
IF I WERE A REAL HERO...

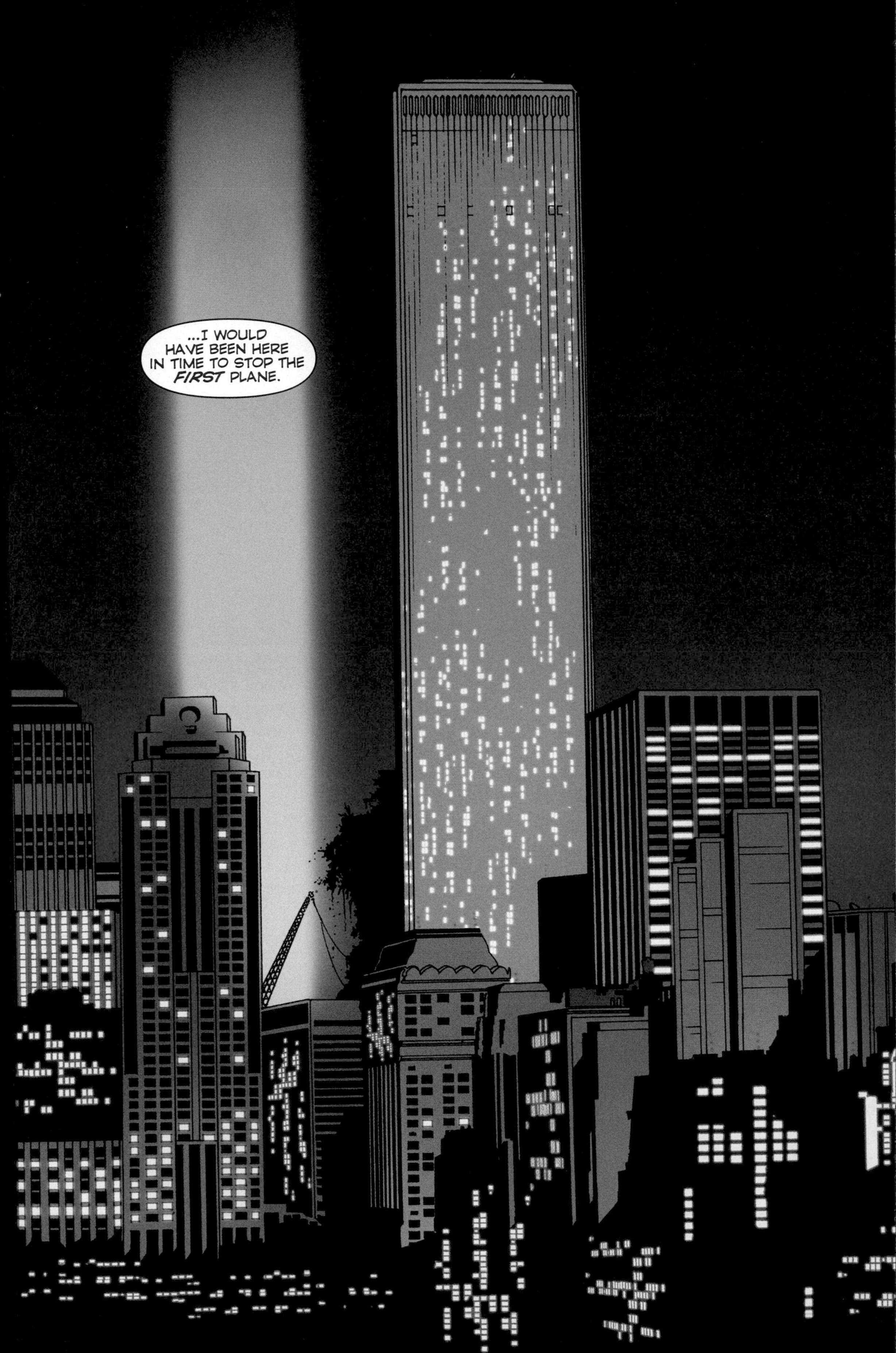
...I WOULD HAVE BEEN HERE IN TIME TO STOP THE *FIRST* PLANE.

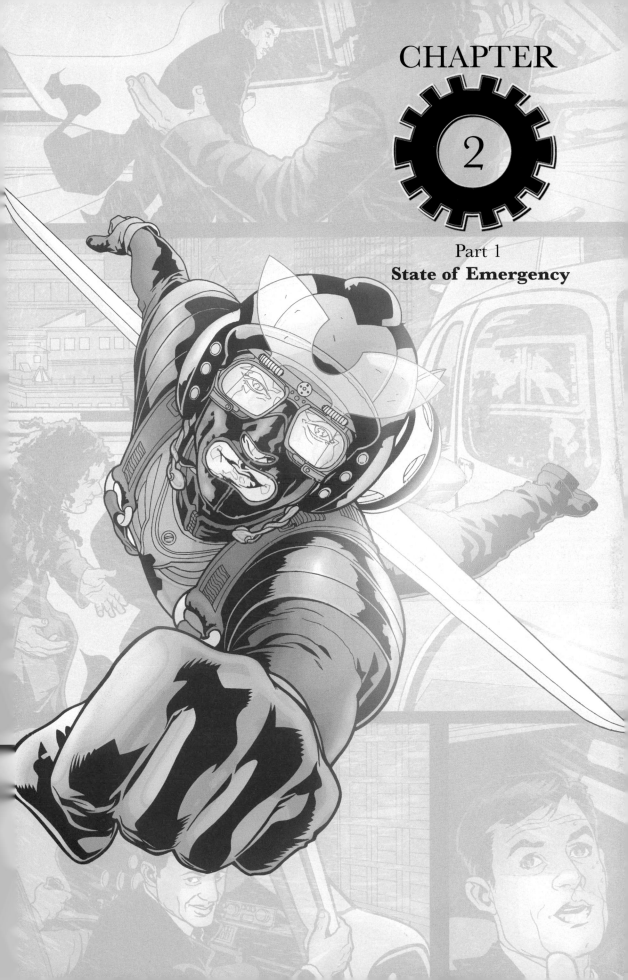

CHAPTER

2

Part 1
State of Emergency

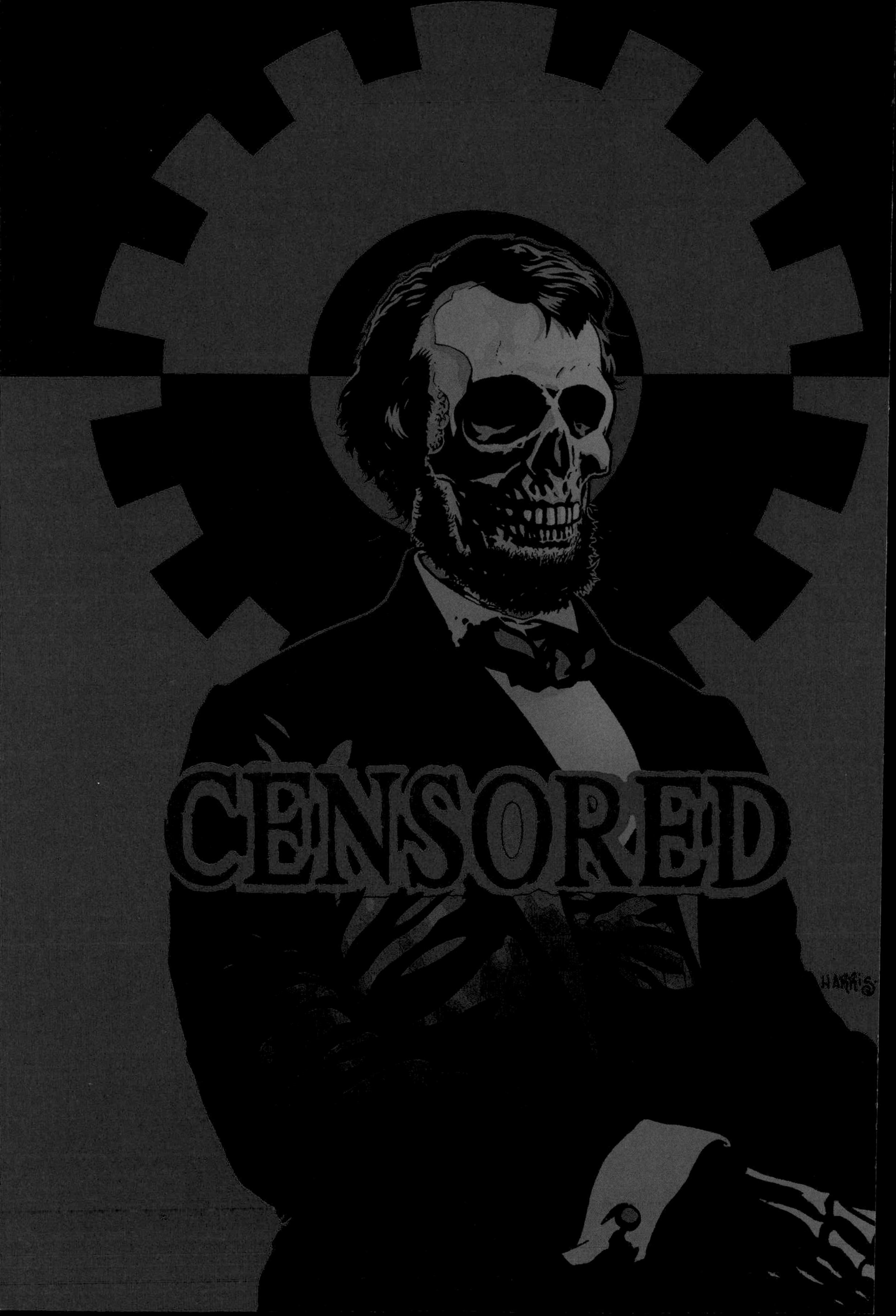
CENSORED
HARRIS

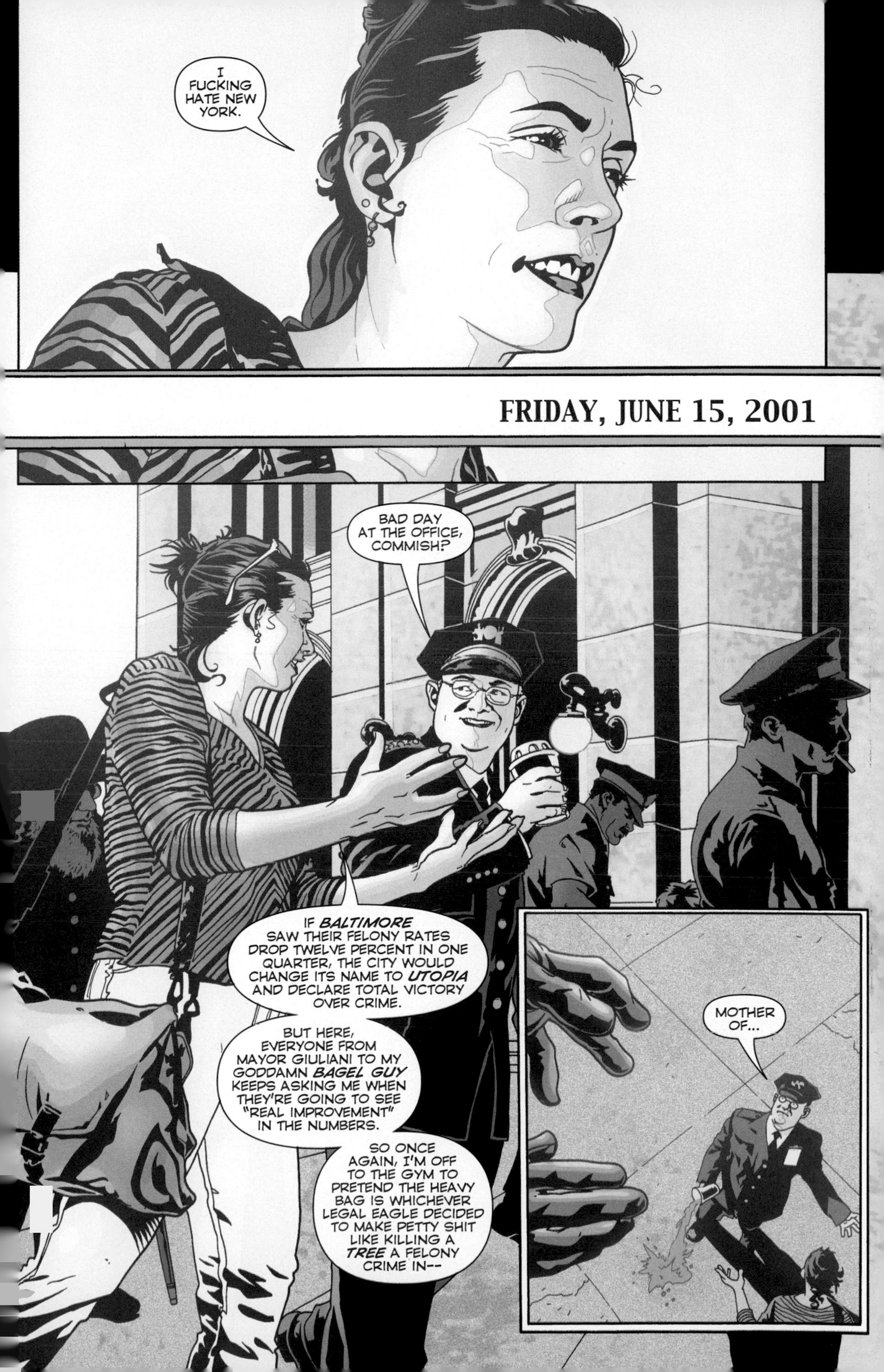
I FUCKING HATE NEW YORK.
FRIDAY, JUNE 15, 2001
BAD DAY AT THE OFFICE, COMMISH?
IF BALTIMORE SAW THEIR FELONY RATES DROP TWELVE PERCENT IN ONE QUARTER, THE CITY WOULD CHANGE ITS NAME TO UTOPIA AND DECLARE TOTAL VICTORY OVER CRIME.
BUT HERE, EVERYONE FROM MAYOR GIULIANI TO MY GODDAMN BAGEL GUY KEEPS ASKING ME WHEN THEY'RE GOING TO SEE "REAL IMPROVEMENT" IN THE NUMBERS.
SO ONCE AGAIN, I'M OFF TO THE GYM TO PRETEND THE HEAVY BAG IS WHICHEVER LEGAL EAGLE DECIDED TO MAKE PETTY SHIT LIKE KILLING A TREE A FELONY CRIME IN--
MOTHER OF...

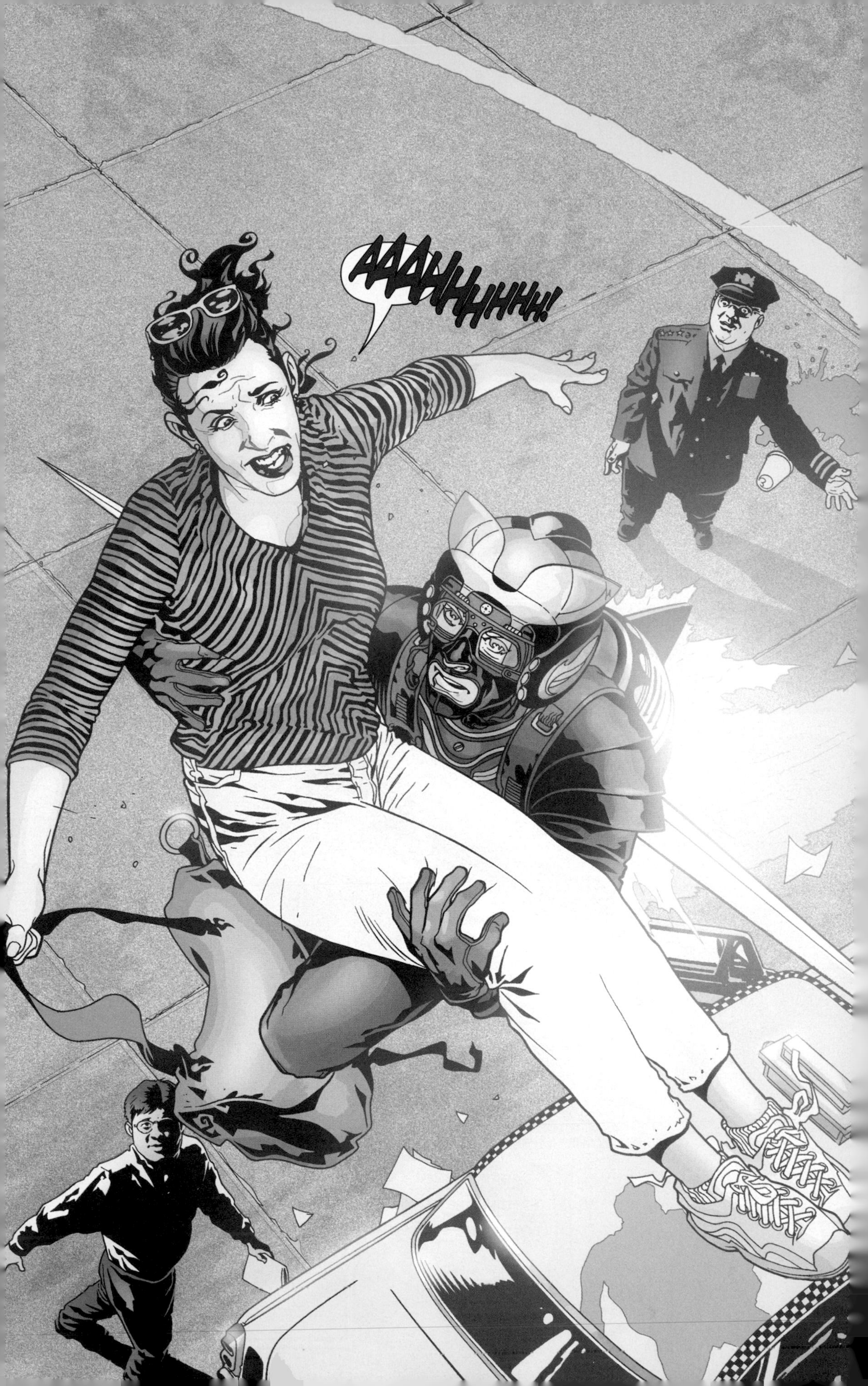
AAAHHHHHH!

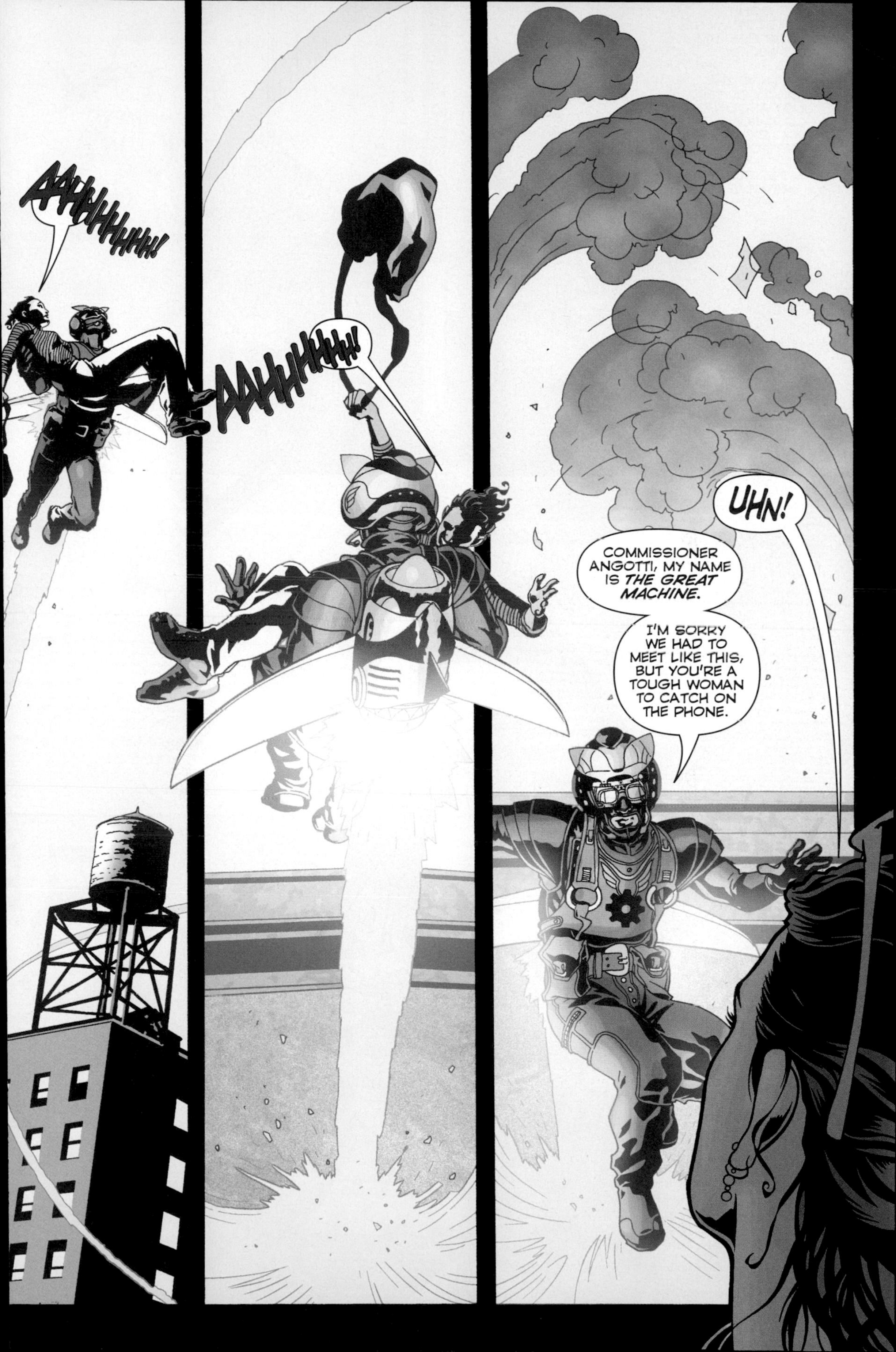
AAHHHHHHH!
AAHHHHHHH!
UHN!
COMMISSIONER ANGOTTI, MY NAME IS *THE GREAT MACHINE*.
I'M SORRY WE HAD TO MEET LIKE THIS, BUT YOU'RE A TOUGH WOMAN TO CATCH ON THE PHONE.

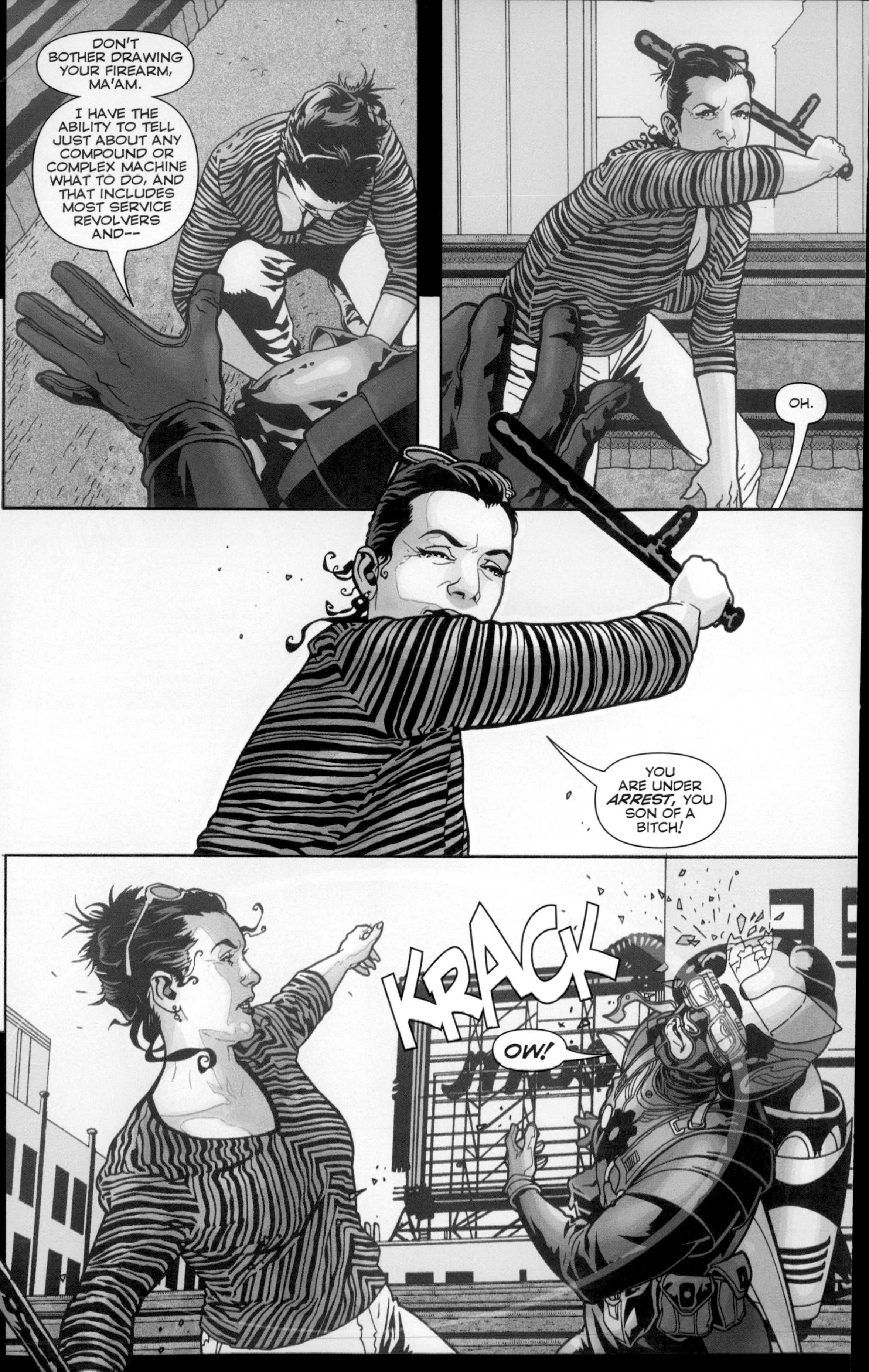
DON'T BOTHER DRAWING YOUR FIREARM, MA'AM.
I HAVE THE ABILITY TO TELL JUST ABOUT ANY COMPOUND OR COMPLEX MACHINE WHAT TO DO, AND THAT INCLUDES MOST SERVICE REVOLVERS AND--
OH.
YOU ARE UNDER *ARREST*, YOU SON OF A BITCH!
KRACK
OW!

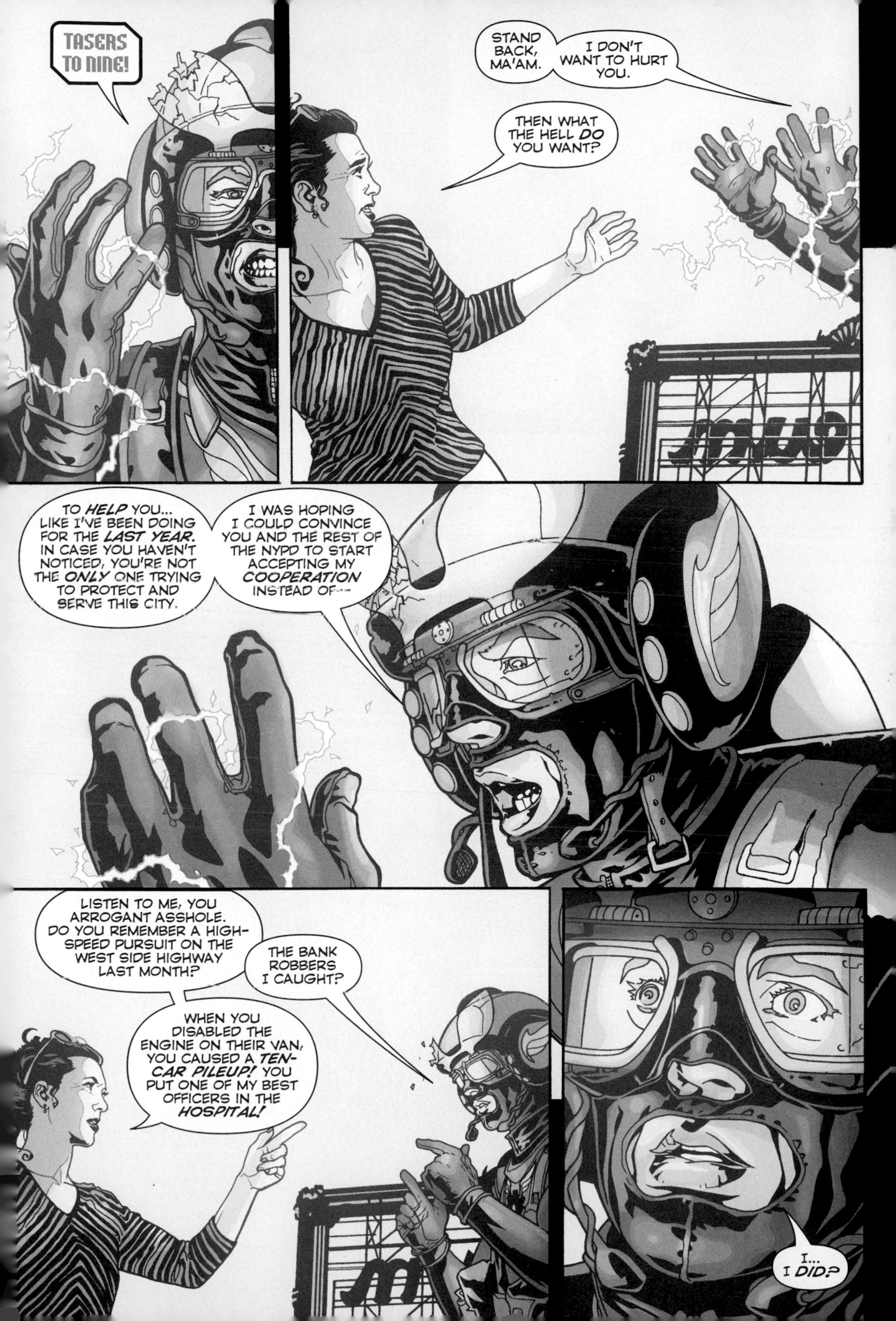
TASERS TO NINE!
STAND BACK, MA'AM.
I DON'T WANT TO HURT YOU.
THEN WHAT THE HELL *DO* YOU WANT?
TO *HELP* YOU... LIKE I'VE BEEN DOING FOR THE *LAST YEAR.* IN CASE YOU HAVEN'T NOTICED, YOU'RE NOT THE *ONLY* ONE TRYING TO PROTECT AND SERVE THIS CITY.
I WAS HOPING I COULD CONVINCE YOU AND THE REST OF THE NYPD TO START ACCEPTING MY *COOPERATION* INSTEAD OF--
LISTEN TO ME, YOU ARROGANT ASSHOLE. DO YOU REMEMBER A HIGH-SPEED PURSUIT ON THE WEST SIDE HIGHWAY LAST MONTH?
THE BANK ROBBERS I CAUGHT?
WHEN YOU DISABLED THE ENGINE ON THEIR VAN, YOU CAUSED A *TEN-CAR PILEUP!* YOU PUT ONE OF MY BEST OFFICERS IN THE *HOSPITAL!*
I... I *DID?*

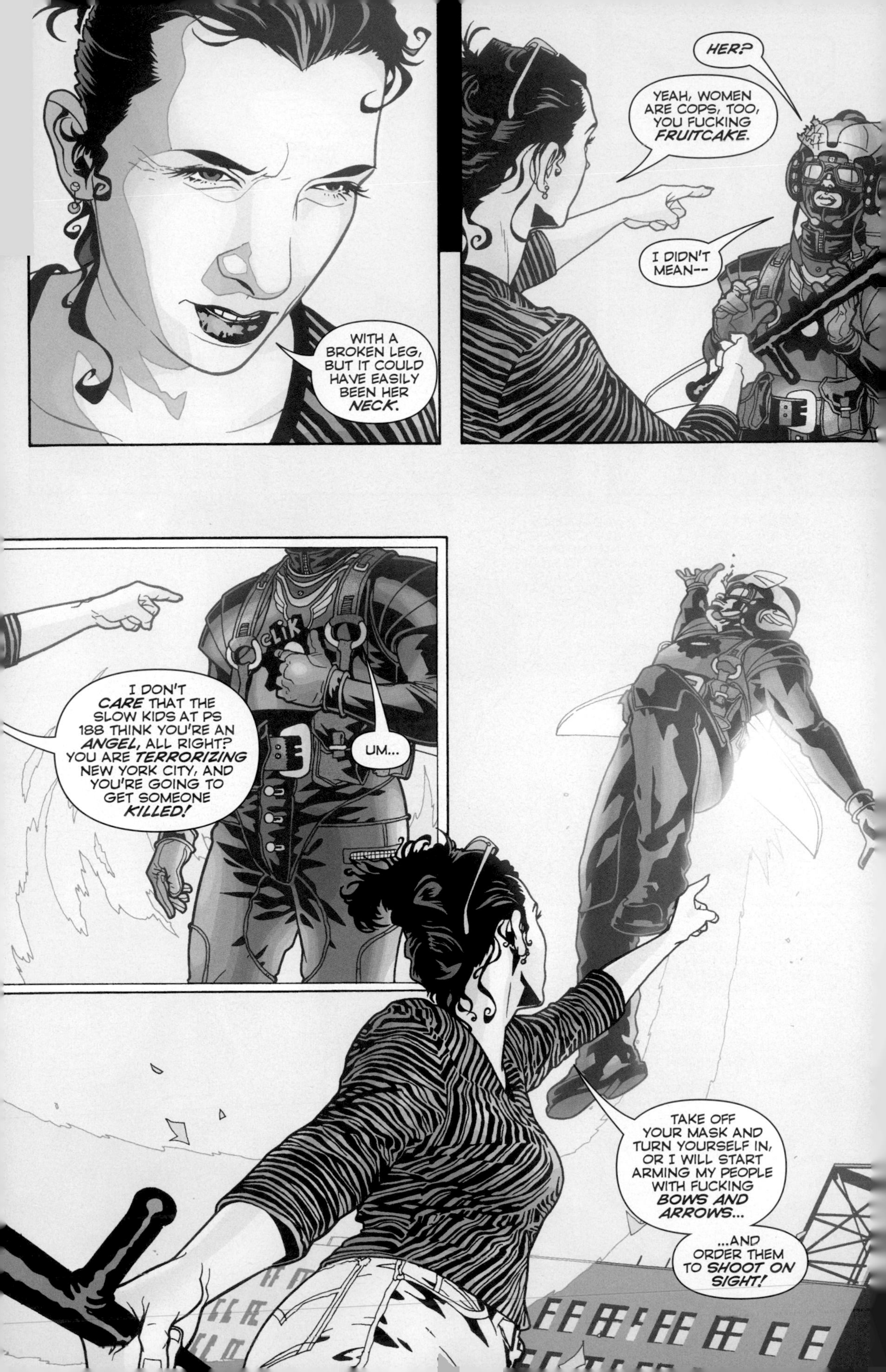
WITH A BROKEN LEG, BUT IT COULD HAVE EASILY BEEN HER *NECK*.
HER?
YEAH, WOMEN ARE COPS, TOO, YOU FUCKING *FRUITCAKE*.
I DIDN'T MEAN--
CLIK
I DON'T *CARE* THAT THE SLOW KIDS AT PS 188 THINK YOU'RE AN *ANGEL*, ALL RIGHT? YOU ARE *TERRORIZING* NEW YORK CITY, AND YOU'RE GOING TO GET SOMEONE *KILLED!*
UM...
TAKE OFF YOUR MASK AND TURN YOURSELF IN, OR I WILL START ARMING MY PEOPLE WITH FUCKING *BOWS AND ARROWS*...
...AND ORDER THEM TO *SHOOT ON SIGHT!*

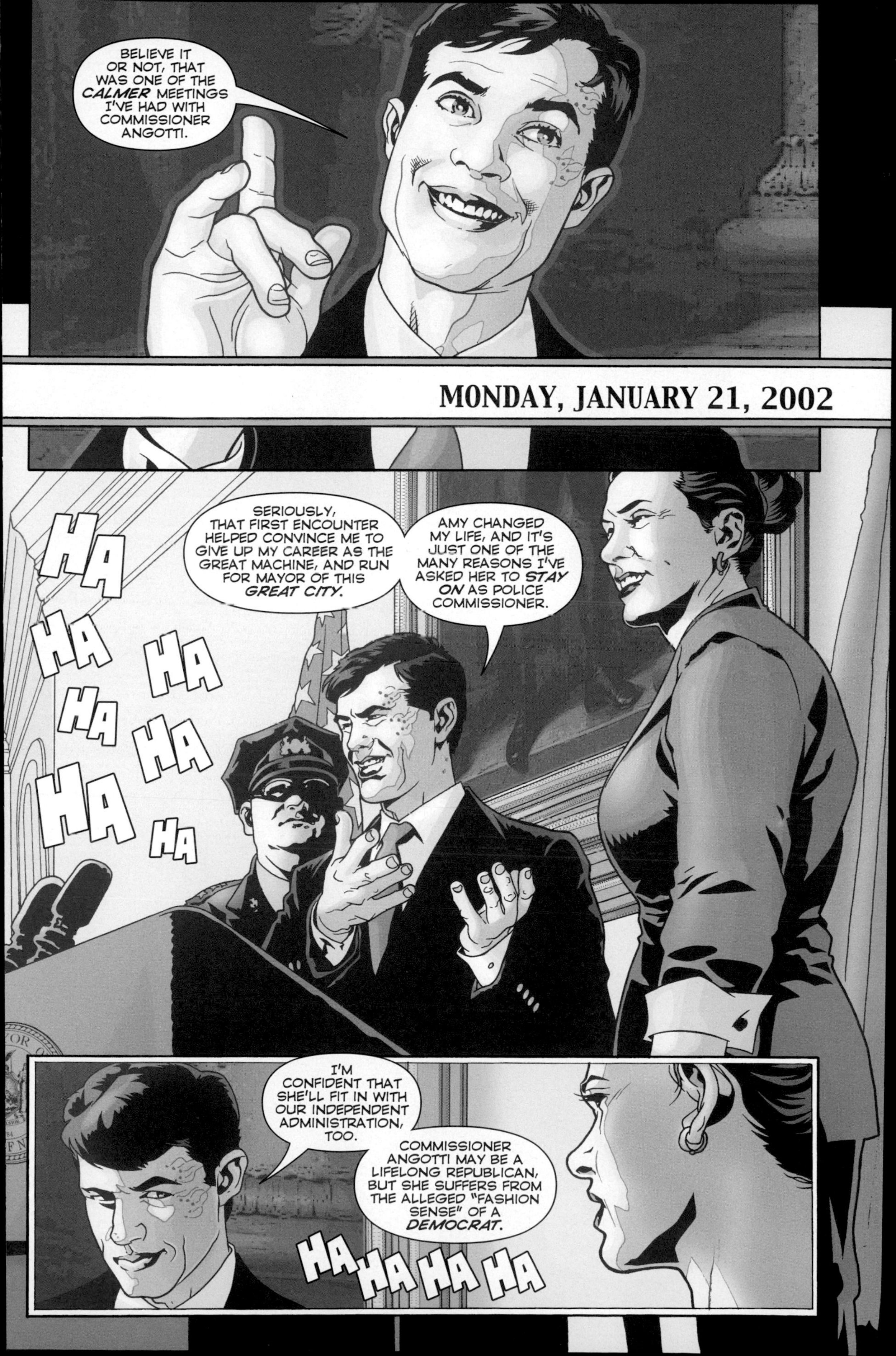
BELIEVE IT OR NOT, THAT WAS ONE OF THE CALMER MEETINGS I'VE HAD WITH COMMISSIONER ANGOTTI.
MONDAY, JANUARY 21, 2002
HA HA HA HA HA HA HA HA
SERIOUSLY, THAT FIRST ENCOUNTER HELPED CONVINCE ME TO GIVE UP MY CAREER AS THE GREAT MACHINE, AND RUN FOR MAYOR OF THIS GREAT CITY.
AMY CHANGED MY LIFE, AND IT'S JUST ONE OF THE MANY REASONS I'VE ASKED HER TO STAY ON AS POLICE COMMISSIONER.
I'M CONFIDENT THAT SHE'LL FIT IN WITH OUR INDEPENDENT ADMINISTRATION, TOO.
COMMISSIONER ANGOTTI MAY BE A LIFELONG REPUBLICAN, BUT SHE SUFFERS FROM THE ALLEGED "FASHION SENSE" OF A DEMOCRAT.
HA HA HA HA HA

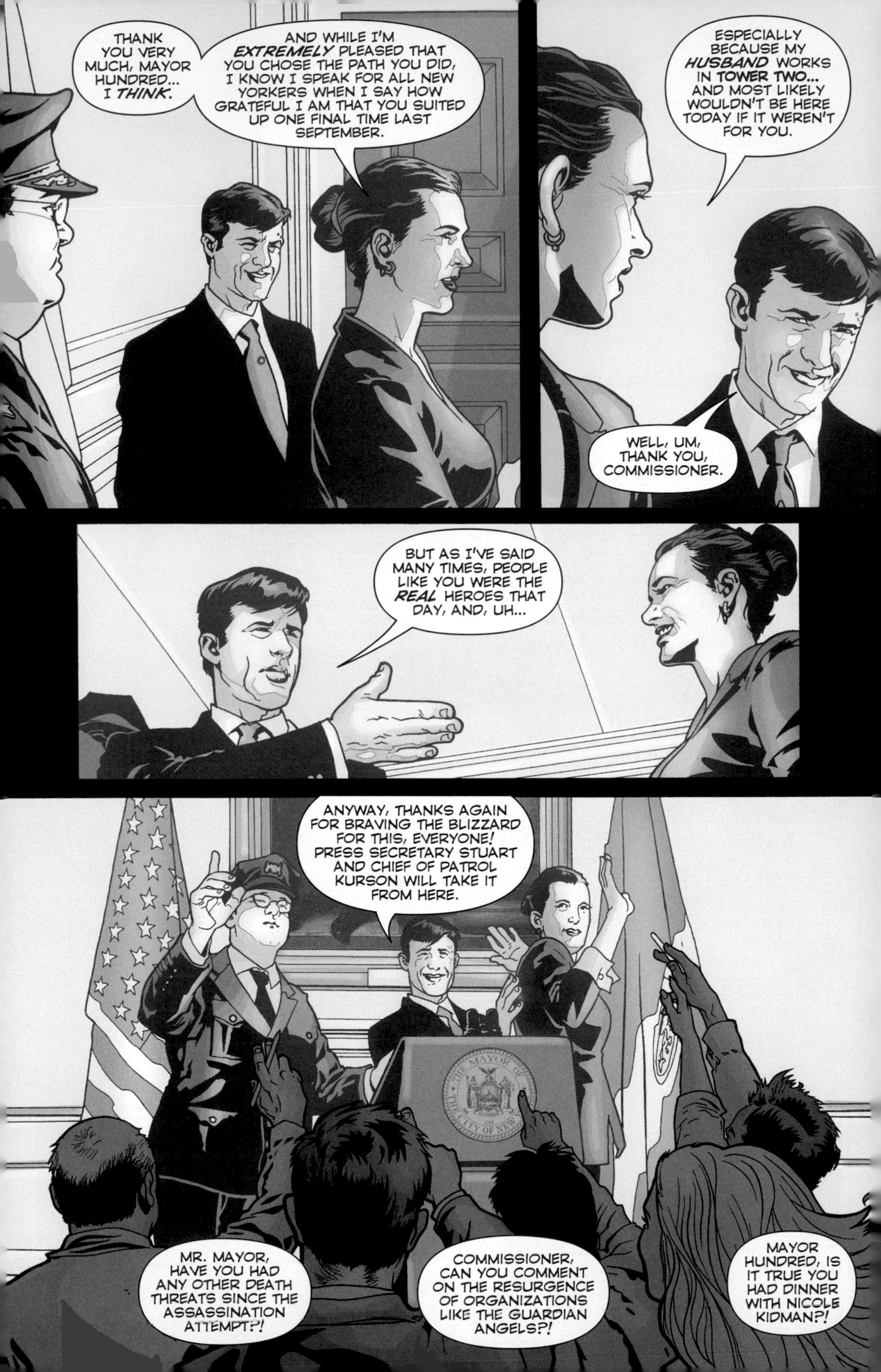
THANK YOU VERY MUCH, MAYOR HUNDRED... I *THINK*.
AND WHILE I'M *EXTREMELY* PLEASED THAT YOU CHOSE THE PATH YOU DID, I KNOW I SPEAK FOR ALL NEW YORKERS WHEN I SAY HOW GRATEFUL I AM THAT YOU SUITED UP ONE FINAL TIME LAST SEPTEMBER.
ESPECIALLY BECAUSE MY ***HUSBAND*** WORKS IN **TOWER TWO...** AND MOST LIKELY WOULDN'T BE HERE TODAY IF IT WEREN'T FOR YOU.
WELL, UM, THANK YOU, COMMISSIONER.
BUT AS I'VE SAID MANY TIMES, PEOPLE LIKE YOU WERE THE *REAL* HEROES THAT DAY, AND, UH...
ANYWAY, THANKS AGAIN FOR BRAVING THE BLIZZARD FOR THIS, EVERYONE! PRESS SECRETARY STUART AND CHIEF OF PATROL KURSON WILL TAKE IT FROM HERE.
MR. MAYOR, HAVE YOU HAD ANY OTHER DEATH THREATS SINCE THE ASSASSINATION ATTEMPT?!
COMMISSIONER, CAN YOU COMMENT ON THE RESURGENCE OF ORGANIZATIONS LIKE THE GUARDIAN ANGELS?!
MAYOR HUNDRED, IS IT TRUE YOU HAD DINNER WITH NICOLE KIDMAN?!

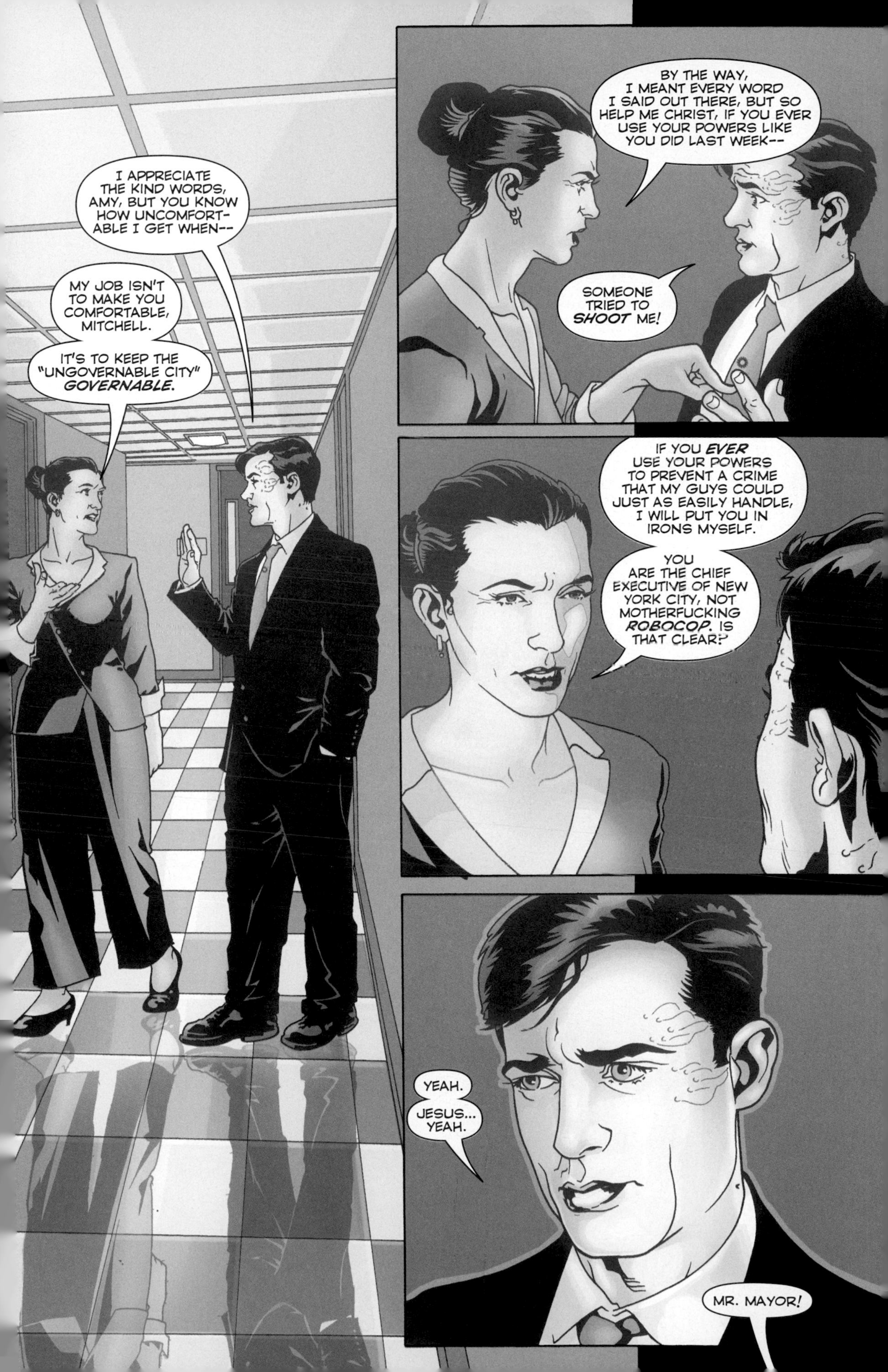
I APPRECIATE THE KIND WORDS, AMY, BUT YOU KNOW HOW UNCOMFORT-ABLE I GET WHEN--
MY JOB ISN'T TO MAKE YOU COMFORTABLE, MITCHELL.
IT'S TO KEEP THE "UNGOVERNABLE CITY" *GOVERNABLE*.
BY THE WAY, I MEANT EVERY WORD I SAID OUT THERE, BUT SO HELP ME CHRIST, IF YOU EVER USE YOUR POWERS LIKE YOU DID LAST WEEK--
SOMEONE TRIED TO *SHOOT* ME!
IF YOU *EVER* USE YOUR POWERS TO PREVENT A CRIME THAT MY GUYS COULD JUST AS EASILY HANDLE, I WILL PUT YOU IN IRONS MYSELF.
YOU ARE THE CHIEF EXECUTIVE OF NEW YORK CITY, NOT MOTHERFUCKING *ROBOCOP*. IS THAT CLEAR?
YEAH.
JESUS... YEAH.
MR. MAYOR!

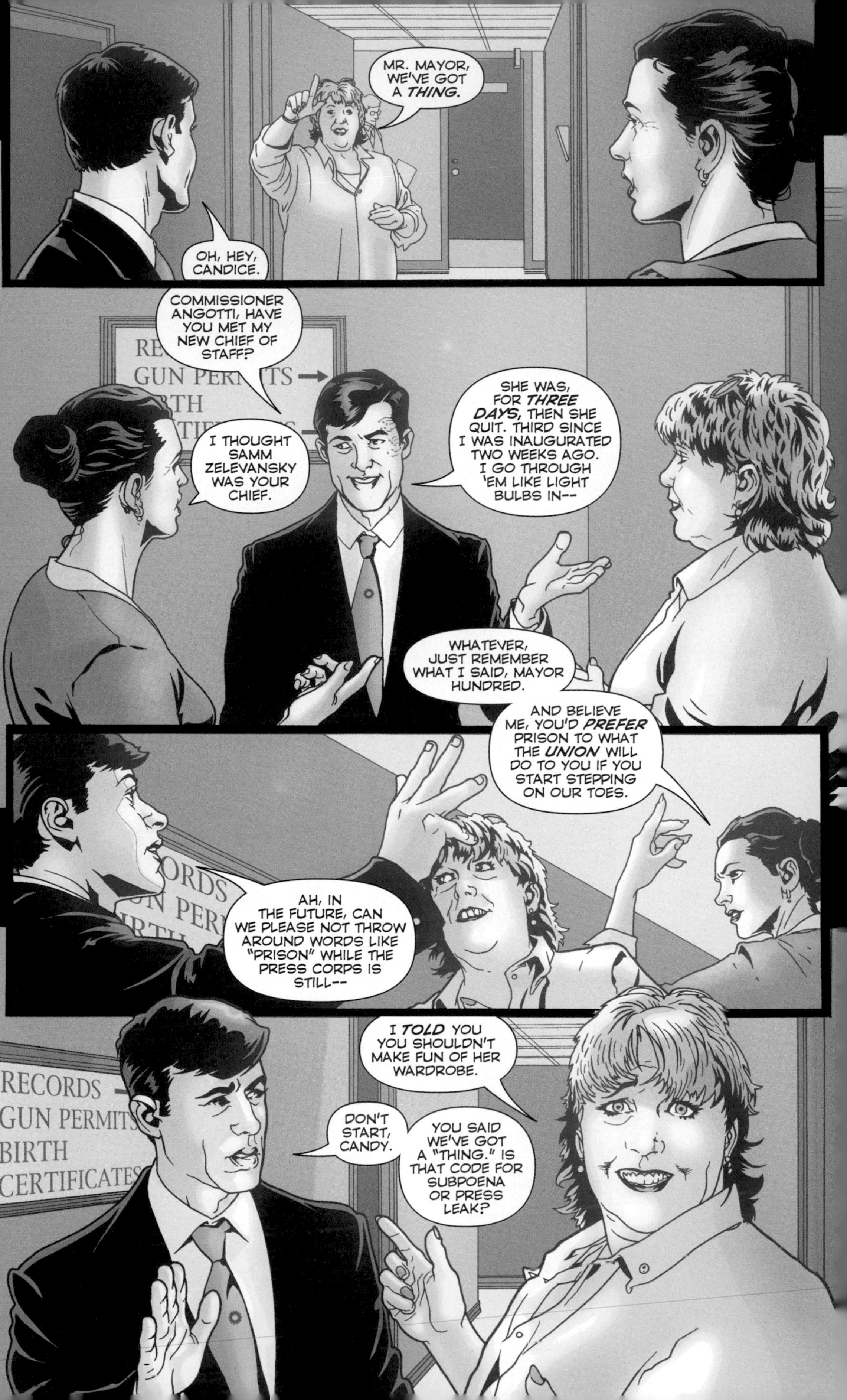
MR. MAYOR, WE'VE GOT A *THING.*
OH, HEY, CANDICE.
COMMISSIONER ANGOTTI, HAVE YOU MET MY NEW CHIEF OF STAFF?
I THOUGHT SAMM ZELEVANSKY WAS YOUR CHIEF.
SHE WAS, FOR *THREE DAYS,* THEN SHE QUIT. THIRD SINCE I WAS INAUGURATED TWO WEEKS AGO. I GO THROUGH 'EM LIKE LIGHT BULBS IN--
RECORDS
GUN PERMITS
BIRTH
CERTIFICATES
WHATEVER, JUST REMEMBER WHAT I SAID, MAYOR HUNDRED.
AND BELIEVE ME, YOU'D *PREFER* PRISON TO WHAT THE *UNION* WILL DO TO YOU IF YOU START STEPPING ON OUR TOES.
AH, IN THE FUTURE, CAN WE PLEASE NOT THROW AROUND WORDS LIKE "PRISON" WHILE THE PRESS CORPS IS STILL--
I *TOLD* YOU YOU SHOULDN'T MAKE FUN OF HER WARDROBE.
DON'T START, CANDY.
YOU SAID WE'VE GOT A "THING." IS THAT CODE FOR SUBPOENA OR PRESS LEAK?
RECORDS
GUN PERMITS
BIRTH
CERTIFICATES

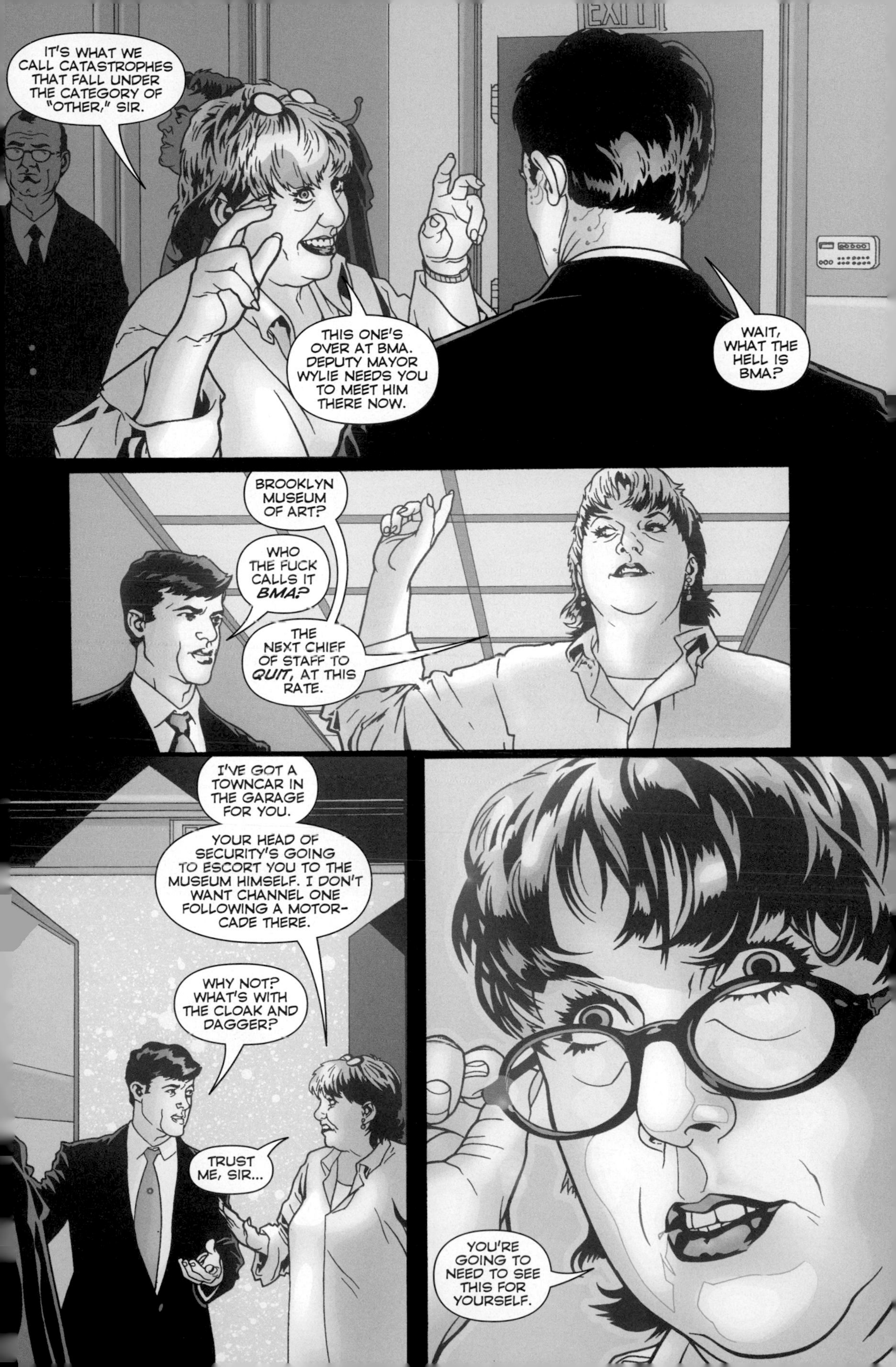
IT'S WHAT WE CALL CATASTROPHES THAT FALL UNDER THE CATEGORY OF "OTHER," SIR.
THIS ONE'S OVER AT BMA. DEPUTY MAYOR WYLIE NEEDS YOU TO MEET HIM THERE NOW.
WAIT, WHAT THE HELL IS BMA?
BROOKLYN MUSEUM OF ART?
WHO THE FUCK CALLS IT *BMA?*
THE NEXT CHIEF OF STAFF TO *QUIT,* AT THIS RATE.
I'VE GOT A TOWNCAR IN THE GARAGE FOR YOU.
YOUR HEAD OF SECURITY'S GOING TO ESCORT YOU TO THE MUSEUM HIMSELF. I DON'T WANT CHANNEL ONE FOLLOWING A MOTOR-CADE THERE.
WHY NOT? WHAT'S WITH THE CLOAK AND DAGGER?
TRUST ME, SIR...
YOU'RE GOING TO NEED TO SEE THIS FOR YOURSELF.

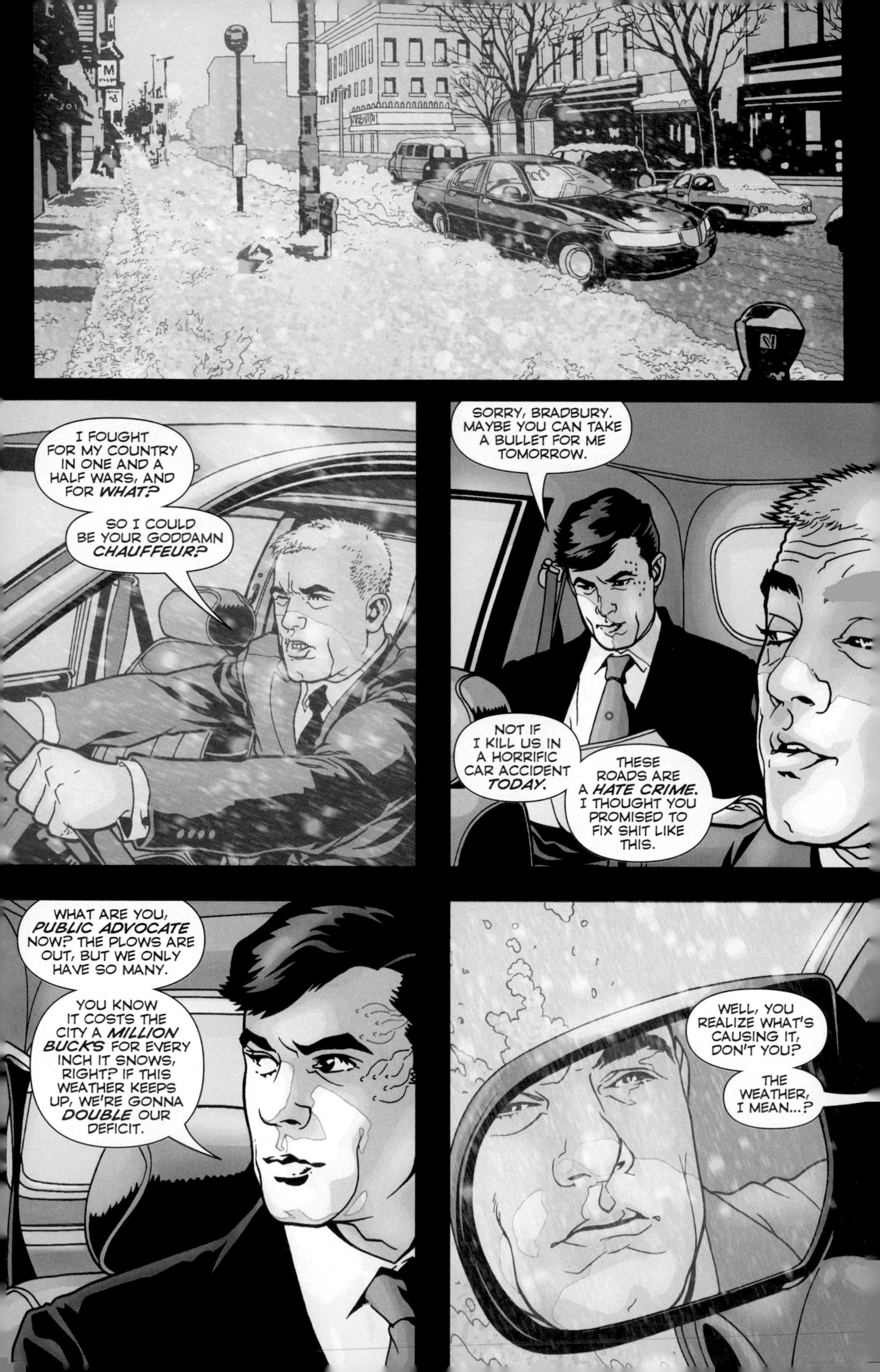
I FOUGHT FOR MY COUNTRY IN ONE AND A HALF WARS, AND FOR *WHAT?*
SO I COULD BE YOUR GODDAMN *CHAUFFEUR?*
SORRY, BRADBURY. MAYBE YOU CAN TAKE A BULLET FOR ME TOMORROW.
NOT IF I KILL US IN A HORRIFIC CAR ACCIDENT *TODAY.*
THESE ROADS ARE A *HATE CRIME.* I THOUGHT YOU PROMISED TO FIX SHIT LIKE THIS.
WHAT ARE YOU, *PUBLIC ADVOCATE* NOW? THE PLOWS ARE OUT, BUT WE ONLY HAVE SO MANY.
YOU KNOW IT COSTS THE CITY A *MILLION BUCKS* FOR EVERY INCH IT SNOWS, RIGHT? IF THIS WEATHER KEEPS UP, WE'RE GONNA *DOUBLE* OUR DEFICIT.
WELL, YOU REALIZE WHAT'S CAUSING IT, DON'T YOU?
THE WEATHER, I MEAN...?

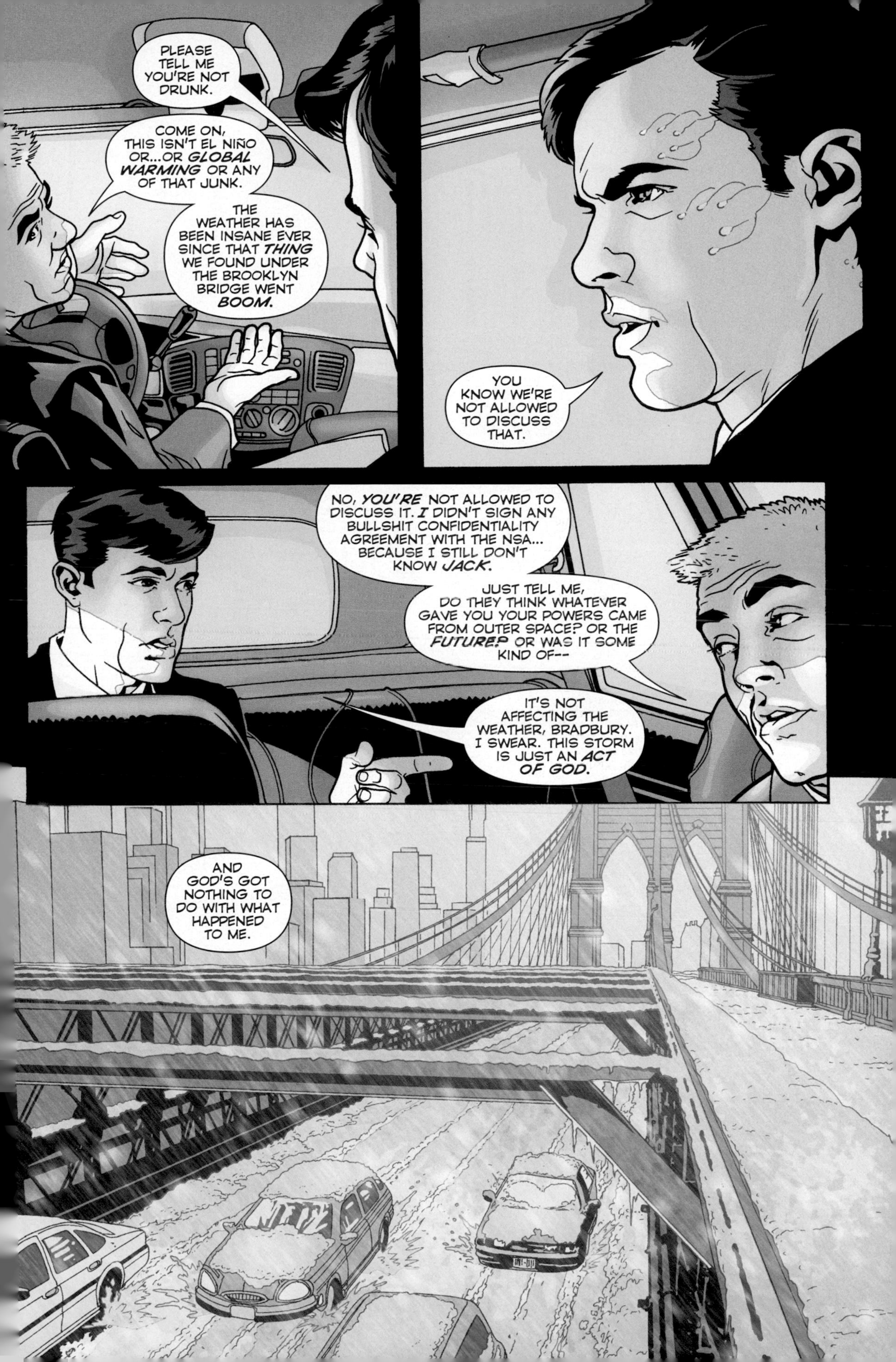
PLEASE TELL ME YOU'RE NOT DRUNK.
COME ON, THIS ISN'T EL NIÑO OR...OR *GLOBAL WARMING* OR ANY OF THAT JUNK.
THE WEATHER HAS BEEN INSANE EVER SINCE THAT *THING* WE FOUND UNDER THE BROOKLYN BRIDGE WENT *BOOM*.
YOU KNOW WE'RE NOT ALLOWED TO DISCUSS THAT.
NO, *YOU'RE* NOT ALLOWED TO DISCUSS IT. *I* DIDN'T SIGN ANY BULLSHIT CONFIDENTIALITY AGREEMENT WITH THE NSA... BECAUSE I STILL DON'T KNOW *JACK*.
JUST TELL ME, DO THEY THINK WHATEVER GAVE YOU YOUR POWERS CAME FROM OUTER SPACE? OR THE *FUTURE?* OR WAS IT SOME KIND OF--
IT'S NOT AFFECTING THE WEATHER, BRADBURY. I SWEAR. THIS STORM IS JUST AN *ACT OF GOD*.
AND GOD'S GOT NOTHING TO DO WITH WHAT HAPPENED TO ME.

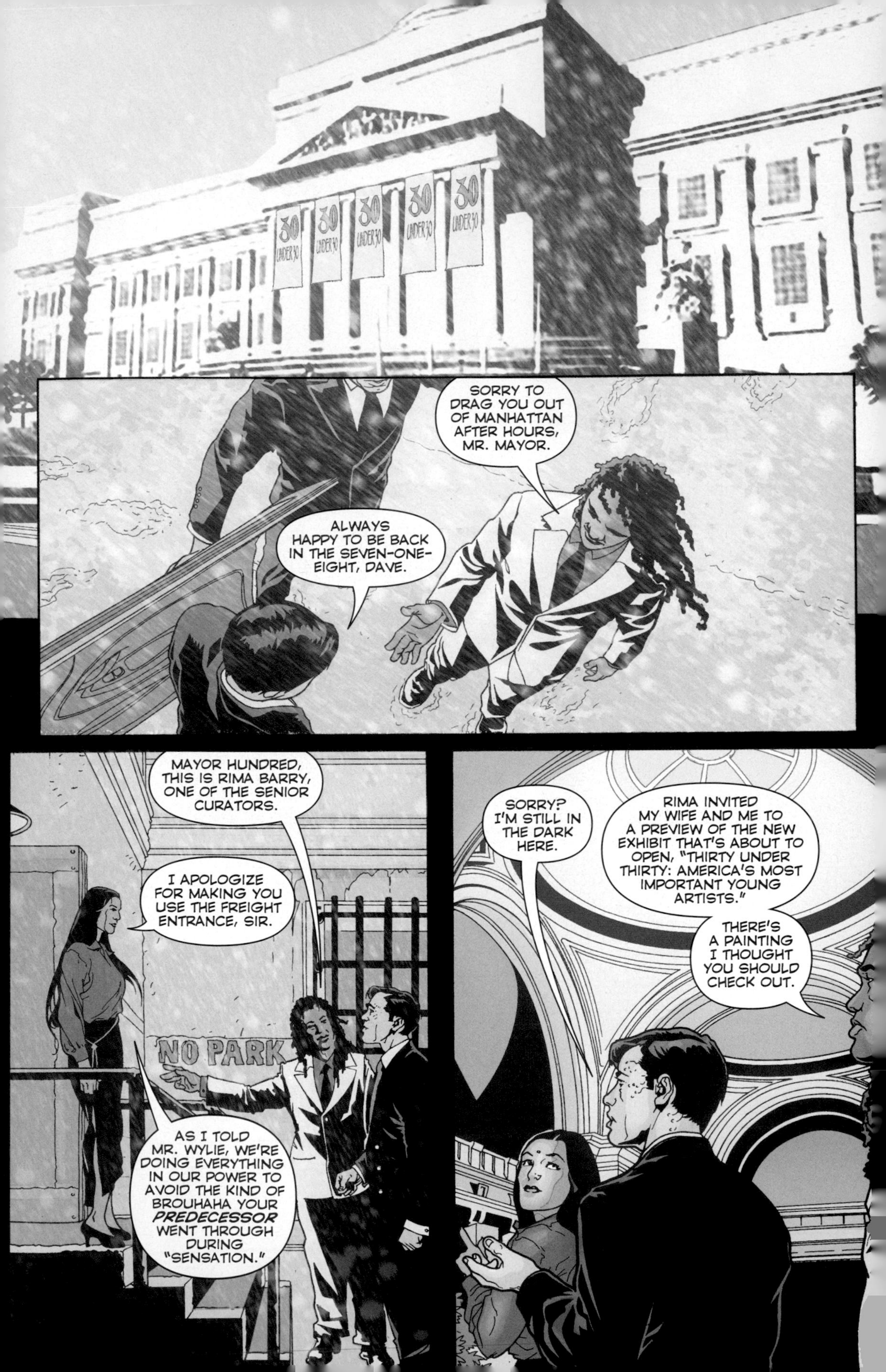
30 UNDER 30
SORRY TO DRAG YOU OUT OF MANHATTAN AFTER HOURS, MR. MAYOR.
ALWAYS HAPPY TO BE BACK IN THE SEVEN-ONE-EIGHT, DAVE.
MAYOR HUNDRED, THIS IS RIMA BARRY, ONE OF THE SENIOR CURATORS.
I APOLOGIZE FOR MAKING YOU USE THE FREIGHT ENTRANCE, SIR.
NO PARK
AS I TOLD MR. WYLIE, WE'RE DOING EVERYTHING IN OUR POWER TO AVOID THE KIND OF BROUHAHA YOUR *PREDECESSOR* WENT THROUGH DURING "SENSATION."
SORRY? I'M STILL IN THE DARK HERE.
RIMA INVITED MY WIFE AND ME TO A PREVIEW OF THE NEW EXHIBIT THAT'S ABOUT TO OPEN, "THIRTY UNDER THIRTY: AMERICA'S MOST IMPORTANT YOUNG ARTISTS."
THERE'S A PAINTING I THOUGHT YOU SHOULD CHECK OUT.

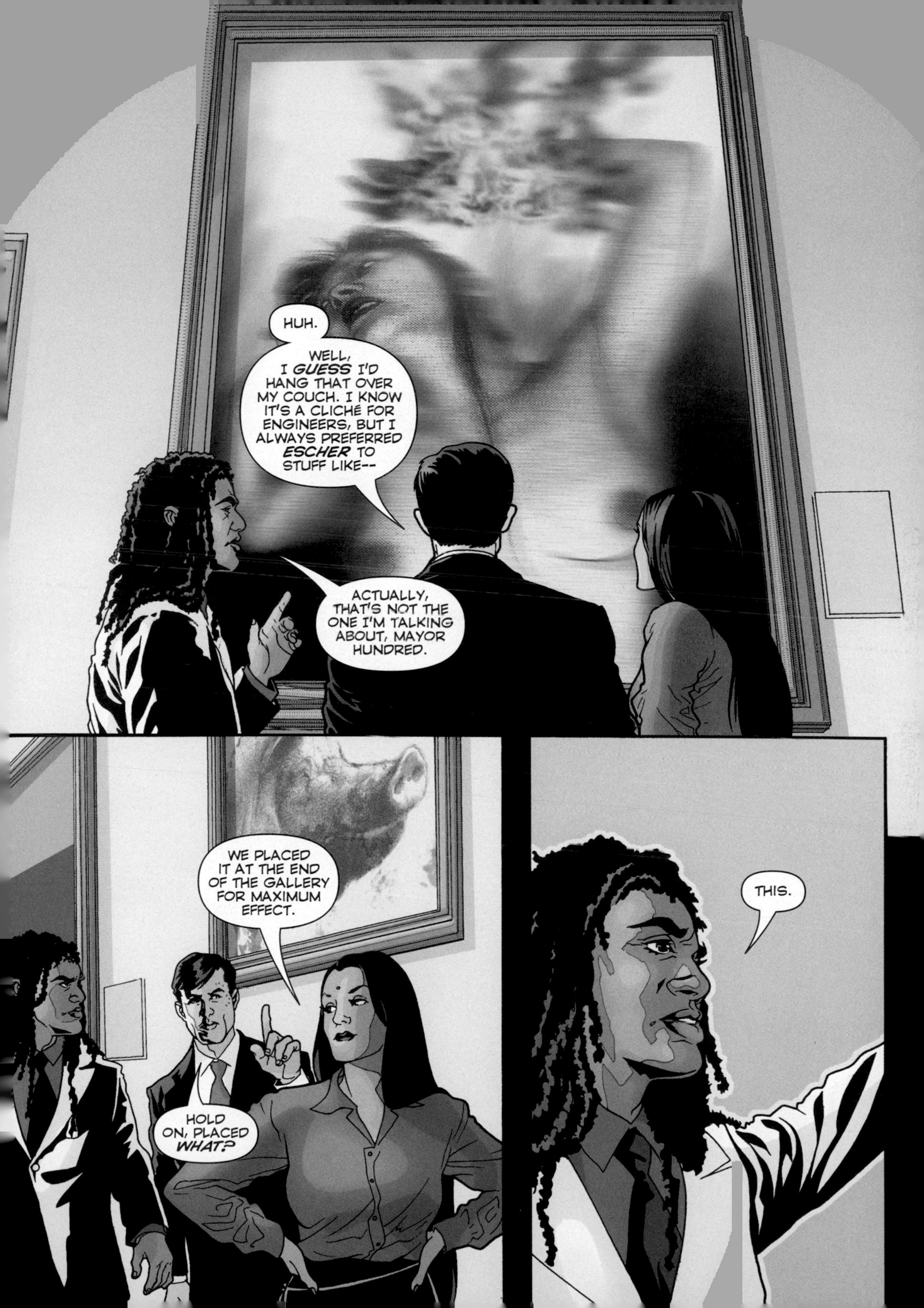
HUH.
WELL, I GUESS I'D HANG THAT OVER MY COUCH. I KNOW IT'S A CLICHÉ FOR ENGINEERS, BUT I ALWAYS PREFERRED ESCHER TO STUFF LIKE--
ACTUALLY, THAT'S NOT THE ONE I'M TALKING ABOUT, MAYOR HUNDRED.
WE PLACED IT AT THE END OF THE GALLERY FOR MAXIMUM EFFECT.
HOLD ON, PLACED WHAT?
THIS.

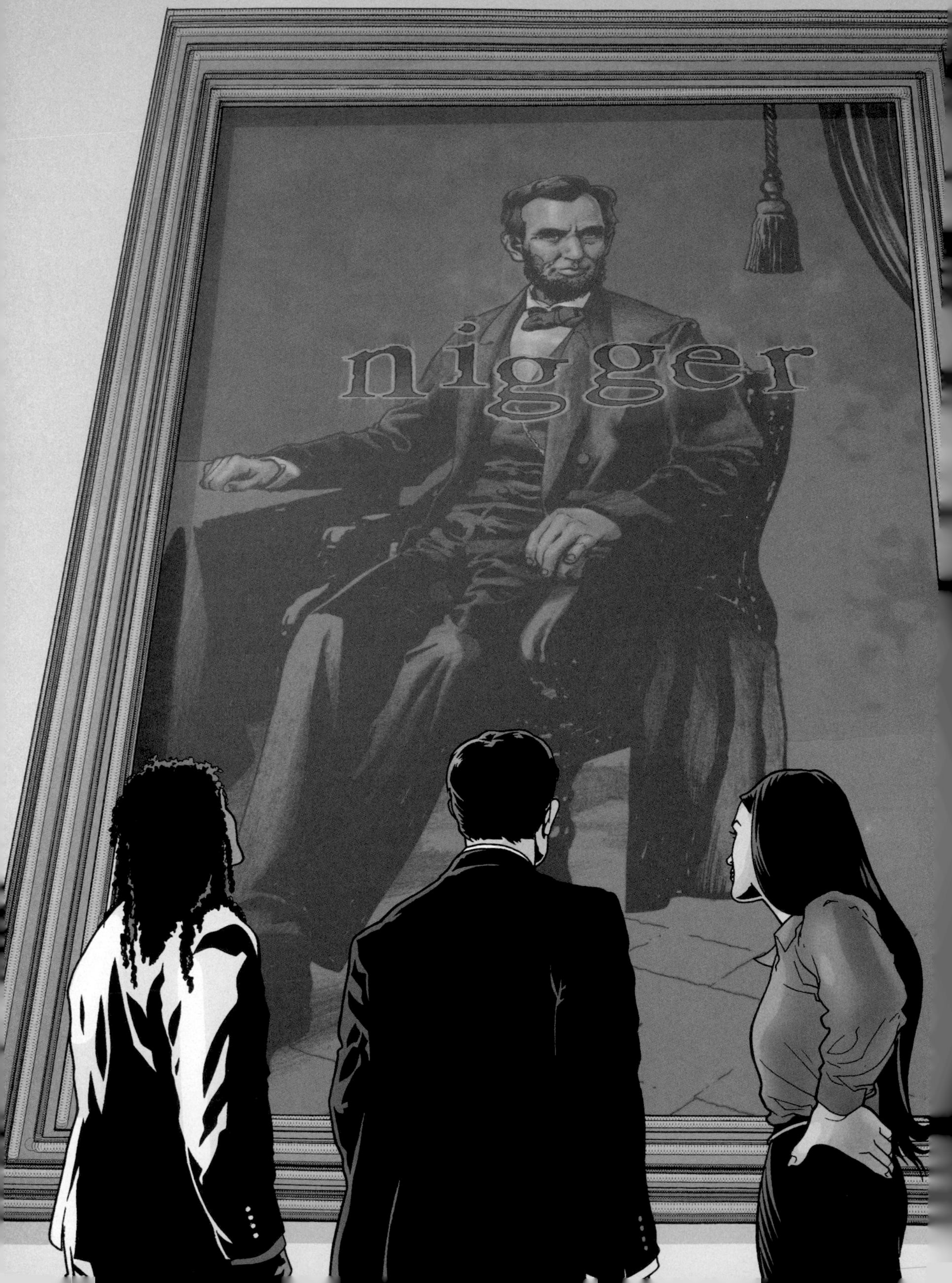
nigger

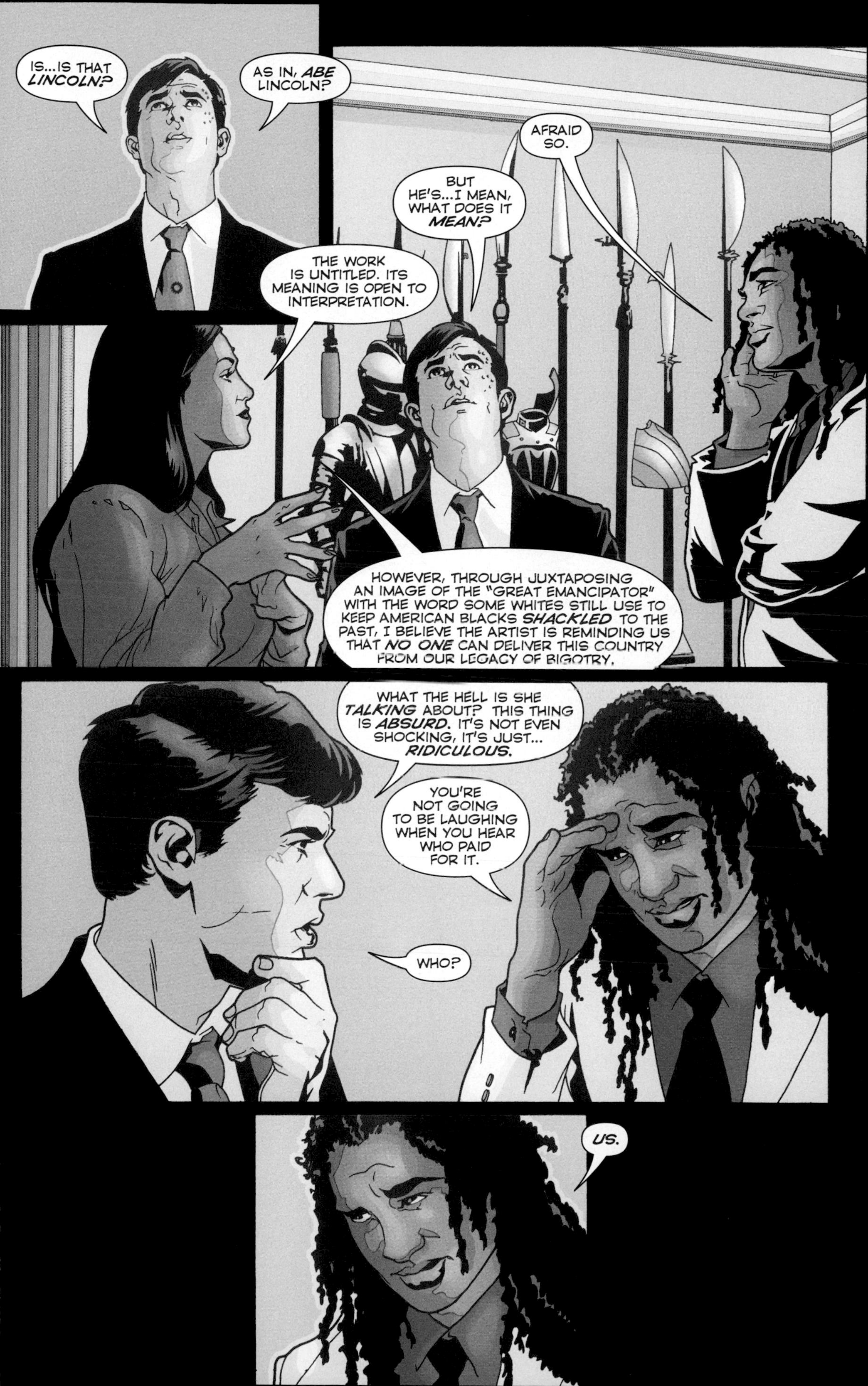
IS...IS THAT LINCOLN?
AS IN, ABE LINCOLN?
AFRAID SO.
BUT HE'S...I MEAN, WHAT DOES IT MEAN?
THE WORK IS UNTITLED. ITS MEANING IS OPEN TO INTERPRETATION.
HOWEVER, THROUGH JUXTAPOSING AN IMAGE OF THE "GREAT EMANCIPATOR" WITH THE WORD SOME WHITES STILL USE TO KEEP AMERICAN BLACKS SHACKLED TO THE PAST, I BELIEVE THE ARTIST IS REMINDING US THAT NO ONE CAN DELIVER THIS COUNTRY FROM OUR LEGACY OF BIGOTRY.
WHAT THE HELL IS SHE TALKING ABOUT? THIS THING IS ABSURD. IT'S NOT EVEN SHOCKING, IT'S JUST... RIDICULOUS.
YOU'RE NOT GOING TO BE LAUGHING WHEN YOU HEAR WHO PAID FOR IT.
WHO?
US.

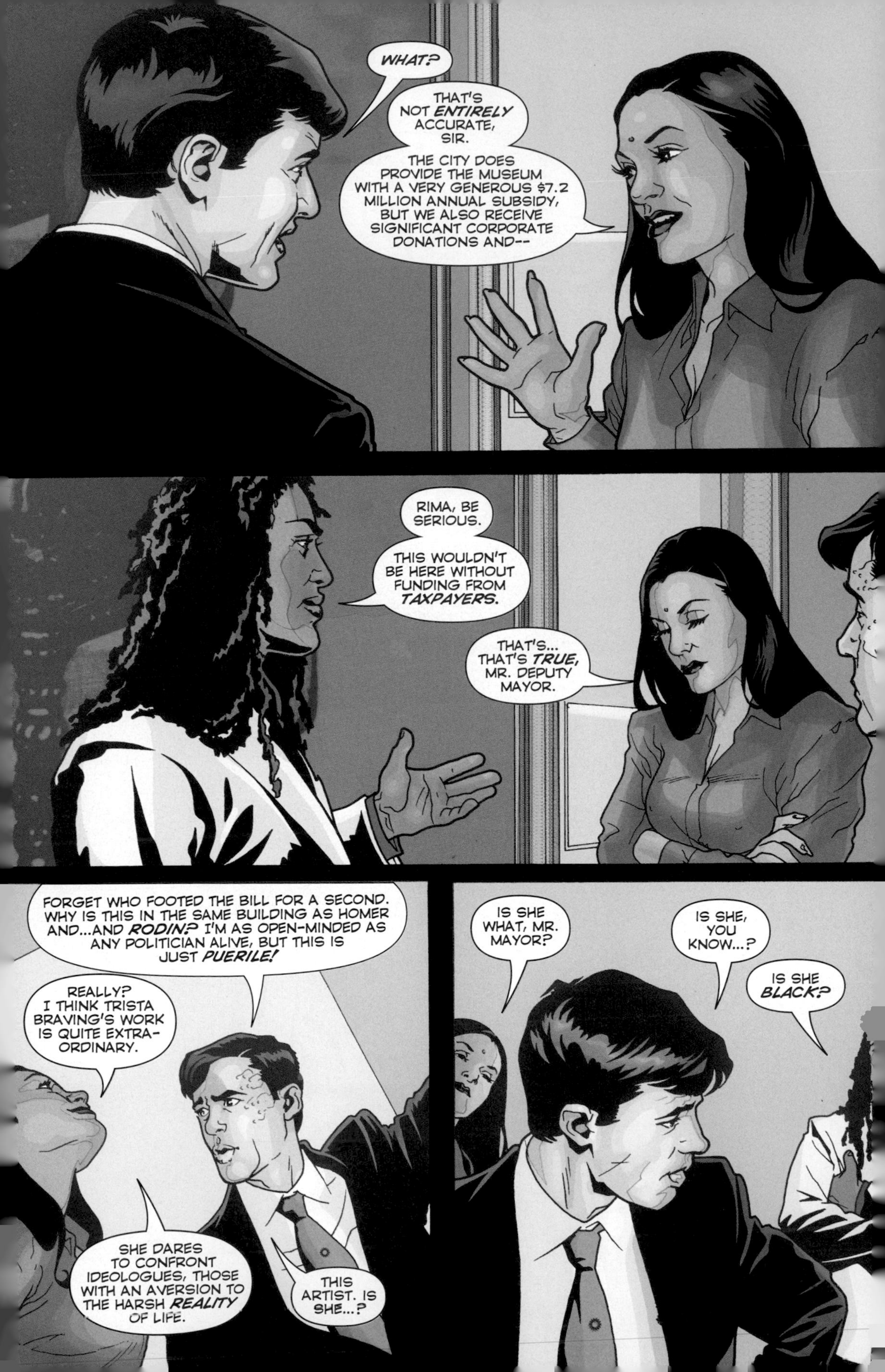
WHAT?
THAT'S NOT ENTIRELY ACCURATE, SIR.
THE CITY DOES PROVIDE THE MUSEUM WITH A VERY GENEROUS $7.2 MILLION ANNUAL SUBSIDY, BUT WE ALSO RECEIVE SIGNIFICANT CORPORATE DONATIONS AND--
RIMA, BE SERIOUS.
THIS WOULDN'T BE HERE WITHOUT FUNDING FROM TAXPAYERS.
THAT'S... THAT'S TRUE, MR. DEPUTY MAYOR.
FORGET WHO FOOTED THE BILL FOR A SECOND. WHY IS THIS IN THE SAME BUILDING AS HOMER AND...AND RODIN? I'M AS OPEN-MINDED AS ANY POLITICIAN ALIVE, BUT THIS IS JUST PUERILE!
REALLY? I THINK TRISTA BRAVING'S WORK IS QUITE EXTRA-ORDINARY.
SHE DARES TO CONFRONT IDEOLOGUES, THOSE WITH AN AVERSION TO THE HARSH REALITY OF LIFE.
THIS ARTIST. IS SHE...?
IS SHE WHAT, MR. MAYOR?
IS SHE, YOU KNOW...?
IS SHE BLACK?

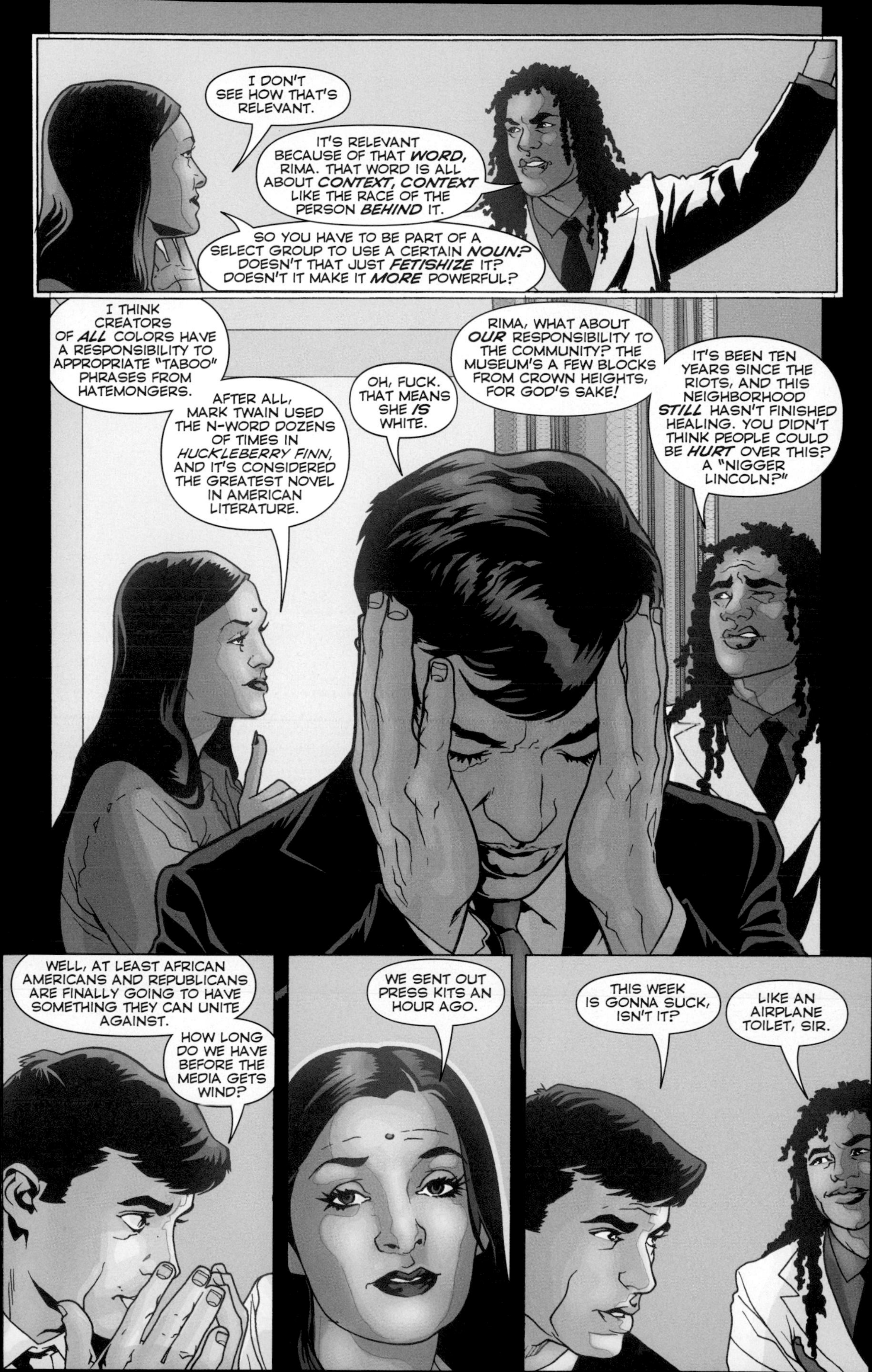
I DON'T SEE HOW THAT'S RELEVANT.
IT'S RELEVANT BECAUSE OF THAT WORD, RIMA. THAT WORD IS ALL ABOUT CONTEXT, CONTEXT LIKE THE RACE OF THE PERSON BEHIND IT.
SO YOU HAVE TO BE PART OF A SELECT GROUP TO USE A CERTAIN NOUN? DOESN'T THAT JUST FETISHIZE IT? DOESN'T IT MAKE IT MORE POWERFUL?
I THINK CREATORS OF ALL COLORS HAVE A RESPONSIBILITY TO APPROPRIATE "TABOO" PHRASES FROM HATEMONGERS.
AFTER ALL, MARK TWAIN USED THE N-WORD DOZENS OF TIMES IN HUCKLEBERRY FINN, AND IT'S CONSIDERED THE GREATEST NOVEL IN AMERICAN LITERATURE.
OH, FUCK. THAT MEANS SHE IS WHITE.
RIMA, WHAT ABOUT OUR RESPONSIBILITY TO THE COMMUNITY? THE MUSEUM'S A FEW BLOCKS FROM CROWN HEIGHTS, FOR GOD'S SAKE!
IT'S BEEN TEN YEARS SINCE THE RIOTS, AND THIS NEIGHBORHOOD STILL HASN'T FINISHED HEALING. YOU DIDN'T THINK PEOPLE COULD BE HURT OVER THIS? A "NIGGER LINCOLN?"
WELL, AT LEAST AFRICAN AMERICANS AND REPUBLICANS ARE FINALLY GOING TO HAVE SOMETHING THEY CAN UNITE AGAINST.
HOW LONG DO WE HAVE BEFORE THE MEDIA GETS WIND?
WE SENT OUT PRESS KITS AN HOUR AGO.
THIS WEEK IS GONNA SUCK, ISN'T IT?
LIKE AN AIRPLANE TOILET, SIR.

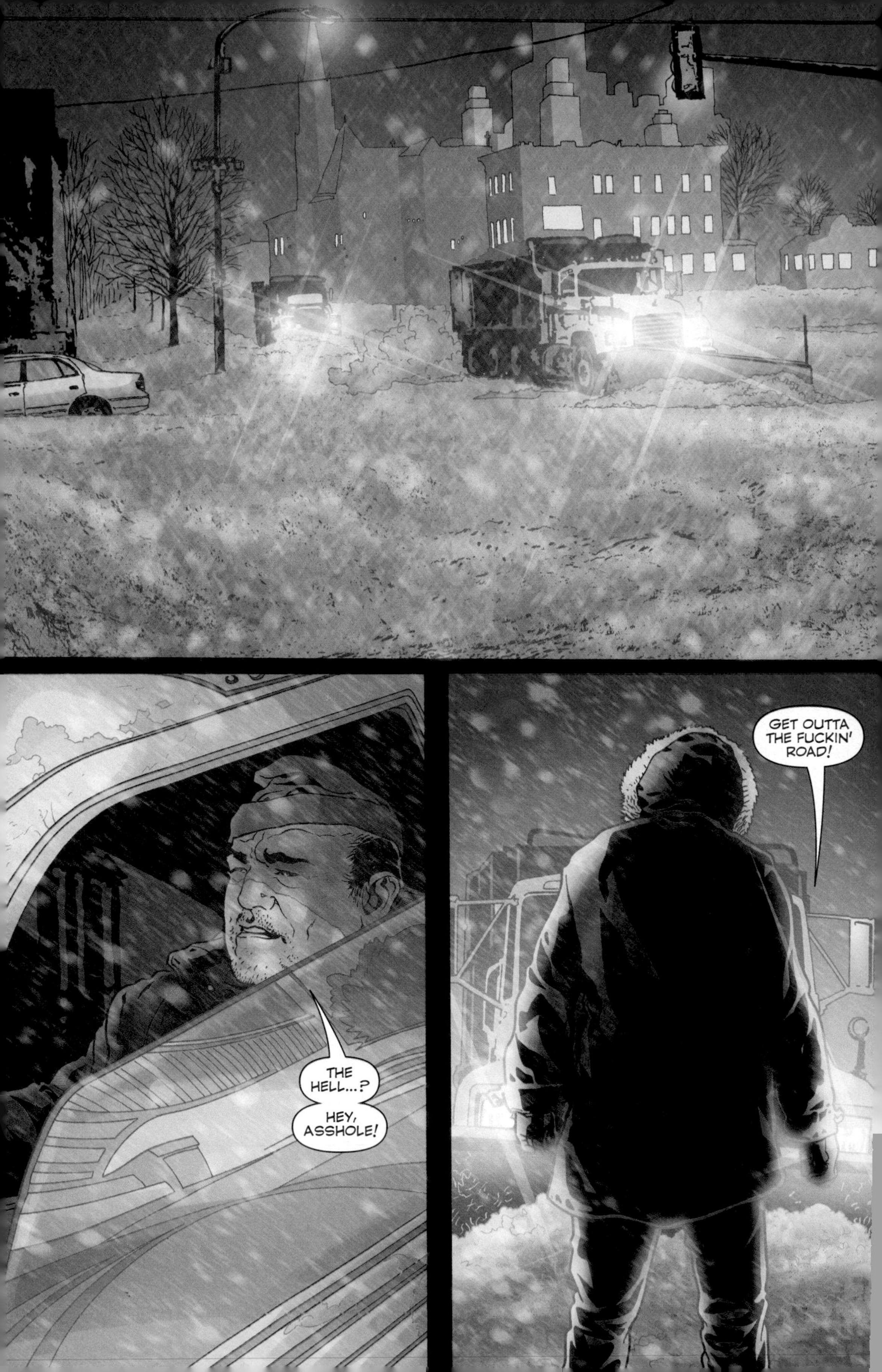
THE HELL...?
HEY, ASSHOLE!
GET OUTTA THE FUCKIN' ROAD!

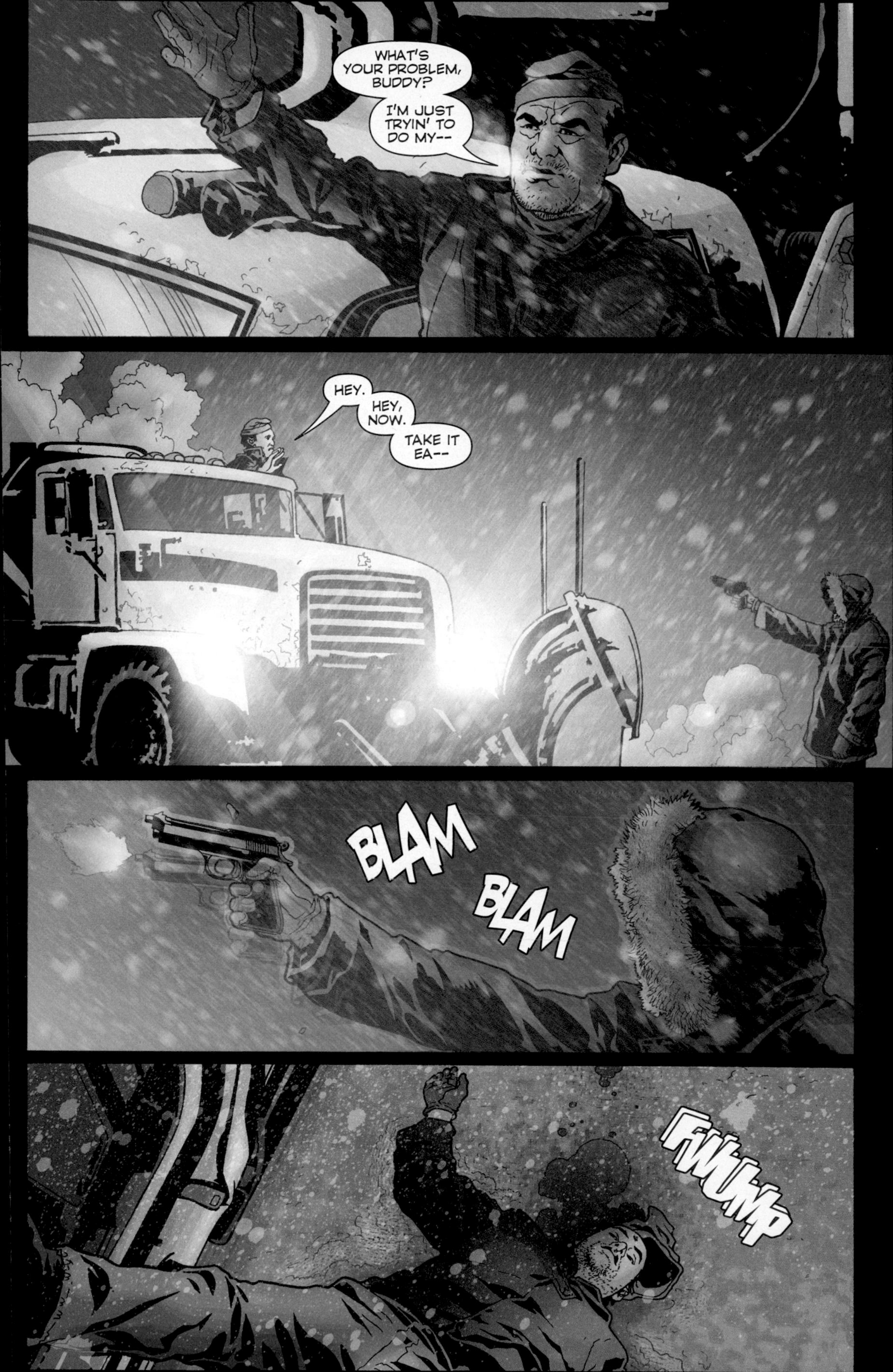
WHAT'S YOUR PROBLEM, BUDDY?
I'M JUST TRYIN' TO DO MY--
HEY.
HEY, NOW.
TAKE IT EA--
BLAM
BLAM
FWUMP

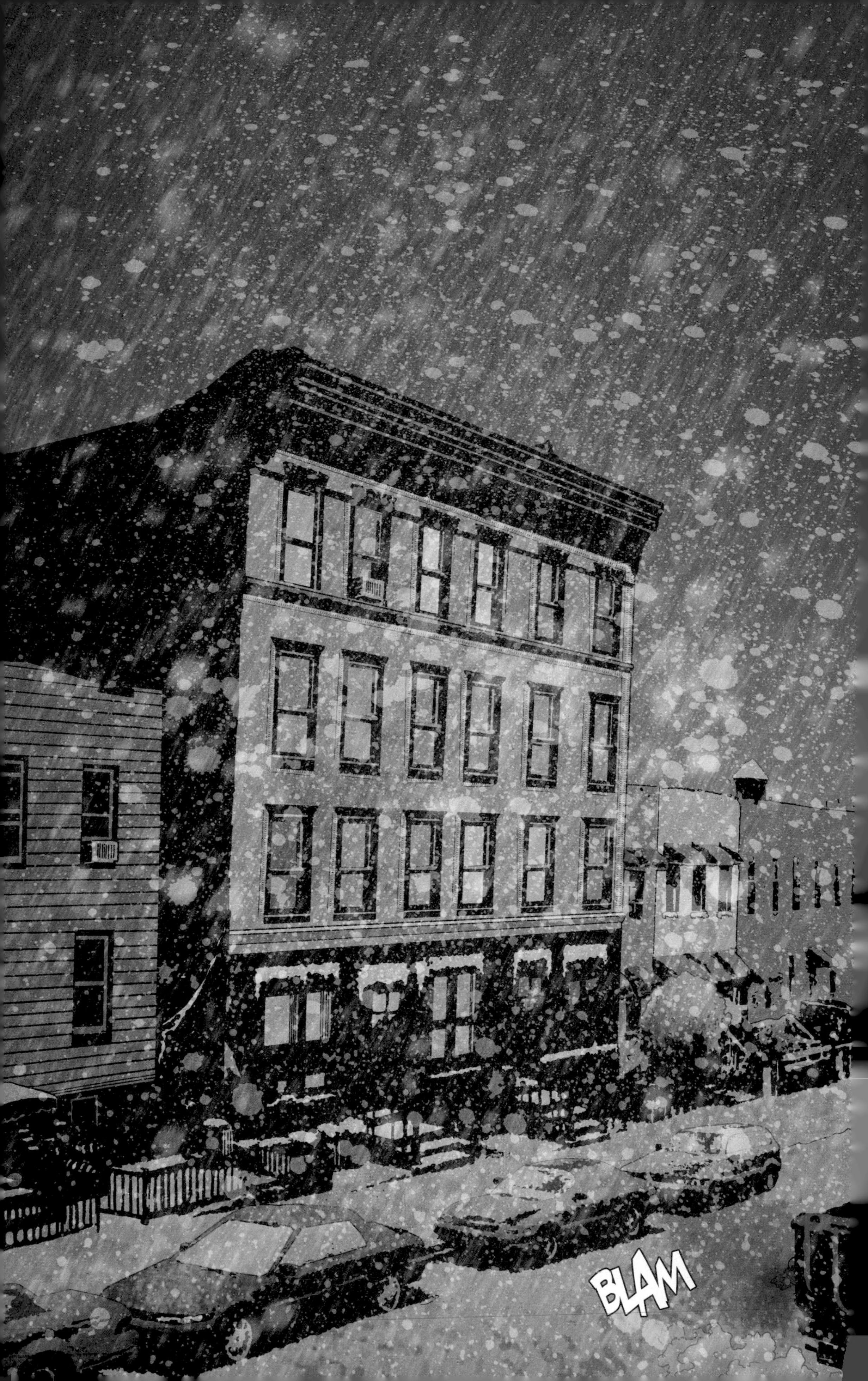
BLAM

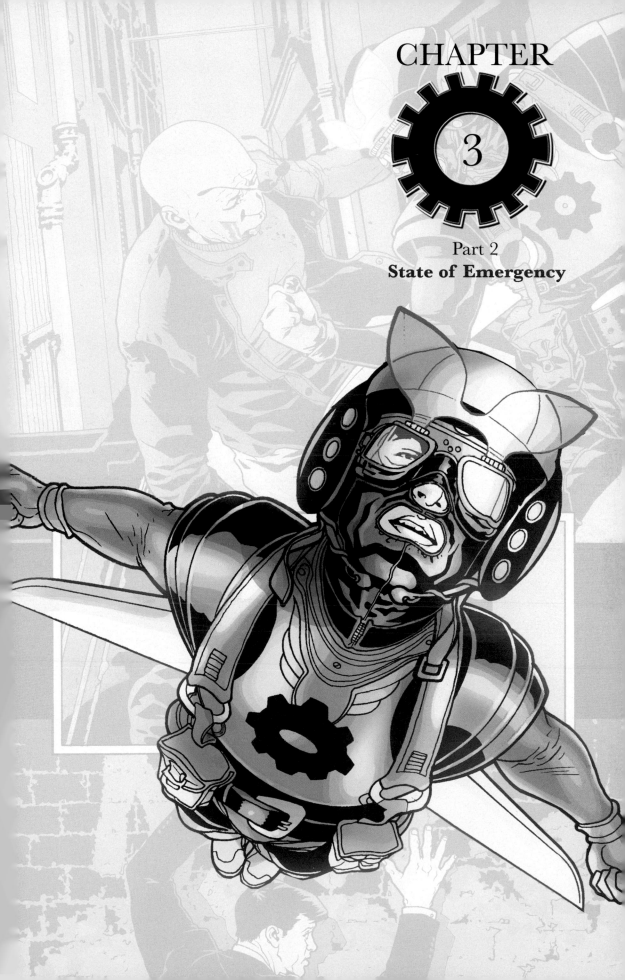

CHAPTER 3

Part 2
State of Emergency

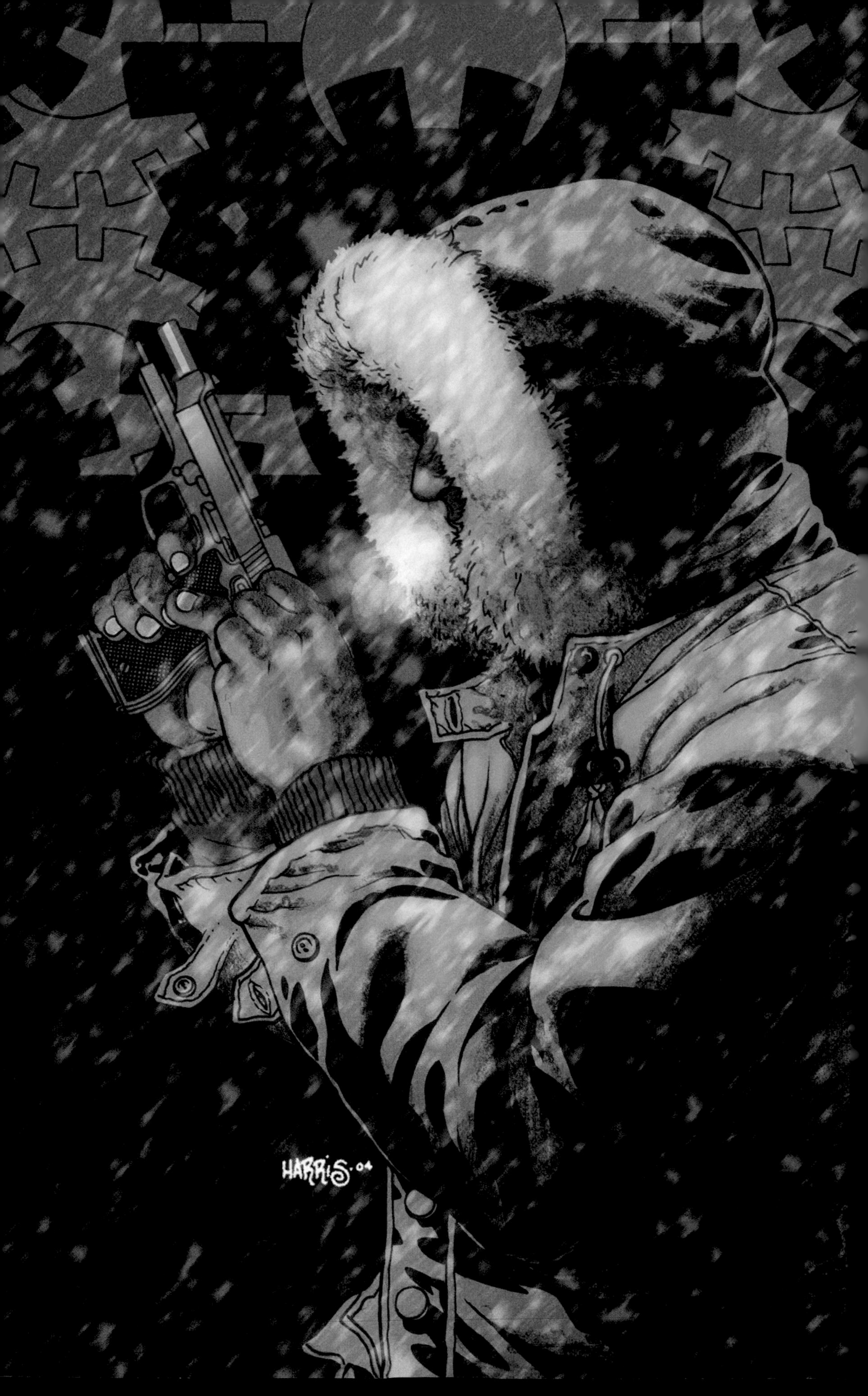
HARRIS·04

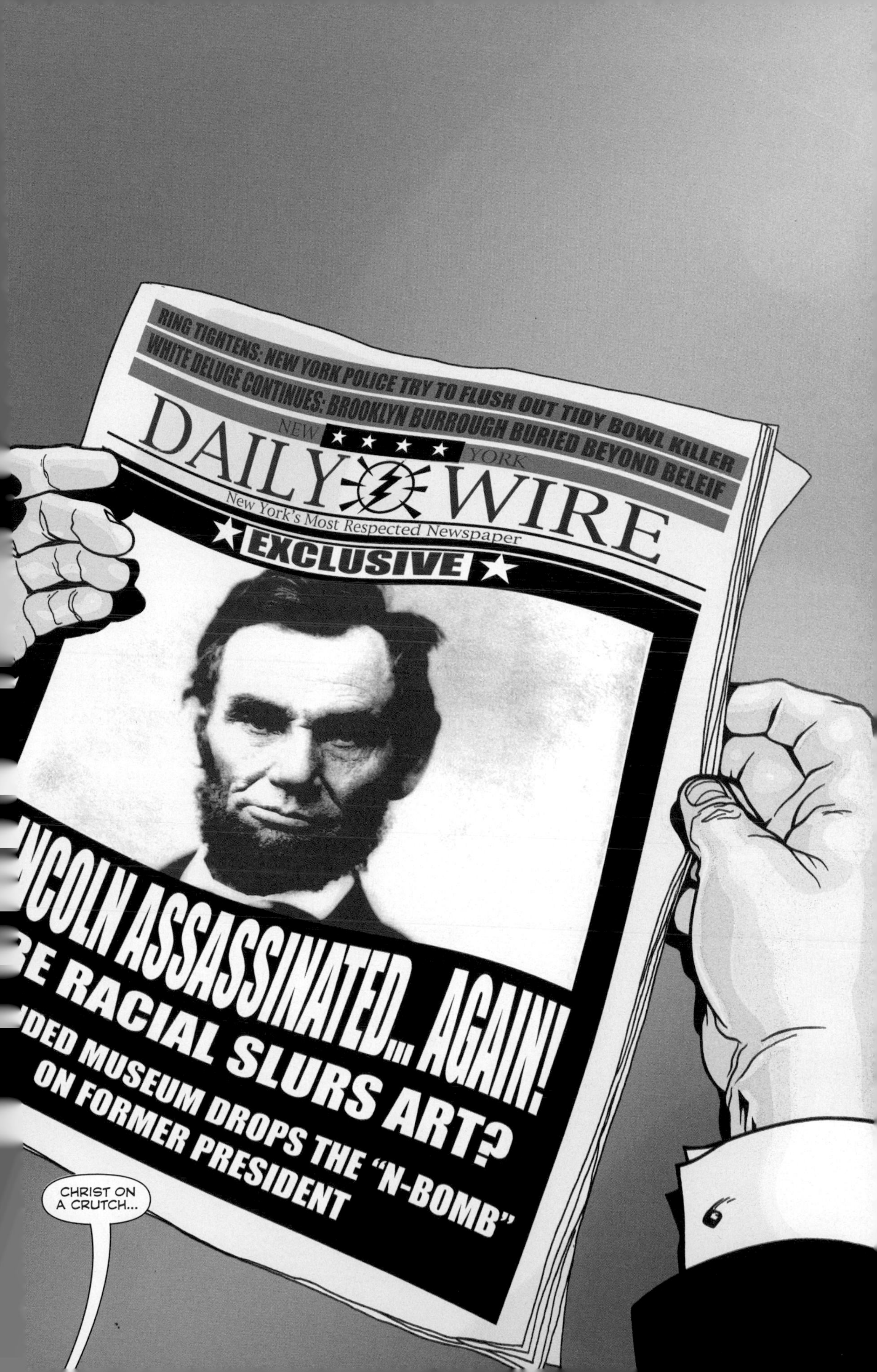
RING TIGHTENS: NEW YORK POLICE TRY TO FLUSH OUT TIDY BOWL KILLER
WHITE DELUGE CONTINUES: BROOKLYN BURROUGH BURIED BEYOND BELEIF
NEW YORK
DAILY WIRE
New York's Most Respected Newspaper
EXCLUSIVE
NCOLN ASSASSINATED... AGAIN!
E RACIAL SLURS ART?
DED MUSEUM DROPS THE "N-BOMB"
ON FORMER PRESIDENT
CHRIST ON A CRUTCH...

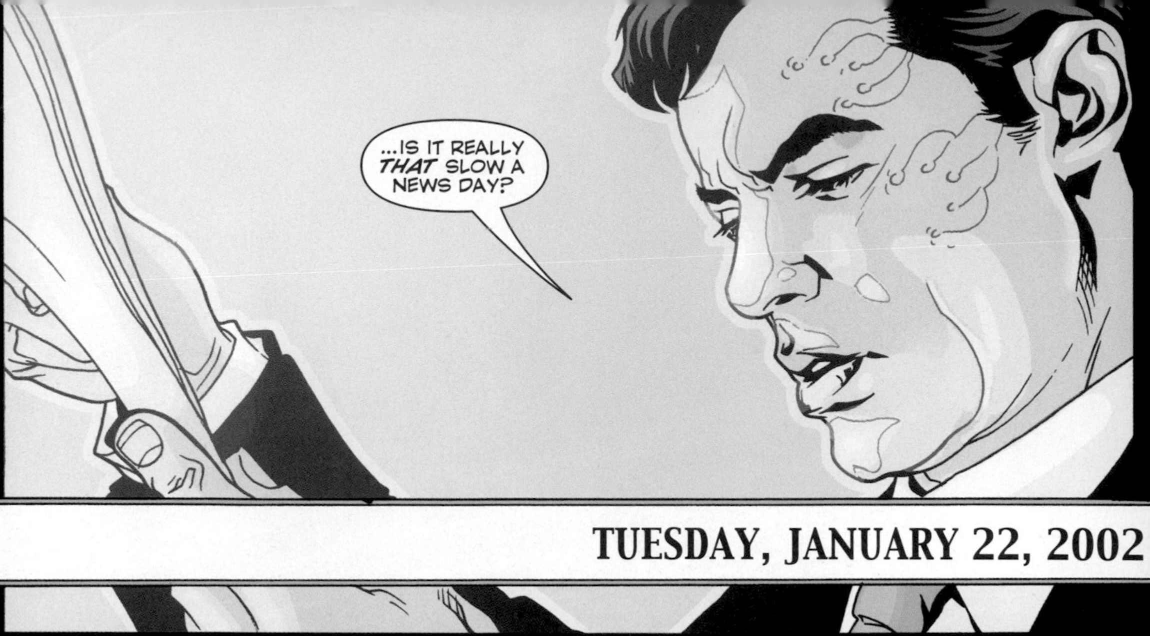
...IS IT REALLY THAT SLOW A NEWS DAY?
TUESDAY, JANUARY 22, 2002

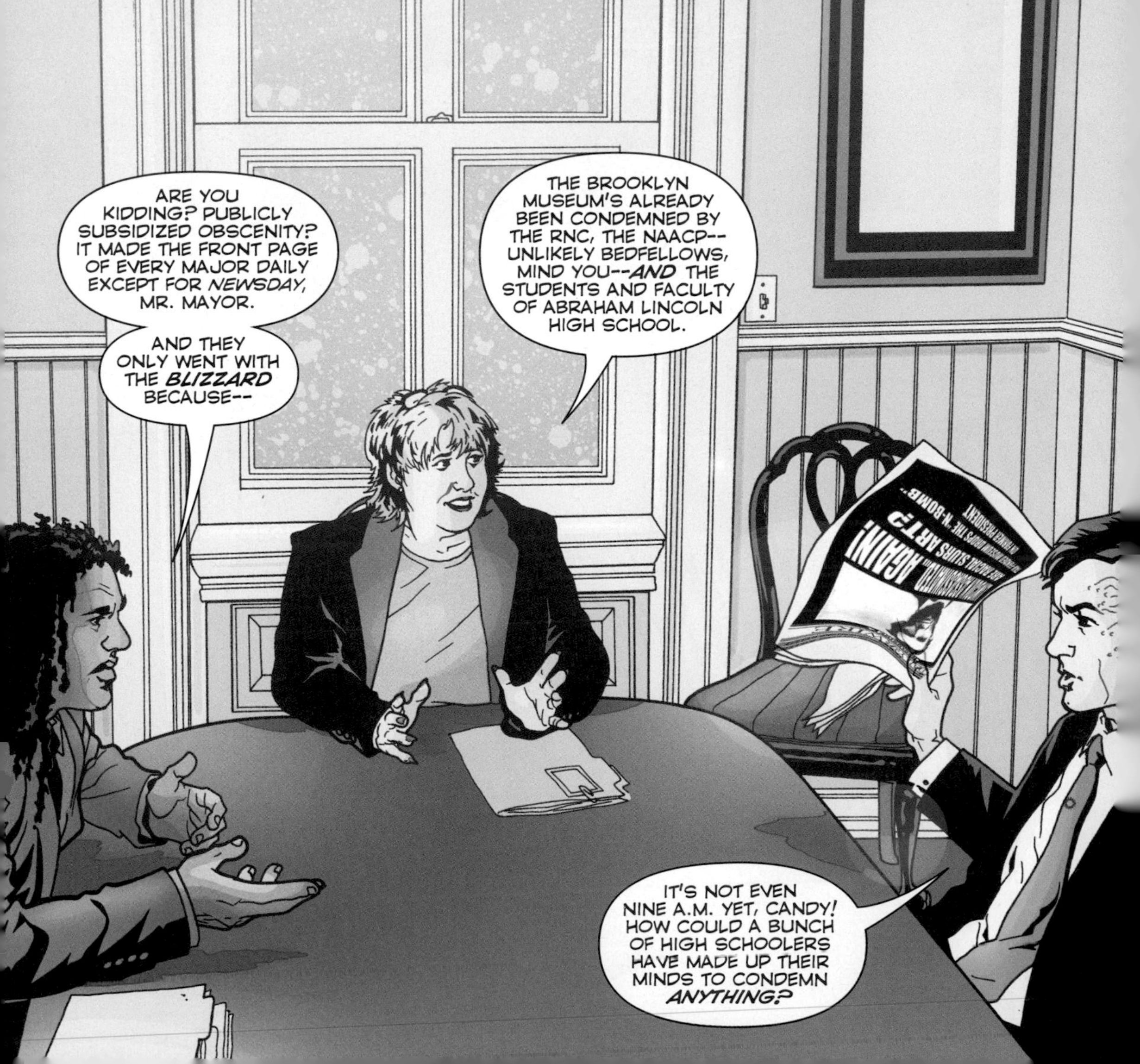
ARE YOU KIDDING? PUBLICLY SUBSIDIZED OBSCENITY? IT MADE THE FRONT PAGE OF EVERY MAJOR DAILY EXCEPT FOR NEWSDAY, MR. MAYOR.
AND THEY ONLY WENT WITH THE BLIZZARD BECAUSE--
THE BROOKLYN MUSEUM'S ALREADY BEEN CONDEMNED BY THE RNC, THE NAACP-- UNLIKELY BEDFELLOWS, MIND YOU--AND THE STUDENTS AND FACULTY OF ABRAHAM LINCOLN HIGH SCHOOL.
IT'S NOT EVEN NINE A.M. YET, CANDY! HOW COULD A BUNCH OF HIGH SCHOOLERS HAVE MADE UP THEIR MINDS TO CONDEMN ANYTHING?

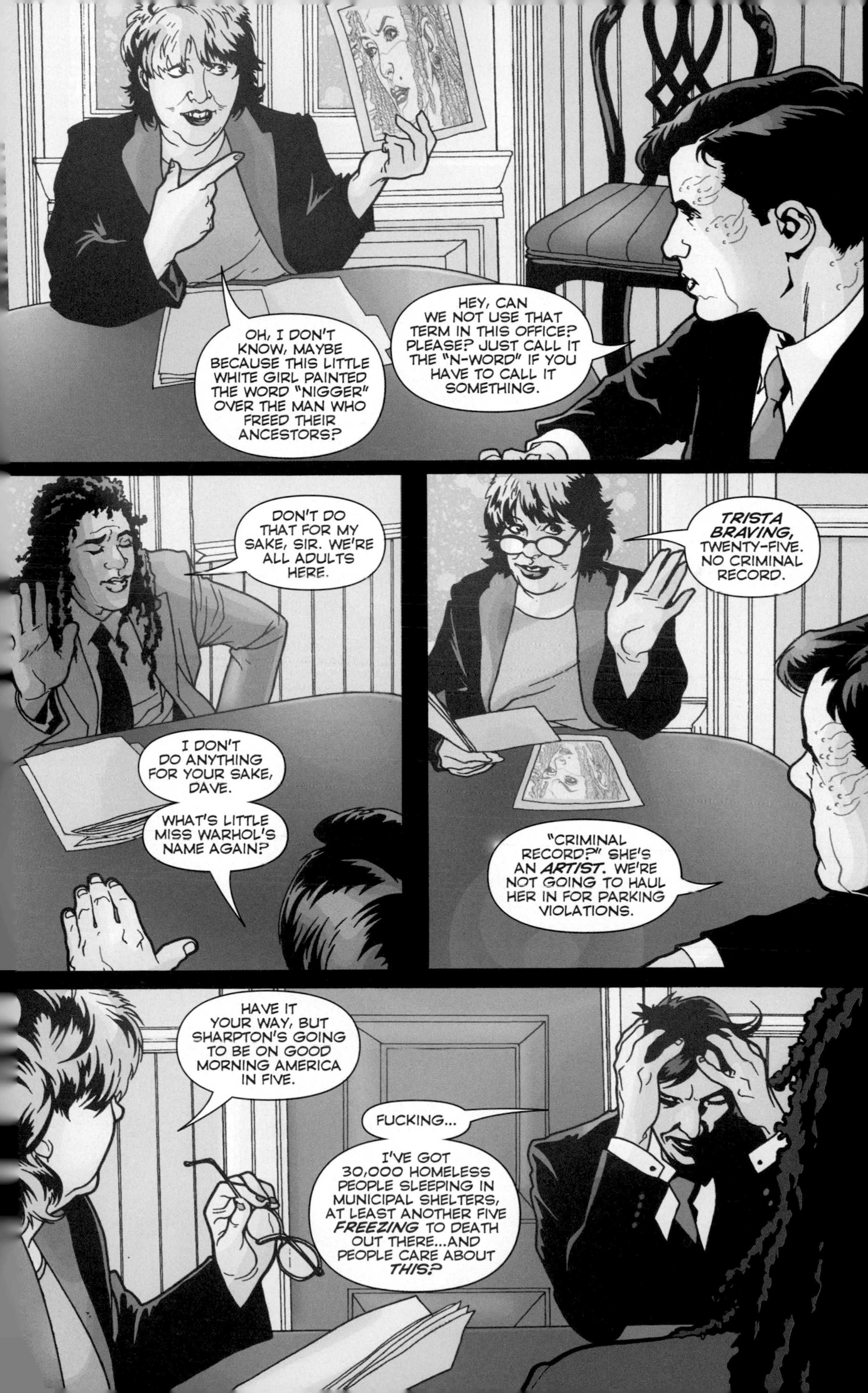
OH, I DON'T KNOW, MAYBE BECAUSE THIS LITTLE WHITE GIRL PAINTED THE WORD "NIGGER" OVER THE MAN WHO FREED THEIR ANCESTORS?
HEY, CAN WE NOT USE THAT TERM IN THIS OFFICE? PLEASE? JUST CALL IT THE "N-WORD" IF YOU HAVE TO CALL IT SOMETHING.
DON'T DO THAT FOR MY SAKE, SIR. WE'RE ALL ADULTS HERE.
I DON'T DO ANYTHING FOR YOUR SAKE, DAVE.
WHAT'S LITTLE MISS WARHOL'S NAME AGAIN?
TRISTA BRAVING, TWENTY-FIVE. NO CRIMINAL RECORD.
"CRIMINAL RECORD?" SHE'S AN *ARTIST*. WE'RE NOT GOING TO HAUL HER IN FOR PARKING VIOLATIONS.
HAVE IT YOUR WAY, BUT SHARPTON'S GOING TO BE ON GOOD MORNING AMERICA IN FIVE.
FUCKING...
I'VE GOT 30,000 HOMELESS PEOPLE SLEEPING IN MUNICIPAL SHELTERS, AT LEAST ANOTHER FIVE *FREEZING* TO DEATH OUT THERE...AND PEOPLE CARE ABOUT *THIS?*

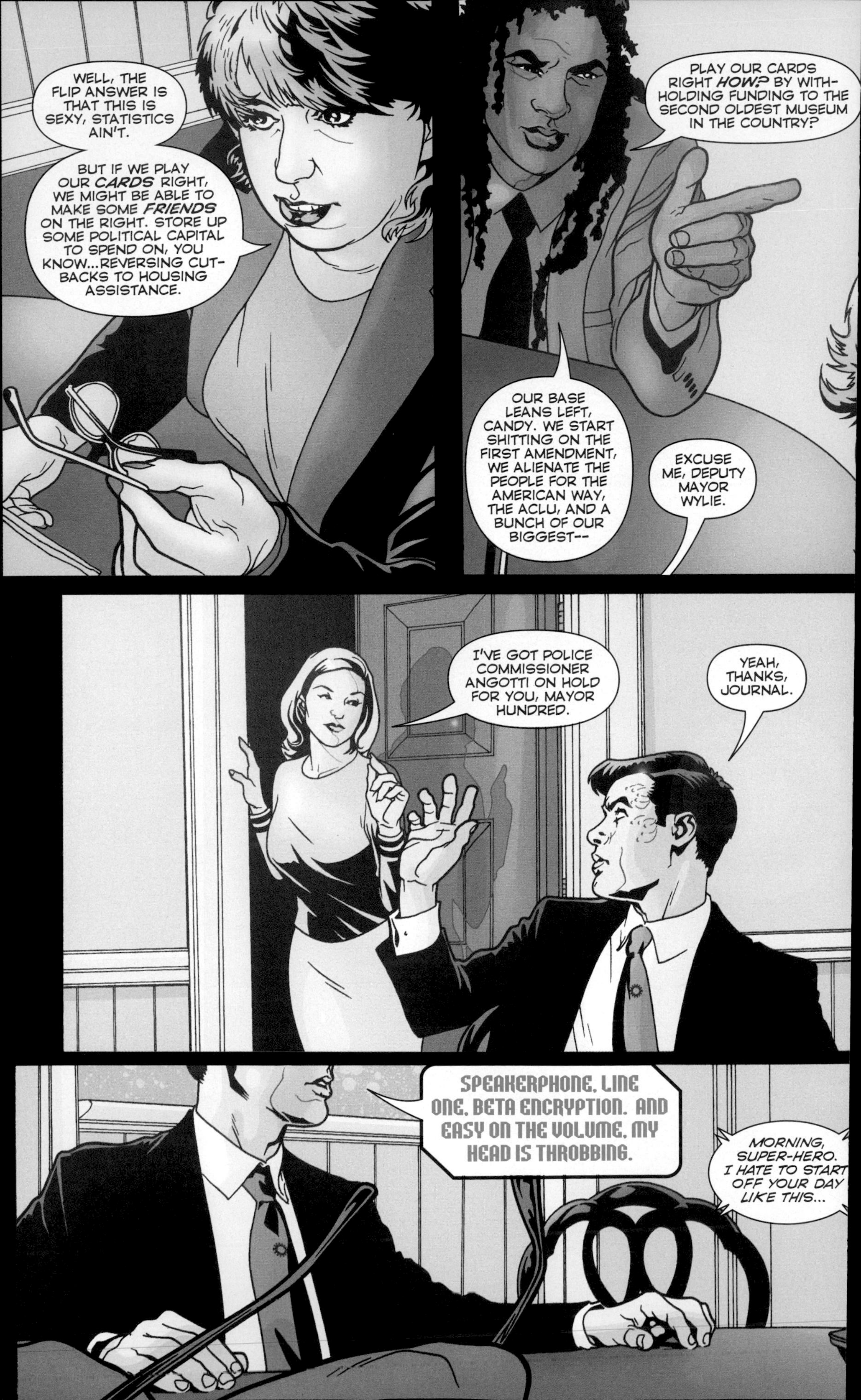
WELL, THE FLIP ANSWER IS THAT THIS IS SEXY, STATISTICS AIN'T.
BUT IF WE PLAY OUR CARDS RIGHT, WE MIGHT BE ABLE TO MAKE SOME FRIENDS ON THE RIGHT. STORE UP SOME POLITICAL CAPITAL TO SPEND ON, YOU KNOW...REVERSING CUT-BACKS TO HOUSING ASSISTANCE.
PLAY OUR CARDS RIGHT HOW? BY WITH-HOLDING FUNDING TO THE SECOND OLDEST MUSEUM IN THE COUNTRY?
OUR BASE LEANS LEFT, CANDY. WE START SHITTING ON THE FIRST AMENDMENT, WE ALIENATE THE PEOPLE FOR THE AMERICAN WAY, THE ACLU, AND A BUNCH OF OUR BIGGEST--
EXCUSE ME, DEPUTY MAYOR WYLIE.
I'VE GOT POLICE COMMISSIONER ANGOTTI ON HOLD FOR YOU, MAYOR HUNDRED.
YEAH, THANKS, JOURNAL.
SPEAKERPHONE, LINE ONE, BETA ENCRYPTION. AND EASY ON THE VOLUME, MY HEAD IS THROBBING.
MORNING, SUPER-HERO. I HATE TO START OFF YOUR DAY LIKE THIS...

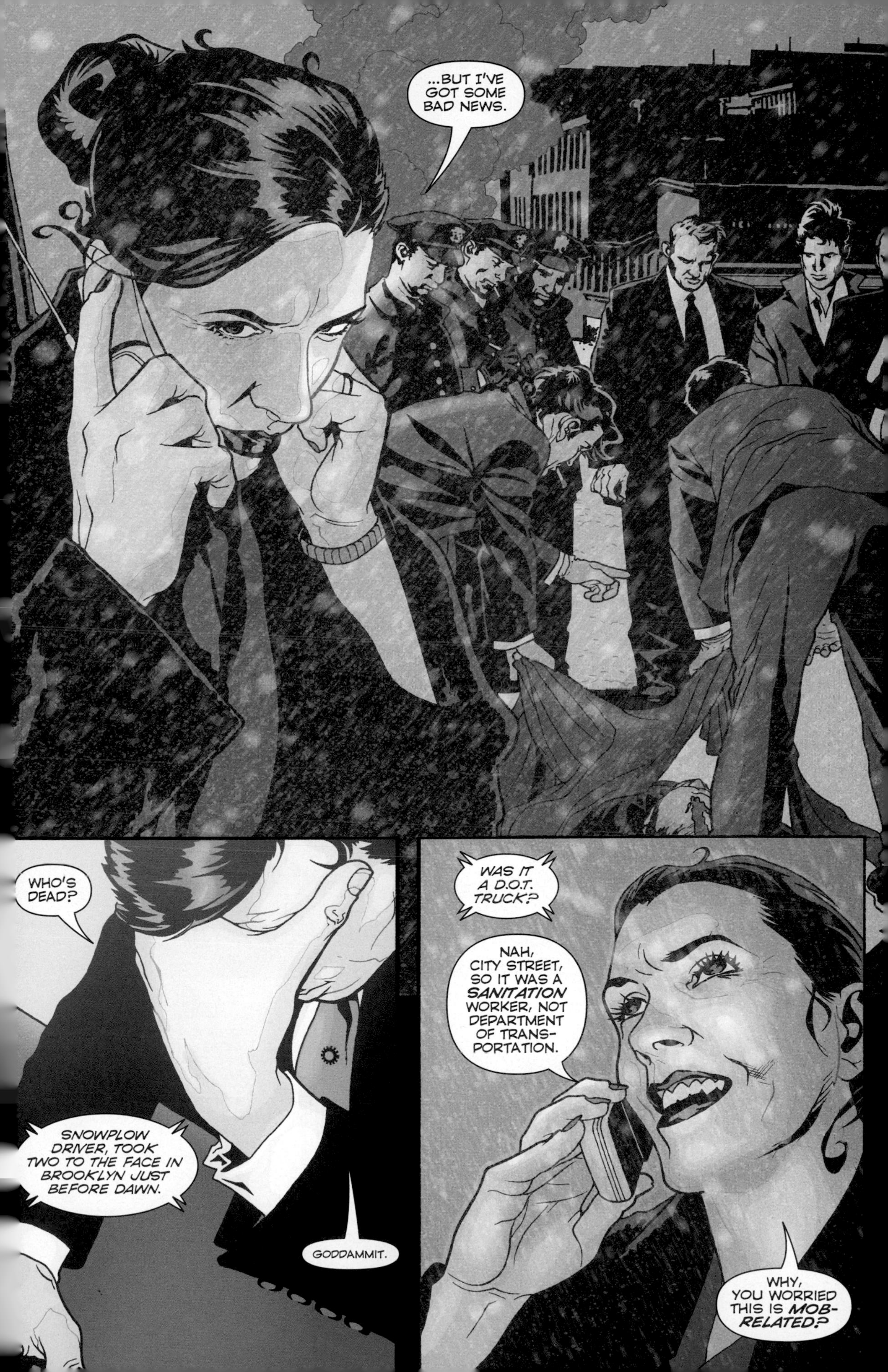
...BUT I'VE GOT SOME BAD NEWS.
WHO'S DEAD?
SNOWPLOW DRIVER, TOOK TWO TO THE FACE IN BROOKLYN JUST BEFORE DAWN.
GODDAMMIT.
WAS IT A D.O.T. TRUCK?
NAH, CITY STREET, SO IT WAS A SANITATION WORKER, NOT DEPARTMENT OF TRANS-PORTATION.
WHY, YOU WORRIED THIS IS MOB-RELATED?

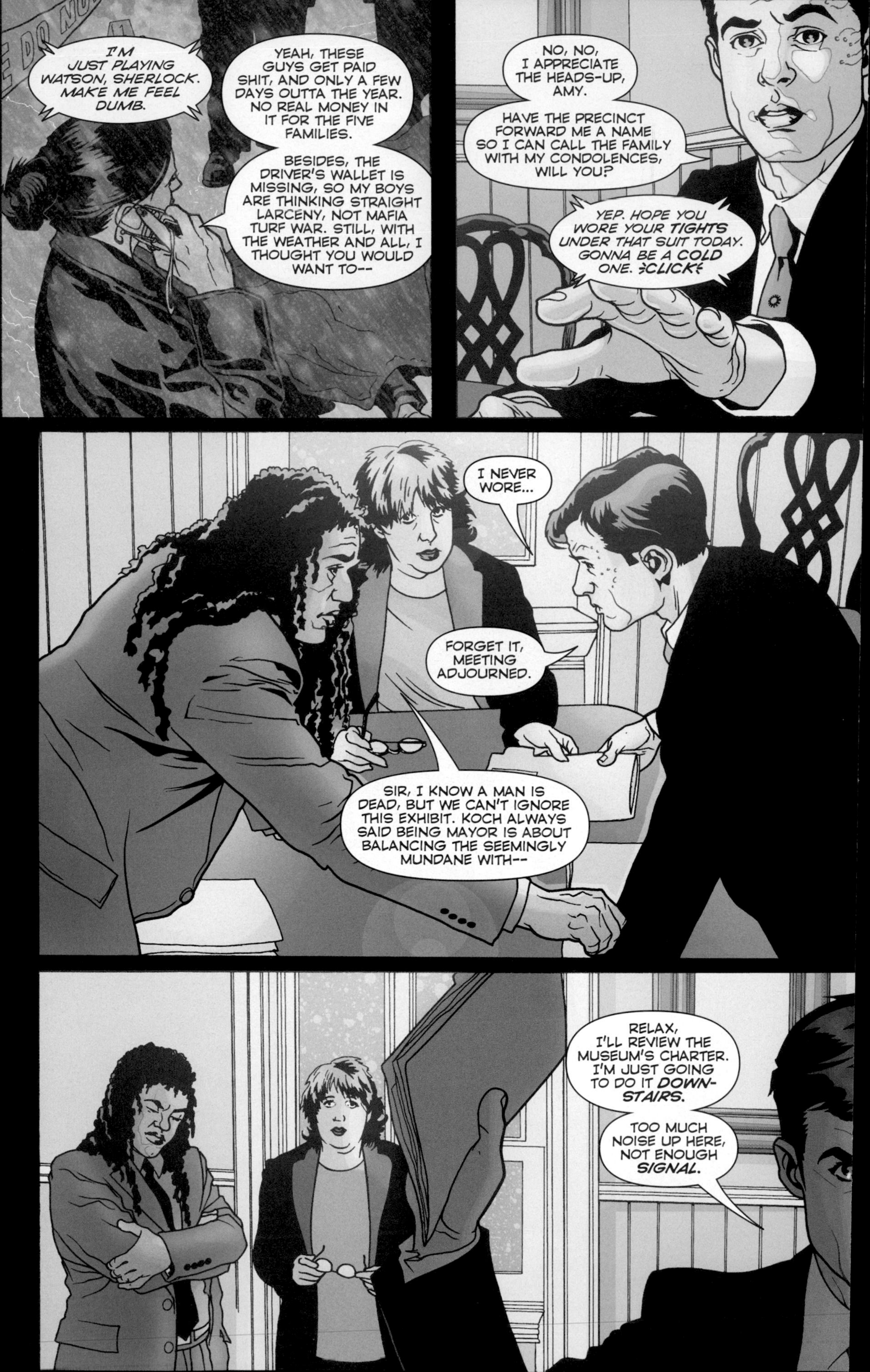
I'M JUST PLAYING WATSON, SHERLOCK. MAKE ME FEEL DUMB.
YEAH, THESE GUYS GET PAID SHIT, AND ONLY A FEW DAYS OUTTA THE YEAR. NO REAL MONEY IN IT FOR THE FIVE FAMILIES.
BESIDES, THE DRIVER'S WALLET IS MISSING, SO MY BOYS ARE THINKING STRAIGHT LARCENY, NOT MAFIA TURF WAR. STILL, WITH THE WEATHER AND ALL, I THOUGHT YOU WOULD WANT TO--
NO, NO, I APPRECIATE THE HEADS-UP, AMY.
HAVE THE PRECINCT FORWARD ME A NAME SO I CAN CALL THE FAMILY WITH MY CONDOLENCES, WILL YOU?
YEP. HOPE YOU WORE YOUR TIGHTS UNDER THAT SUIT TODAY. GONNA BE A COLD ONE. ≶CLICK≶
I NEVER WORE...
FORGET IT, MEETING ADJOURNED.
SIR, I KNOW A MAN IS DEAD, BUT WE CAN'T IGNORE THIS EXHIBIT. KOCH ALWAYS SAID BEING MAYOR IS ABOUT BALANCING THE SEEMINGLY MUNDANE WITH--
RELAX, I'LL REVIEW THE MUSEUM'S CHARTER. I'M JUST GOING TO DO IT DOWN-STAIRS.
TOO MUCH NOISE UP HERE, NOT ENOUGH SIGNAL.

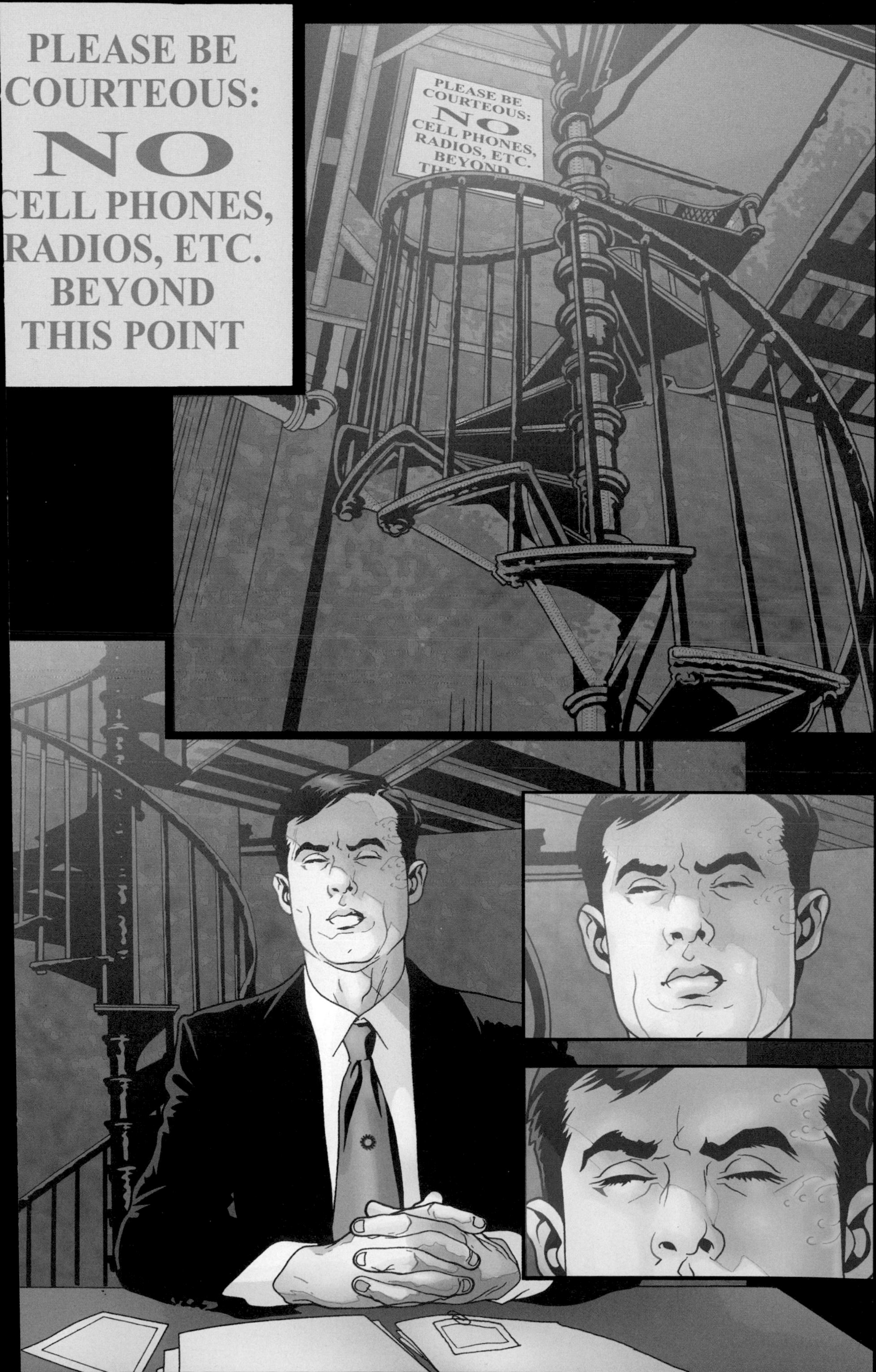
PLEASE BE
COURTEOUS:
NO
CELL PHONES,
RADIOS, ETC.
BEYOND
THIS POINT

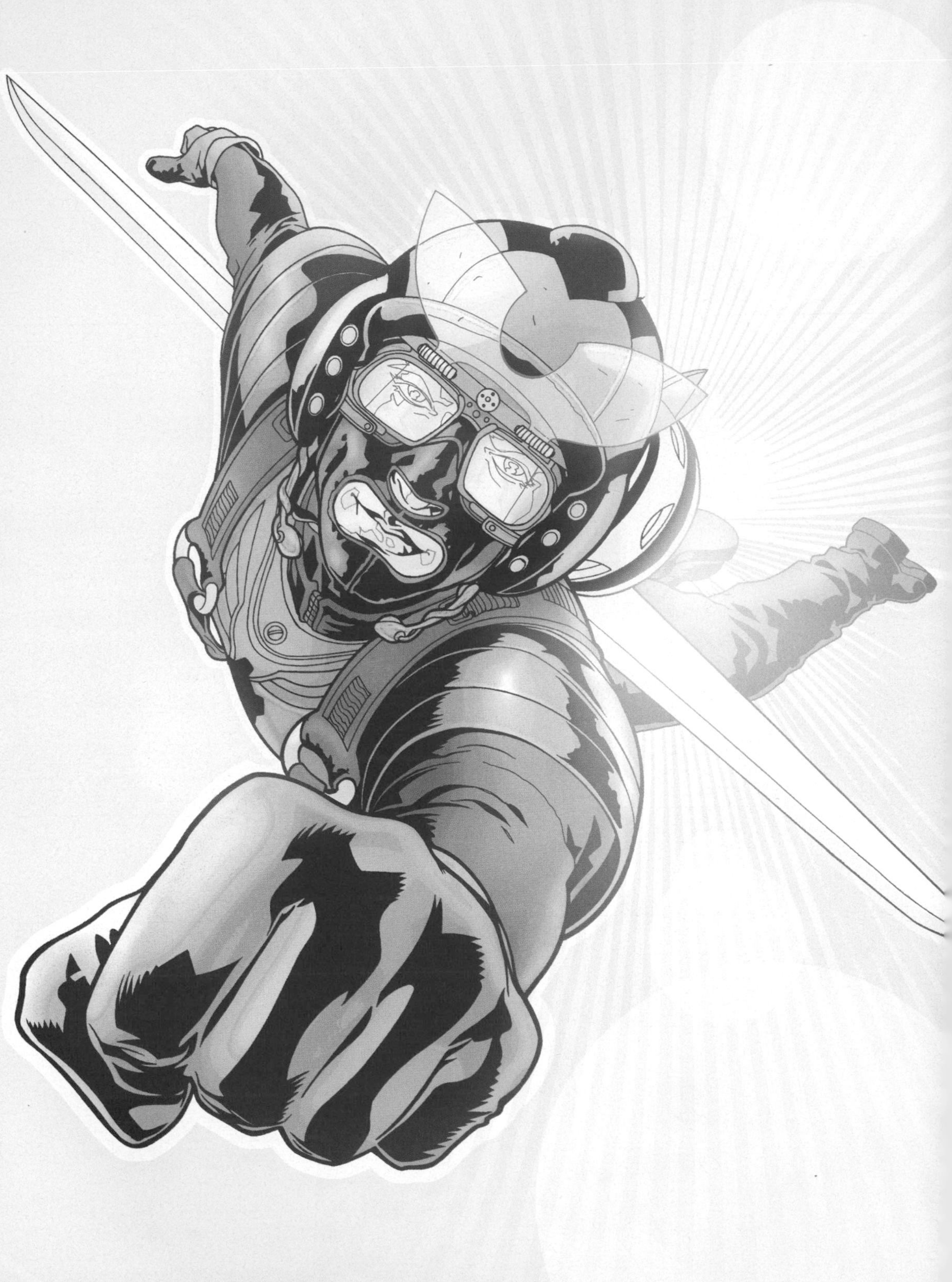

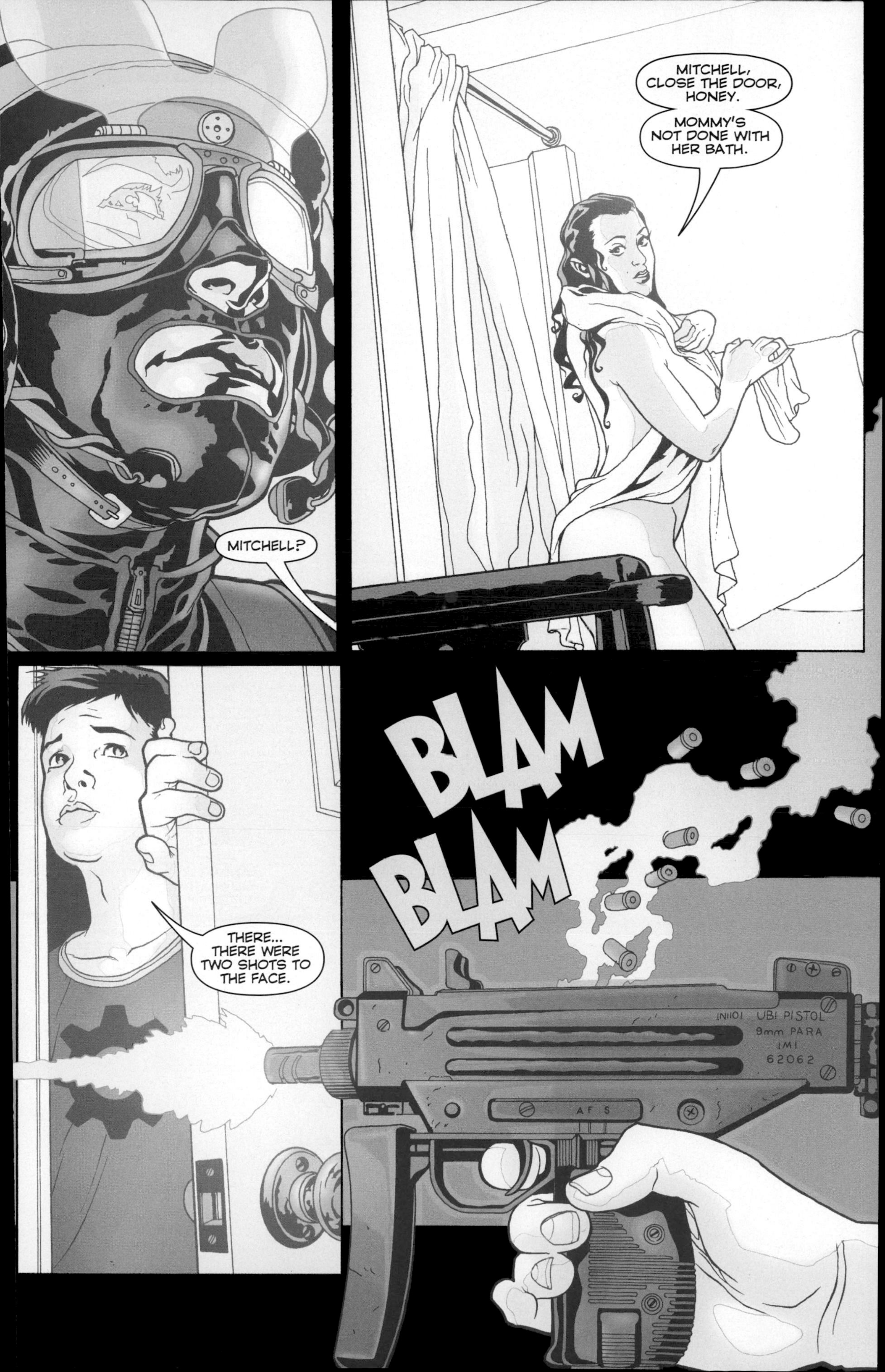
MITCHELL?
MITCHELL, CLOSE THE DOOR, HONEY.
MOMMY'S NOT DONE WITH HER BATH.
THERE... THERE WERE TWO SHOTS TO THE FACE.
BLAM
BLAM
UBI PISTOL
9mm PARA
IMI
62062
AF S

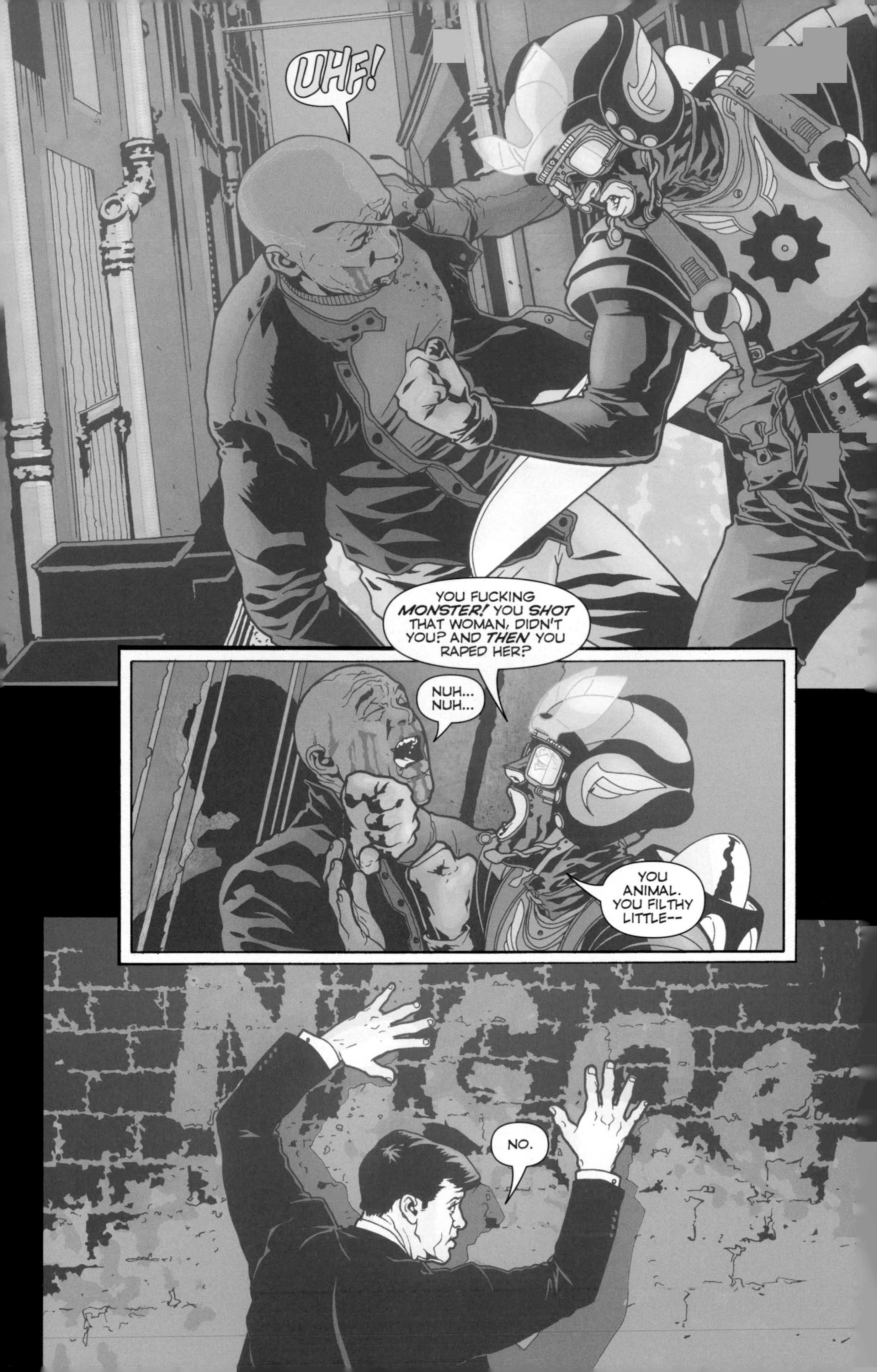
UHF!
YOU FUCKING MONSTER! YOU SHOT THAT WOMAN, DIDN'T YOU? AND THEN YOU RAPED HER?
NUH... NUH...
YOU ANIMAL. YOU FILTHY LITTLE--
NO.

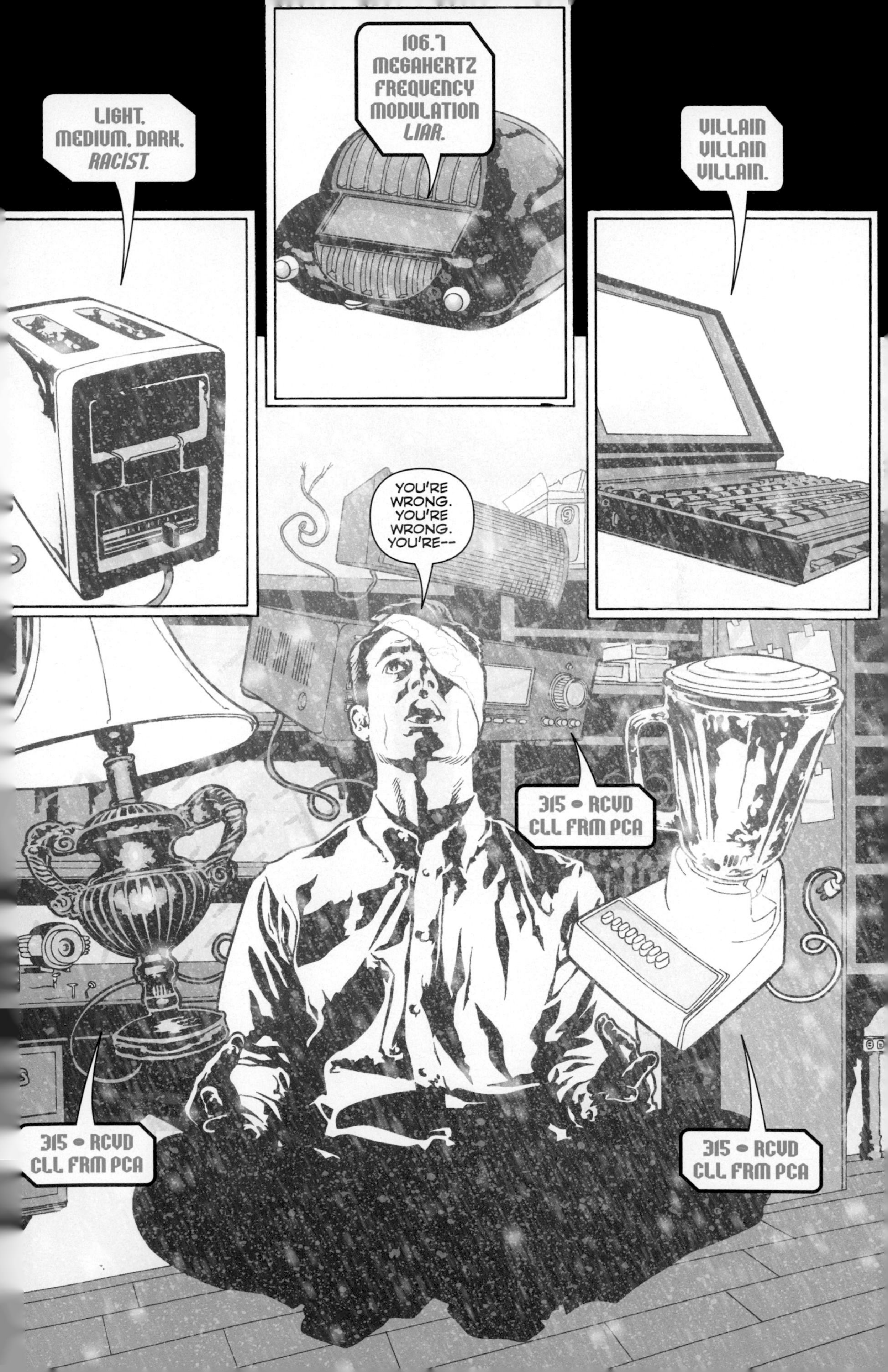
LIGHT. MEDIUM. DARK. RACIST.
106.7 MEGAHERTZ FREQUENCY MODULATION LIAR.
VILLAIN VILLAIN VILLAIN.
YOU'RE WRONG. YOU'RE WRONG. YOU'RE--
315 - RCVD CLL FRM PCA
315 - RCVD CLL FRM PCA
315 - RCVD CLL FRM PCA

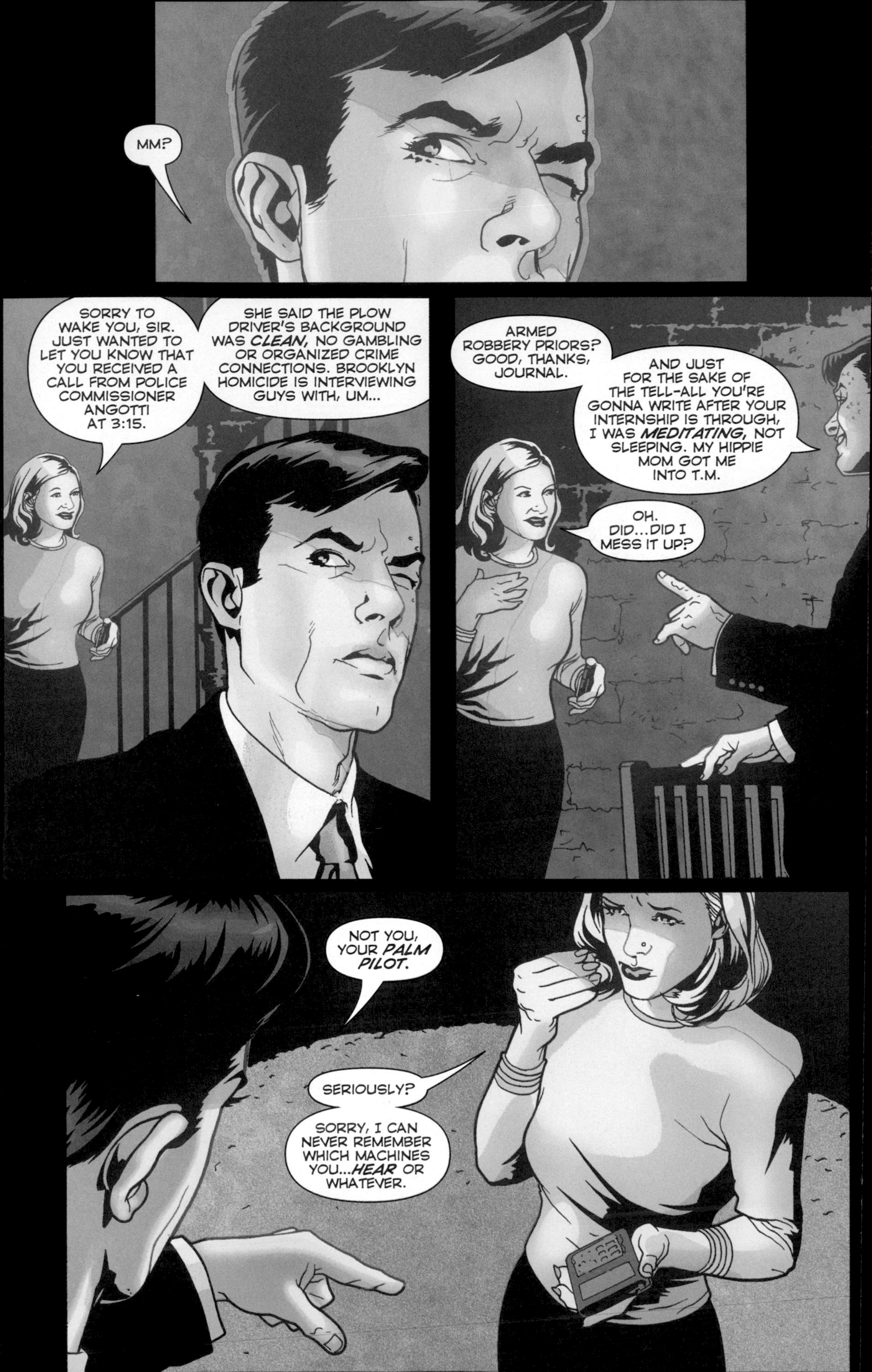
MM?
SORRY TO WAKE YOU, SIR. JUST WANTED TO LET YOU KNOW THAT YOU RECEIVED A CALL FROM POLICE COMMISSIONER ANGOTTI AT 3:15.
SHE SAID THE PLOW DRIVER'S BACKGROUND WAS *CLEAN,* NO GAMBLING OR ORGANIZED CRIME CONNECTIONS. BROOKLYN HOMICIDE IS INTERVIEWING GUYS WITH, UM...
ARMED ROBBERY PRIORS? GOOD, THANKS, JOURNAL.
AND JUST FOR THE SAKE OF THE TELL-ALL YOU'RE GONNA WRITE AFTER YOUR INTERNSHIP IS THROUGH, I WAS *MEDITATING,* NOT SLEEPING. MY HIPPIE MOM GOT ME INTO T.M.
OH. DID...DID I MESS IT UP?
NOT YOU, YOUR *PALM PILOT*.
SERIOUSLY?
SORRY, I CAN NEVER REMEMBER WHICH MACHINES YOU...*HEAR* OR WHATEVER.

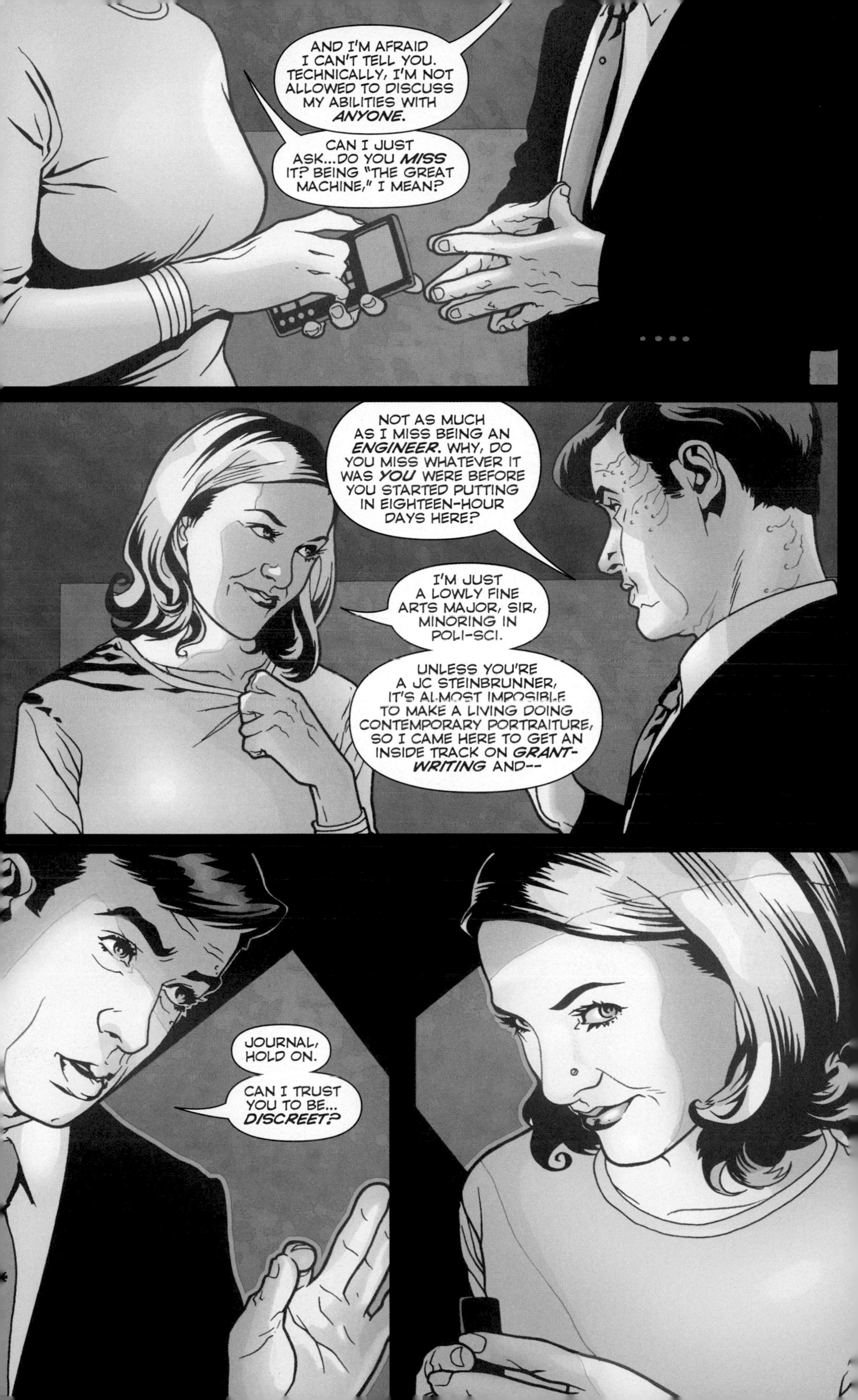
AND I'M AFRAID I CAN'T TELL YOU. TECHNICALLY, I'M NOT ALLOWED TO DISCUSS MY ABILITIES WITH ANYONE.
CAN I JUST ASK...DO YOU MISS IT? BEING "THE GREAT MACHINE," I MEAN?
NOT AS MUCH AS I MISS BEING AN ENGINEER. WHY, DO YOU MISS WHATEVER IT WAS YOU WERE BEFORE YOU STARTED PUTTING IN EIGHTEEN-HOUR DAYS HERE?
I'M JUST A LOWLY FINE ARTS MAJOR, SIR, MINORING IN POLI-SCI.
UNLESS YOU'RE A JC STEINBRUNNER, IT'S ALMOST IMPOSIBLE TO MAKE A LIVING DOING CONTEMPORARY PORTRAITURE, SO I CAME HERE TO GET AN INSIDE TRACK ON GRANT-WRITING AND--
JOURNAL, HOLD ON.
CAN I TRUST YOU TO BE... DISCREET?

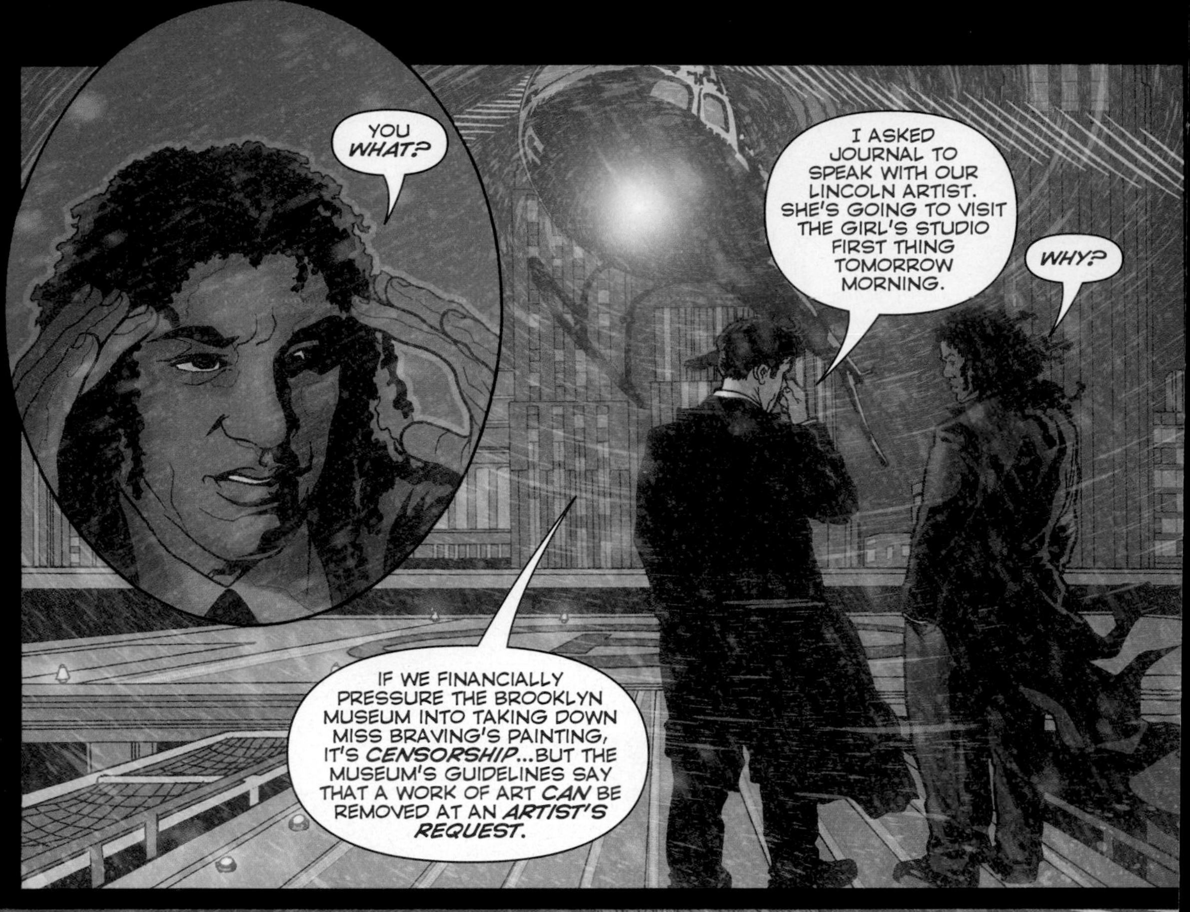
YOU WHAT?
I ASKED JOURNAL TO SPEAK WITH OUR LINCOLN ARTIST. SHE'S GOING TO VISIT THE GIRL'S STUDIO FIRST THING TOMORROW MORNING.
WHY?
IF WE FINANCIALLY PRESSURE THE BROOKLYN MUSEUM INTO TAKING DOWN MISS BRAVING'S PAINTING, IT'S CENSORSHIP...BUT THE MUSEUM'S GUIDELINES SAY THAT A WORK OF ART CAN BE REMOVED AT AN ARTIST'S REQUEST.

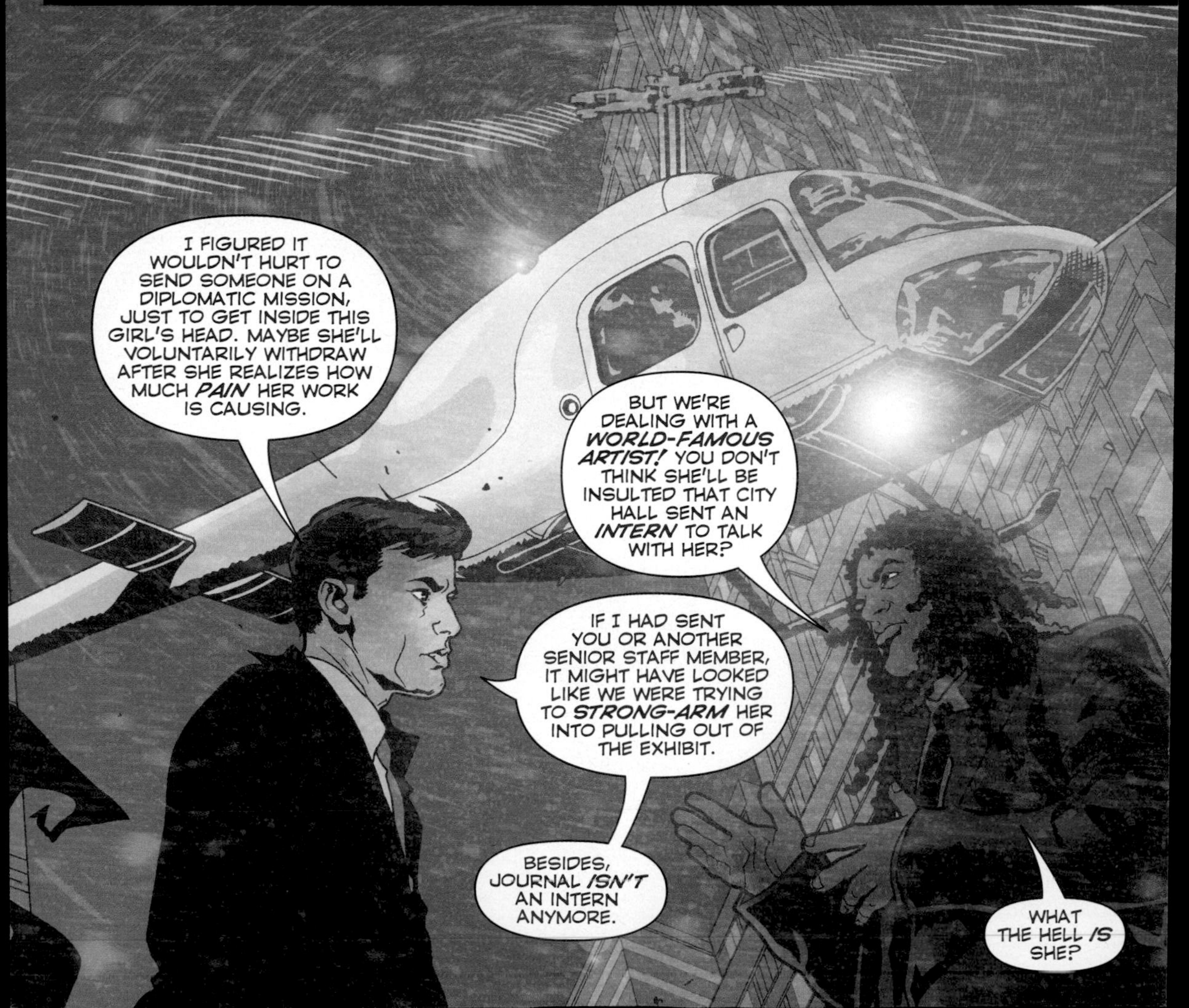
I FIGURED IT WOULDN'T HURT TO SEND SOMEONE ON A DIPLOMATIC MISSION, JUST TO GET INSIDE THIS GIRL'S HEAD. MAYBE SHE'LL VOLUNTARILY WITHDRAW AFTER SHE REALIZES HOW MUCH PAIN HER WORK IS CAUSING.
BUT WE'RE DEALING WITH A WORLD-FAMOUS ARTIST! YOU DON'T THINK SHE'LL BE INSULTED THAT CITY HALL SENT AN INTERN TO TALK WITH HER?
IF I HAD SENT YOU OR ANOTHER SENIOR STAFF MEMBER, IT MIGHT HAVE LOOKED LIKE WE WERE TRYING TO STRONG-ARM HER INTO PULLING OUT OF THE EXHIBIT.
BESIDES, JOURNAL ISN'T AN INTERN ANYMORE.
WHAT THE HELL IS SHE?

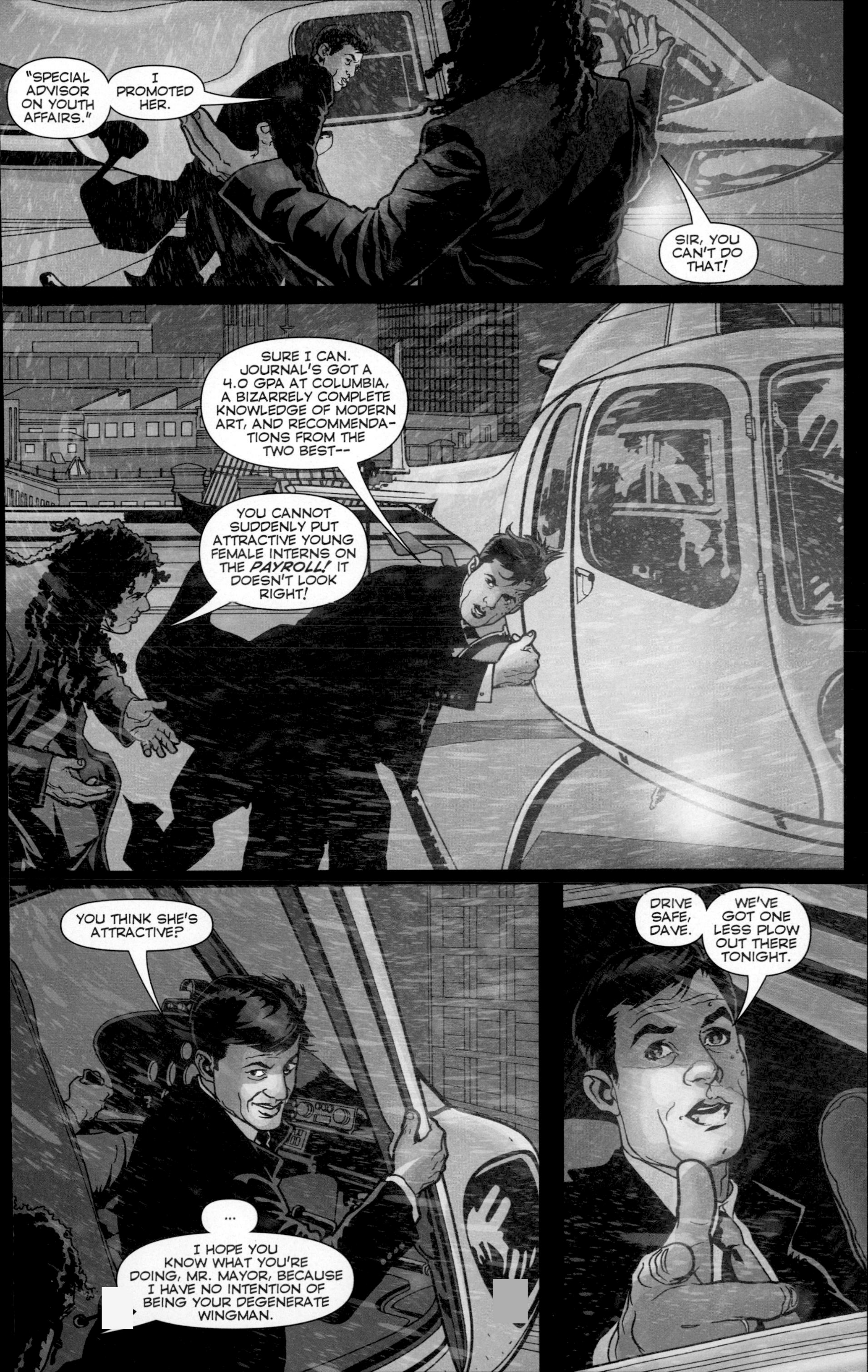
"SPECIAL ADVISOR ON YOUTH AFFAIRS."
I PROMOTED HER.
SIR, YOU CAN'T DO THAT!
SURE I CAN. JOURNAL'S GOT A 4.0 GPA AT COLUMBIA, A BIZARRELY COMPLETE KNOWLEDGE OF MODERN ART, AND RECOMMENDATIONS FROM THE TWO BEST--
YOU CANNOT SUDDENLY PUT ATTRACTIVE YOUNG FEMALE INTERNS ON THE *PAYROLL!* IT DOESN'T LOOK RIGHT!
YOU THINK SHE'S ATTRACTIVE?
...
I HOPE YOU KNOW WHAT YOU'RE DOING, MR. MAYOR, BECAUSE I HAVE NO INTENTION OF BEING YOUR DEGENERATE WINGMAN.
DRIVE SAFE, DAVE.
WE'VE GOT ONE LESS PLOW OUT THERE TONIGHT.

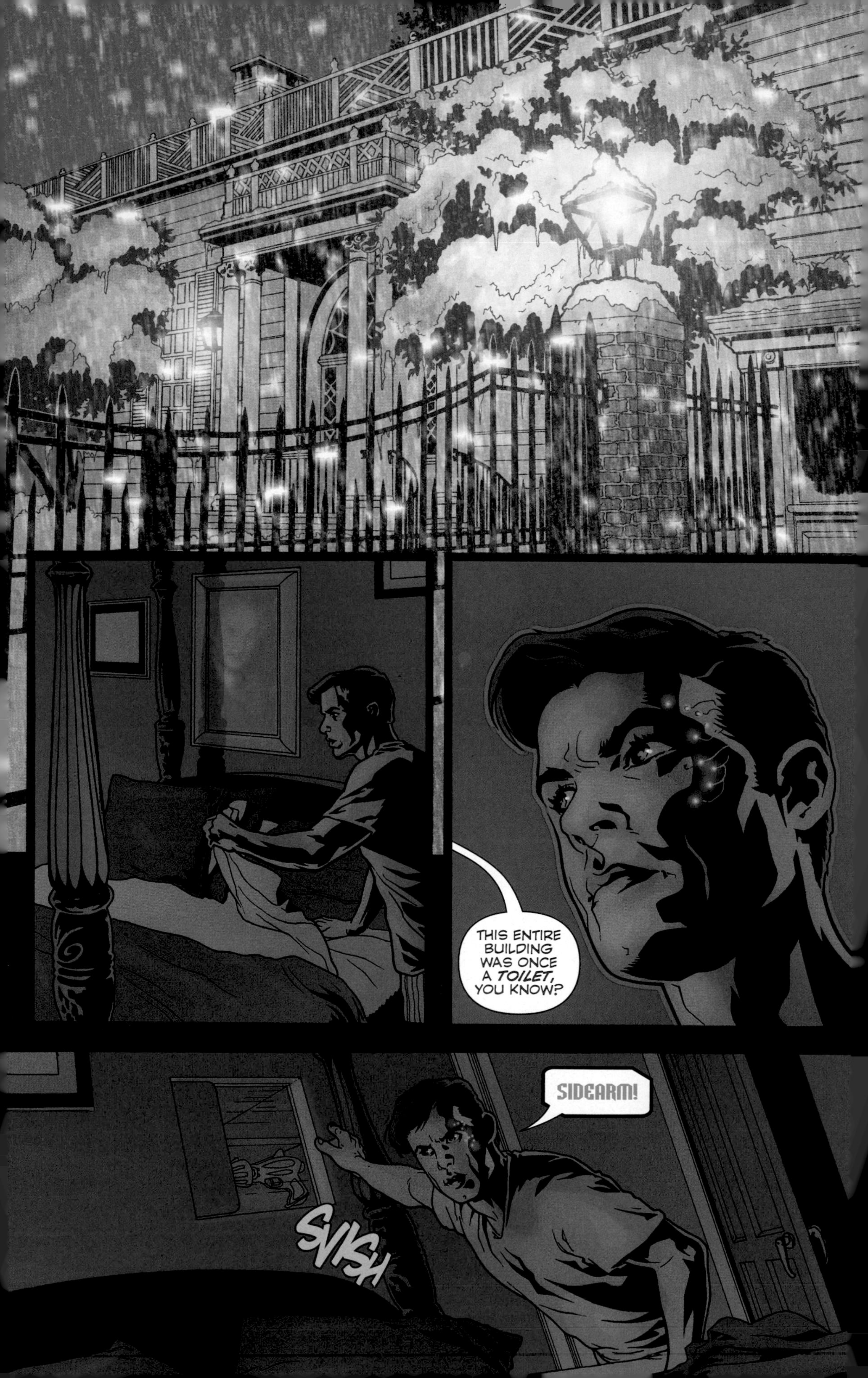
THIS ENTIRE BUILDING WAS ONCE A *TOILET*, YOU KNOW?
SIDEARM!
SWISH

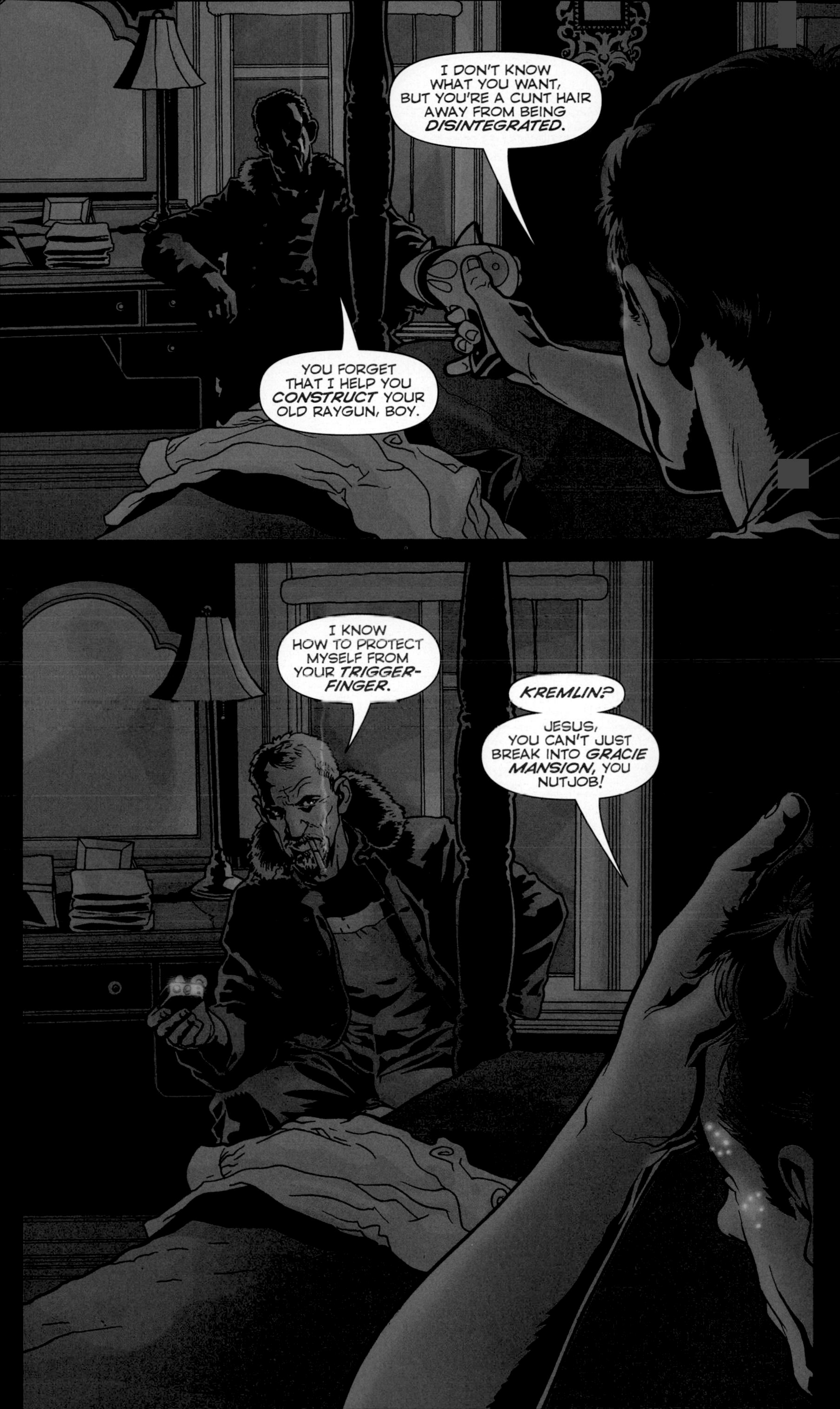
I DON'T KNOW WHAT YOU WANT, BUT YOU'RE A CUNT HAIR AWAY FROM BEING *DISINTEGRATED*.
YOU FORGET THAT I HELP YOU *CONSTRUCT* YOUR OLD RAYGUN, BOY.
I KNOW HOW TO PROTECT MYSELF FROM YOUR *TRIGGER-FINGER*.
KREMLIN?
JESUS, YOU CAN'T JUST BREAK INTO *GRACIE MANSION*, YOU NUTJOB!

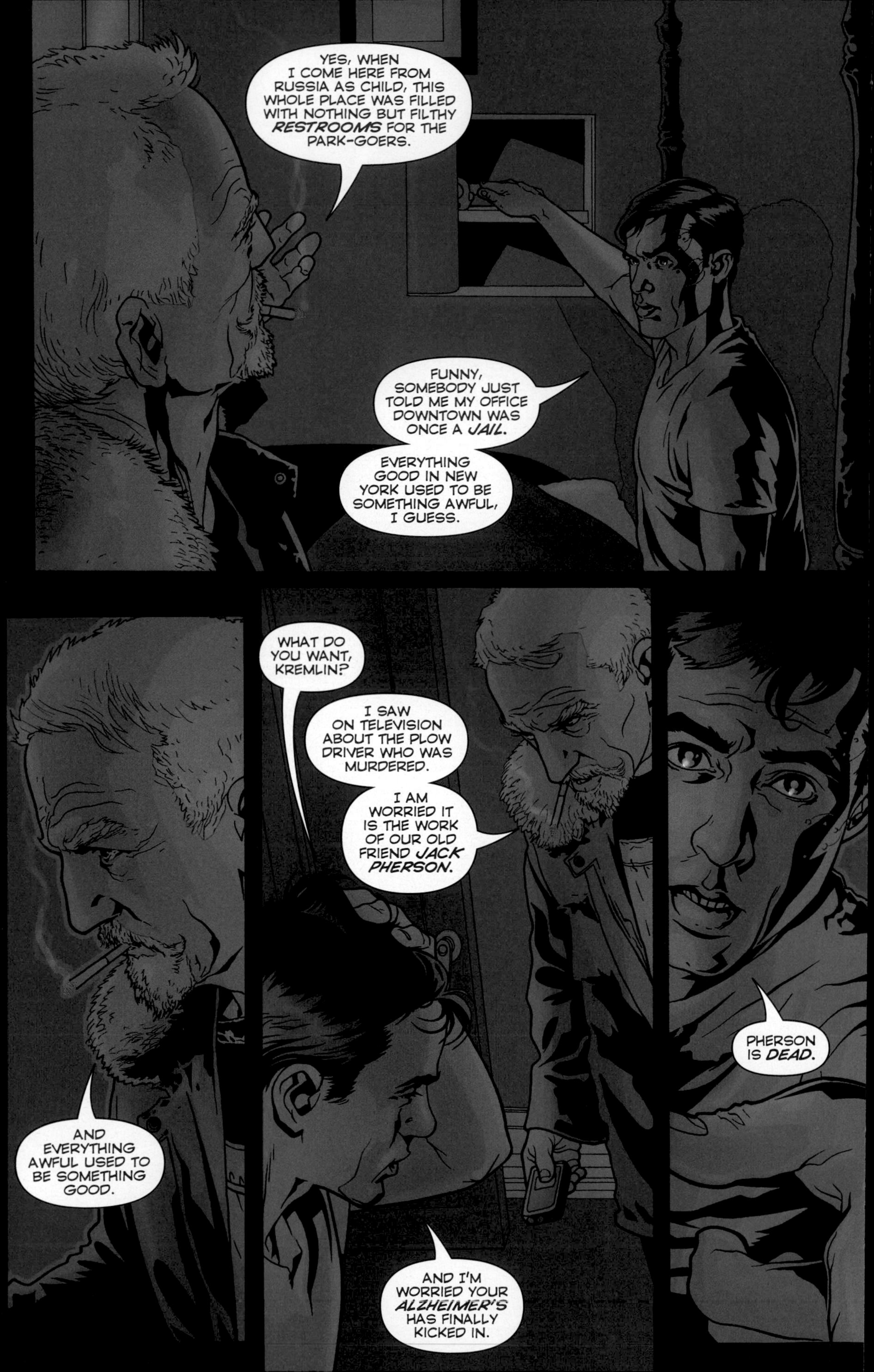
YES, WHEN I COME HERE FROM RUSSIA AS CHILD, THIS WHOLE PLACE WAS FILLED WITH NOTHING BUT FILTHY *RESTROOMS* FOR THE PARK-GOERS.
FUNNY, SOMEBODY JUST TOLD ME MY OFFICE DOWNTOWN WAS ONCE A *JAIL*.
EVERYTHING GOOD IN NEW YORK USED TO BE SOMETHING AWFUL, I GUESS.
AND EVERYTHING AWFUL USED TO BE SOMETHING GOOD.
WHAT DO YOU WANT, KREMLIN?
I SAW ON TELEVISION ABOUT THE PLOW DRIVER WHO WAS MURDERED.
I AM WORRIED IT IS THE WORK OF OUR OLD FRIEND *JACK PHERSON*.
AND I'M WORRIED YOUR *ALZHEIMER'S* HAS FINALLY KICKED IN.
PHERSON IS *DEAD*.

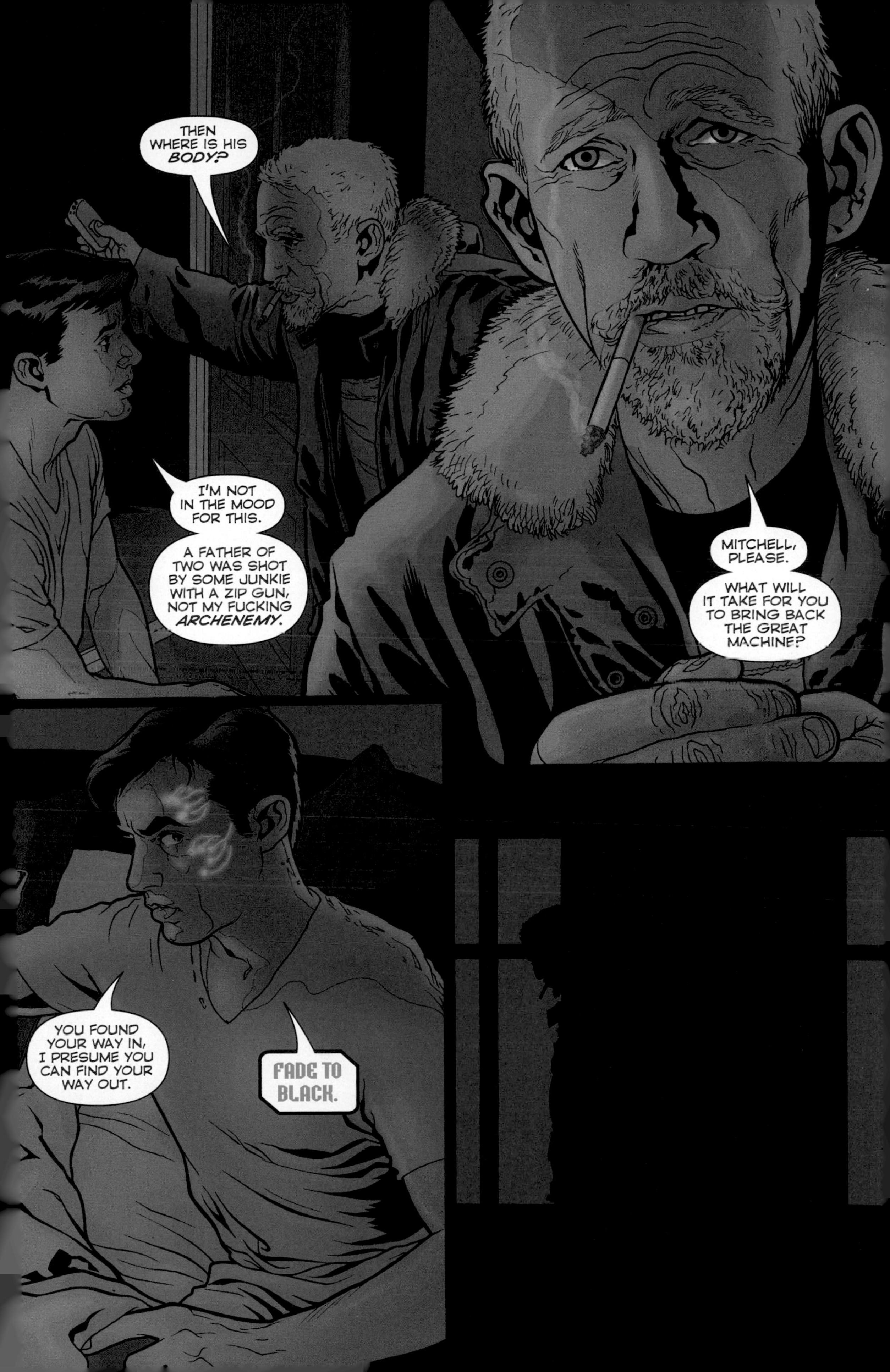
THEN WHERE IS HIS BODY?
I'M NOT IN THE MOOD FOR THIS.
A FATHER OF TWO WAS SHOT BY SOME JUNKIE WITH A ZIP GUN, NOT MY FUCKING ARCHENEMY.
MITCHELL, PLEASE.
WHAT WILL IT TAKE FOR YOU TO BRING BACK THE GREAT MACHINE?
YOU FOUND YOUR WAY IN, I PRESUME YOU CAN FIND YOUR WAY OUT.
FADE TO BLACK.

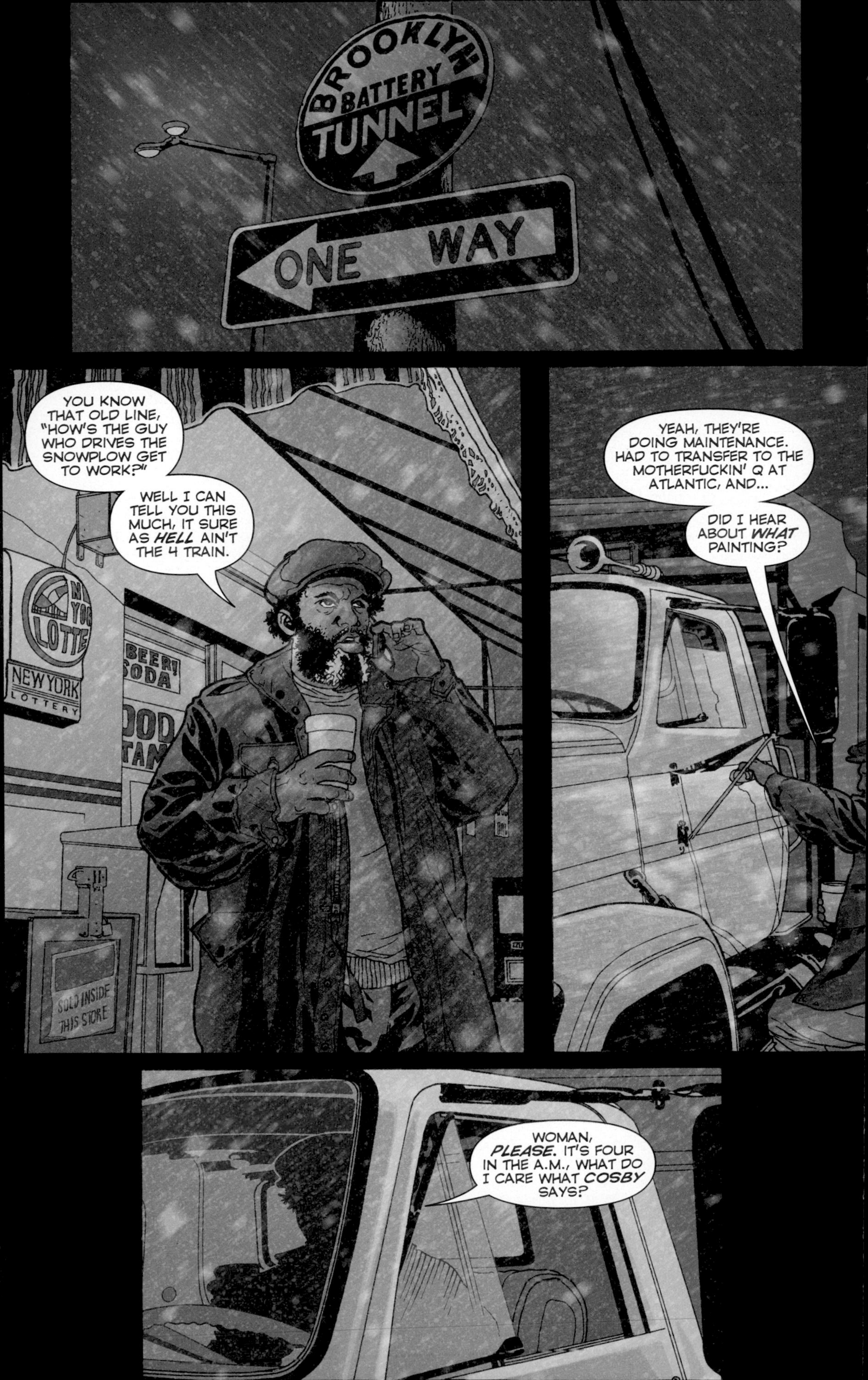
BROOKLYN BATTERY TUNNEL
ONE WAY
YOU KNOW THAT OLD LINE, "HOW'S THE GUY WHO DRIVES THE SNOWPLOW GET TO WORK?"
WELL I CAN TELL YOU THIS MUCH, IT SURE AS HELL AIN'T THE 4 TRAIN.
NEW YORK LOTTERY
BEER! SODA
SOLD INSIDE THIS STORE
YEAH, THEY'RE DOING MAINTENANCE. HAD TO TRANSFER TO THE MOTHERFUCKIN' Q AT ATLANTIC, AND...
DID I HEAR ABOUT WHAT PAINTING?
WOMAN, PLEASE. IT'S FOUR IN THE A.M., WHAT DO I CARE WHAT COSBY SAYS?

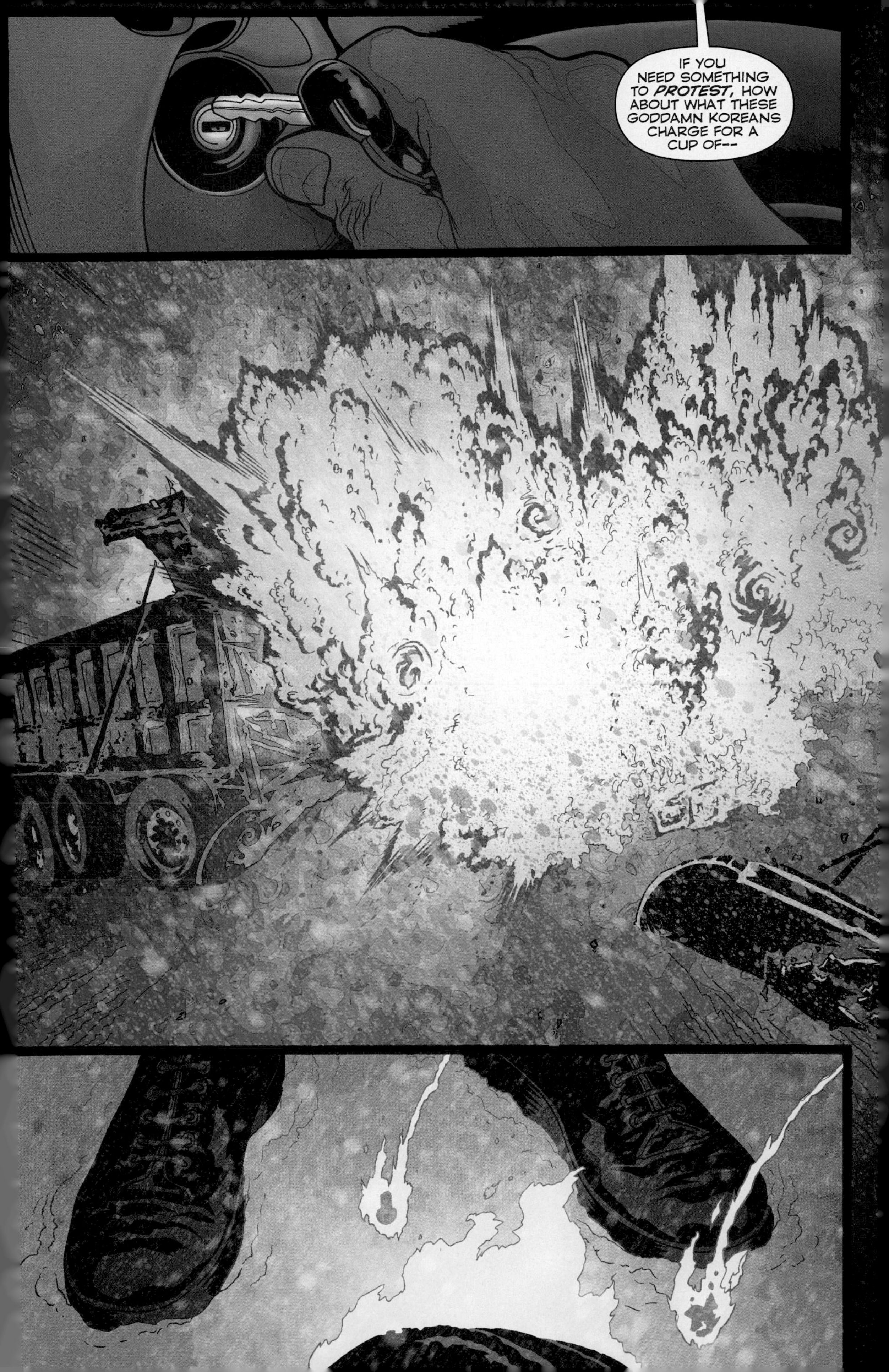
IF YOU NEED SOMETHING TO *PROTEST,* HOW ABOUT WHAT THESE GODDAMN KOREANS CHARGE FOR A CUP OF--

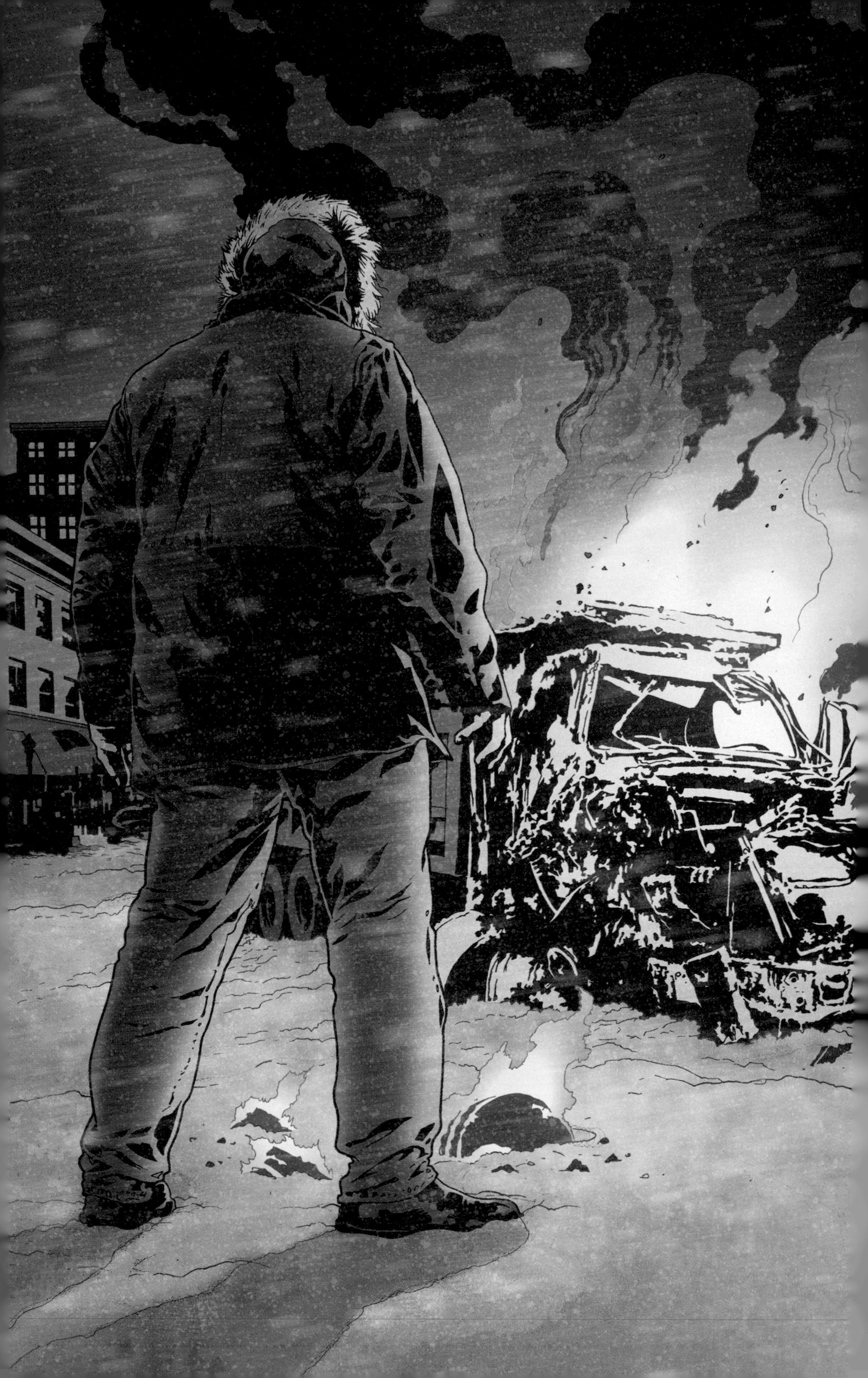

CHAPTER 4

Part 3
State of Emergency

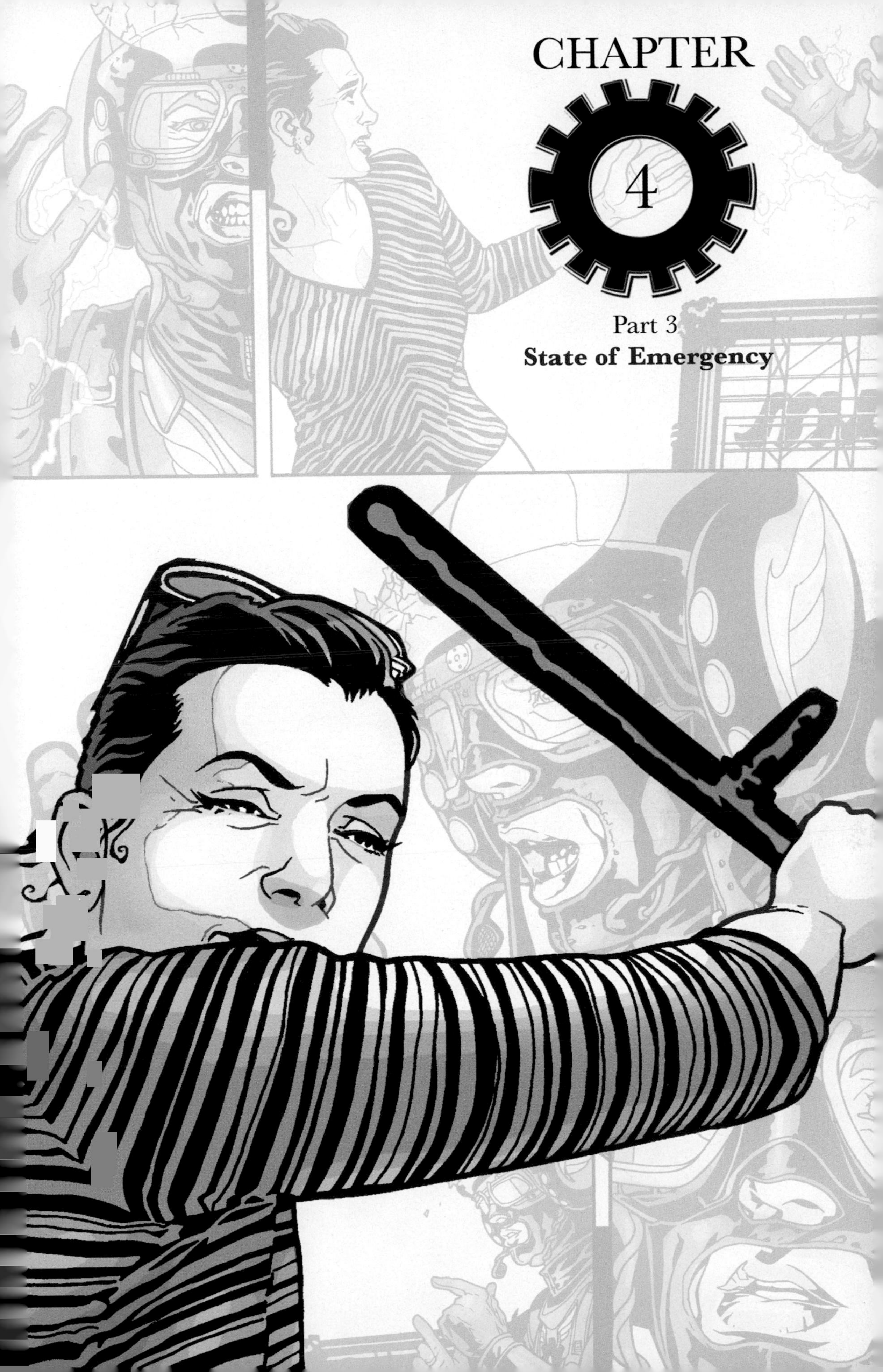

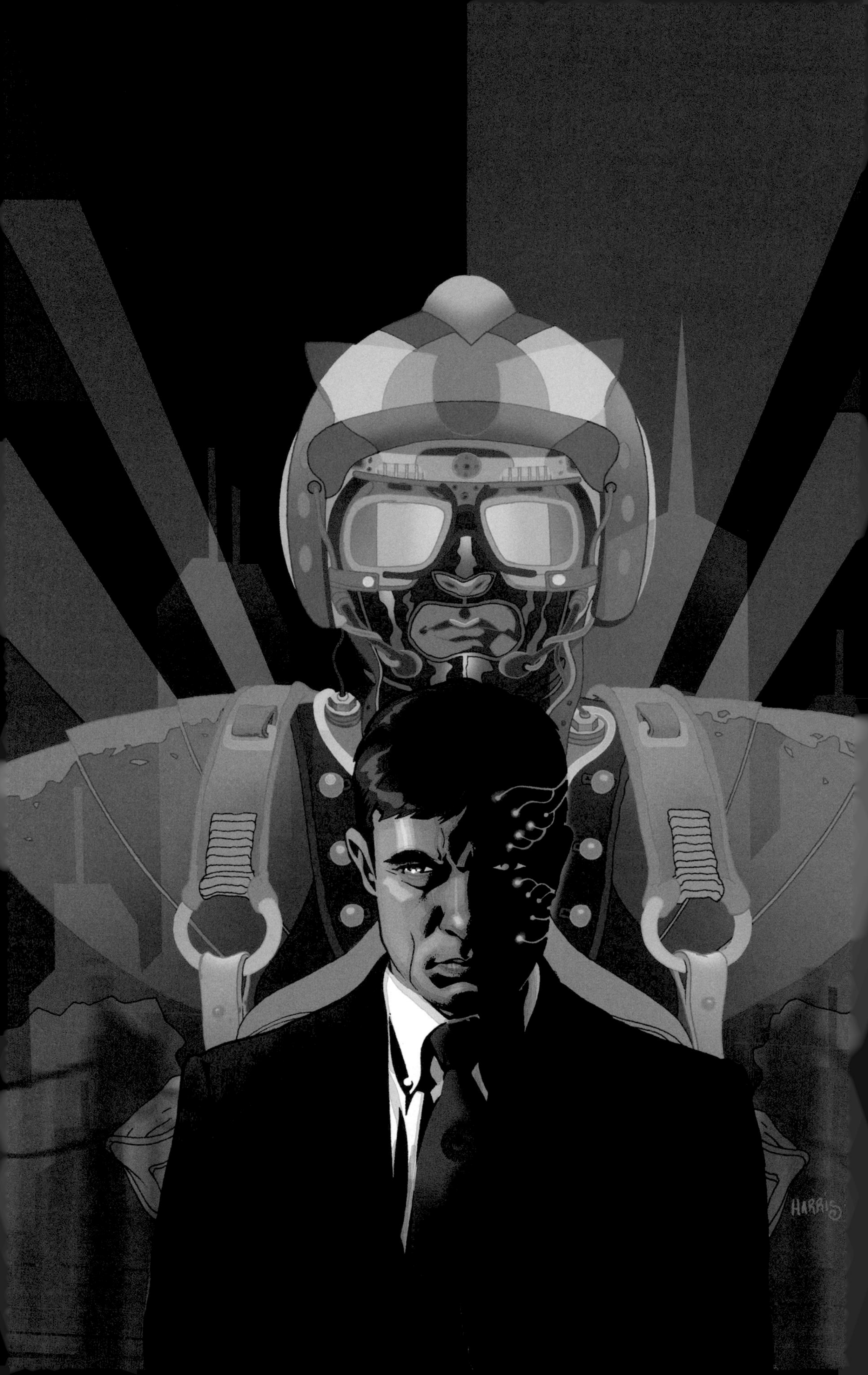
HARRIS

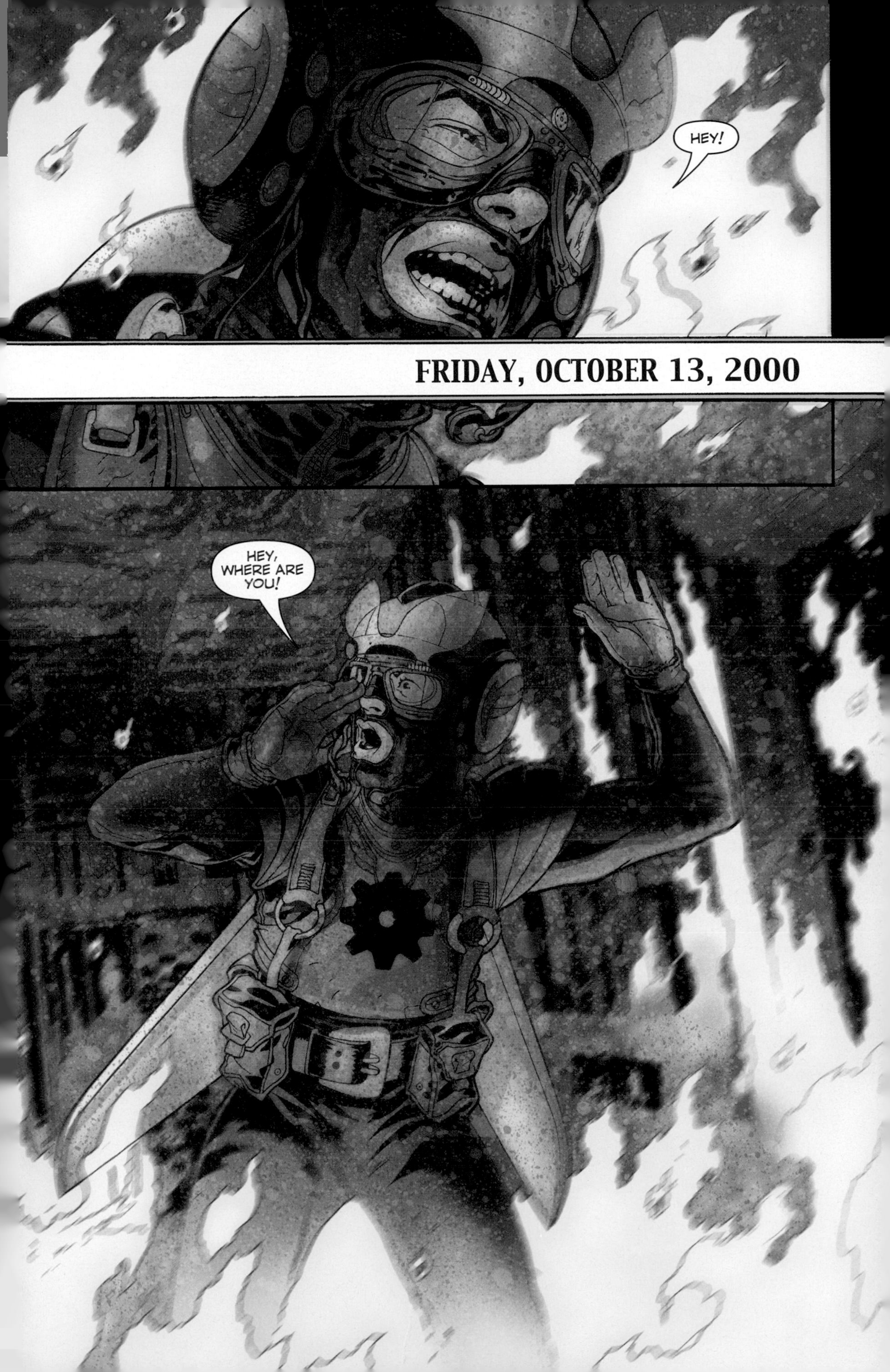
HEY!
FRIDAY, OCTOBER 13, 2000
HEY, WHERE ARE YOU!

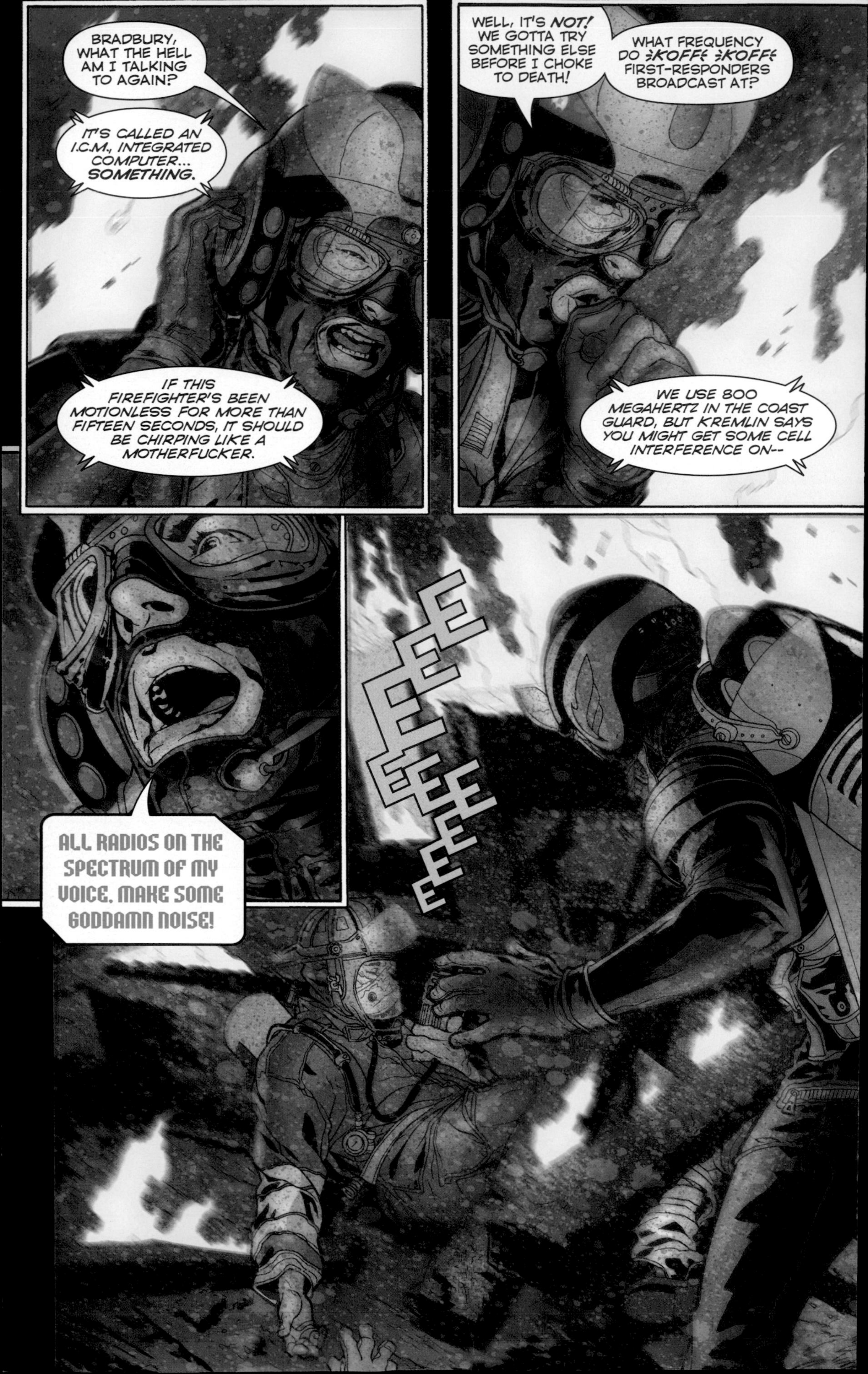
BRADBURY, WHAT THE HELL AM I TALKING TO AGAIN?
IT'S CALLED AN I.C.M., INTEGRATED COMPUTER... SOMETHING.
IF THIS FIREFIGHTER'S BEEN MOTIONLESS FOR MORE THAN FIFTEEN SECONDS, IT SHOULD BE CHIRPING LIKE A MOTHERFUCKER.
WELL, IT'S NOT! WE GOTTA TRY SOMETHING ELSE BEFORE I CHOKE TO DEATH!
WHAT FREQUENCY DO KOFF KOFF FIRST-RESPONDERS BROADCAST AT?
WE USE 800 MEGAHERTZ IN THE COAST GUARD, BUT KREMLIN SAYS YOU MIGHT GET SOME CELL INTERFERENCE ON--
ALL RADIOS ON THE SPECTRUM OF MY VOICE. MAKE SOME GODDAMN NOISE!
EEEEEEEEE

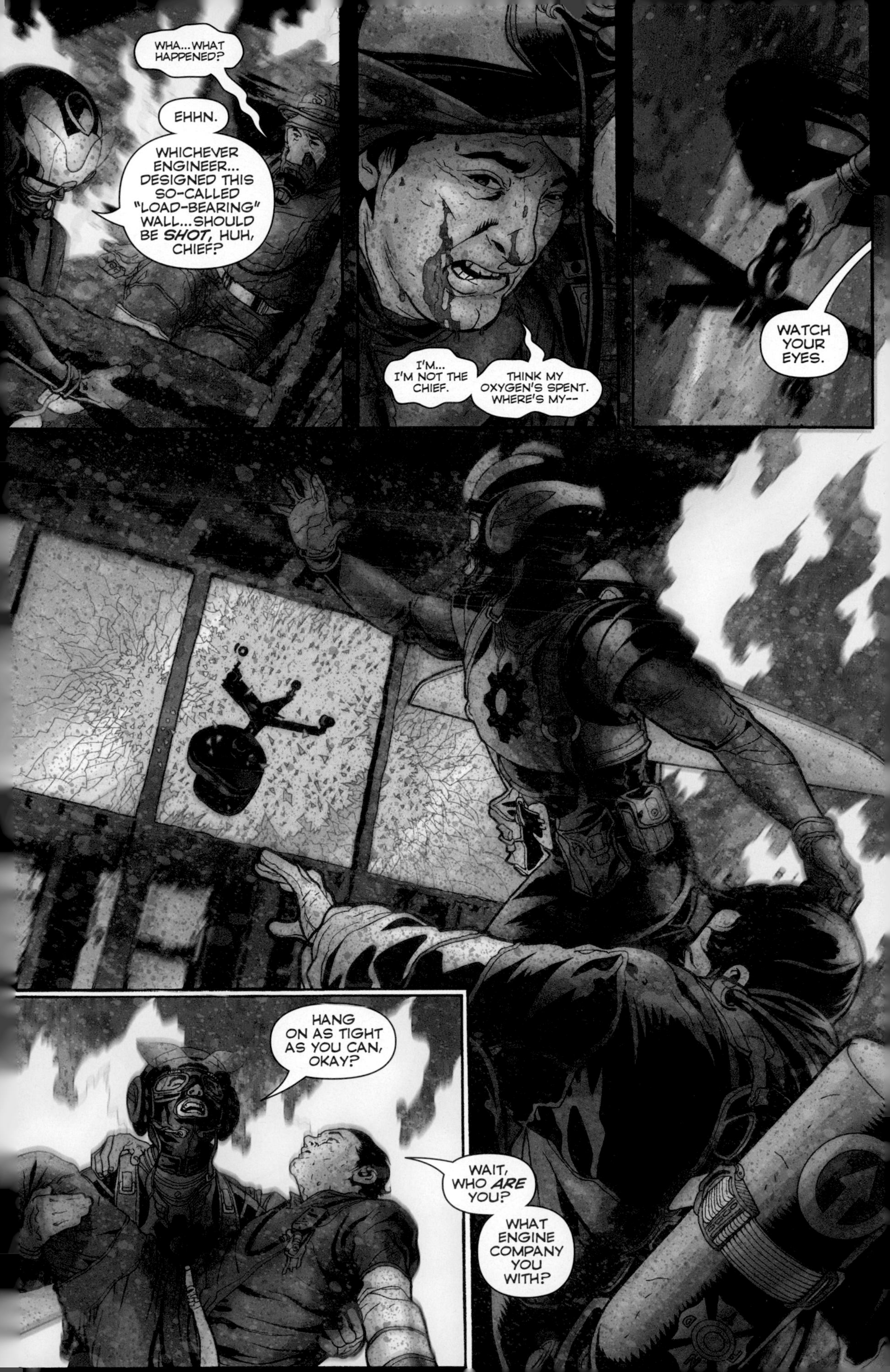
WHA...WHAT HAPPENED?
EHHN.
WHICHEVER ENGINEER... DESIGNED THIS SO-CALLED "LOAD-BEARING" WALL...SHOULD BE *SHOT*, HUH, CHIEF?
I'M... I'M NOT THE CHIEF.
THINK MY OXYGEN'S SPENT. WHERE'S MY--
WATCH YOUR EYES.
HANG ON AS TIGHT AS YOU CAN, OKAY?
WAIT, WHO *ARE* YOU?
WHAT ENGINE COMPANY YOU WITH?

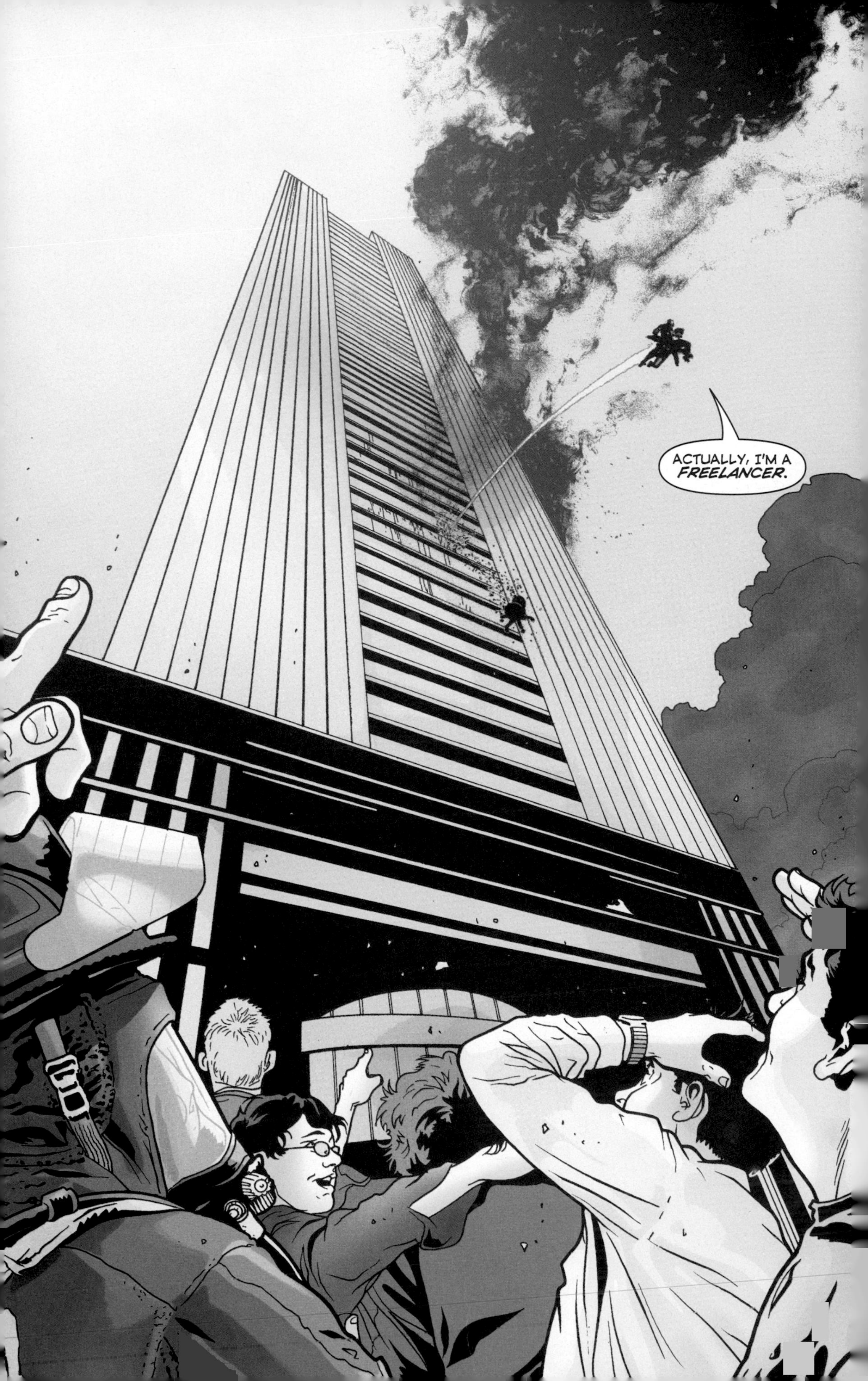
ACTUALLY, I'M A *FREELANCER*.

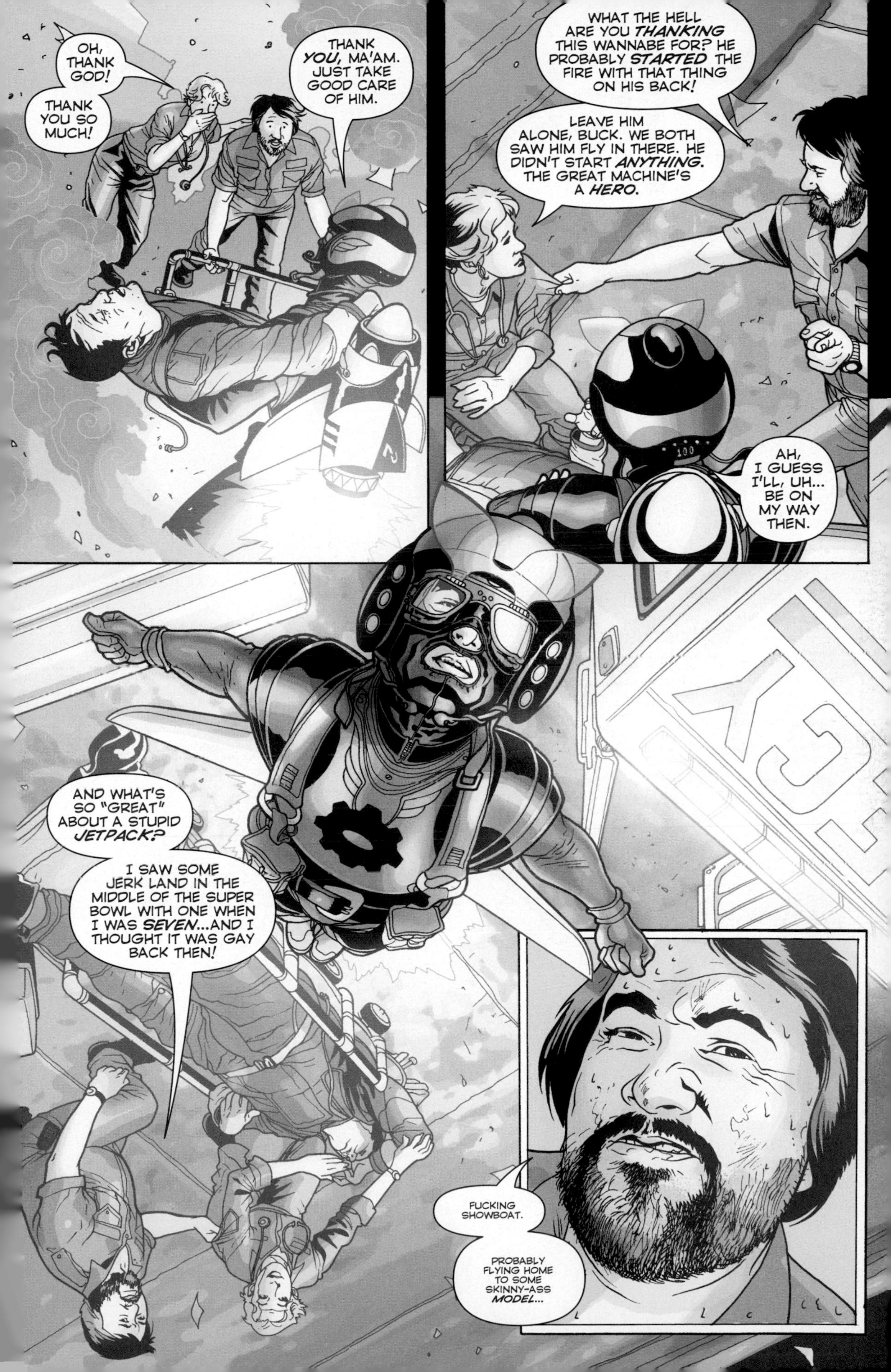
OH, THANK GOD!
THANK YOU SO MUCH!
THANK *YOU*, MA'AM. JUST TAKE GOOD CARE OF HIM.
WHAT THE HELL ARE YOU *THANKING* THIS WANNABE FOR? HE PROBABLY *STARTED* THE FIRE WITH THAT THING ON HIS BACK!
LEAVE HIM ALONE, BUCK. WE BOTH SAW HIM FLY IN THERE. HE DIDN'T START *ANYTHING*. THE GREAT MACHINE'S A *HERO*.
AH, I GUESS I'LL, UH... BE ON MY WAY THEN.
AND WHAT'S SO "GREAT" ABOUT A STUPID *JETPACK?*
I SAW SOME JERK LAND IN THE MIDDLE OF THE SUPER BOWL WITH ONE WHEN I WAS *SEVEN*...AND I THOUGHT IT WAS GAY BACK THEN!
FUCKING SHOWBOAT.
PROBABLY FLYING HOME TO SOME SKINNY-ASS *MODEL*...

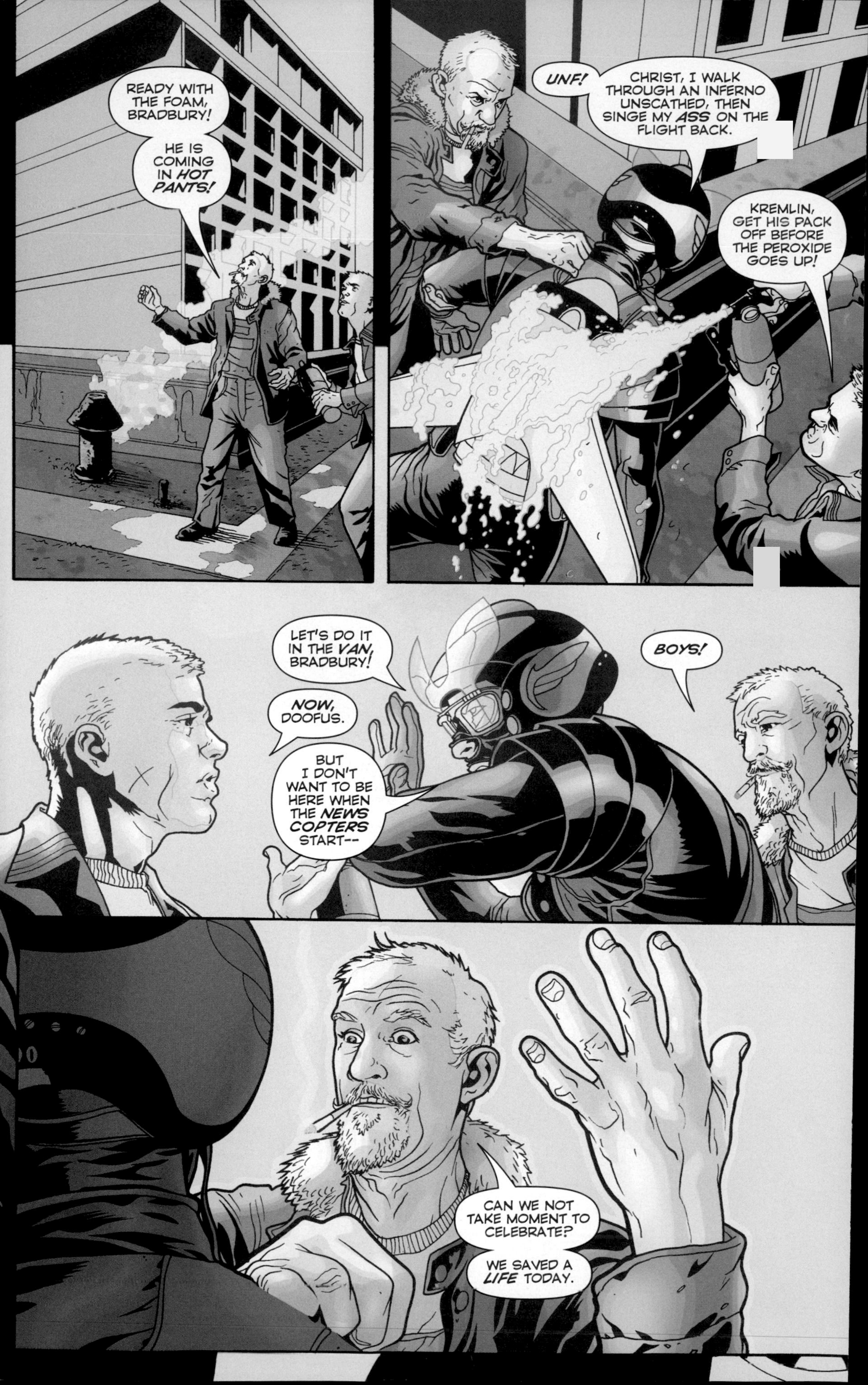
READY WITH THE FOAM, BRADBURY!
HE IS COMING IN HOT PANTS!
UNF!
CHRIST, I WALK THROUGH AN INFERNO UNSCATHED, THEN SINGE MY ASS ON THE FLIGHT BACK.
KREMLIN, GET HIS PACK OFF BEFORE THE PEROXIDE GOES UP!
LET'S DO IT IN THE VAN, BRADBURY!
NOW, DOOFUS.
BUT I DON'T WANT TO BE HERE WHEN THE NEWS COPTERS START--
BOYS!
CAN WE NOT TAKE MOMENT TO CELEBRATE?
WE SAVED A LIFE TODAY.

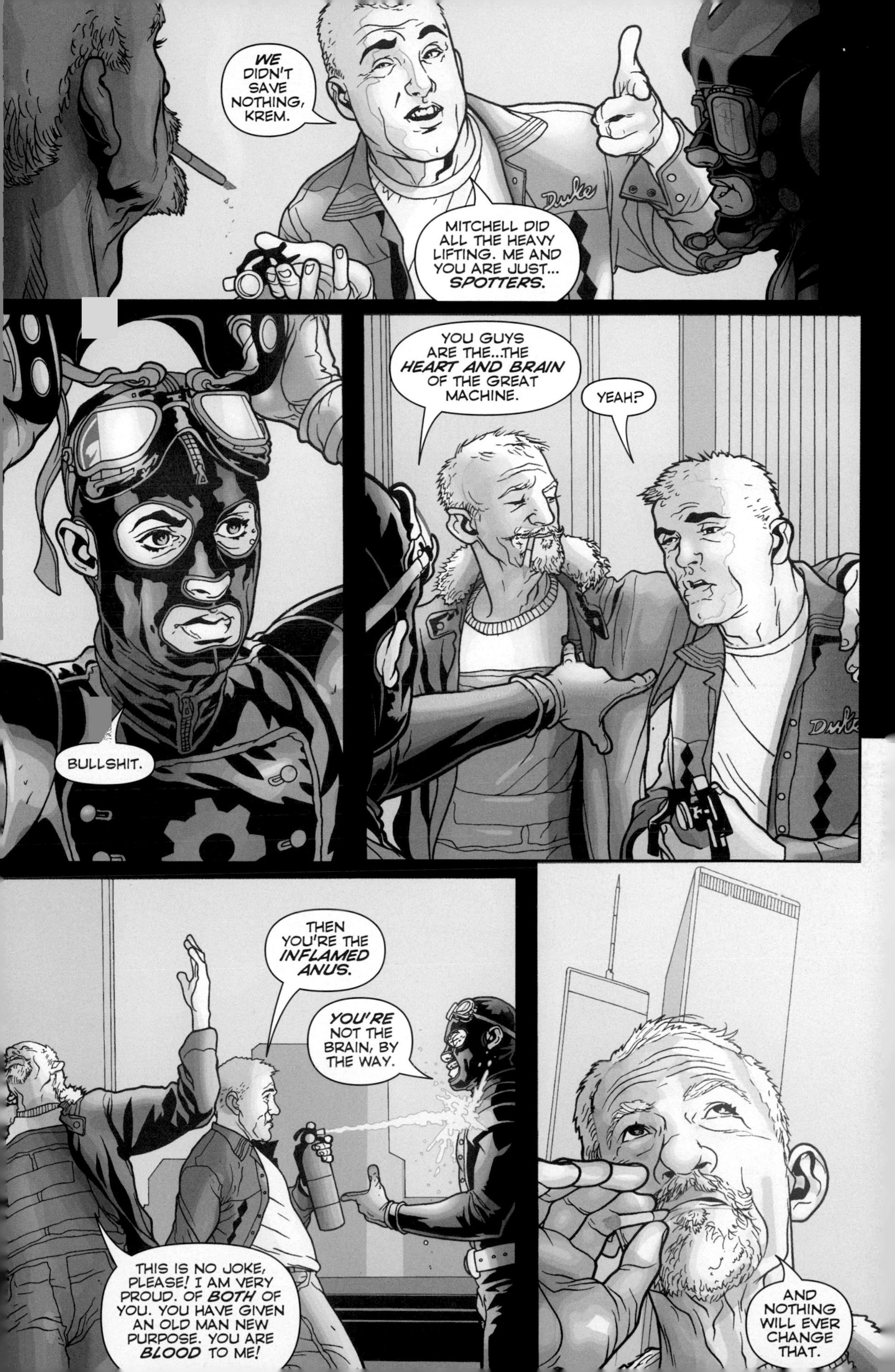
WE DIDN'T SAVE NOTHING, KREM.
MITCHELL DID ALL THE HEAVY LIFTING. ME AND YOU ARE JUST... SPOTTERS.
Duke
BULLSHIT.
YOU GUYS ARE THE...THE HEART AND BRAIN OF THE GREAT MACHINE.
YEAH?
THEN YOU'RE THE INFLAMED ANUS.
YOU'RE NOT THE BRAIN, BY THE WAY.
THIS IS NO JOKE, PLEASE! I AM VERY PROUD. OF BOTH OF YOU. YOU HAVE GIVEN AN OLD MAN NEW PURPOSE. YOU ARE BLOOD TO ME!
AND NOTHING WILL EVER CHANGE THAT.

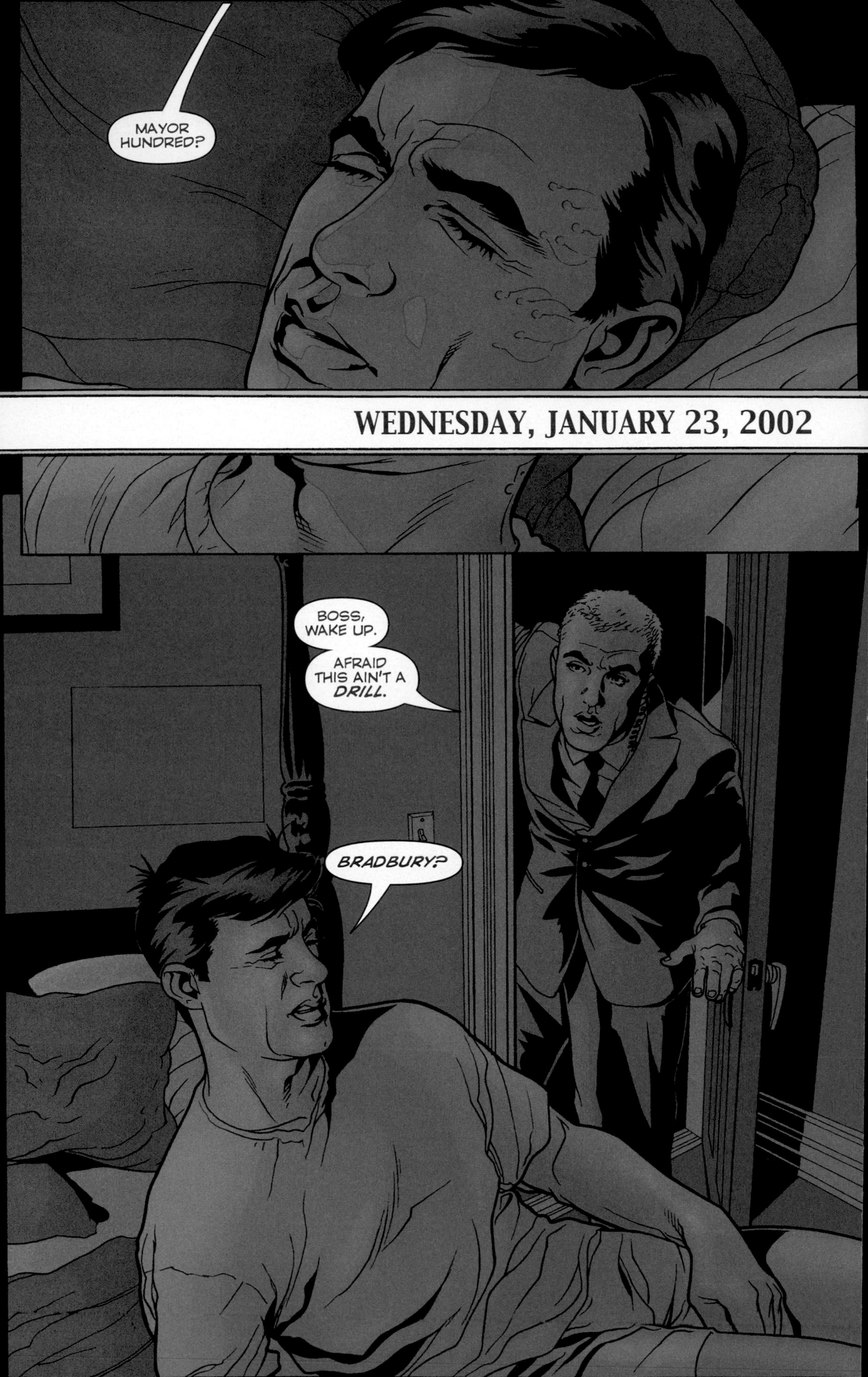
MAYOR HUNDRED?
WEDNESDAY, JANUARY 23, 2002
BOSS, WAKE UP.
AFRAID THIS AIN'T A *DRILL*.
BRADBURY?

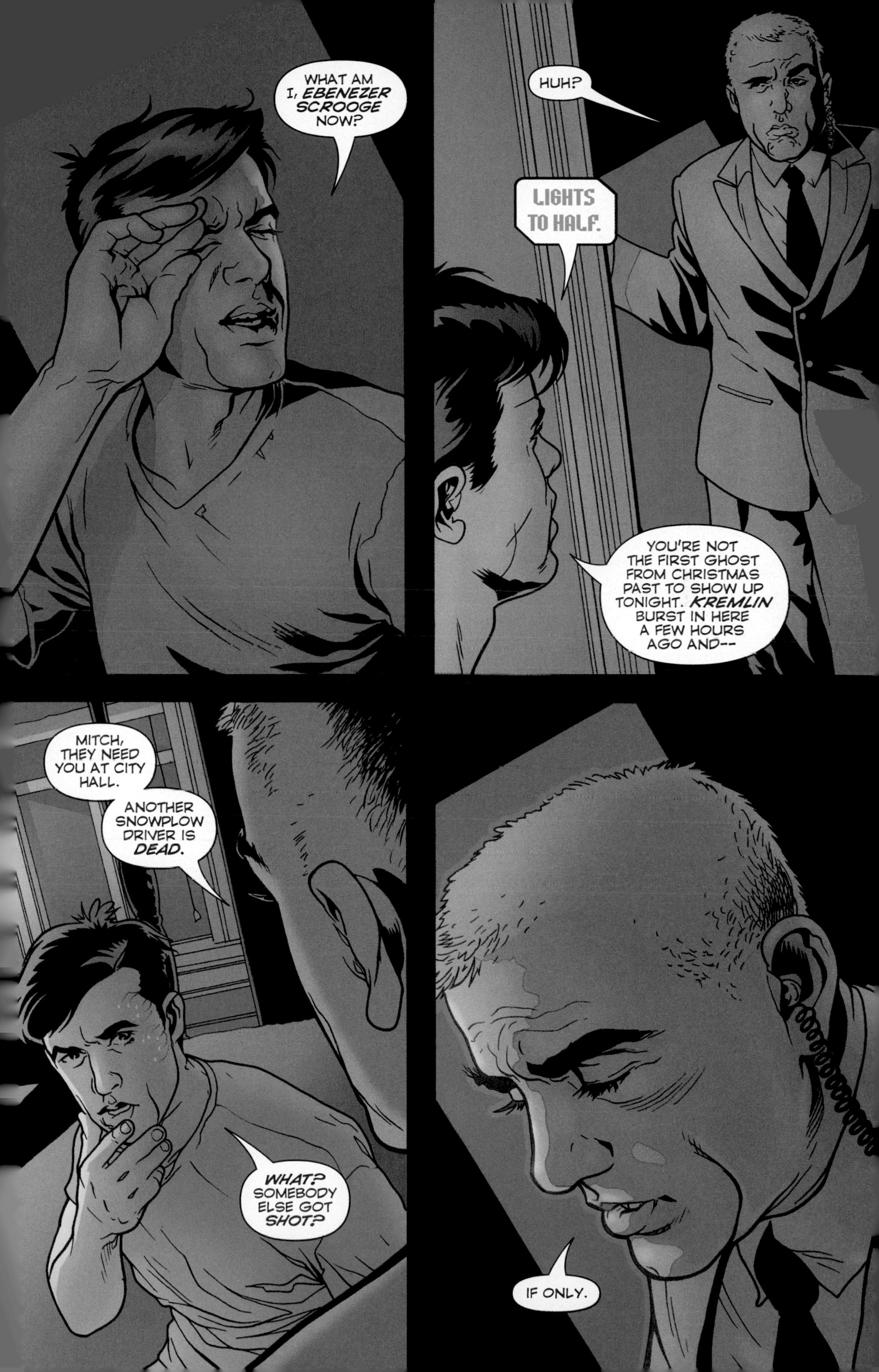
WHAT AM I, *EBENEZER SCROOGE* NOW?
HUH?
LIGHTS TO HALF.
YOU'RE NOT THE FIRST GHOST FROM CHRISTMAS PAST TO SHOW UP TONIGHT. *KREMLIN* BURST IN HERE A FEW HOURS AGO AND--
MITCH, THEY NEED YOU AT CITY HALL.
ANOTHER SNOWPLOW DRIVER IS *DEAD*.
WHAT? SOMEBODY ELSE GOT *SHOT?*
IF ONLY.

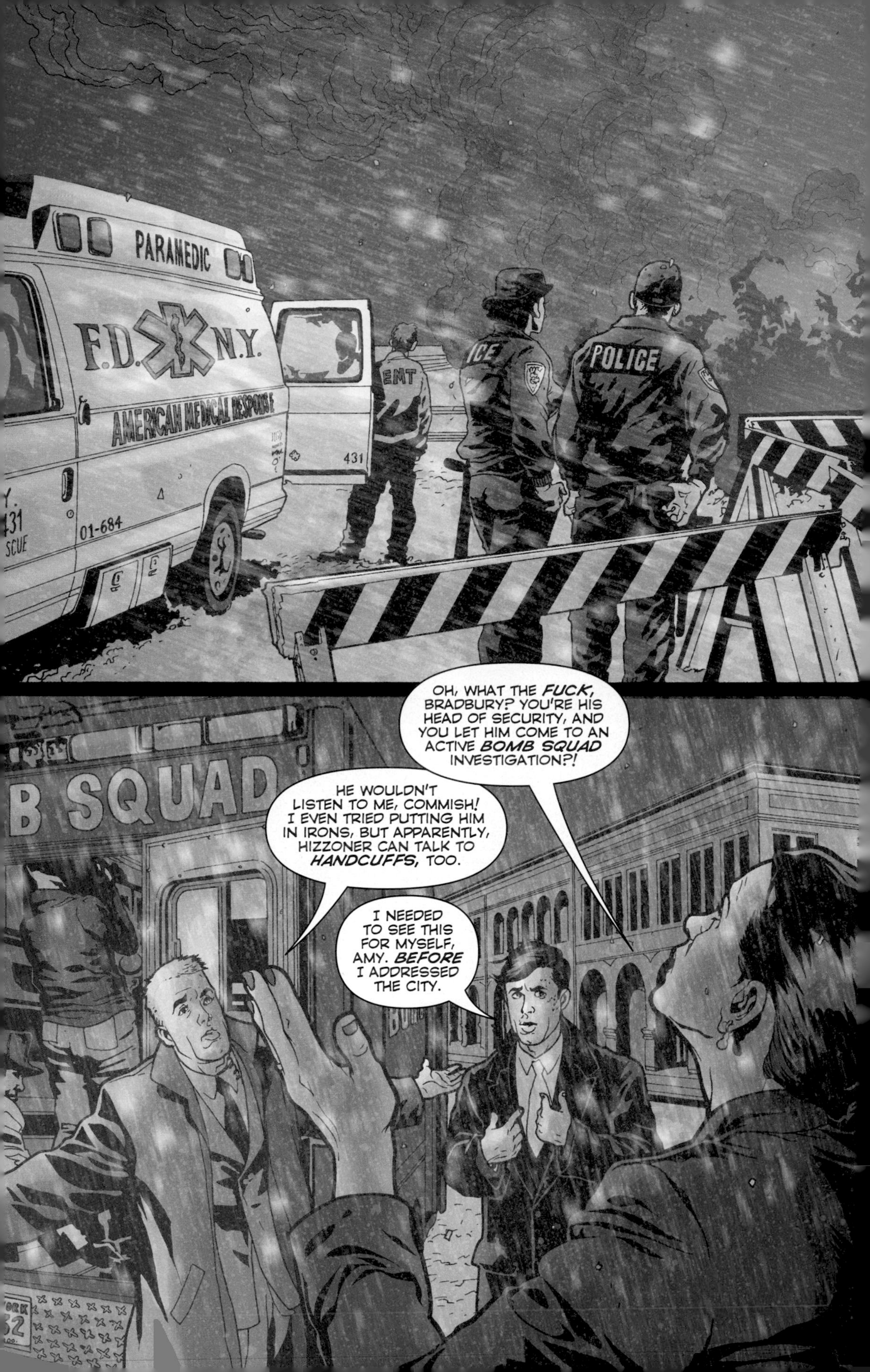
PARAMEDIC
F.D. N.Y.
AMERICAN MEDICAL RESPONSE
01-684
431
EMT
ICE
POLICE
B SQUAD
OH, WHAT THE *FUCK,* BRADBURY? YOU'RE HIS HEAD OF SECURITY, AND YOU LET HIM COME TO AN ACTIVE ***BOMB SQUAD*** INVESTIGATION?!
HE WOULDN'T LISTEN TO ME, COMMISH! I EVEN TRIED PUTTING HIM IN IRONS, BUT APPARENTLY, HIZZONER CAN TALK TO ***HANDCUFFS,*** TOO.
I NEEDED TO SEE THIS FOR MYSELF, AMY. ***BEFORE*** I ADDRESSED THE CITY.

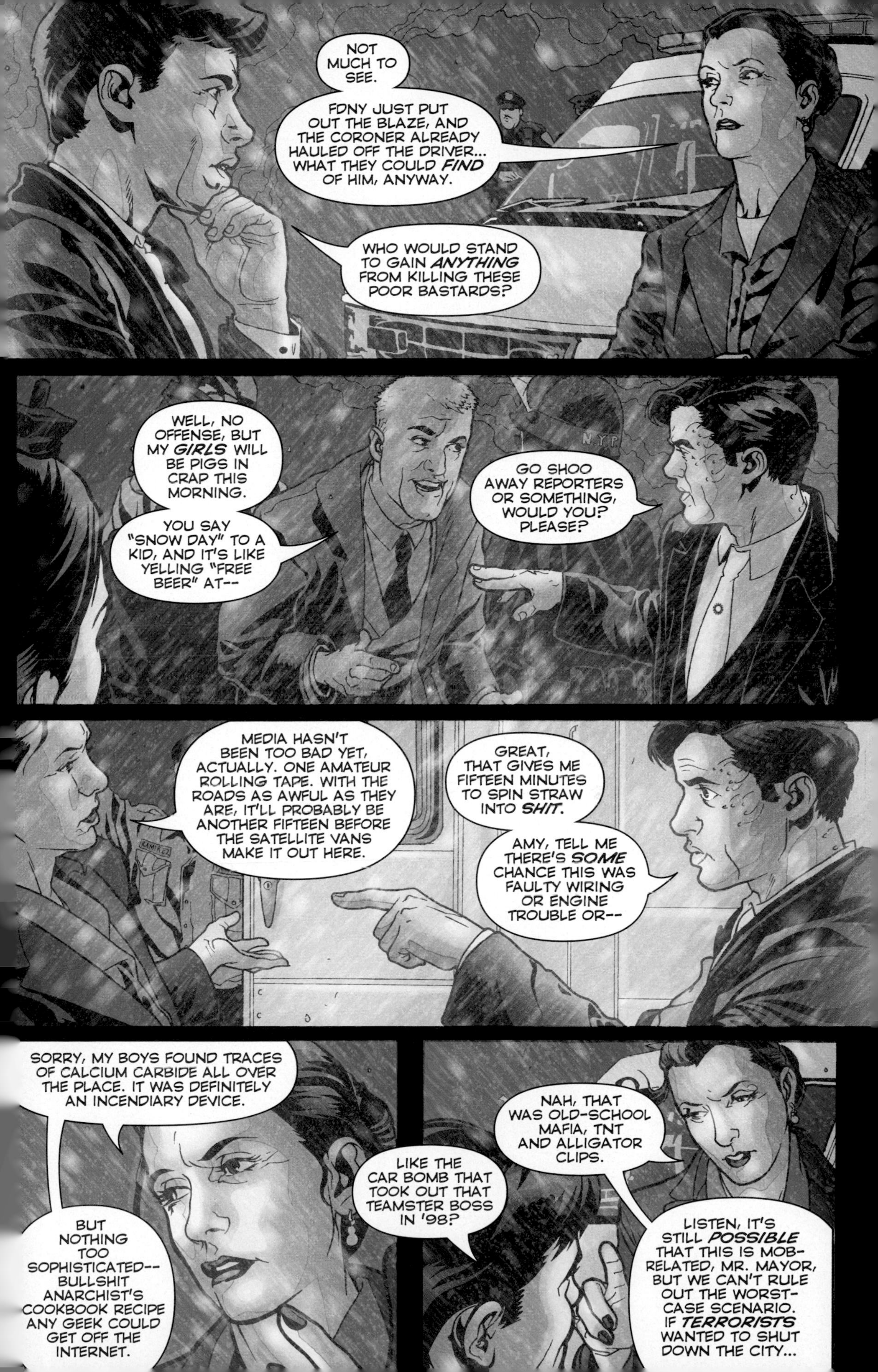
NOT MUCH TO SEE.
FDNY JUST PUT OUT THE BLAZE, AND THE CORONER ALREADY HAULED OFF THE DRIVER... WHAT THEY COULD *FIND* OF HIM, ANYWAY.
WHO WOULD STAND TO GAIN *ANYTHING* FROM KILLING THESE POOR BASTARDS?
WELL, NO OFFENSE, BUT MY *GIRLS* WILL BE PIGS IN CRAP THIS MORNING.
YOU SAY "SNOW DAY" TO A KID, AND IT'S LIKE YELLING "FREE BEER" AT--
GO SHOO AWAY REPORTERS OR SOMETHING, WOULD YOU? PLEASE?
MEDIA HASN'T BEEN TOO BAD YET, ACTUALLY. ONE AMATEUR ROLLING TAPE. WITH THE ROADS AS AWFUL AS THEY ARE, IT'LL PROBABLY BE ANOTHER FIFTEEN BEFORE THE SATELLITE VANS MAKE IT OUT HERE.
GREAT, THAT GIVES ME FIFTEEN MINUTES TO SPIN STRAW INTO *SHIT*.
AMY, TELL ME THERE'S *SOME* CHANCE THIS WAS FAULTY WIRING OR ENGINE TROUBLE OR--
SORRY, MY BOYS FOUND TRACES OF CALCIUM CARBIDE ALL OVER THE PLACE. IT WAS DEFINITELY AN INCENDIARY DEVICE.
BUT NOTHING TOO SOPHISTICATED-- BULLSHIT ANARCHIST'S COOKBOOK RECIPE ANY GEEK COULD GET OFF THE INTERNET.
LIKE THE CAR BOMB THAT TOOK OUT THAT TEAMSTER BOSS IN '98?
NAH, THAT WAS OLD-SCHOOL MAFIA, TNT AND ALLIGATOR CLIPS.
LISTEN, IT'S STILL *POSSIBLE* THAT THIS IS MOB-RELATED, MR. MAYOR, BUT WE CAN'T RULE OUT THE WORST-CASE SCENARIO. IF *TERRORISTS* WANTED TO SHUT DOWN THE CITY...

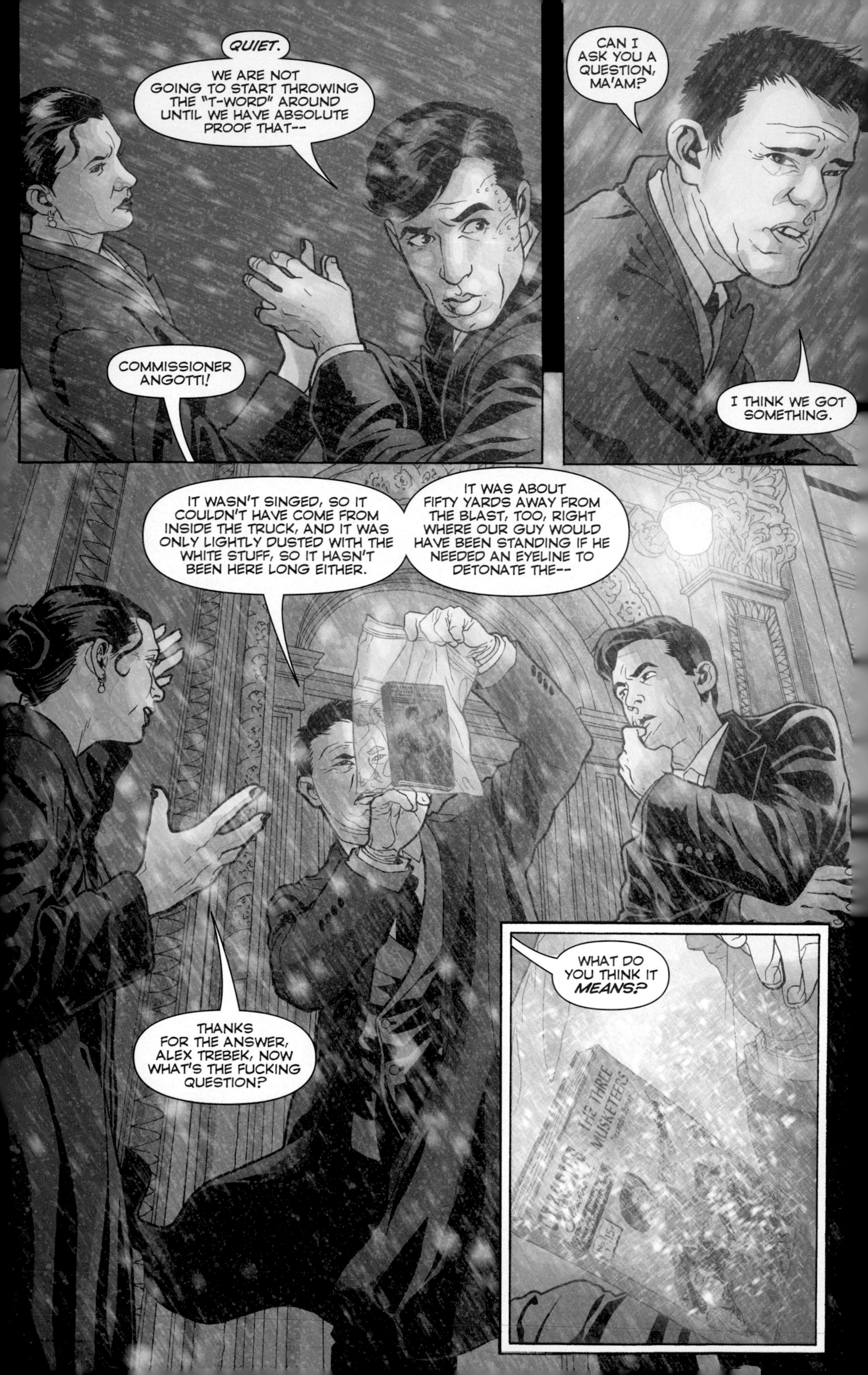
QUIET.
WE ARE NOT GOING TO START THROWING THE "T-WORD" AROUND UNTIL WE HAVE ABSOLUTE PROOF THAT--
COMMISSIONER ANGOTTI!
CAN I ASK YOU A QUESTION, MA'AM?
I THINK WE GOT SOMETHING.
IT WASN'T SINGED, SO IT COULDN'T HAVE COME FROM INSIDE THE TRUCK, AND IT WAS ONLY LIGHTLY DUSTED WITH THE WHITE STUFF, SO IT HASN'T BEEN HERE LONG EITHER.
IT WAS ABOUT FIFTY YARDS AWAY FROM THE BLAST, TOO, RIGHT WHERE OUR GUY WOULD HAVE BEEN STANDING IF HE NEEDED AN EYELINE TO DETONATE THE--
THANKS FOR THE ANSWER, ALEX TREBEK, NOW WHAT'S THE FUCKING QUESTION?
WHAT DO YOU THINK IT MEANS?
THE THREE MUSKETEERS

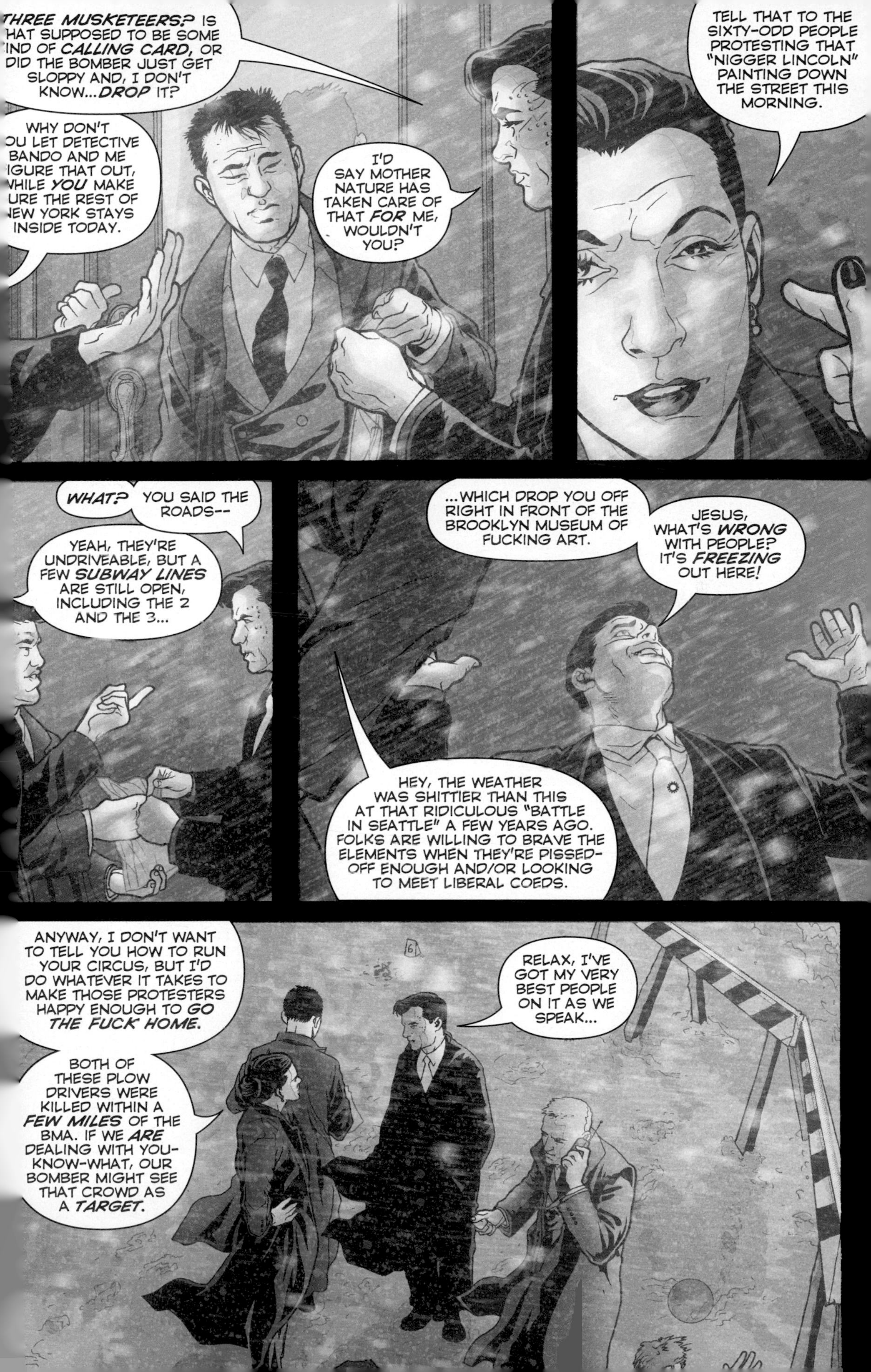
THREE MUSKETEERS? IS HAT SUPPOSED TO BE SOME IND OF CALLING CARD, OR DID THE BOMBER JUST GET SLOPPY AND, I DON'T KNOW...DROP IT?
WHY DON'T OU LET DETECTIVE BANDO AND ME IGURE THAT OUT, HILE YOU MAKE URE THE REST OF NEW YORK STAYS INSIDE TODAY.
I'D SAY MOTHER NATURE HAS TAKEN CARE OF THAT FOR ME, WOULDN'T YOU?
TELL THAT TO THE SIXTY-ODD PEOPLE PROTESTING THAT "NIGGER LINCOLN" PAINTING DOWN THE STREET THIS MORNING.
WHAT?
YOU SAID THE ROADS--
YEAH, THEY'RE UNDRIVEABLE, BUT A FEW SUBWAY LINES ARE STILL OPEN, INCLUDING THE 2 AND THE 3...
...WHICH DROP YOU OFF RIGHT IN FRONT OF THE BROOKLYN MUSEUM OF FUCKING ART.
JESUS, WHAT'S WRONG WITH PEOPLE? IT'S FREEZING OUT HERE!
HEY, THE WEATHER WAS SHITTIER THAN THIS AT THAT RIDICULOUS "BATTLE IN SEATTLE" A FEW YEARS AGO. FOLKS ARE WILLING TO BRAVE THE ELEMENTS WHEN THEY'RE PISSED-OFF ENOUGH AND/OR LOOKING TO MEET LIBERAL COEDS.
ANYWAY, I DON'T WANT TO TELL YOU HOW TO RUN YOUR CIRCUS, BUT I'D DO WHATEVER IT TAKES TO MAKE THOSE PROTESTERS HAPPY ENOUGH TO GO THE FUCK HOME.
BOTH OF THESE PLOW DRIVERS WERE KILLED WITHIN A FEW MILES OF THE BMA. IF WE ARE DEALING WITH YOU-KNOW-WHAT, OUR BOMBER MIGHT SEE THAT CROWD AS A TARGET.
RELAX, I'VE GOT MY VERY BEST PEOPLE ON IT AS WE SPEAK...

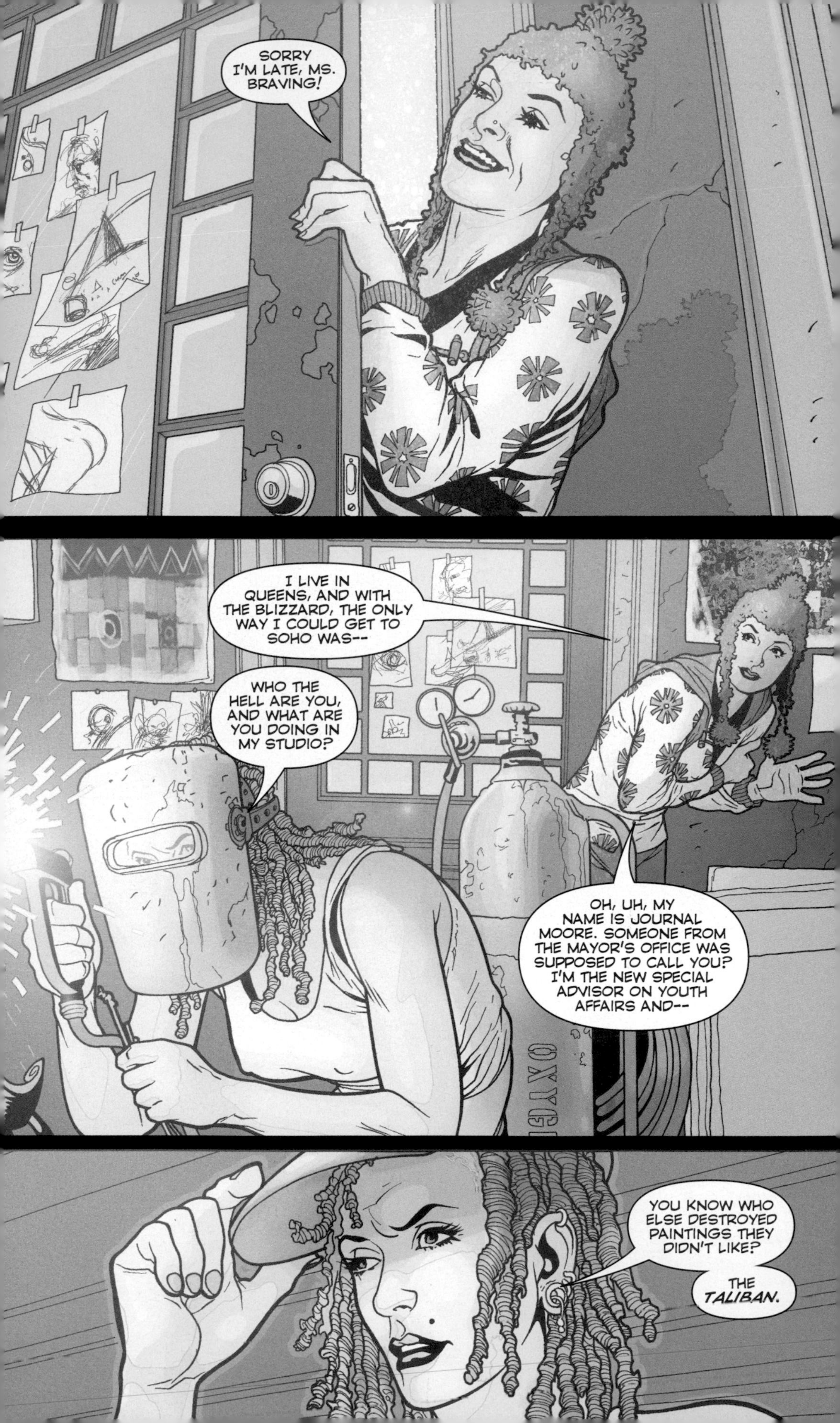
SORRY I'M LATE, MS. BRAVING!
I LIVE IN QUEENS, AND WITH THE BLIZZARD, THE ONLY WAY I COULD GET TO SOHO WAS--
WHO THE HELL ARE YOU, AND WHAT ARE YOU DOING IN MY STUDIO?
OH, UH, MY NAME IS JOURNAL MOORE. SOMEONE FROM THE MAYOR'S OFFICE WAS SUPPOSED TO CALL YOU? I'M THE NEW SPECIAL ADVISOR ON YOUTH AFFAIRS AND--
OXYGEN
YOU KNOW WHO ELSE DESTROYED PAINTINGS THEY DIDN'T LIKE?
THE *TALIBAN*.

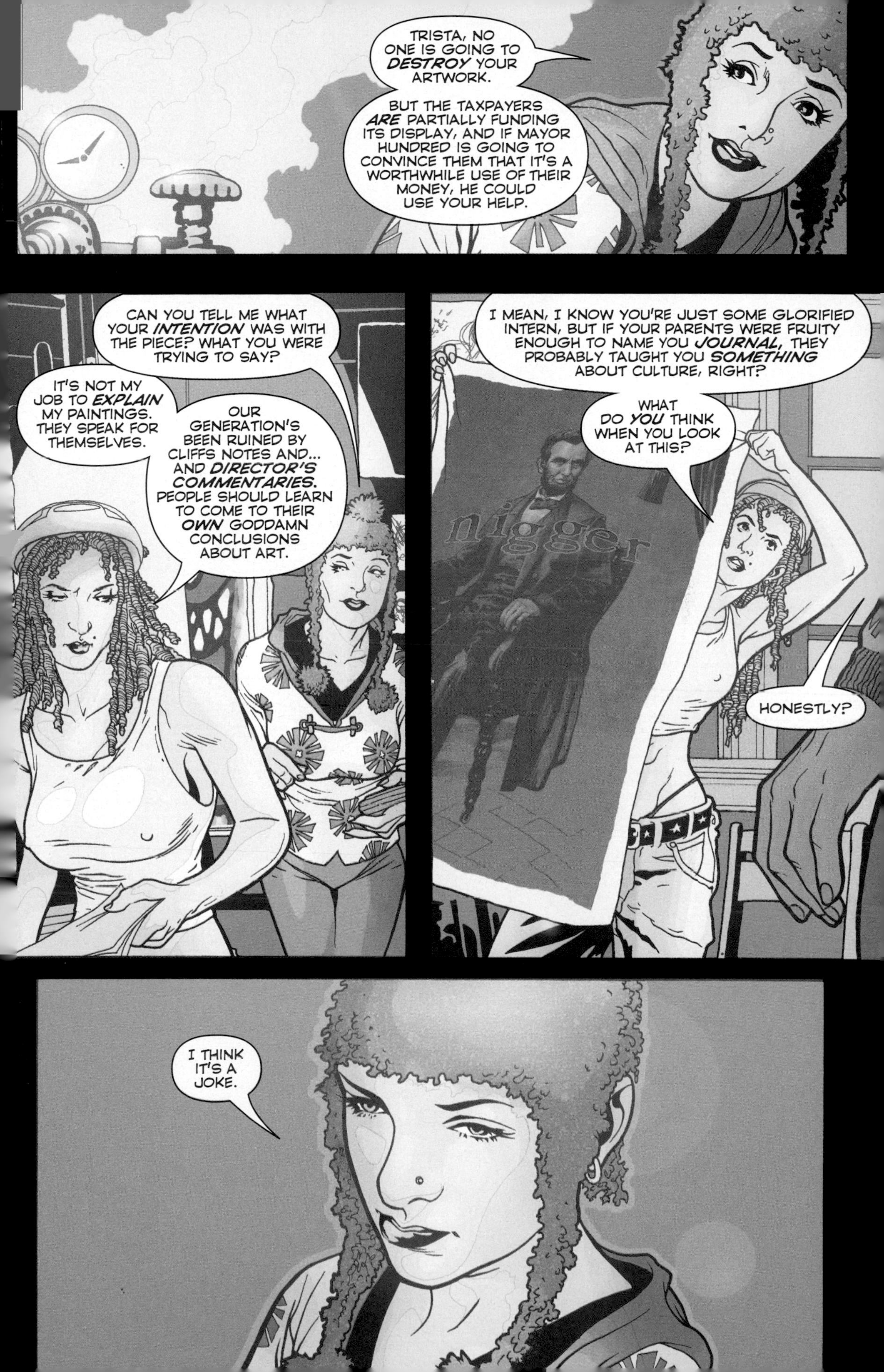

TRISTA, NO ONE IS GOING TO *DESTROY* YOUR ARTWORK.
BUT THE TAXPAYERS *ARE* PARTIALLY FUNDING ITS DISPLAY, AND IF MAYOR HUNDRED IS GOING TO CONVINCE THEM THAT IT'S A WORTHWHILE USE OF THEIR MONEY, HE COULD USE YOUR HELP.
CAN YOU TELL ME WHAT YOUR *INTENTION* WAS WITH THE PIECE? WHAT YOU WERE TRYING TO SAY?
IT'S NOT MY JOB TO *EXPLAIN* MY PAINTINGS. THEY SPEAK FOR THEMSELVES.
OUR GENERATION'S BEEN RUINED BY CLIFFS NOTES AND... AND *DIRECTOR'S COMMENTARIES.* PEOPLE SHOULD LEARN TO COME TO THEIR *OWN* GODDAMN CONCLUSIONS ABOUT ART.
I MEAN, I KNOW YOU'RE JUST SOME GLORIFIED INTERN, BUT IF YOUR PARENTS WERE FRUITY ENOUGH TO NAME YOU *JOURNAL,* THEY PROBABLY TAUGHT YOU *SOMETHING* ABOUT CULTURE, RIGHT?
WHAT DO *YOU* THINK WHEN YOU LOOK AT THIS?
nigger
HONESTLY?
I THINK IT'S A JOKE.

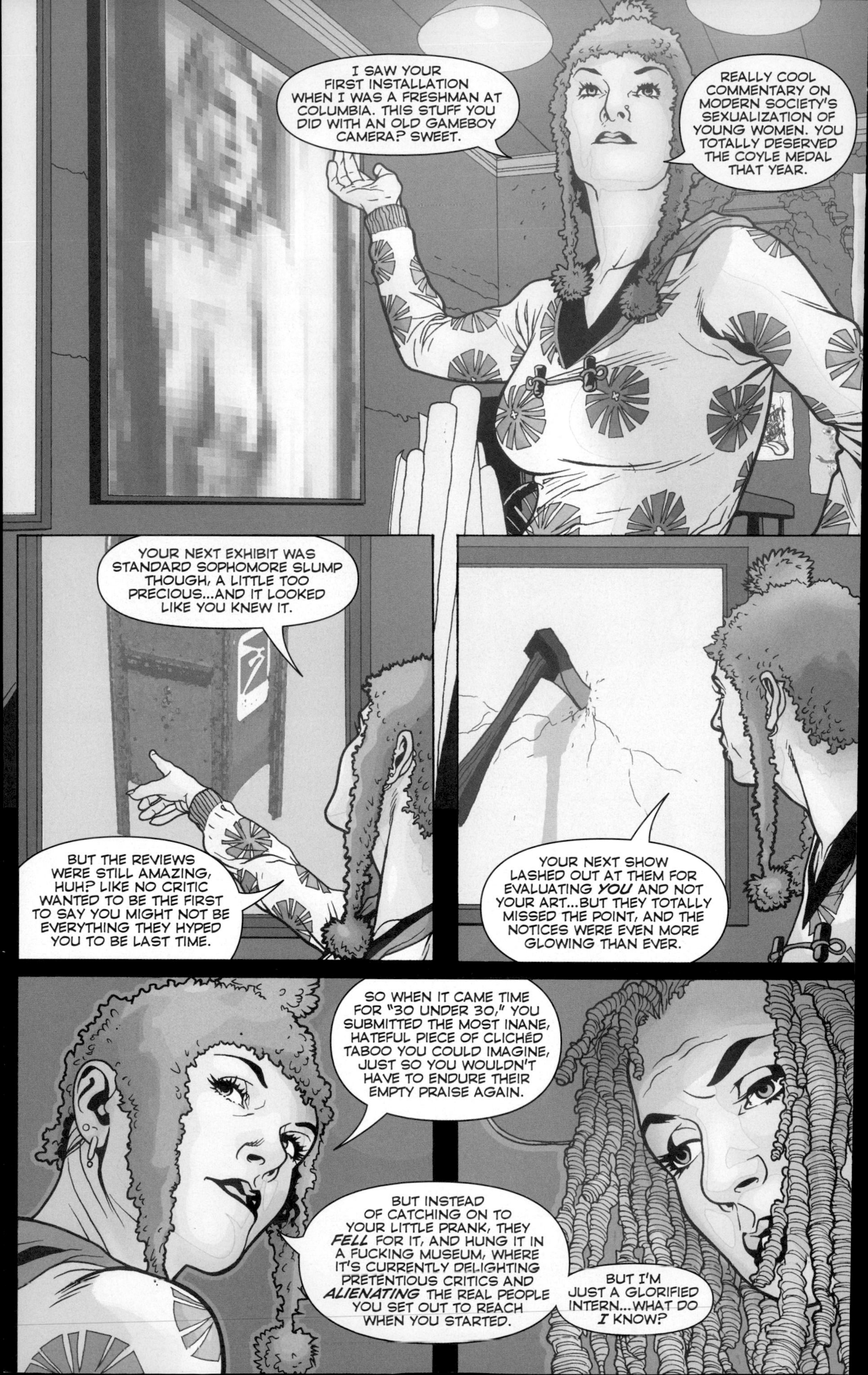
I SAW YOUR FIRST INSTALLATION WHEN I WAS A FRESHMAN AT COLUMBIA. THIS STUFF YOU DID WITH AN OLD GAMEBOY CAMERA? SWEET.
REALLY COOL COMMENTARY ON MODERN SOCIETY'S SEXUALIZATION OF YOUNG WOMEN. YOU TOTALLY DESERVED THE COYLE MEDAL THAT YEAR.
YOUR NEXT EXHIBIT WAS STANDARD SOPHOMORE SLUMP THOUGH, A LITTLE TOO PRECIOUS...AND IT LOOKED LIKE YOU KNEW IT.
BUT THE REVIEWS WERE STILL AMAZING, HUH? LIKE NO CRITIC WANTED TO BE THE FIRST TO SAY YOU MIGHT NOT BE EVERYTHING THEY HYPED YOU TO BE LAST TIME.
YOUR NEXT SHOW LASHED OUT AT THEM FOR EVALUATING *YOU* AND NOT YOUR ART...BUT THEY TOTALLY MISSED THE POINT, AND THE NOTICES WERE EVEN MORE GLOWING THAN EVER.
SO WHEN IT CAME TIME FOR "30 UNDER 30," YOU SUBMITTED THE MOST INANE, HATEFUL PIECE OF CLICHÉD TABOO YOU COULD IMAGINE, JUST SO YOU WOULDN'T HAVE TO ENDURE THEIR EMPTY PRAISE AGAIN.
BUT INSTEAD OF CATCHING ON TO YOUR LITTLE PRANK, THEY *FELL* FOR IT, AND HUNG IT IN A FUCKING MUSEUM, WHERE IT'S CURRENTLY DELIGHTING PRETENTIOUS CRITICS AND *ALIENATING* THE REAL PEOPLE YOU SET OUT TO REACH WHEN YOU STARTED.
BUT I'M JUST A GLORIFIED INTERN...WHAT DO *I* KNOW?

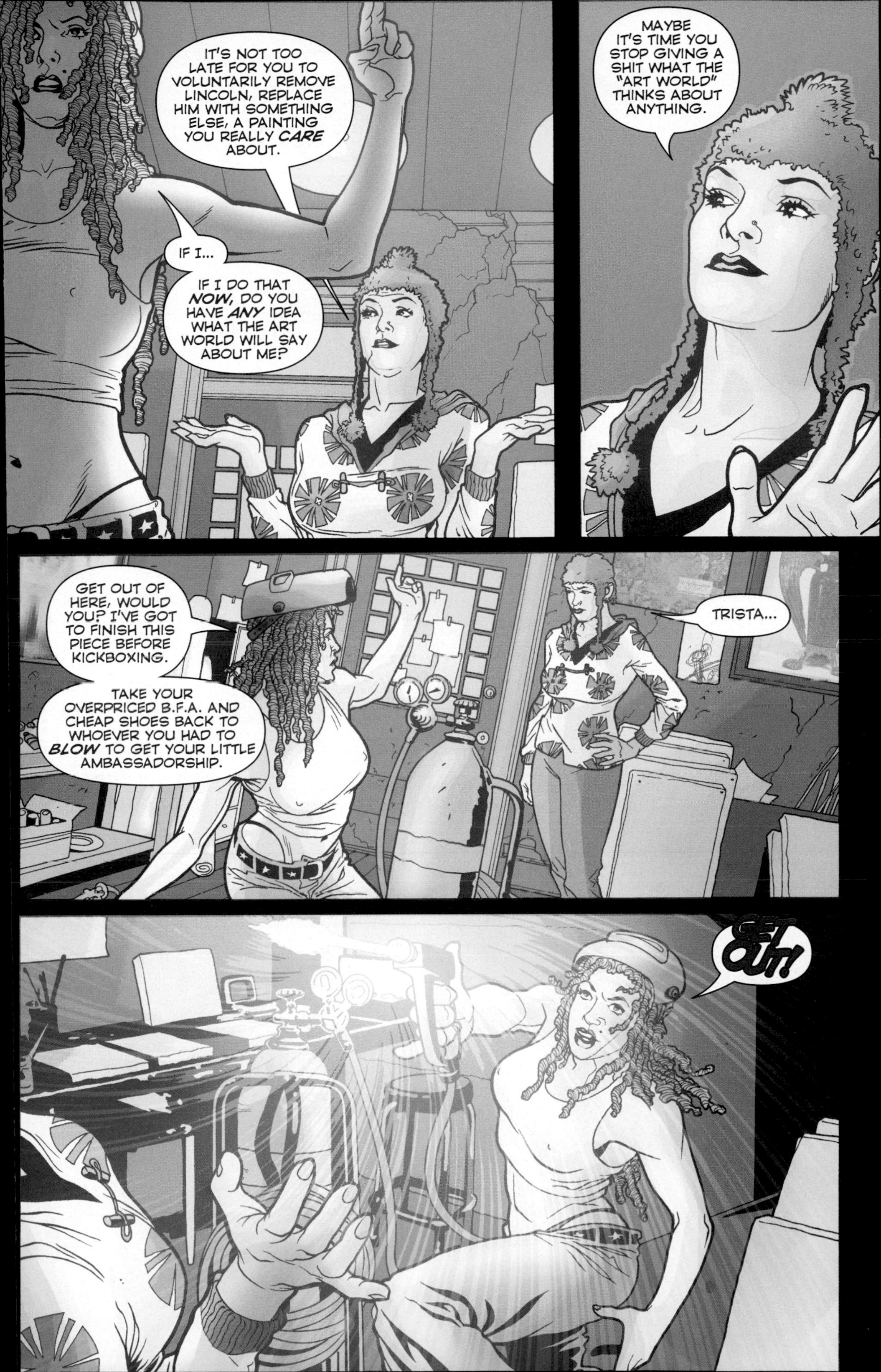
IT'S NOT TOO LATE FOR YOU TO VOLUNTARILY REMOVE LINCOLN, REPLACE HIM WITH SOMETHING ELSE, A PAINTING YOU REALLY CARE ABOUT.
IF I...
IF I DO THAT NOW, DO YOU HAVE ANY IDEA WHAT THE ART WORLD WILL SAY ABOUT ME?
MAYBE IT'S TIME YOU STOP GIVING A SHIT WHAT THE "ART WORLD" THINKS ABOUT ANYTHING.
GET OUT OF HERE, WOULD YOU? I'VE GOT TO FINISH THIS PIECE BEFORE KICKBOXING.
TAKE YOUR OVERPRICED B.F.A. AND CHEAP SHOES BACK TO WHOEVER YOU HAD TO BLOW TO GET YOUR LITTLE AMBASSADORSHIP.
TRISTA...
GET OUT!

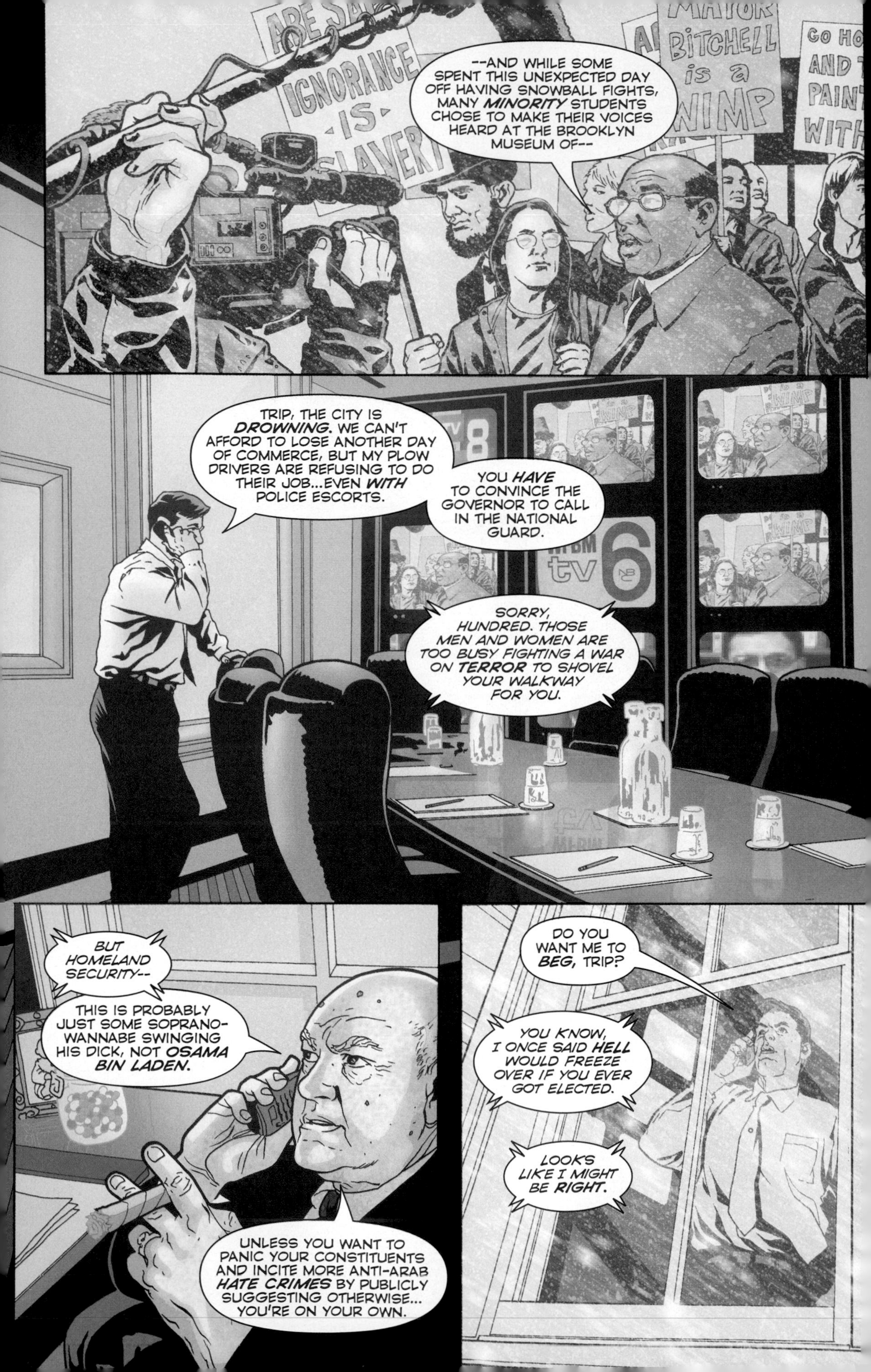
--AND WHILE SOME SPENT THIS UNEXPECTED DAY OFF HAVING SNOWBALL FIGHTS, MANY MINORITY STUDENTS CHOSE TO MAKE THEIR VOICES HEARD AT THE BROOKLYN MUSEUM OF--
TRIP, THE CITY IS DROWNING. WE CAN'T AFFORD TO LOSE ANOTHER DAY OF COMMERCE, BUT MY PLOW DRIVERS ARE REFUSING TO DO THEIR JOB...EVEN WITH POLICE ESCORTS.
YOU HAVE TO CONVINCE THE GOVERNOR TO CALL IN THE NATIONAL GUARD.
SORRY, HUNDRED. THOSE MEN AND WOMEN ARE TOO BUSY FIGHTING A WAR ON TERROR TO SHOVEL YOUR WALKWAY FOR YOU.
BUT HOMELAND SECURITY--
THIS IS PROBABLY JUST SOME SOPRANO-WANNABE SWINGING HIS DICK, NOT OSAMA BIN LADEN.
UNLESS YOU WANT TO PANIC YOUR CONSTITUENTS AND INCITE MORE ANTI-ARAB HATE CRIMES BY PUBLICLY SUGGESTING OTHERWISE... YOU'RE ON YOUR OWN.
DO YOU WANT ME TO BEG, TRIP?
YOU KNOW, I ONCE SAID HELL WOULD FREEZE OVER IF YOU EVER GOT ELECTED.
LOOKS LIKE I MIGHT BE RIGHT.

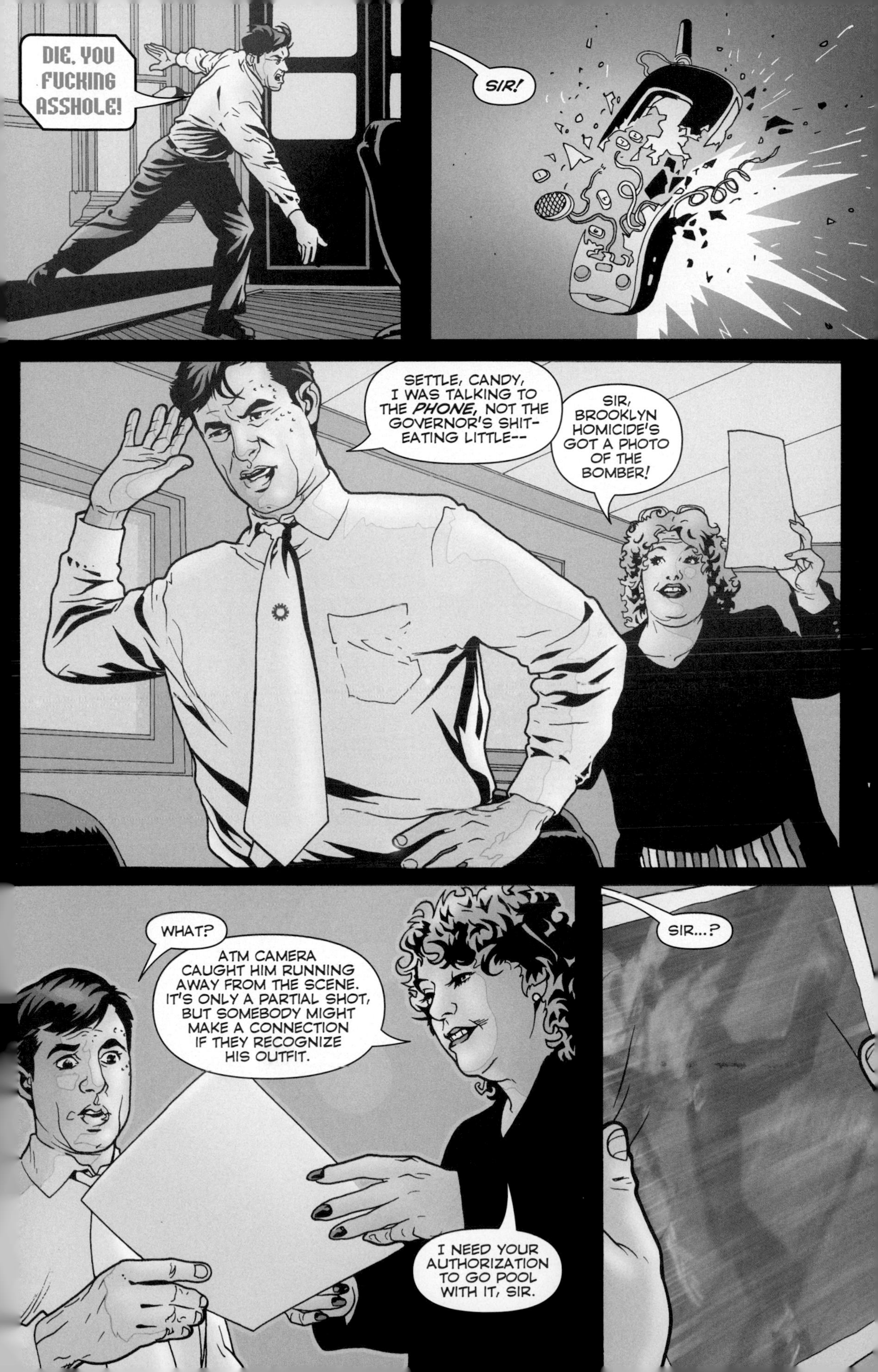
DIE, YOU FUCKING ASSHOLE!
SIR!
SETTLE, CANDY, I WAS TALKING TO THE *PHONE,* NOT THE GOVERNOR'S SHIT-EATING LITTLE--
SIR, BROOKLYN HOMICIDE'S GOT A PHOTO OF THE BOMBER!
WHAT?
ATM CAMERA CAUGHT HIM RUNNING AWAY FROM THE SCENE. IT'S ONLY A PARTIAL SHOT, BUT SOMEBODY MIGHT MAKE A CONNECTION IF THEY RECOGNIZE HIS OUTFIT.
I NEED YOUR AUTHORIZATION TO GO POOL WITH IT, SIR.
SIR...?

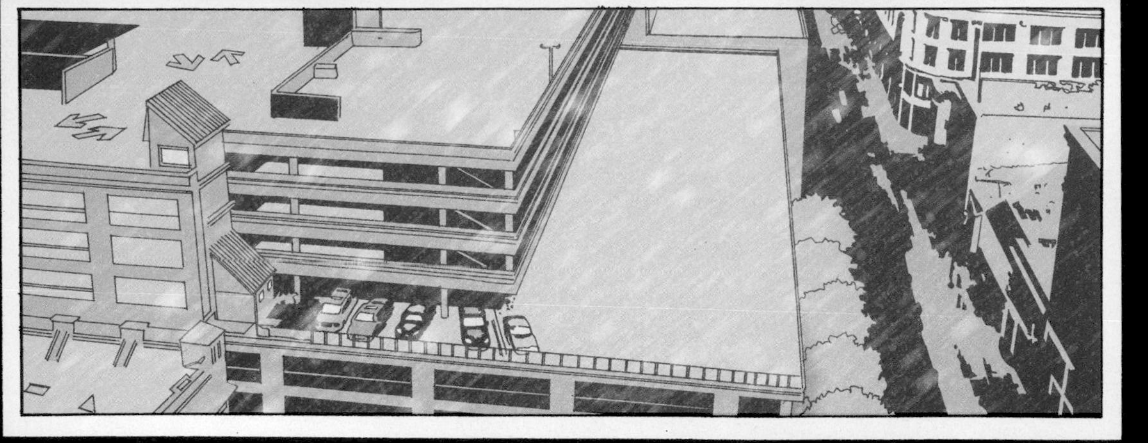

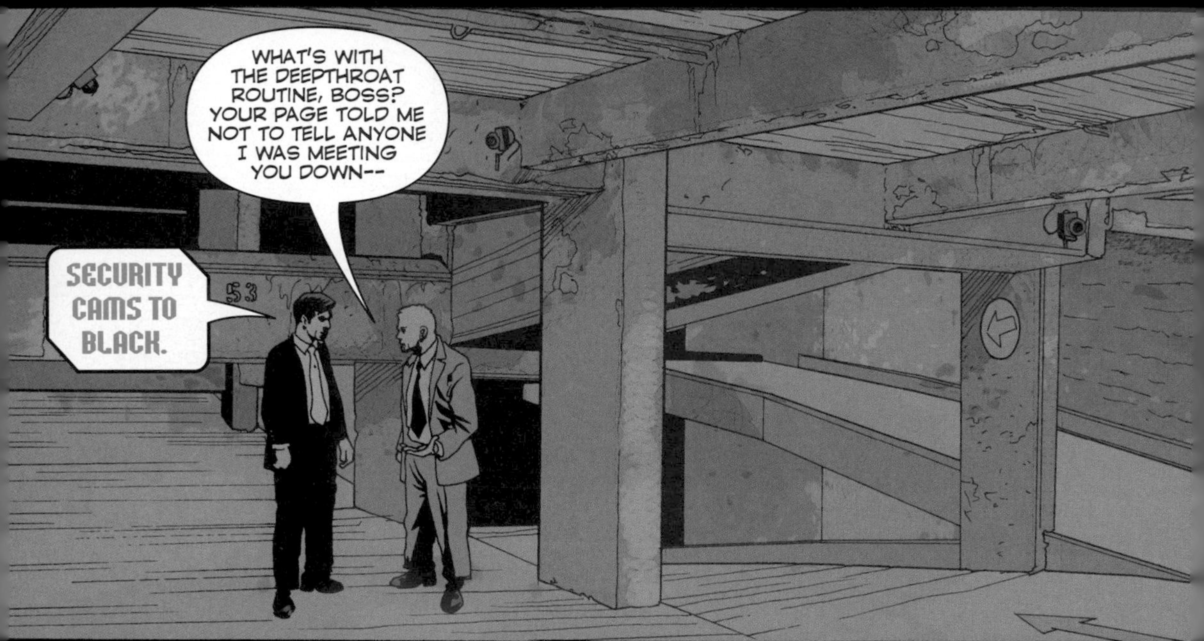
WHAT'S WITH THE DEEPTHROAT ROUTINE, BOSS? YOUR PAGE TOLD ME NOT TO TELL ANYONE I WAS MEETING YOU DOWN--
SECURITY CAMS TO BLACK.
53

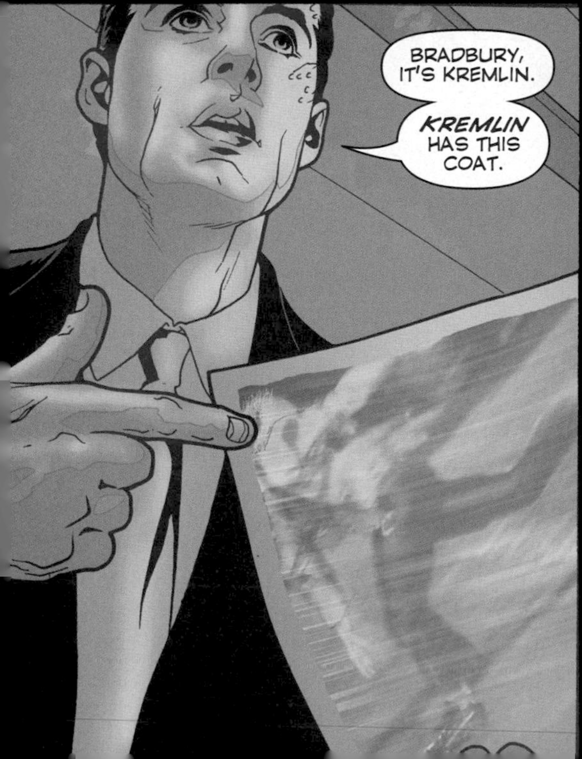
BRADBURY, IT'S KREMLIN.
KREMLIN HAS THIS COAT.

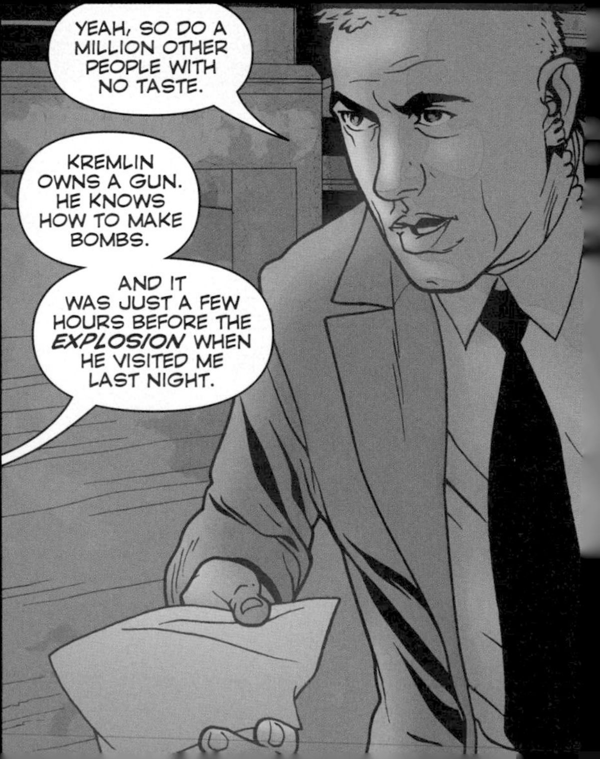
YEAH, SO DO A MILLION OTHER PEOPLE WITH NO TASTE.
KREMLIN OWNS A GUN. HE KNOWS HOW TO MAKE BOMBS.
AND IT WAS JUST A FEW HOURS BEFORE THE *EXPLOSION* WHEN HE VISITED ME LAST NIGHT.

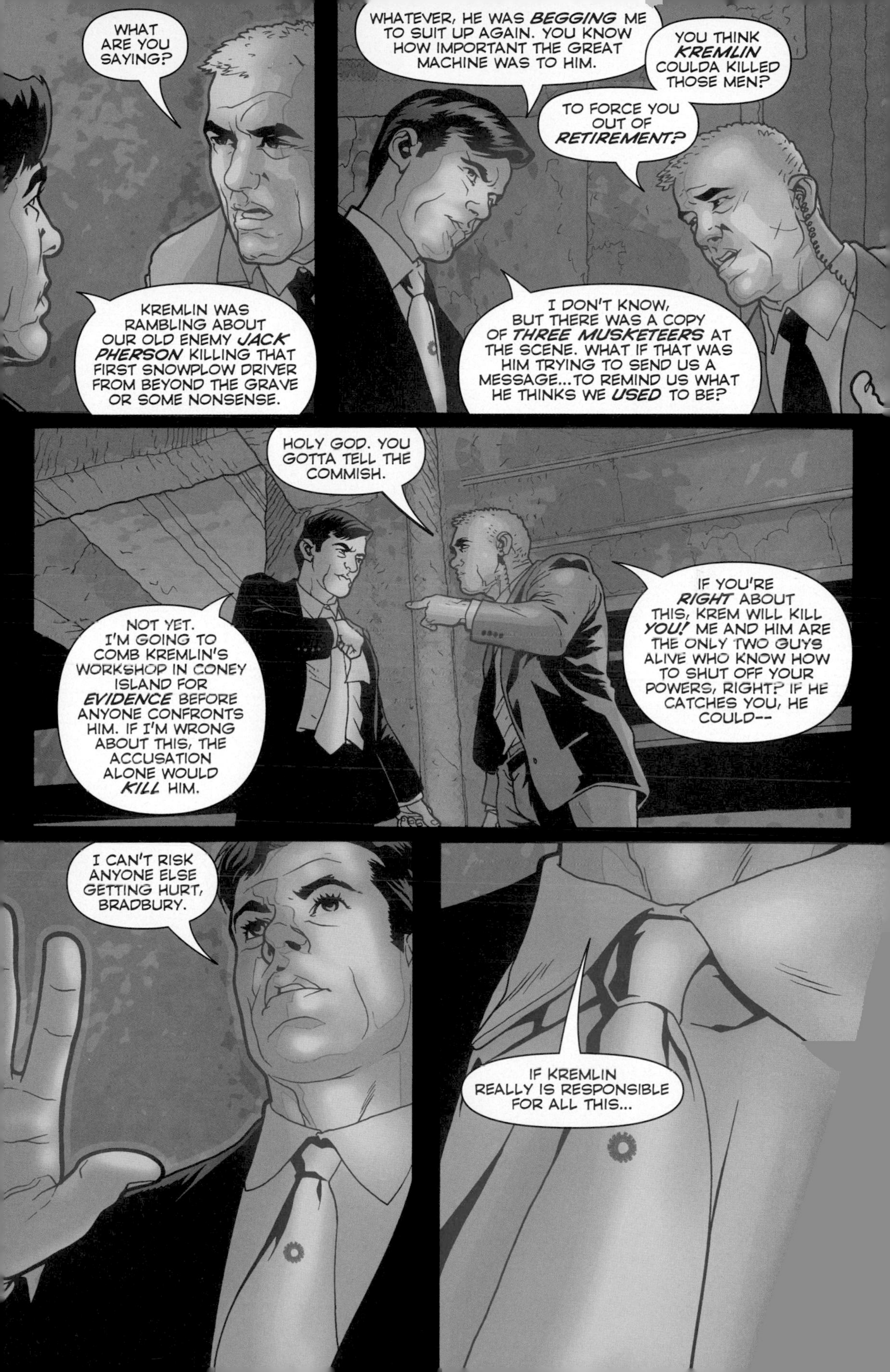
WHAT ARE YOU SAYING?
KREMLIN WAS RAMBLING ABOUT OUR OLD ENEMY JACK PHERSON KILLING THAT FIRST SNOWPLOW DRIVER FROM BEYOND THE GRAVE OR SOME NONSENSE.
WHATEVER, HE WAS BEGGING ME TO SUIT UP AGAIN. YOU KNOW HOW IMPORTANT THE GREAT MACHINE WAS TO HIM.
YOU THINK KREMLIN COULDA KILLED THOSE MEN?
TO FORCE YOU OUT OF RETIREMENT?
I DON'T KNOW, BUT THERE WAS A COPY OF THREE MUSKETEERS AT THE SCENE. WHAT IF THAT WAS HIM TRYING TO SEND US A MESSAGE...TO REMIND US WHAT HE THINKS WE USED TO BE?
HOLY GOD. YOU GOTTA TELL THE COMMISH.
NOT YET. I'M GOING TO COMB KREMLIN'S WORKSHOP IN CONEY ISLAND FOR EVIDENCE BEFORE ANYONE CONFRONTS HIM. IF I'M WRONG ABOUT THIS, THE ACCUSATION ALONE WOULD KILL HIM.
IF YOU'RE RIGHT ABOUT THIS, KREM WILL KILL YOU! ME AND HIM ARE THE ONLY TWO GUYS ALIVE WHO KNOW HOW TO SHUT OFF YOUR POWERS, RIGHT? IF HE CATCHES YOU, HE COULD--
I CAN'T RISK ANYONE ELSE GETTING HURT, BRADBURY.
IF KREMLIN REALLY IS RESPONSIBLE FOR ALL THIS...

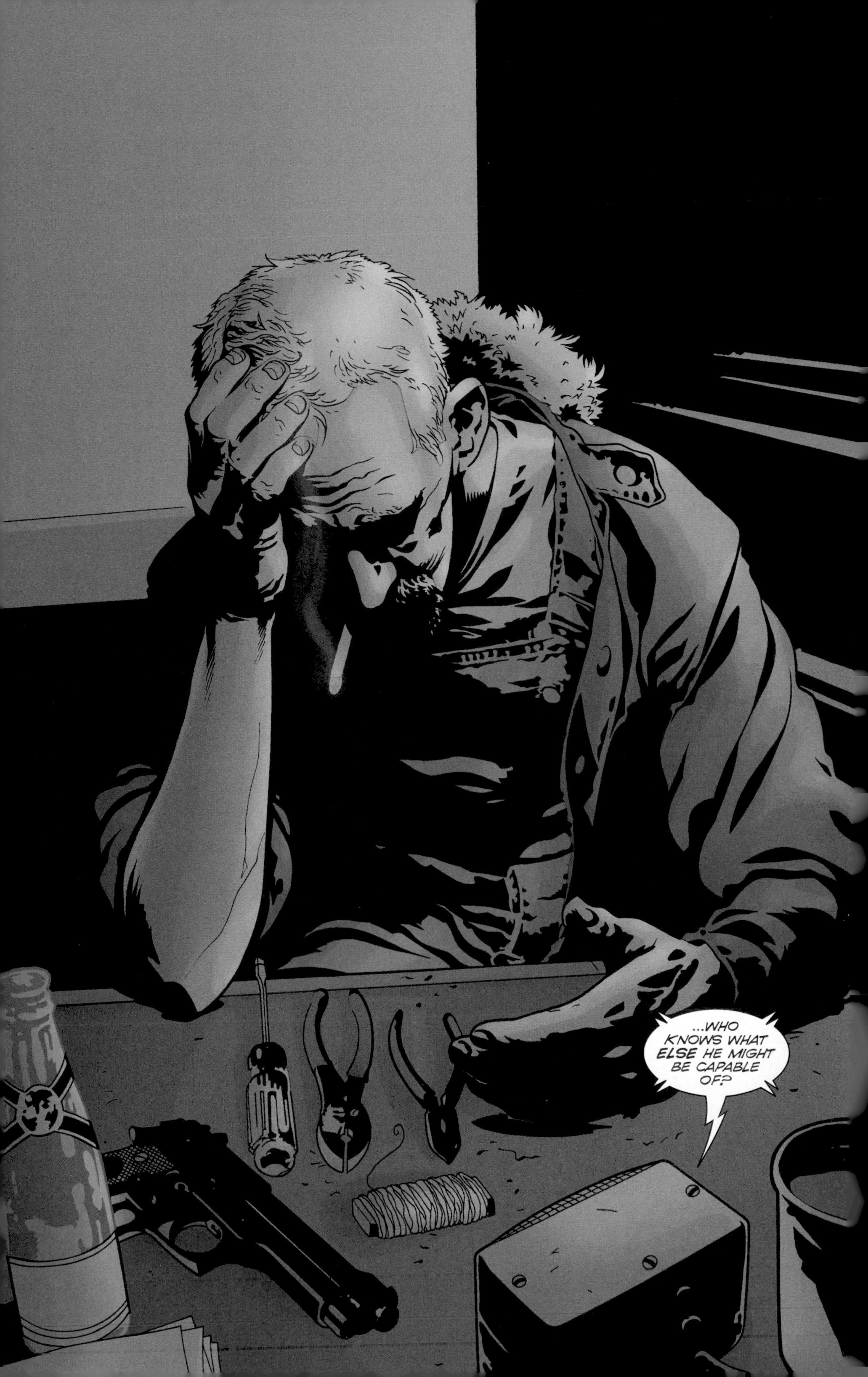
...WHO KNOWS WHAT ELSE HE MIGHT BE CAPABLE OF?

CHAPTER 5

Part 4

State of Emergency

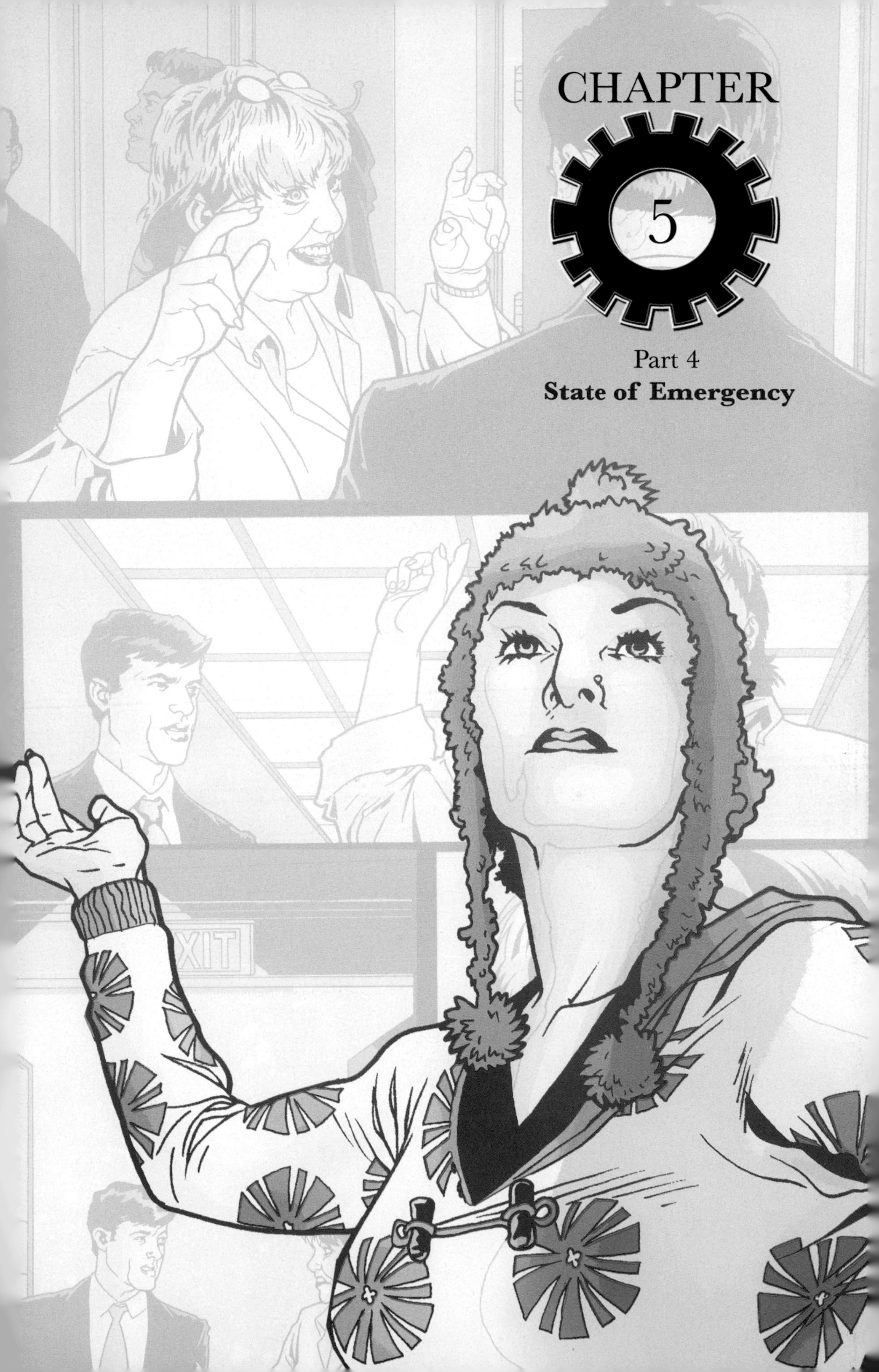

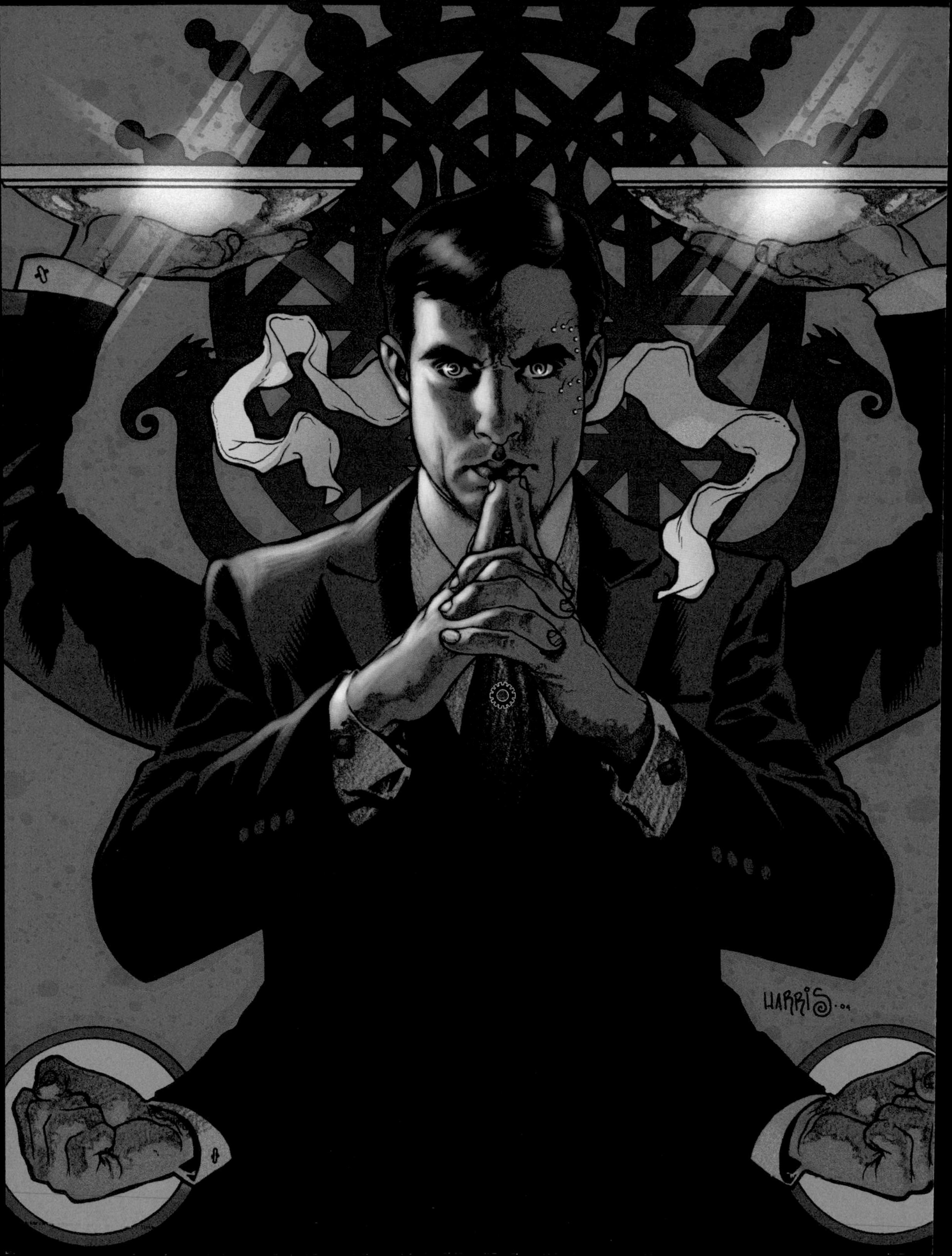
HARRIS.04

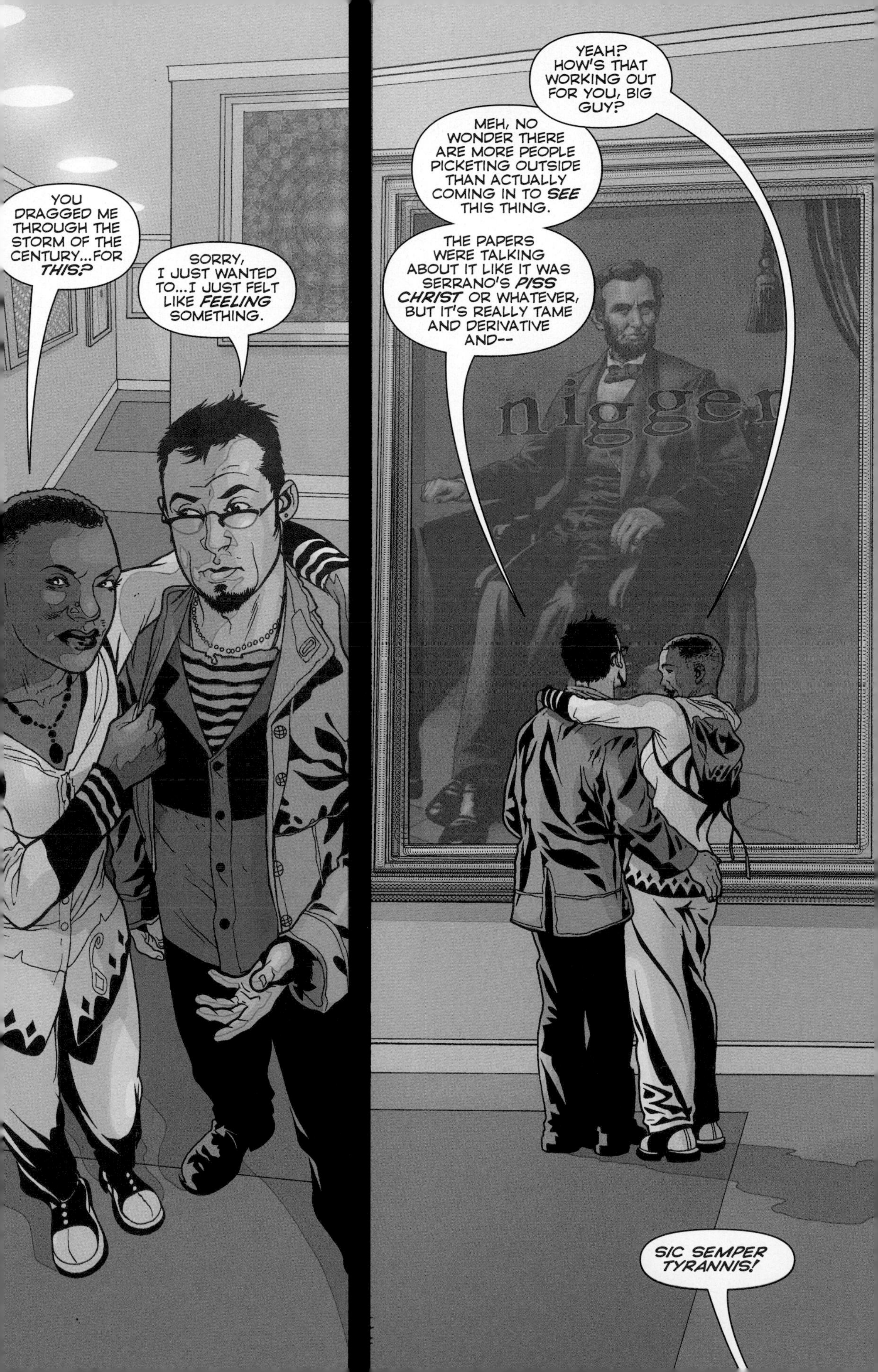
YOU DRAGGED ME THROUGH THE STORM OF THE CENTURY...FOR *THIS?*
SORRY, I JUST WANTED TO...I JUST FELT LIKE *FEELING* SOMETHING.
MEH, NO WONDER THERE ARE MORE PEOPLE PICKETING OUTSIDE THAN ACTUALLY COMING IN TO *SEE* THIS THING.
THE PAPERS WERE TALKING ABOUT IT LIKE IT WAS SERRANO'S *PISS CHRIST* OR WHATEVER, BUT IT'S REALLY TAME AND DERIVATIVE AND--
YEAH? HOW'S THAT WORKING OUT FOR YOU, BIG GUY?
nigger
SIC SEMPER TYRANNIS!

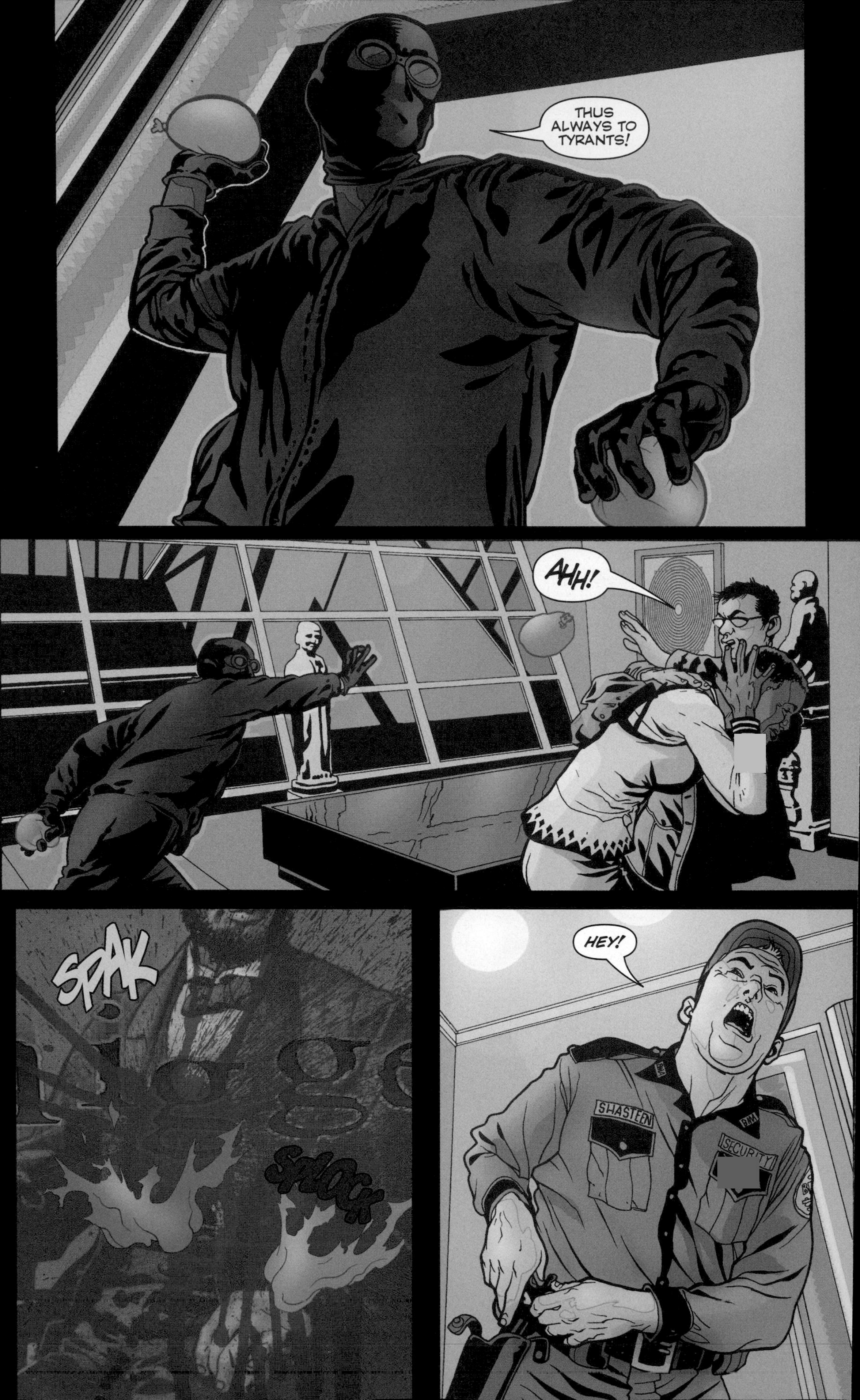
THUS ALWAYS TO TYRANTS!
AHH!
SPAK
SPLOCK
HEY!
SHASTEEN
SECURITY

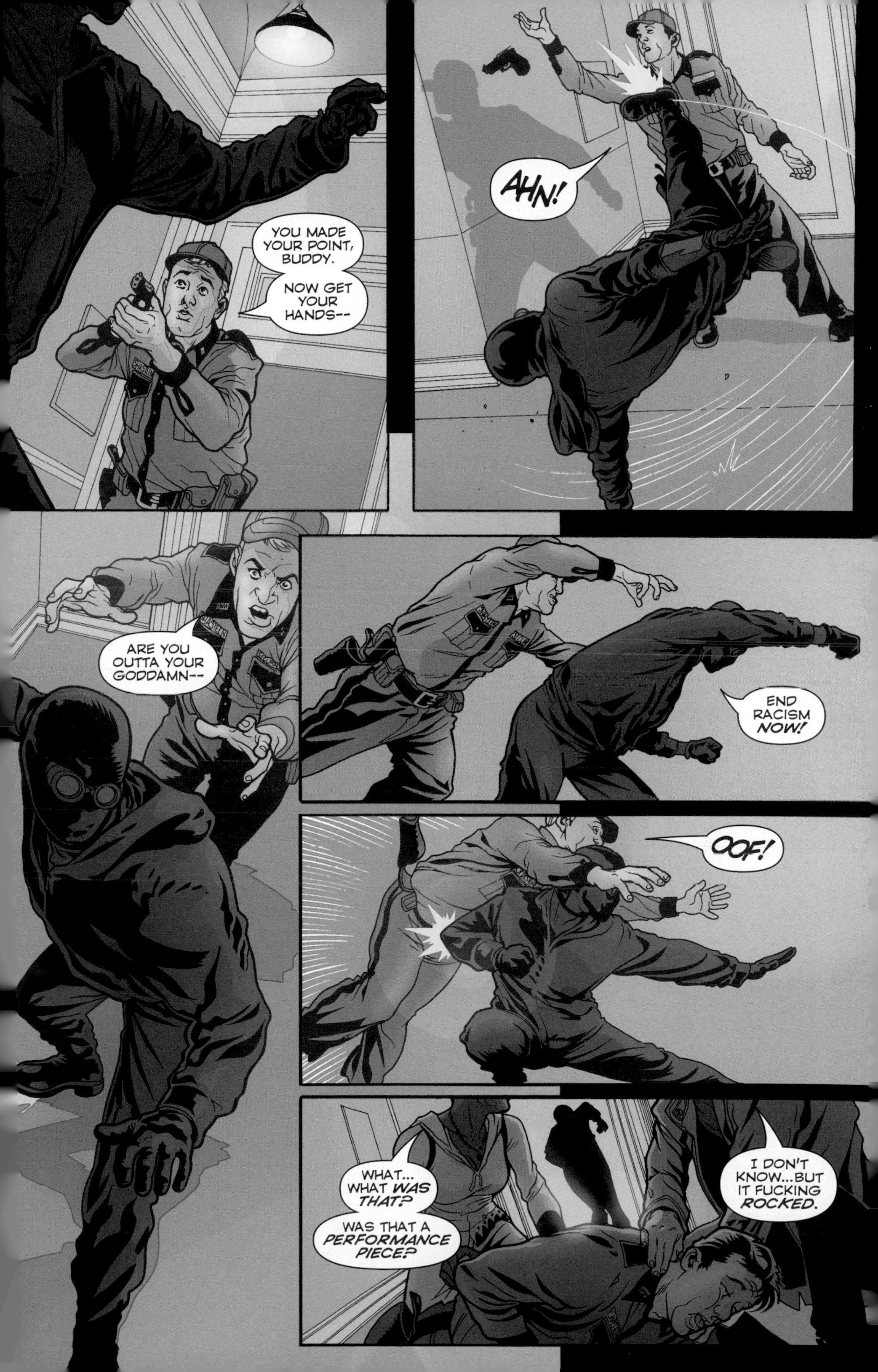
YOU MADE YOUR POINT, BUDDY.
NOW GET YOUR HANDS--
AHN!
ARE YOU OUTTA YOUR GODDAMN--
END RACISM *NOW!*
OOF!
WHAT... WHAT *WAS* THAT?
WAS THAT A *PERFORMANCE PIECE?*
I DON'T KNOW...BUT IT FUCKING *ROCKED*.

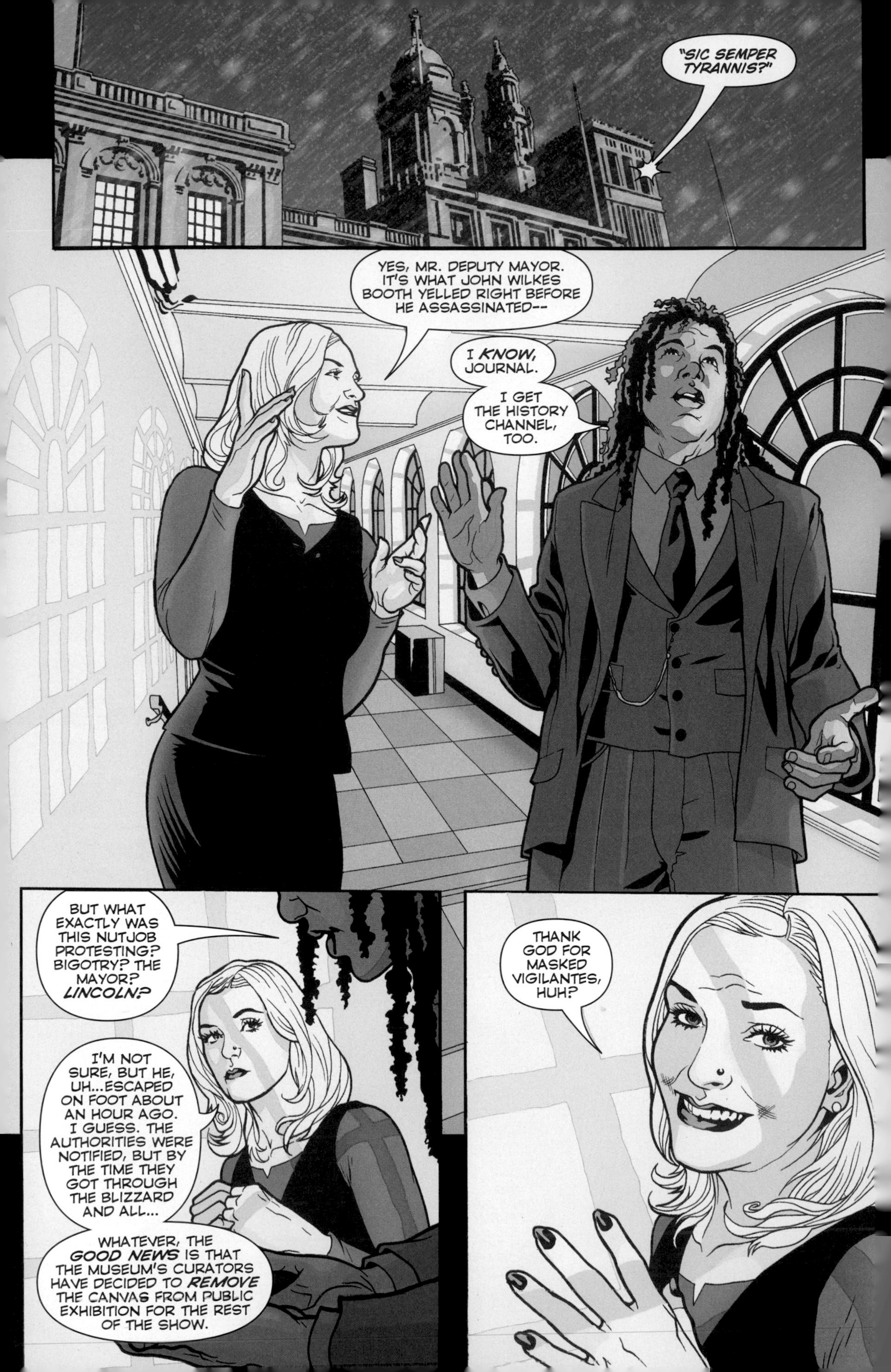
"SIC SEMPER TYRANNIS?"
YES, MR. DEPUTY MAYOR. IT'S WHAT JOHN WILKES BOOTH YELLED RIGHT BEFORE HE ASSASSINATED--
I KNOW, JOURNAL.
I GET THE HISTORY CHANNEL, TOO.
BUT WHAT EXACTLY WAS THIS NUTJOB PROTESTING? BIGOTRY? THE MAYOR? LINCOLN?
I'M NOT SURE, BUT HE, UH...ESCAPED ON FOOT ABOUT AN HOUR AGO. I GUESS. THE AUTHORITIES WERE NOTIFIED, BUT BY THE TIME THEY GOT THROUGH THE BLIZZARD AND ALL...
WHATEVER, THE GOOD NEWS IS THAT THE MUSEUM'S CURATORS HAVE DECIDED TO REMOVE THE CANVAS FROM PUBLIC EXHIBITION FOR THE REST OF THE SHOW.
THANK GOD FOR MASKED VIGILANTES, HUH?

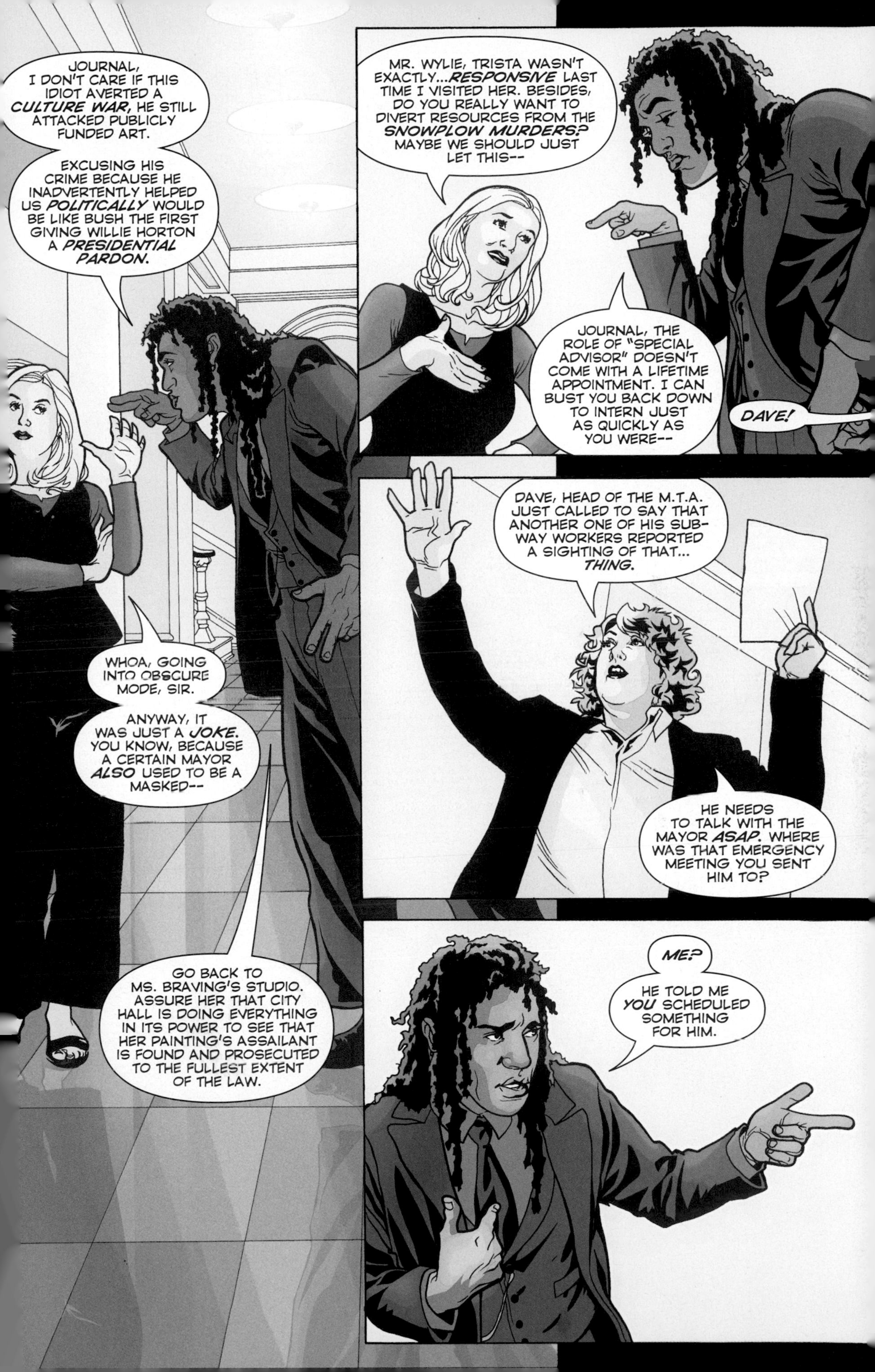
JOURNAL, I DON'T CARE IF THIS IDIOT AVERTED A CULTURE WAR, HE STILL ATTACKED PUBLICLY FUNDED ART.
EXCUSING HIS CRIME BECAUSE HE INADVERTENTLY HELPED US POLITICALLY WOULD BE LIKE BUSH THE FIRST GIVING WILLIE HORTON A PRESIDENTIAL PARDON.
WHOA, GOING INTO OBSCURE MODE, SIR.
ANYWAY, IT WAS JUST A JOKE. YOU KNOW, BECAUSE A CERTAIN MAYOR ALSO USED TO BE A MASKED--
GO BACK TO MS. BRAVING'S STUDIO. ASSURE HER THAT CITY HALL IS DOING EVERYTHING IN ITS POWER TO SEE THAT HER PAINTING'S ASSAILANT IS FOUND AND PROSECUTED TO THE FULLEST EXTENT OF THE LAW.
MR. WYLIE, TRISTA WASN'T EXACTLY...RESPONSIVE LAST TIME I VISITED HER. BESIDES, DO YOU REALLY WANT TO DIVERT RESOURCES FROM THE SNOWPLOW MURDERS? MAYBE WE SHOULD JUST LET THIS--
JOURNAL, THE ROLE OF "SPECIAL ADVISOR" DOESN'T COME WITH A LIFETIME APPOINTMENT. I CAN BUST YOU BACK DOWN TO INTERN JUST AS QUICKLY AS YOU WERE--
DAVE!
DAVE, HEAD OF THE M.T.A. JUST CALLED TO SAY THAT ANOTHER ONE OF HIS SUBWAY WORKERS REPORTED A SIGHTING OF THAT... THING.
HE NEEDS TO TALK WITH THE MAYOR ASAP. WHERE WAS THAT EMERGENCY MEETING YOU SENT HIM TO?
ME?
HE TOLD ME YOU SCHEDULED SOMETHING FOR HIM.

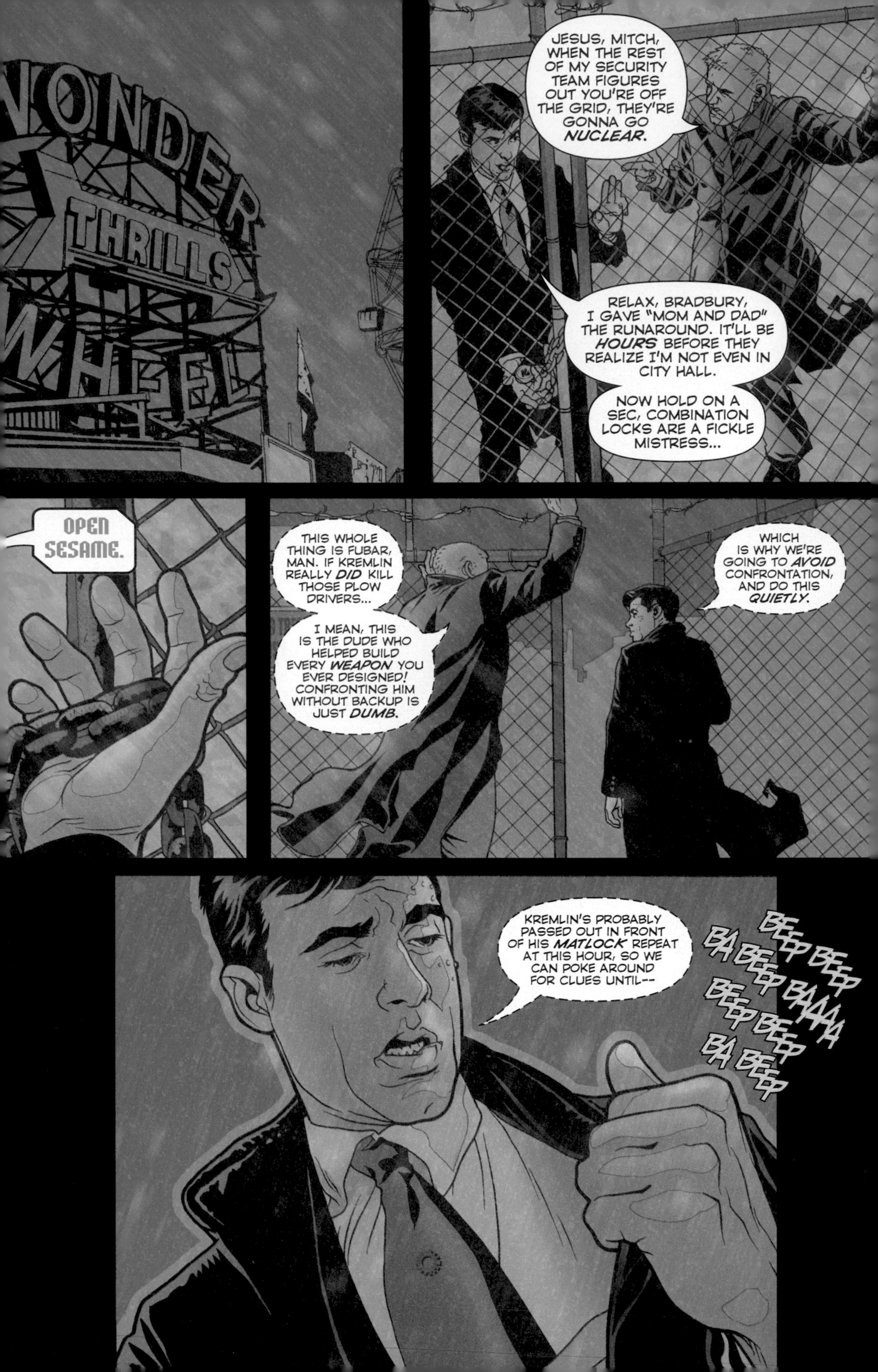
WONDER THRILLS WHEEL
JESUS, MITCH, WHEN THE REST OF MY SECURITY TEAM FIGURES OUT YOU'RE OFF THE GRID, THEY'RE GONNA GO NUCLEAR.
RELAX, BRADBURY, I GAVE "MOM AND DAD" THE RUNAROUND. IT'LL BE HOURS BEFORE THEY REALIZE I'M NOT EVEN IN CITY HALL.
NOW HOLD ON A SEC, COMBINATION LOCKS ARE A FICKLE MISTRESS...
OPEN SESAME.
THIS WHOLE THING IS FUBAR, MAN. IF KREMLIN REALLY DID KILL THOSE PLOW DRIVERS...
I MEAN, THIS IS THE DUDE WHO HELPED BUILD EVERY WEAPON YOU EVER DESIGNED! CONFRONTING HIM WITHOUT BACKUP IS JUST DUMB.
WHICH IS WHY WE'RE GOING TO AVOID CONFRONTATION, AND DO THIS QUIETLY.
KREMLIN'S PROBABLY PASSED OUT IN FRONT OF HIS MATLOCK REPEAT AT THIS HOUR, SO WE CAN POKE AROUND FOR CLUES UNTIL--
BEEP BEEP BA BEEP BAAAA BEEP BEEP BA BEEP

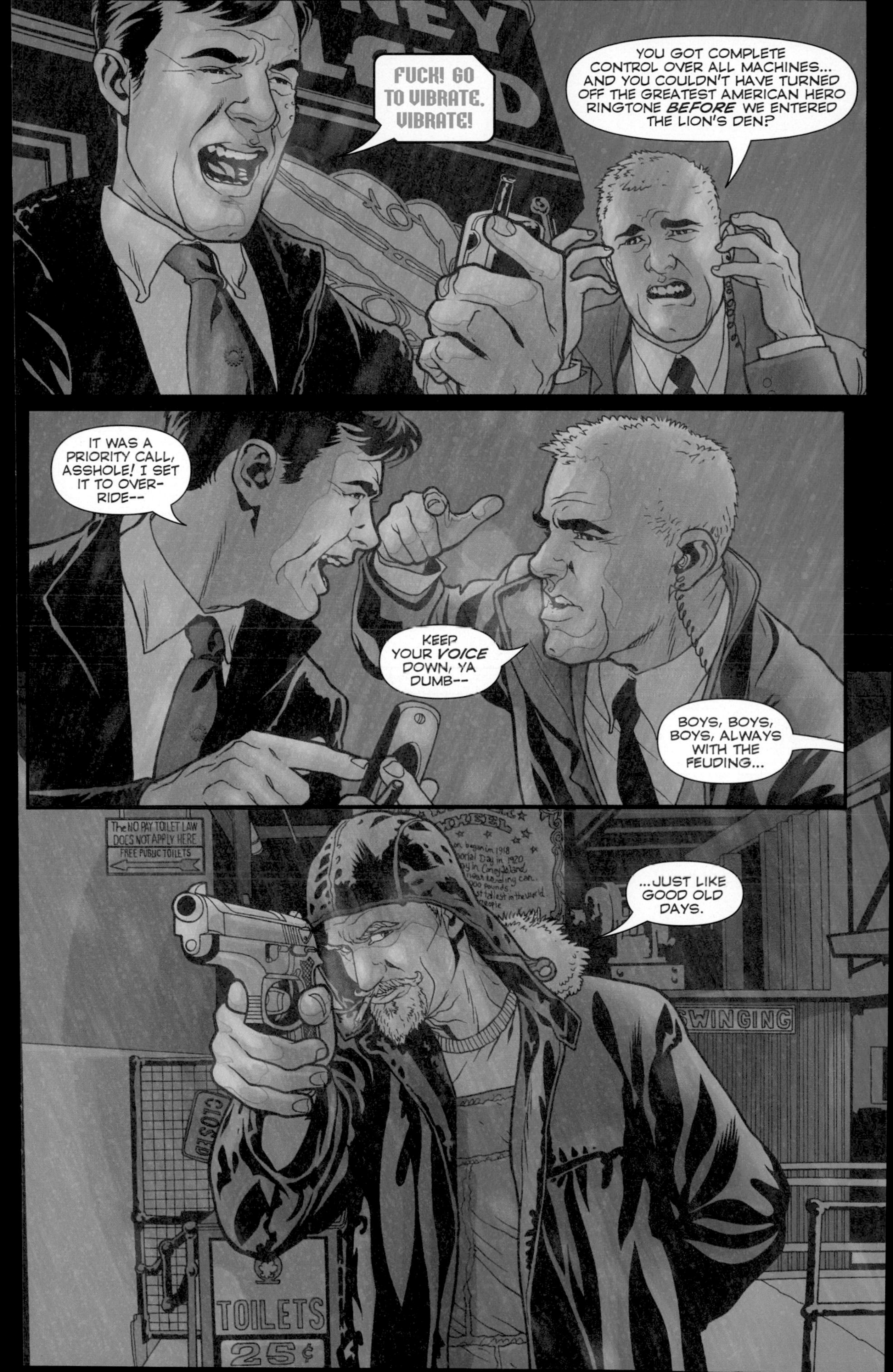
FUCK! GO TO VIBRATE. VIBRATE!
YOU GOT COMPLETE CONTROL OVER ALL MACHINES... AND YOU COULDN'T HAVE TURNED OFF THE GREATEST AMERICAN HERO RINGTONE *BEFORE* WE ENTERED THE LION'S DEN?
IT WAS A PRIORITY CALL, ASSHOLE! I SET IT TO OVER-RIDE--
KEEP YOUR *VOICE* DOWN, YA DUMB--
BOYS, BOYS, BOYS, ALWAYS WITH THE FEUDING...
The NO PAY TOILET LAW DOES NOT APPLY HERE
FREE PUBLIC TOILETS
...JUST LIKE GOOD OLD DAYS.
SWINGING
TOILETS
25¢

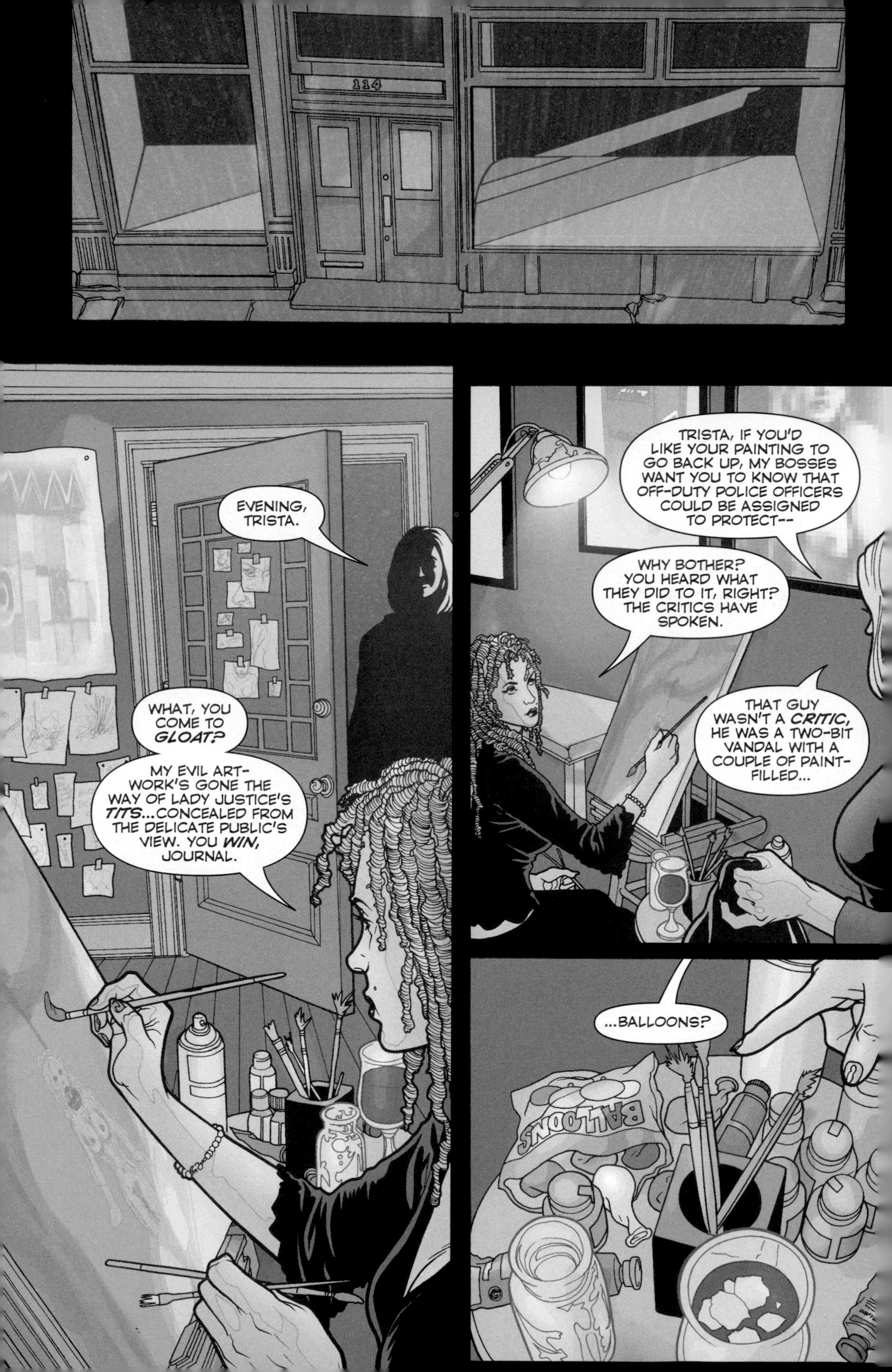
114
EVENING, TRISTA.
WHAT, YOU COME TO GLOAT?
MY EVIL ART-WORK'S GONE THE WAY OF LADY JUSTICE'S TITS...CONCEALED FROM THE DELICATE PUBLIC'S VIEW. YOU WIN, JOURNAL.
TRISTA, IF YOU'D LIKE YOUR PAINTING TO GO BACK UP, MY BOSSES WANT YOU TO KNOW THAT OFF-DUTY POLICE OFFICERS COULD BE ASSIGNED TO PROTECT--
WHY BOTHER? YOU HEARD WHAT THEY DID TO IT, RIGHT? THE CRITICS HAVE SPOKEN.
THAT GUY WASN'T A CRITIC, HE WAS A TWO-BIT VANDAL WITH A COUPLE OF PAINT-FILLED...
...BALLOONS?
BALLOONS

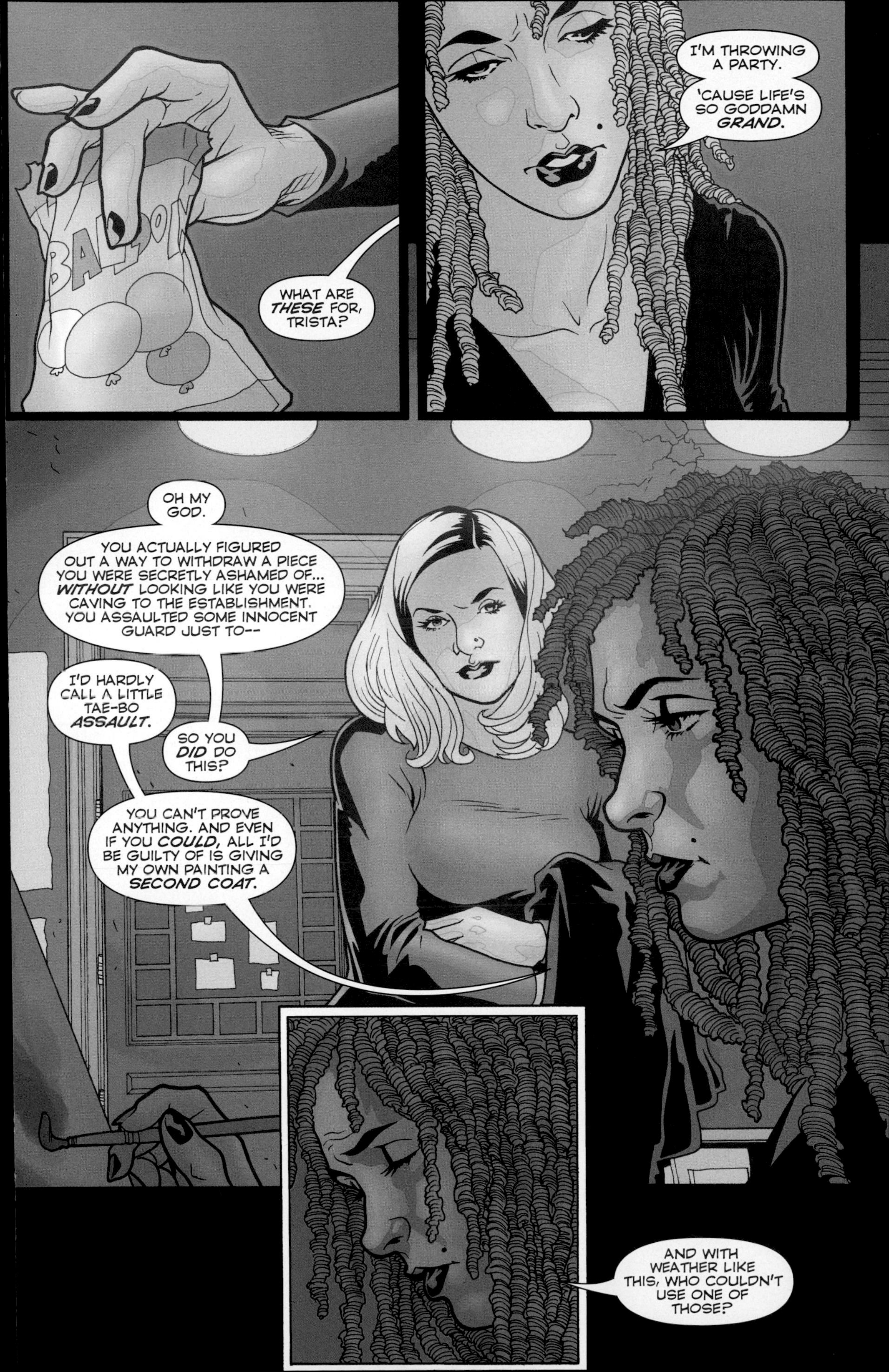

BALLOONS
WHAT ARE THESE FOR, TRISTA?
I'M THROWING A PARTY.
'CAUSE LIFE'S SO GODDAMN GRAND.
OH MY GOD.
YOU ACTUALLY FIGURED OUT A WAY TO WITHDRAW A PIECE YOU WERE SECRETLY ASHAMED OF... WITHOUT LOOKING LIKE YOU WERE CAVING TO THE ESTABLISHMENT. YOU ASSAULTED SOME INNOCENT GUARD JUST TO--
I'D HARDLY CALL A LITTLE TAE-BO ASSAULT.
SO YOU DID DO THIS?
YOU CAN'T PROVE ANYTHING. AND EVEN IF YOU COULD, ALL I'D BE GUILTY OF IS GIVING MY OWN PAINTING A SECOND COAT.
AND WITH WEATHER LIKE THIS, WHO COULDN'T USE ONE OF THOSE?

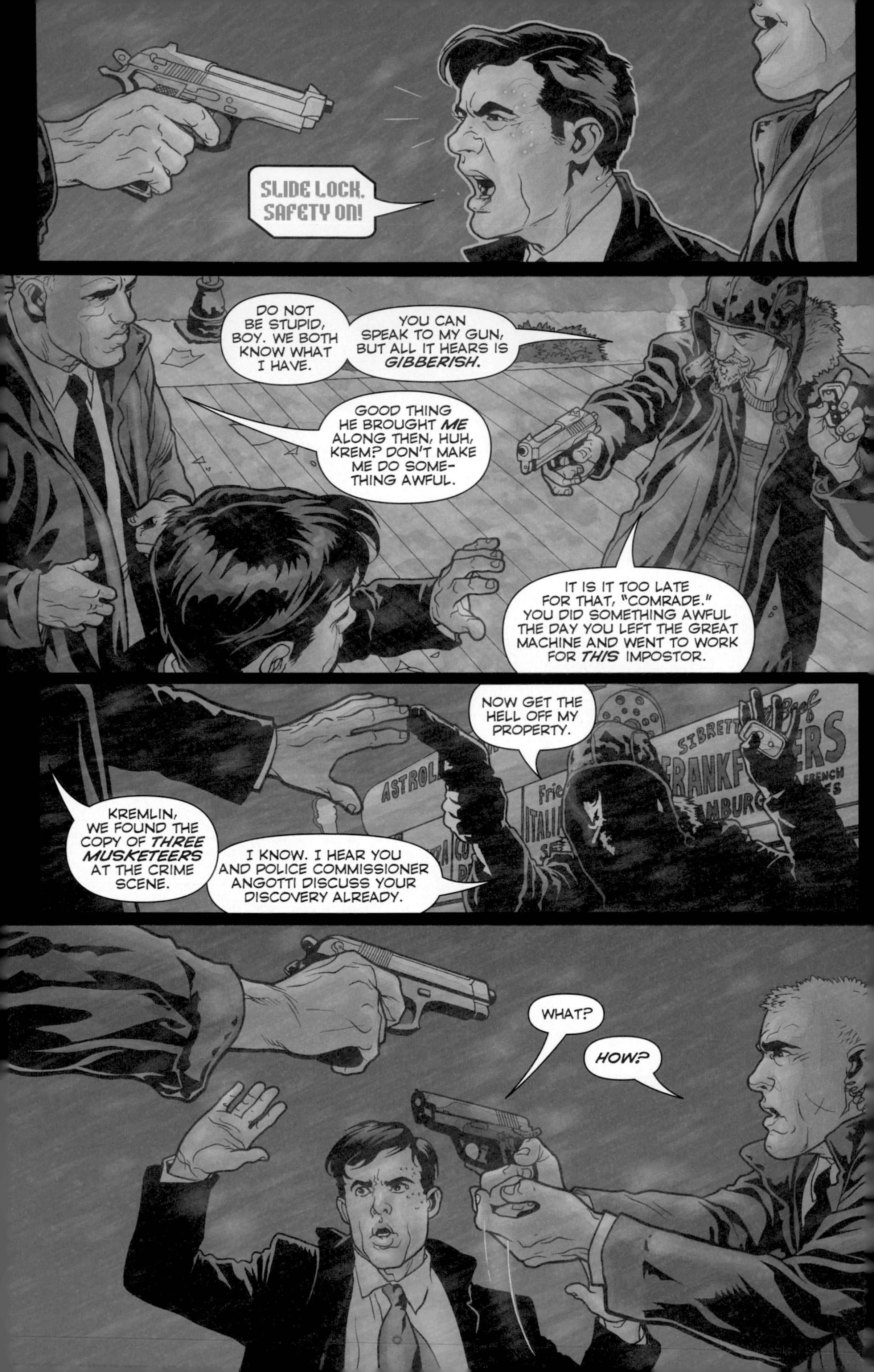
SLIDE LOCK. SAFETY ON!
DO NOT BE STUPID, BOY. WE BOTH KNOW WHAT I HAVE.
YOU CAN SPEAK TO MY GUN, BUT ALL IT HEARS IS *GIBBERISH*.
GOOD THING HE BROUGHT *ME* ALONG THEN, HUH, KREM? DON'T MAKE ME DO SOME-THING AWFUL.
IT IS IT TOO LATE FOR THAT, "COMRADE." YOU DID SOMETHING AWFUL THE DAY YOU LEFT THE GREAT MACHINE AND WENT TO WORK FOR *THIS* IMPOSTOR.
NOW GET THE HELL OFF MY PROPERTY.
KREMLIN, WE FOUND THE COPY OF *THREE MUSKETEERS* AT THE CRIME SCENE.
I KNOW. I HEAR YOU AND POLICE COMMISSIONER ANGOTTI DISCUSS YOUR DISCOVERY ALREADY.
WHAT?
HOW?

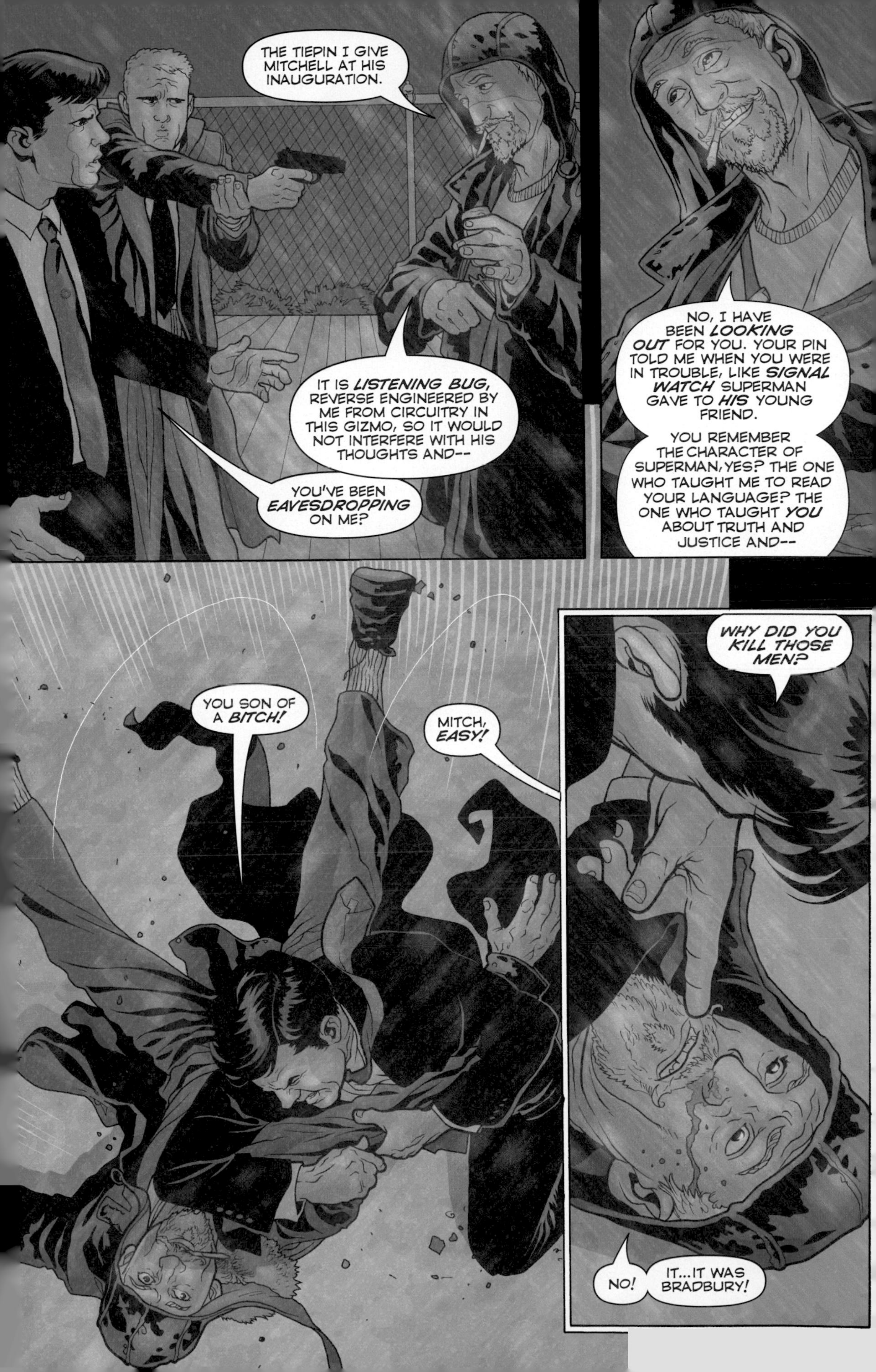
THE TIEPIN I GIVE MITCHELL AT HIS INAUGURATION.
IT IS *LISTENING BUG*, REVERSE ENGINEERED BY ME FROM CIRCUITRY IN THIS GIZMO, SO IT WOULD NOT INTERFERE WITH HIS THOUGHTS AND--
YOU'VE BEEN *EAVESDROPPING* ON ME?
NO, I HAVE BEEN *LOOKING OUT* FOR YOU. YOUR PIN TOLD ME WHEN YOU WERE IN TROUBLE, LIKE *SIGNAL WATCH* SUPERMAN GAVE TO *HIS* YOUNG FRIEND.
YOU REMEMBER THE CHARACTER OF SUPERMAN, YES? THE ONE WHO TAUGHT ME TO READ YOUR LANGUAGE? THE ONE WHO TAUGHT *YOU* ABOUT TRUTH AND JUSTICE AND--
YOU SON OF A *BITCH!*
MITCH, *EASY!*
WHY DID YOU KILL THOSE MEN?
NO!
IT...IT WAS BRADBURY!

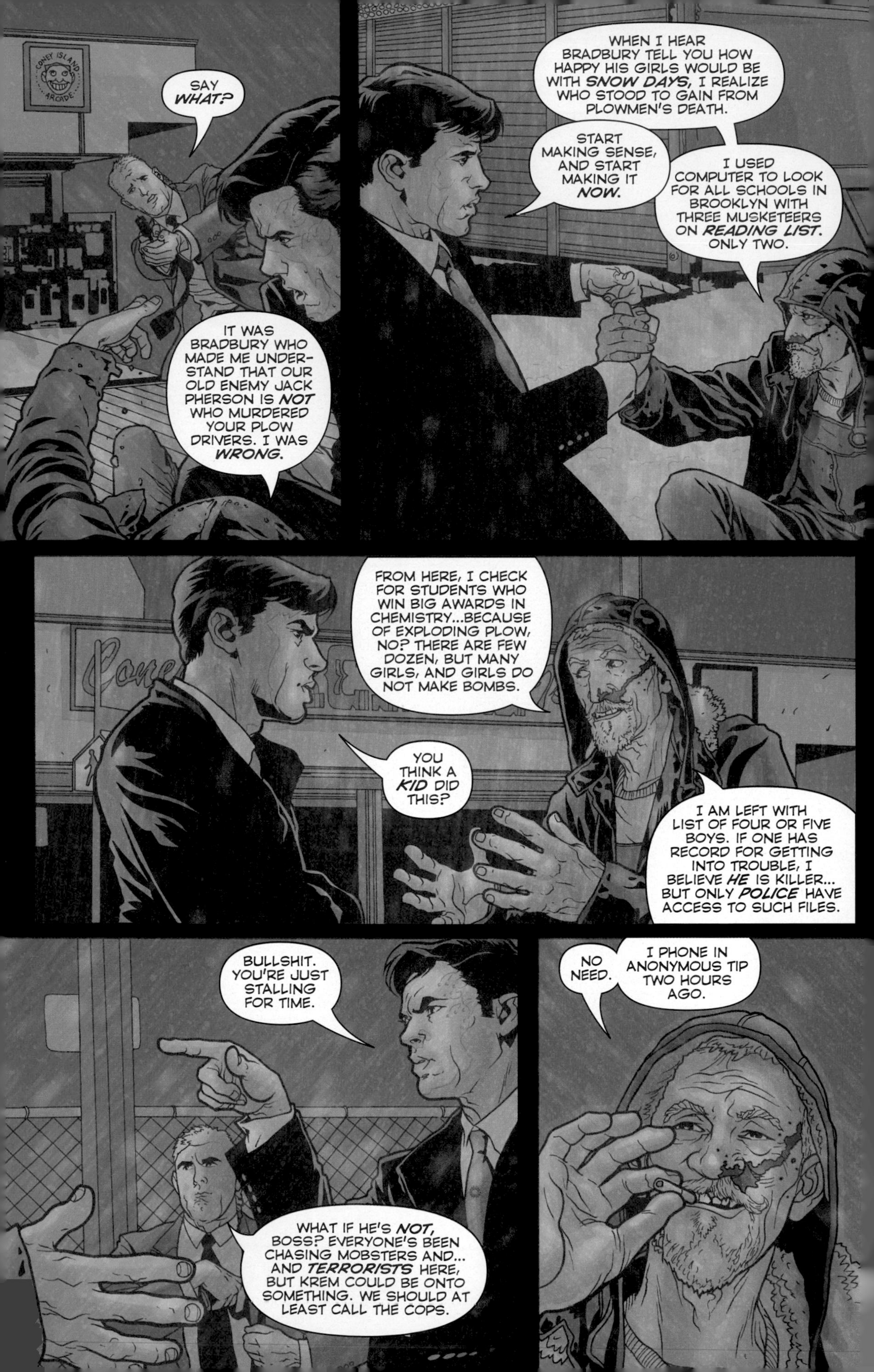

CONEY ISLAND ARCADE
SAY WHAT?
IT WAS BRADBURY WHO MADE ME UNDERSTAND THAT OUR OLD ENEMY JACK PHERSON IS NOT WHO MURDERED YOUR PLOW DRIVERS. I WAS WRONG.
WHEN I HEAR BRADBURY TELL YOU HOW HAPPY HIS GIRLS WOULD BE WITH SNOW DAYS, I REALIZE WHO STOOD TO GAIN FROM PLOWMEN'S DEATH.
START MAKING SENSE, AND START MAKING IT NOW.
I USED COMPUTER TO LOOK FOR ALL SCHOOLS IN BROOKLYN WITH THREE MUSKETEERS ON READING LIST. ONLY TWO.
FROM HERE, I CHECK FOR STUDENTS WHO WIN BIG AWARDS IN CHEMISTRY...BECAUSE OF EXPLODING PLOW, NO? THERE ARE FEW DOZEN, BUT MANY GIRLS, AND GIRLS DO NOT MAKE BOMBS.
YOU THINK A KID DID THIS?
I AM LEFT WITH LIST OF FOUR OR FIVE BOYS. IF ONE HAS RECORD FOR GETTING INTO TROUBLE, I BELIEVE HE IS KILLER... BUT ONLY POLICE HAVE ACCESS TO SUCH FILES.
BULLSHIT. YOU'RE JUST STALLING FOR TIME.
WHAT IF HE'S NOT, BOSS? EVERYONE'S BEEN CHASING MOBSTERS AND... AND TERRORISTS HERE, BUT KREM COULD BE ONTO SOMETHING. WE SHOULD AT LEAST CALL THE COPS.
NO NEED.
I PHONE IN ANONYMOUS TIP TWO HOURS AGO.

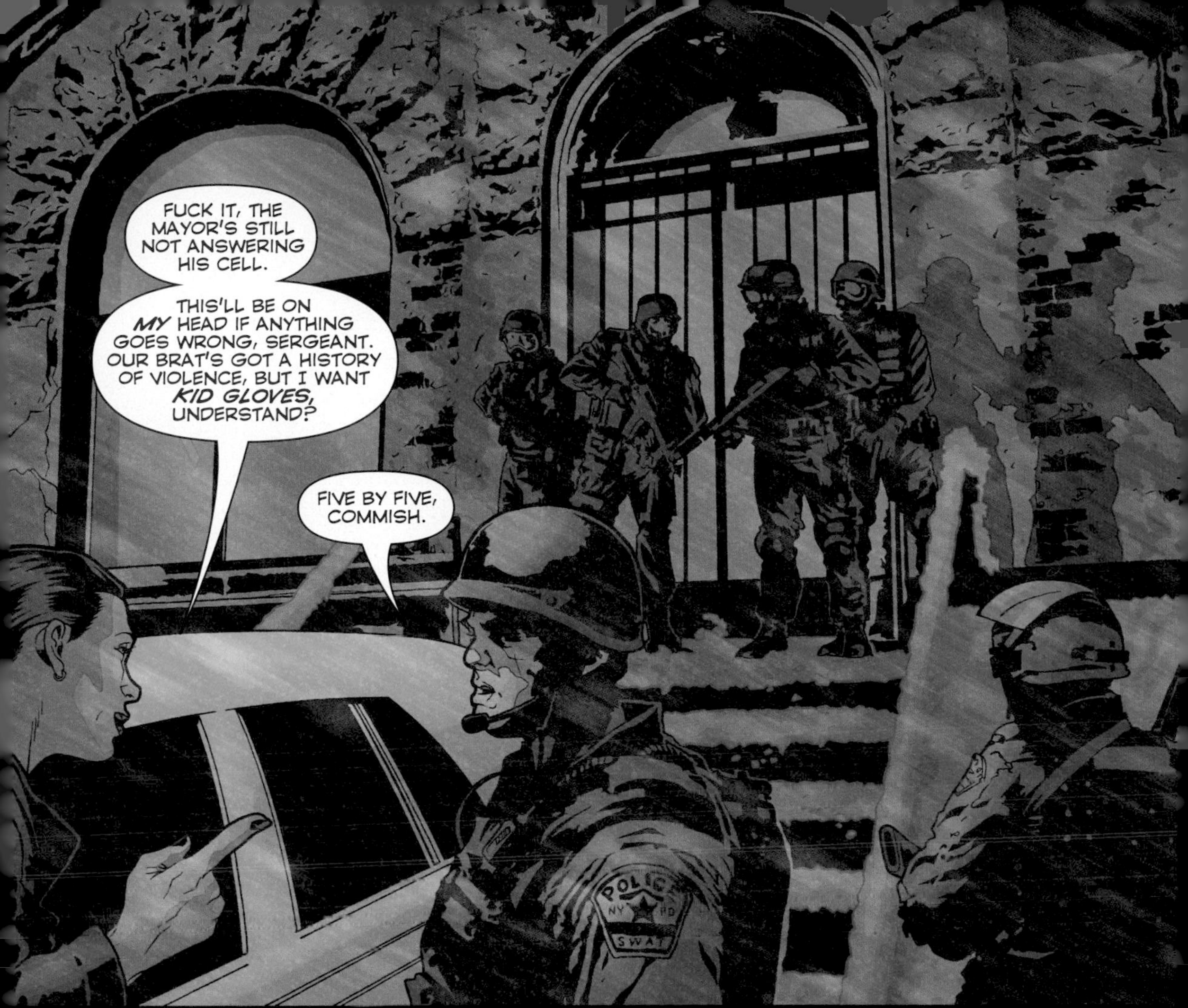
FUCK IT, THE MAYOR'S STILL NOT ANSWERING HIS CELL.
THIS'LL BE ON *MY* HEAD IF ANYTHING GOES WRONG, SERGEANT. OUR BRAT'S GOT A HISTORY OF VIOLENCE, BUT I WANT *KID GLOVES,* UNDERSTAND?
FIVE BY FIVE, COMMISH.
POLICE NYPD SWAT

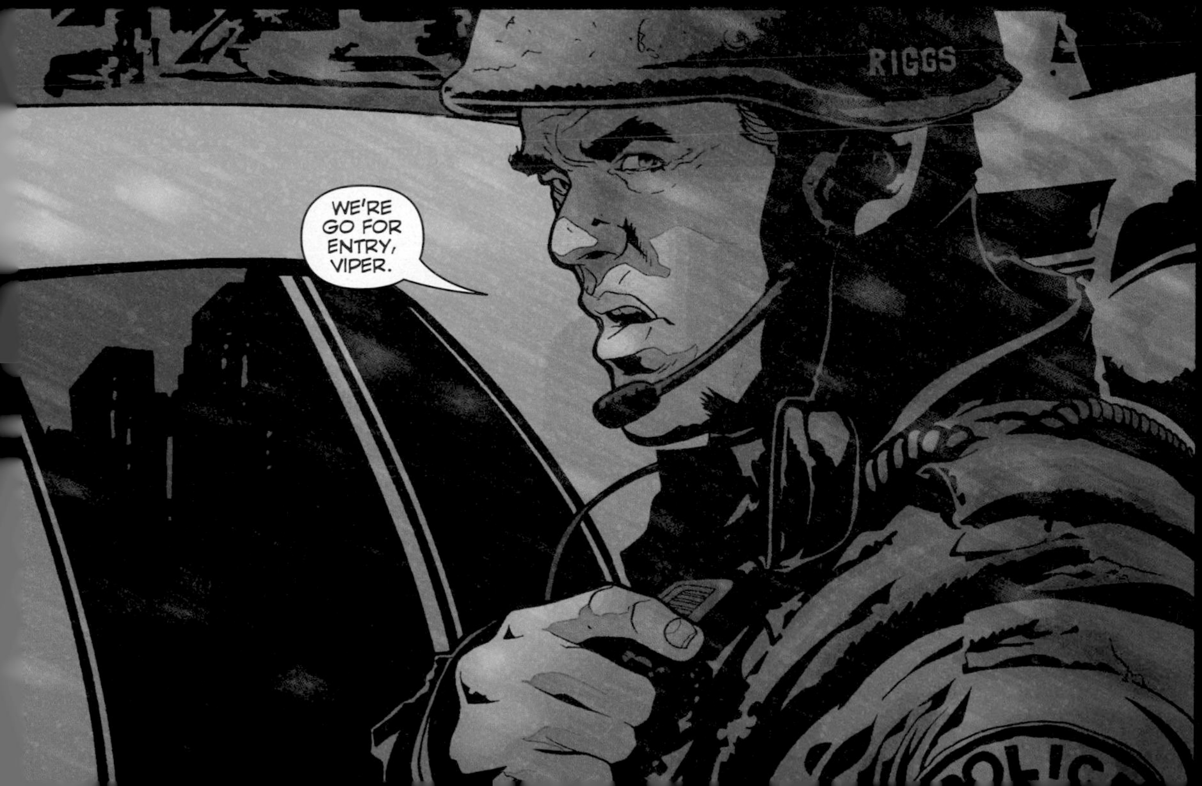
RIGGS
WE'RE GO FOR ENTRY, VIPER.

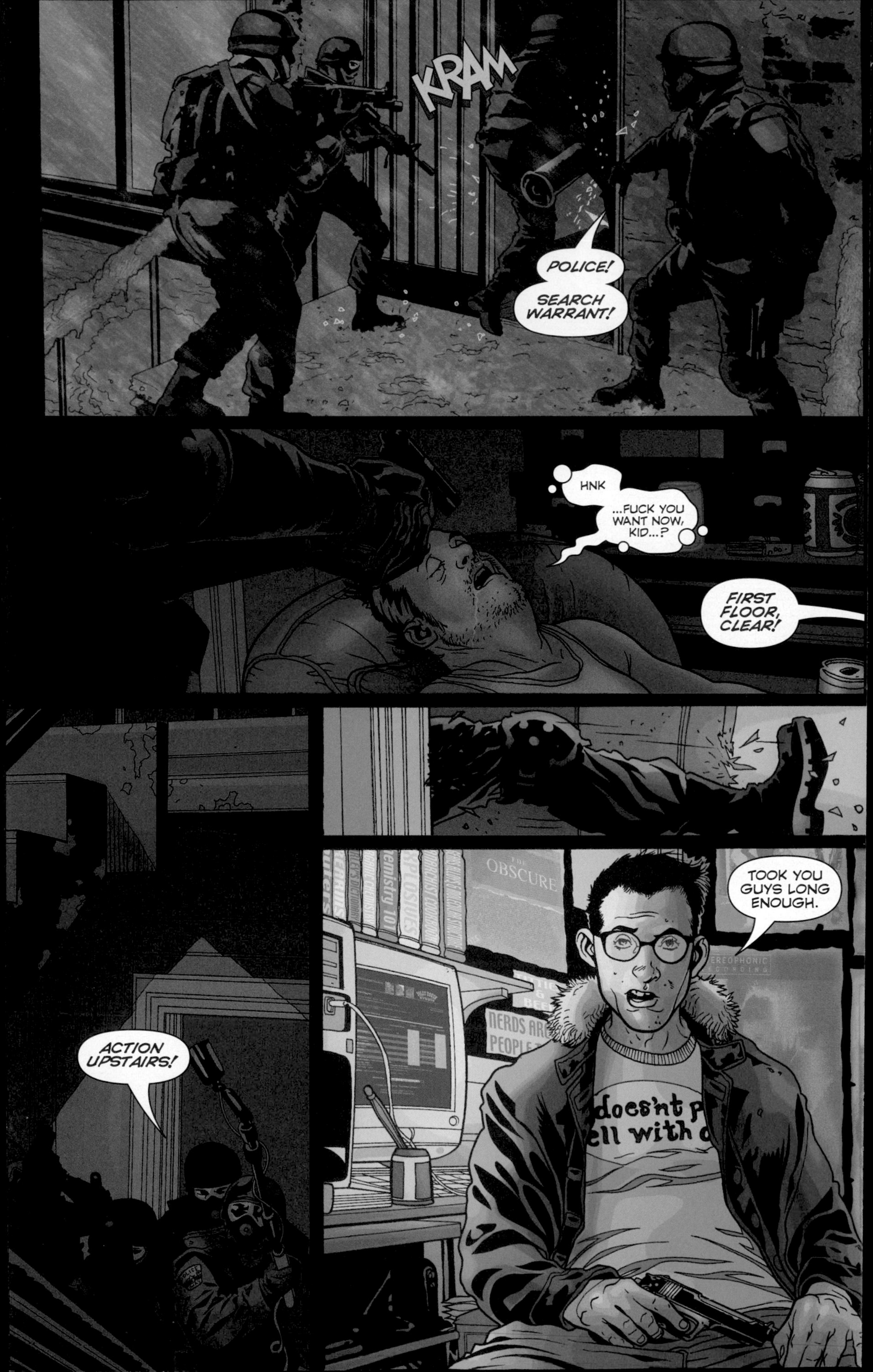
KRAM
POLICE!
SEARCH WARRANT!
HNK
...FUCK YOU WANT NOW, KID...?
FIRST FLOOR, CLEAR!
ACTION UPSTAIRS!
TOOK YOU GUYS LONG ENOUGH.

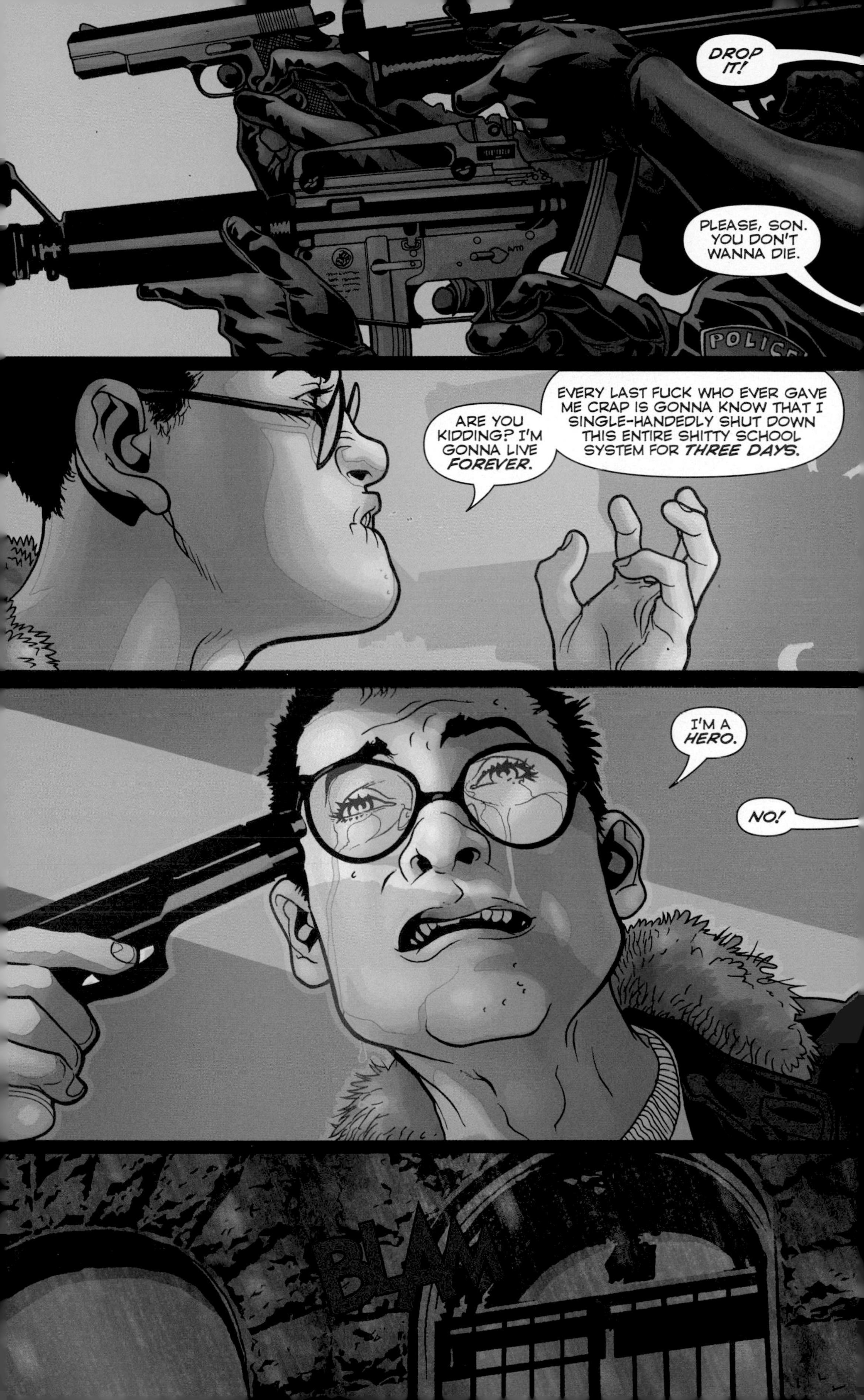
DROP IT!
PLEASE, SON. YOU DON'T WANNA DIE.
POLICE
ARE YOU KIDDING? I'M GONNA LIVE *FOREVER*.
EVERY LAST FUCK WHO EVER GAVE ME CRAP IS GONNA KNOW THAT I SINGLE-HANDEDLY SHUT DOWN THIS ENTIRE SHITTY SCHOOL SYSTEM FOR *THREE DAYS*.
I'M A *HERO*.
NO!
BLAM

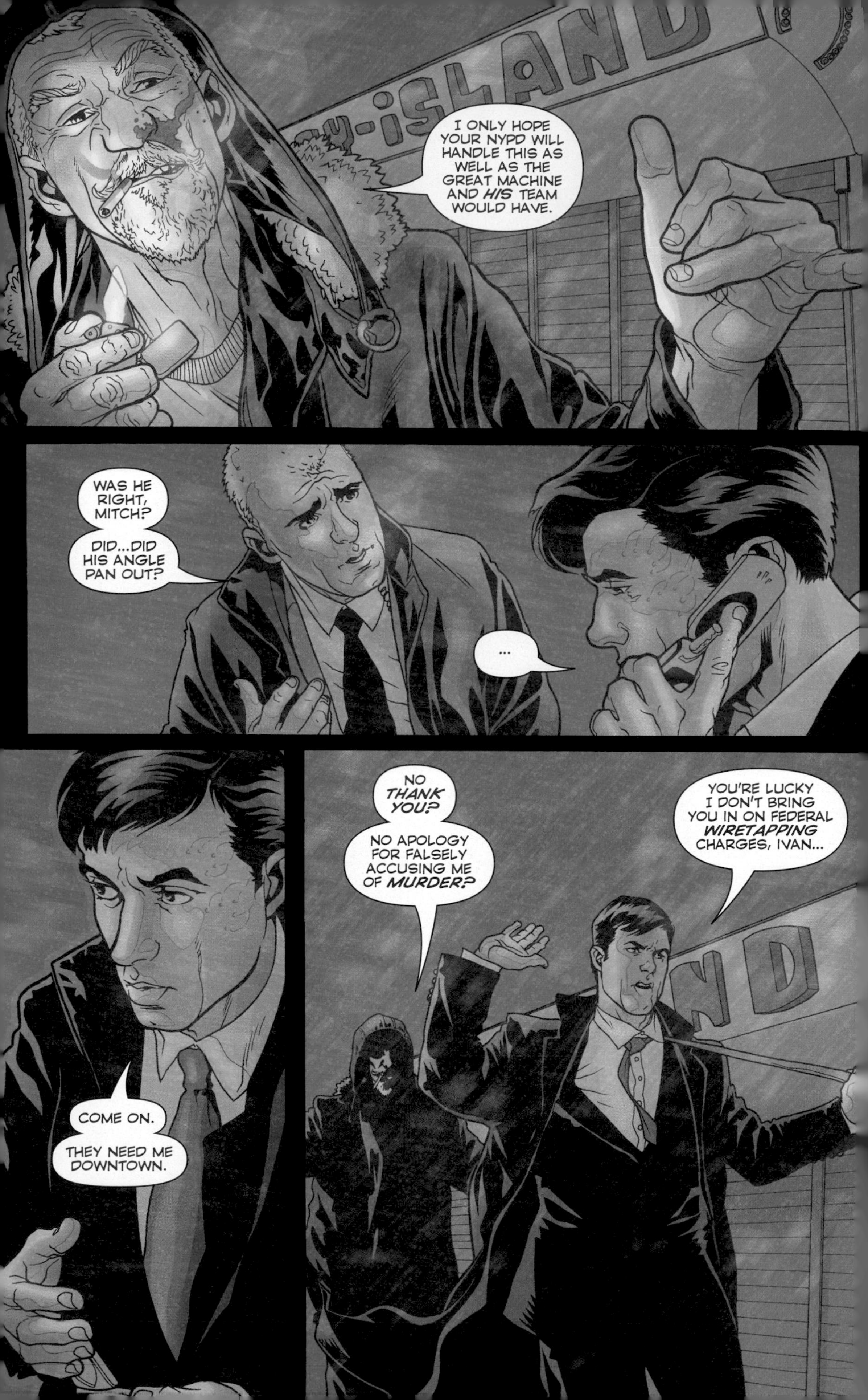

I ONLY HOPE YOUR NYPD WILL HANDLE THIS AS WELL AS THE GREAT MACHINE AND *HIS* TEAM WOULD HAVE.
WAS HE RIGHT, MITCH?
DID...DID HIS ANGLE PAN OUT?
...
COME ON.
THEY NEED ME DOWNTOWN.
NO *THANK YOU?*
NO APOLOGY FOR FALSELY ACCUSING ME OF *MURDER?*
YOU'RE LUCKY I DON'T BRING YOU IN ON FEDERAL *WIRETAPPING* CHARGES, IVAN...

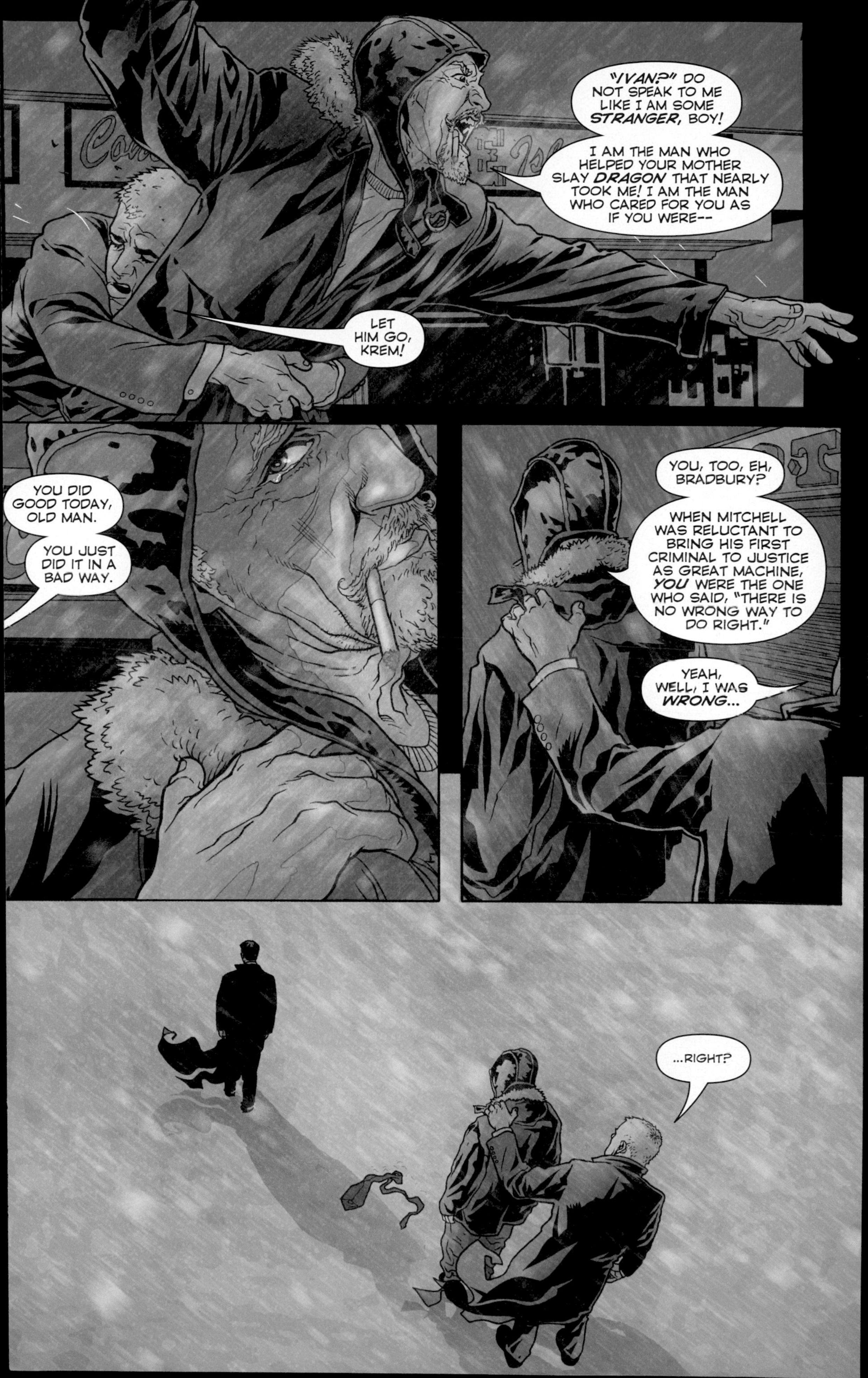
"IVAN?" DO NOT SPEAK TO ME LIKE I AM SOME STRANGER, BOY!
I AM THE MAN WHO HELPED YOUR MOTHER SLAY DRAGON THAT NEARLY TOOK ME! I AM THE MAN WHO CARED FOR YOU AS IF YOU WERE--
LET HIM GO, KREM!
YOU DID GOOD TODAY, OLD MAN.
YOU JUST DID IT IN A BAD WAY.
YOU, TOO, EH, BRADBURY?
WHEN MITCHELL WAS RELUCTANT TO BRING HIS FIRST CRIMINAL TO JUSTICE AS GREAT MACHINE, YOU WERE THE ONE WHO SAID, "THERE IS NO WRONG WAY TO DO RIGHT."
YEAH, WELL, I WAS WRONG...
...RIGHT?

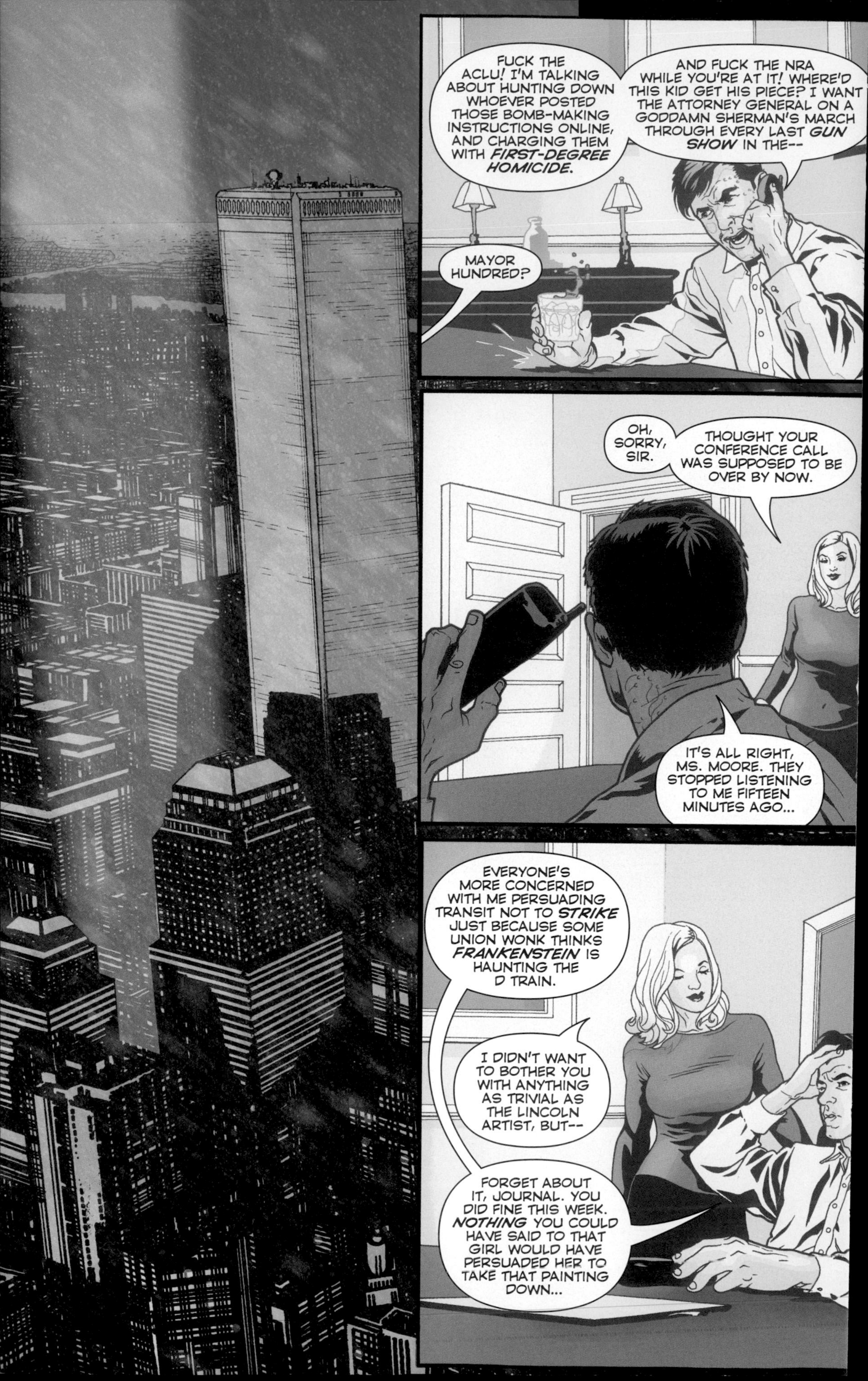
FUCK THE ACLU! I'M TALKING ABOUT HUNTING DOWN WHOEVER POSTED THOSE BOMB-MAKING INSTRUCTIONS ONLINE, AND CHARGING THEM WITH *FIRST-DEGREE HOMICIDE*.
AND FUCK THE NRA WHILE YOU'RE AT IT! WHERE'D THIS KID GET HIS PIECE? I WANT THE ATTORNEY GENERAL ON A GODDAMN SHERMAN'S MARCH THROUGH EVERY LAST *GUN SHOW* IN THE--
MAYOR HUNDRED?
OH, SORRY, SIR.
THOUGHT YOUR CONFERENCE CALL WAS SUPPOSED TO BE OVER BY NOW.
IT'S ALL RIGHT, MS. MOORE. THEY STOPPED LISTENING TO ME FIFTEEN MINUTES AGO...
EVERYONE'S MORE CONCERNED WITH ME PERSUADING TRANSIT NOT TO *STRIKE* JUST BECAUSE SOME UNION WONK THINKS *FRANKENSTEIN* IS HAUNTING THE D TRAIN.
I DIDN'T WANT TO BOTHER YOU WITH ANYTHING AS TRIVIAL AS THE LINCOLN ARTIST, BUT--
FORGET ABOUT IT, JOURNAL. YOU DID FINE THIS WEEK. *NOTHING* YOU COULD HAVE SAID TO THAT GIRL WOULD HAVE PERSUADED HER TO TAKE THAT PAINTING DOWN...

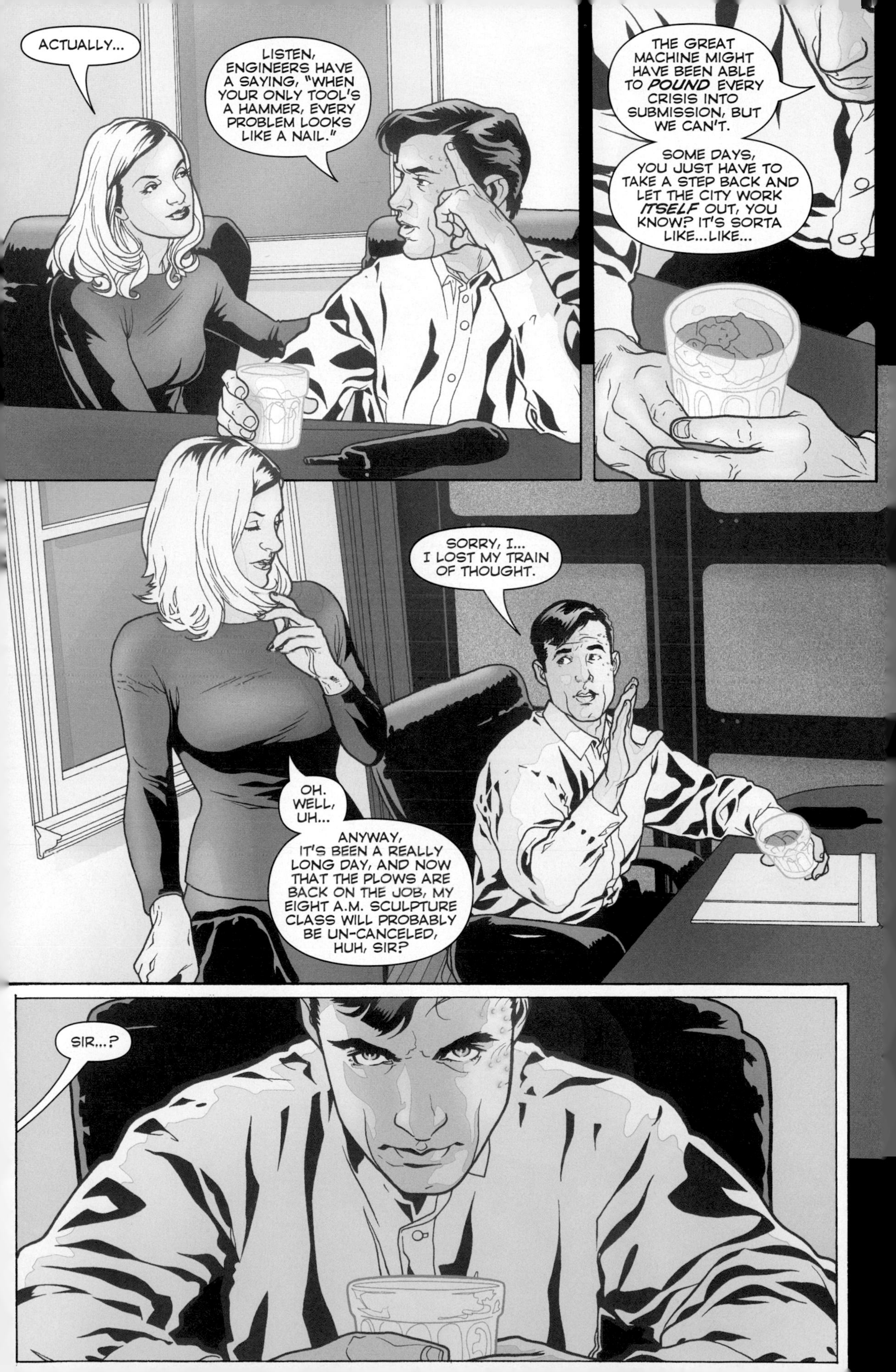
ACTUALLY...
LISTEN, ENGINEERS HAVE A SAYING, "WHEN YOUR ONLY TOOL'S A HAMMER, EVERY PROBLEM LOOKS LIKE A NAIL."
THE GREAT MACHINE MIGHT HAVE BEEN ABLE TO POUND EVERY CRISIS INTO SUBMISSION, BUT WE CAN'T.
SOME DAYS, YOU JUST HAVE TO TAKE A STEP BACK AND LET THE CITY WORK ITSELF OUT, YOU KNOW? IT'S SORTA LIKE...LIKE...
SORRY, I... I LOST MY TRAIN OF THOUGHT.
OH. WELL, UH...
ANYWAY, IT'S BEEN A REALLY LONG DAY, AND NOW THAT THE PLOWS ARE BACK ON THE JOB, MY EIGHT A.M. SCULPTURE CLASS WILL PROBABLY BE UN-CANCELED, HUH, SIR?
SIR...?

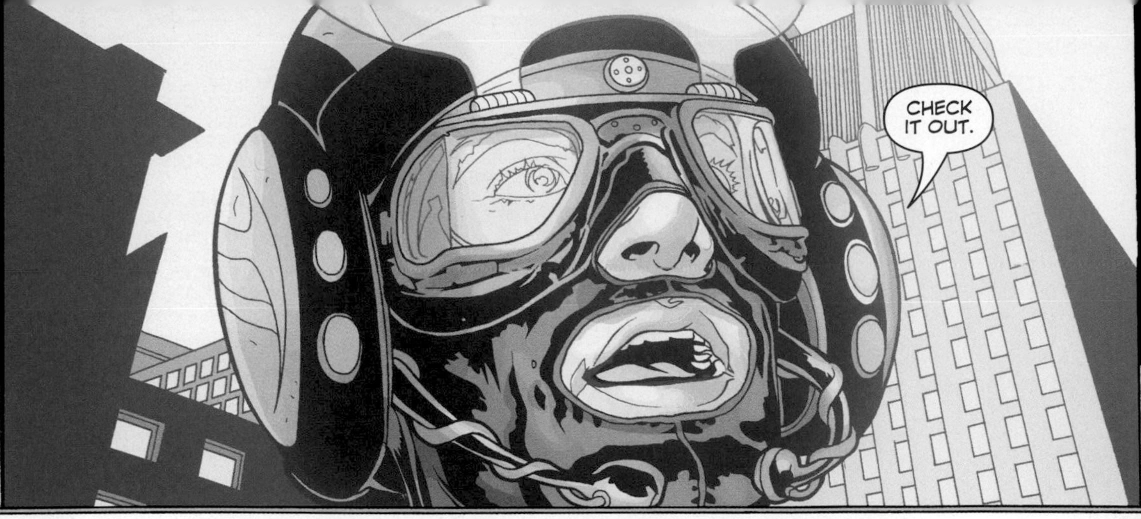
CHECK IT OUT.

TUESDAY, MAY 8, 2001

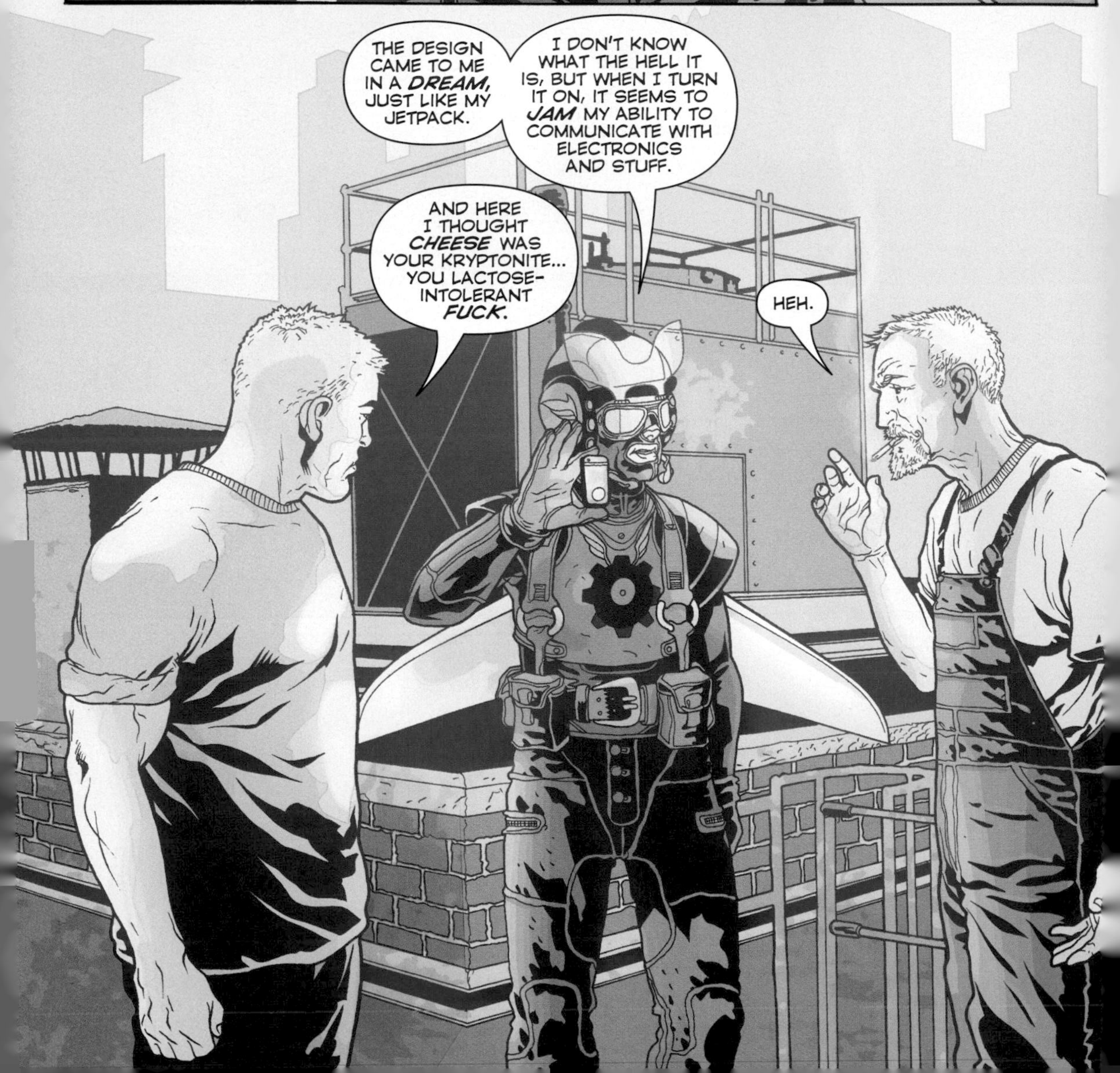
THE DESIGN CAME TO ME IN A *DREAM,* JUST LIKE MY JETPACK.
I DON'T KNOW WHAT THE HELL IT IS, BUT WHEN I TURN IT ON, IT SEEMS TO *JAM* MY ABILITY TO COMMUNICATE WITH ELECTRONICS AND STUFF.
AND HERE I THOUGHT *CHEESE* WAS YOUR KRYPTONITE... YOU LACTOSE-INTOLERANT *FUCK*.
HEH.

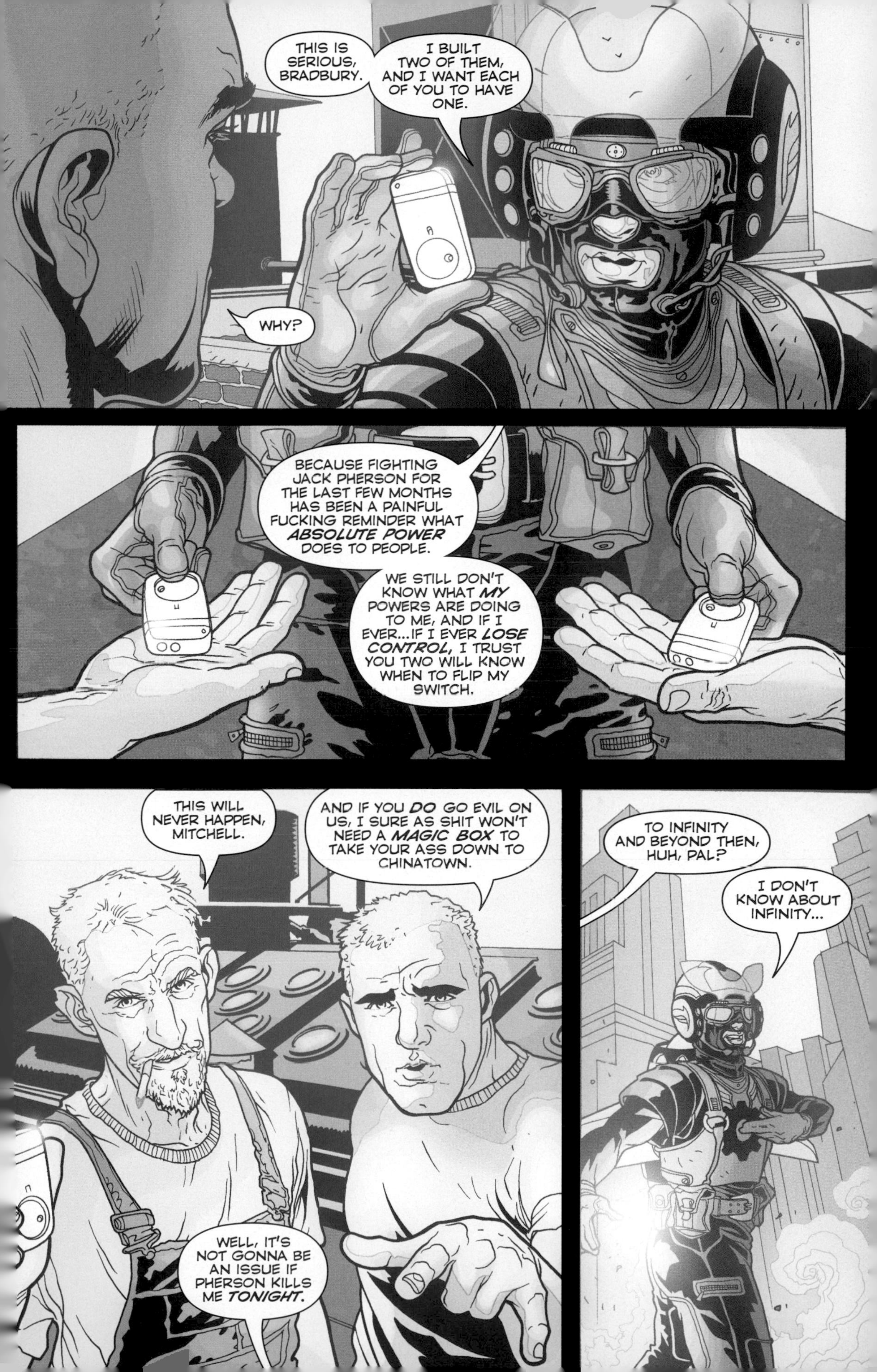
THIS IS SERIOUS, BRADBURY.
I BUILT TWO OF THEM, AND I WANT EACH OF YOU TO HAVE ONE.
WHY?
BECAUSE FIGHTING JACK PHERSON FOR THE LAST FEW MONTHS HAS BEEN A PAINFUL FUCKING REMINDER WHAT *ABSOLUTE POWER* DOES TO PEOPLE.
WE STILL DON'T KNOW WHAT *MY* POWERS ARE DOING TO ME, AND IF I EVER...IF I EVER *LOSE CONTROL,* I TRUST YOU TWO WILL KNOW WHEN TO FLIP MY SWITCH.
THIS WILL NEVER HAPPEN, MITCHELL.
AND IF YOU *DO* GO EVIL ON US, I SURE AS SHIT WON'T NEED A *MAGIC BOX* TO TAKE YOUR ASS DOWN TO CHINATOWN.
WELL, IT'S NOT GONNA BE AN ISSUE IF PHERSON KILLS ME *TONIGHT*.
TO INFINITY AND BEYOND THEN, HUH, PAL?
I DON'T KNOW ABOUT INFINITY...

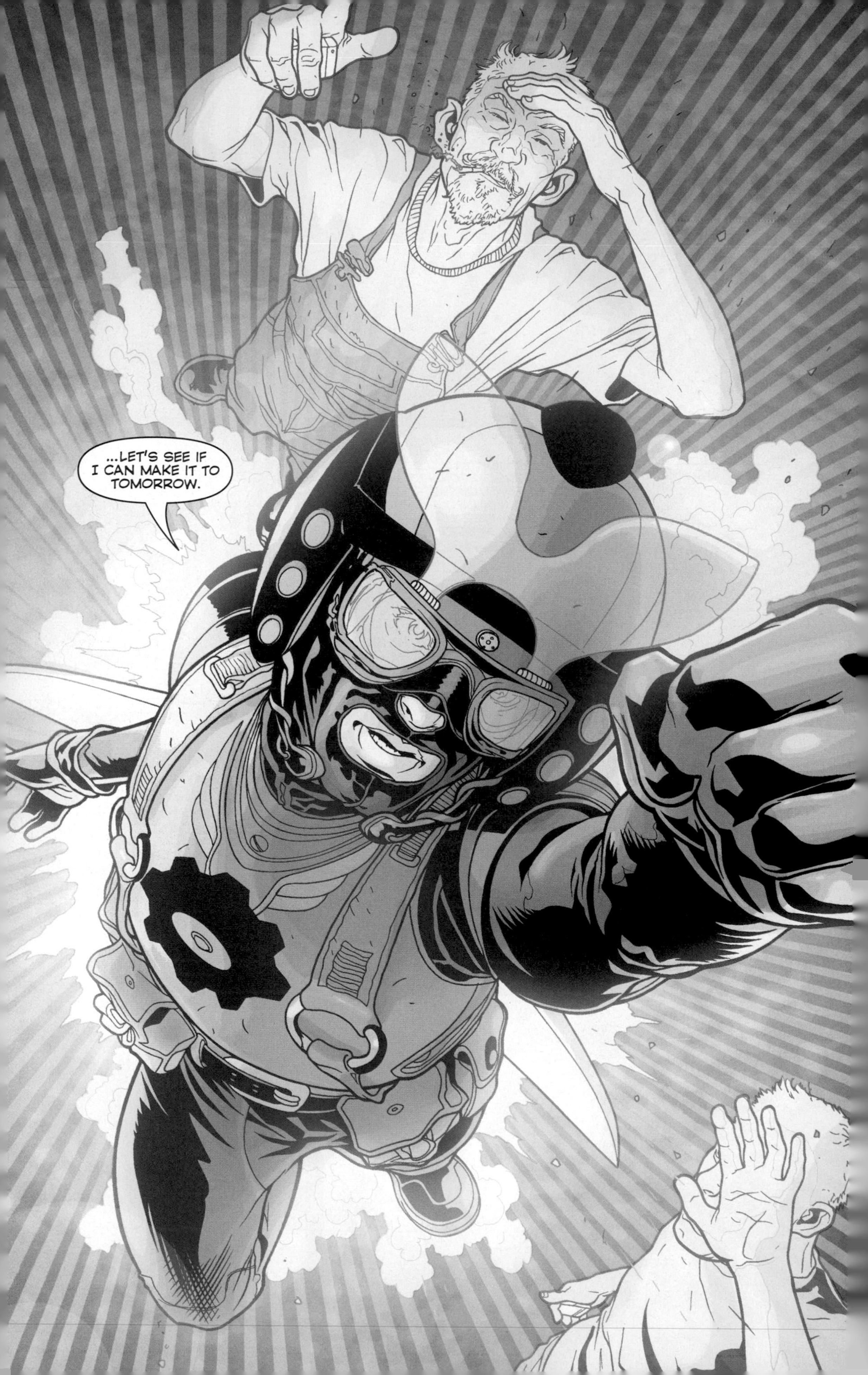
...LET'S SEE IF I CAN MAKE IT TO TOMORROW.

CAST OF CHARACTERS

JIMMY HILL

AS: MITCHELL HUNDRED

DOODLE GRUB

AS: TRIP

ERIC O'DELL

AS: BRADBURY

MARNIE HILL

AS: JOURNAL MOORE

GRETA O'DELL

AS: COMMISSIONER ANGOTTI
AND TRISTA BRAVING

ENZO HARRIS

AS: YOUNG MITCHELL

**LARRY
BRANTLEY**

AS: KREMLIN

STACIE HARRIS

AS: MITCHELL'S MOTHER

TONY HARRIS

AS: VARIOUS

PAT GRAHAM

AS: CANDY WATSON

JIMMY CLARK

AS: JACKSON GEORGES

EDDIE THOMAS

AS: CHIEF OF PATROL KURSON

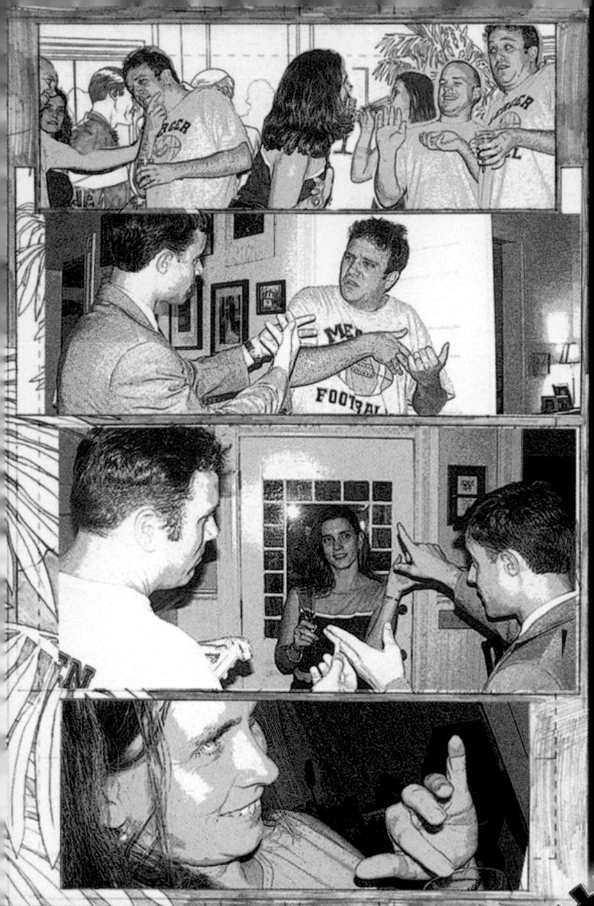

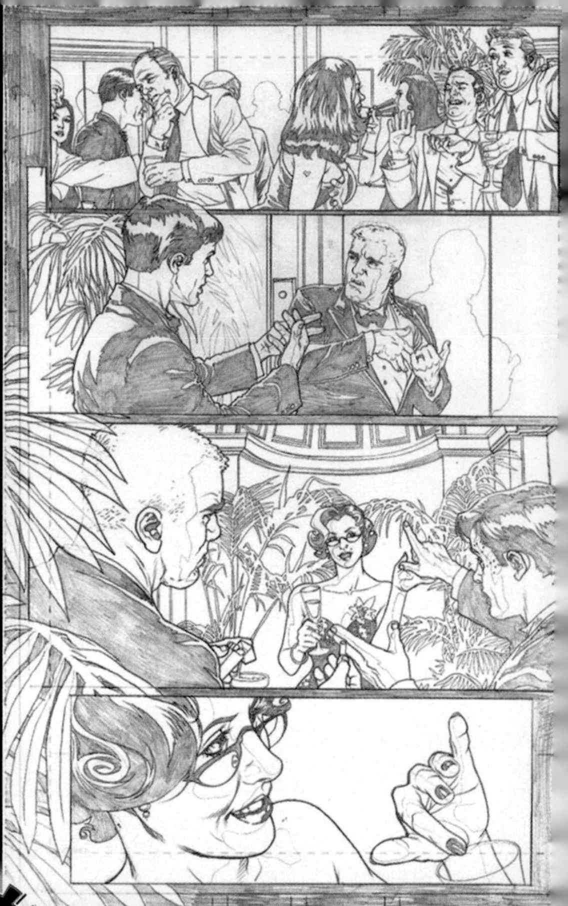

FROM REFERENCE TO FINISH PAGES

PAGE 1

BY HARRIS, FEISTER AND METTLER

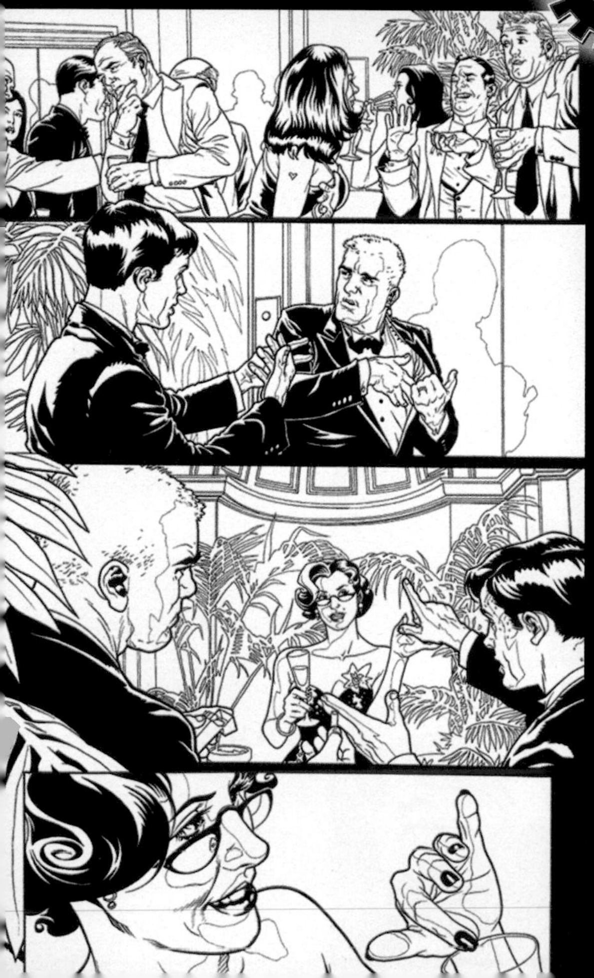

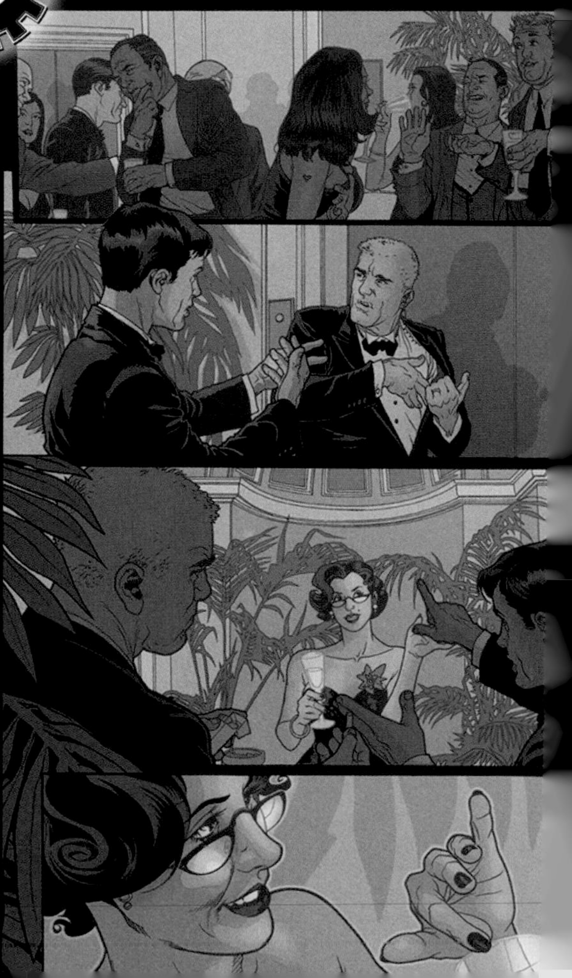

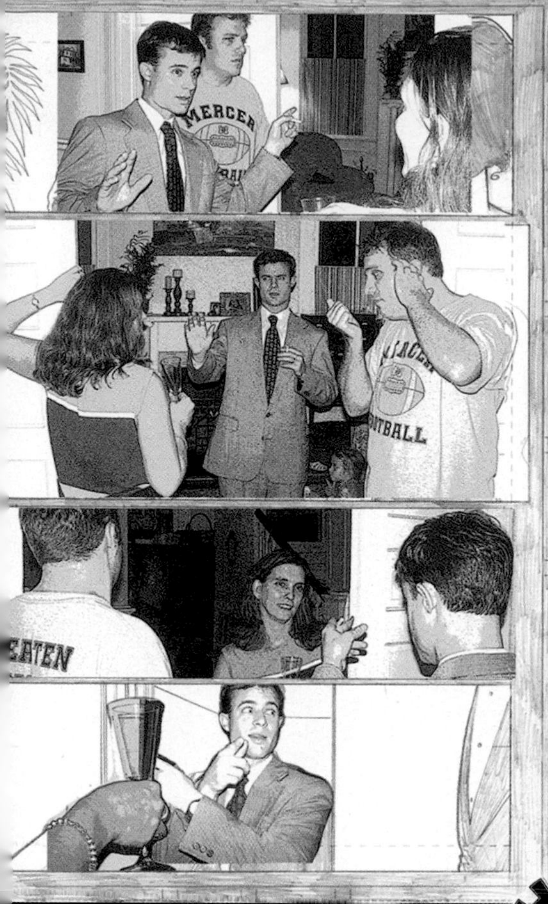
MERCER
FOOTBALL.

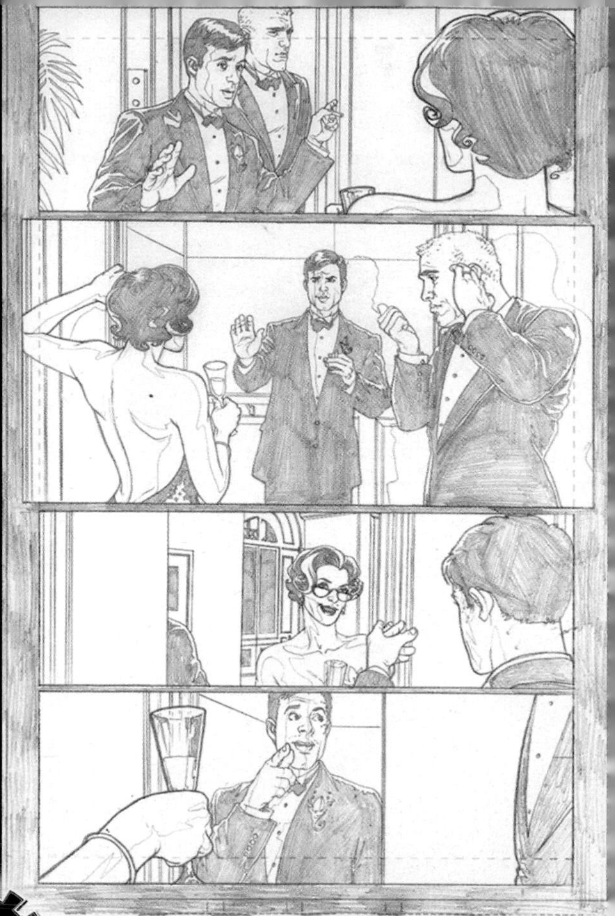

FROM REFERENCE TO FINISH PAGES

PAGE 2

BY HARRIS, FEISTER AND METTLER

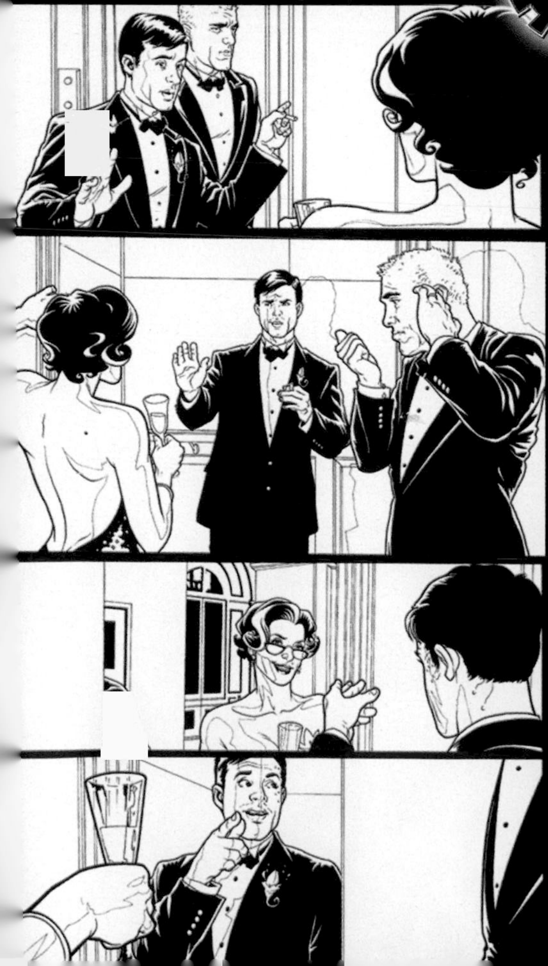

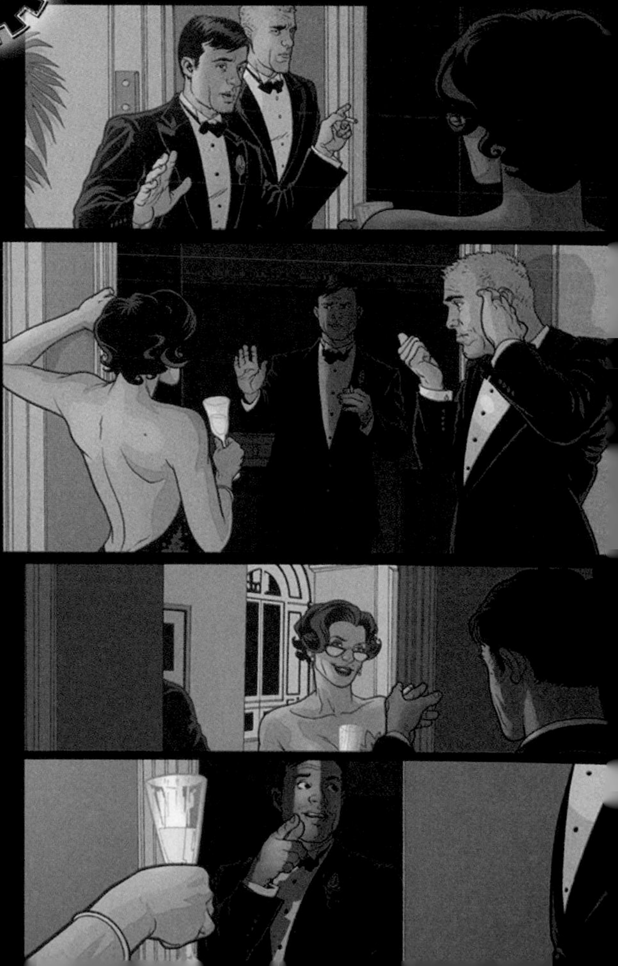

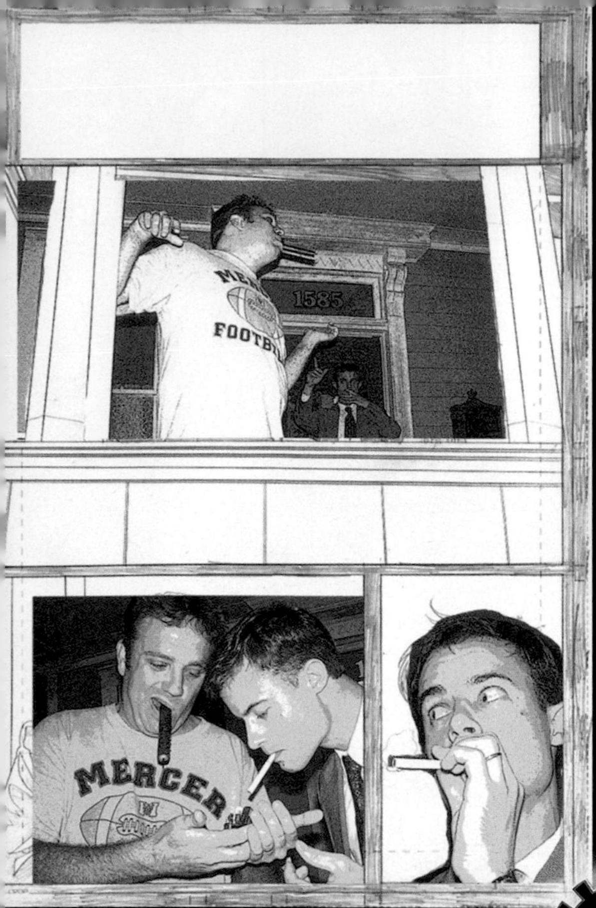
1585
MERCER

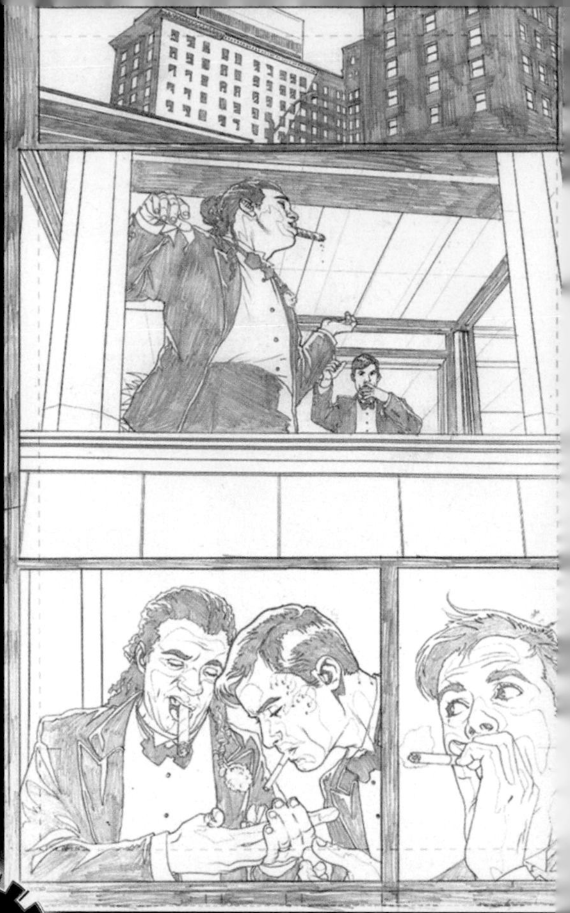

FROM REFERENCE TO FINISH PAGES

PAGE 3

BY HARRIS, FEISTER AND METTLER

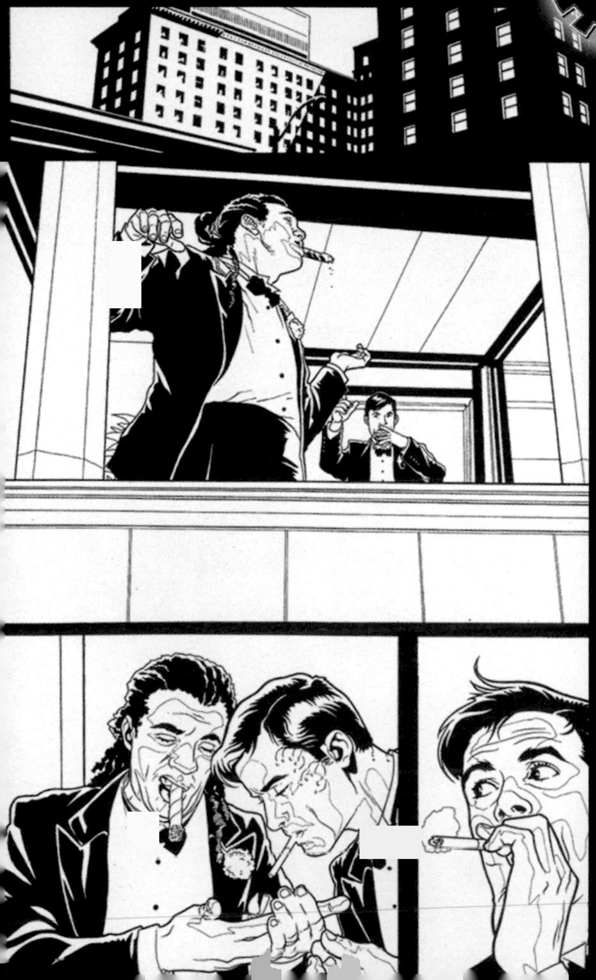

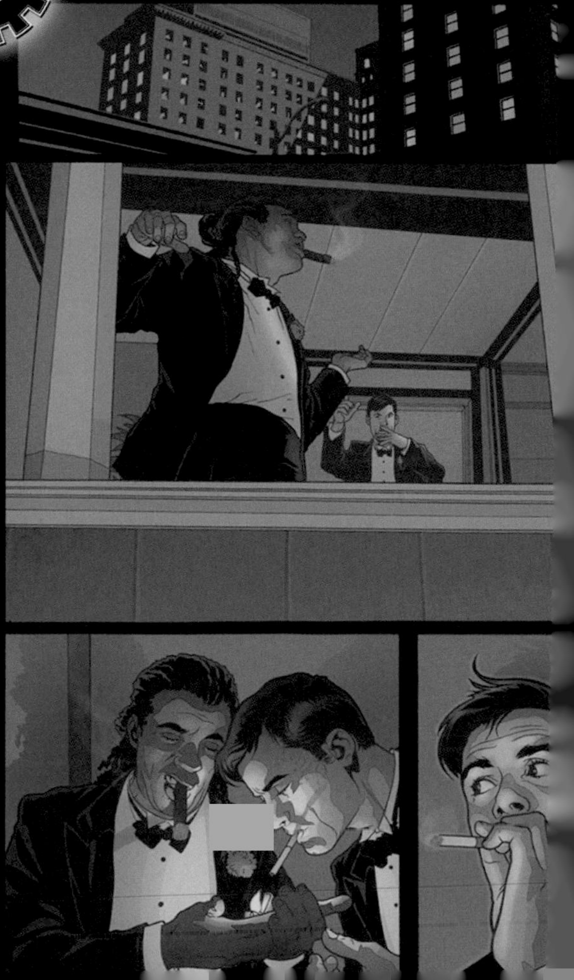

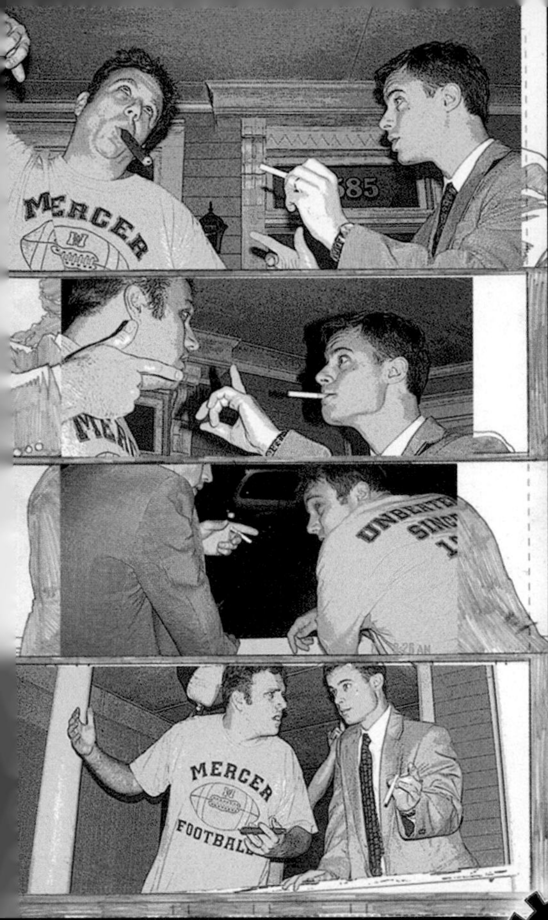
MERCER
MERCER
FOOTBALL

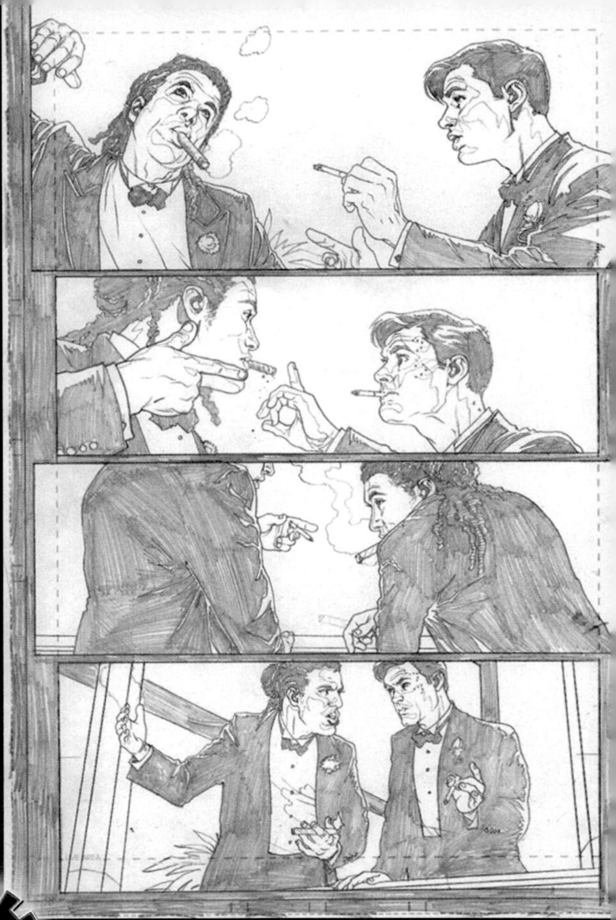

FROM REFERENCE TO FINISH PAGES

PAGE 4

BY HARRIS, FEISTER AND METTLER

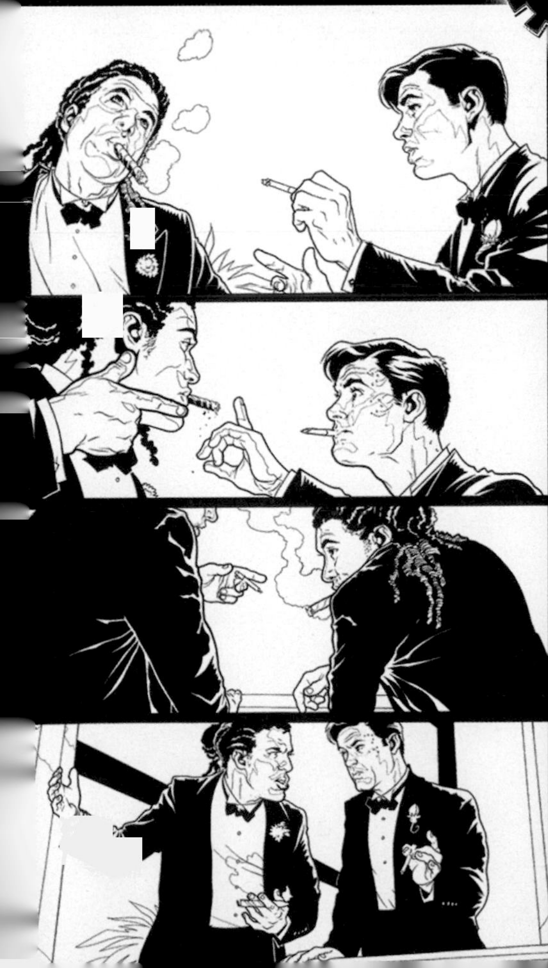

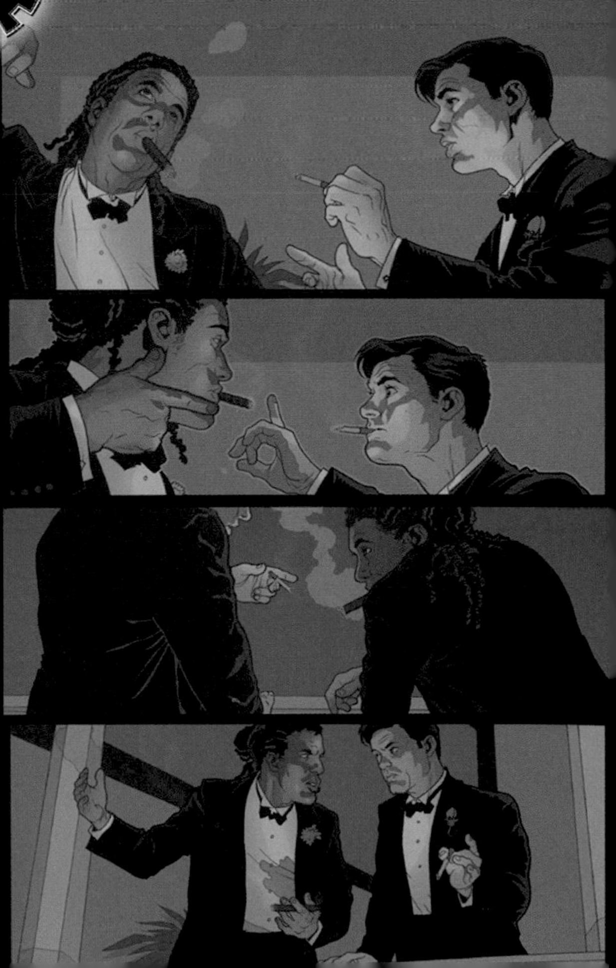

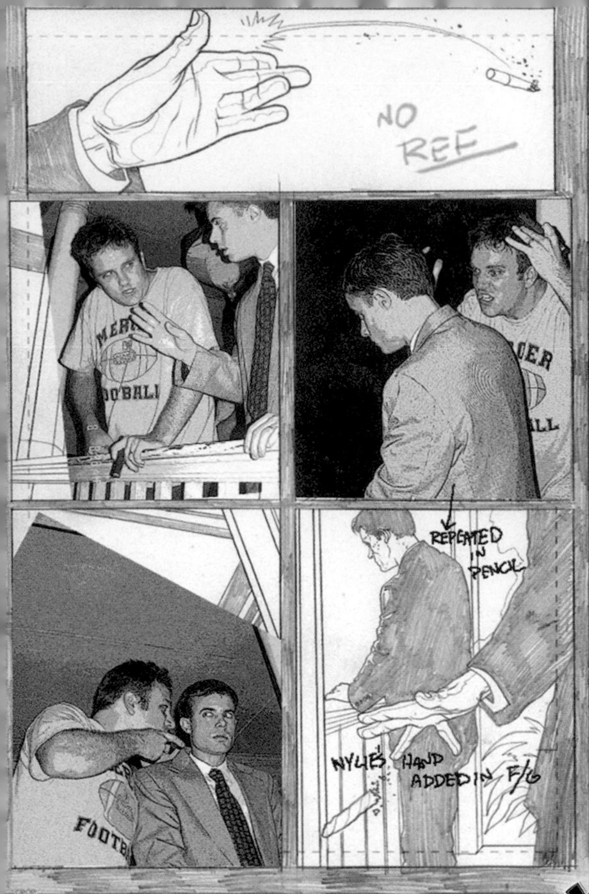
NO REF
REPEATED IN PENCIL
KYLE'S HAND ADDED IN F/G

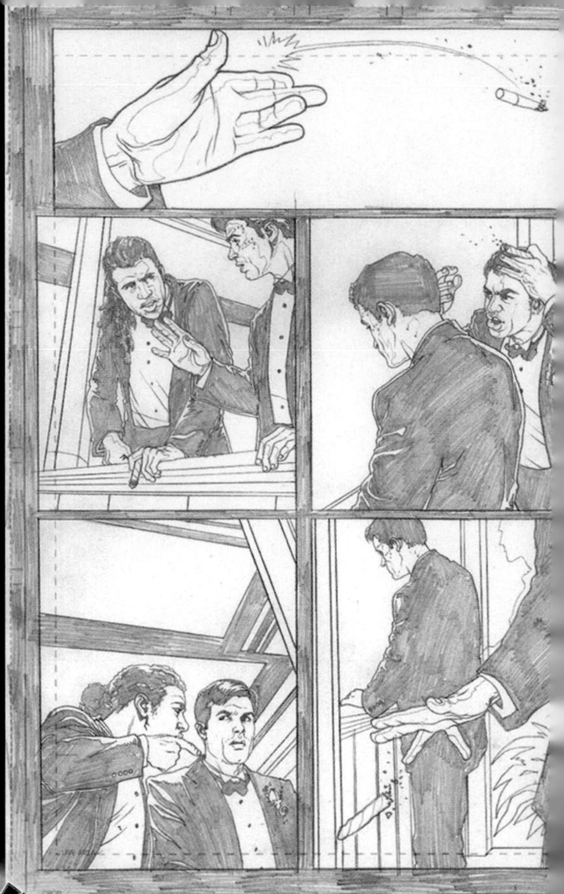

FROM REFERENCE TO FINISH PAGES

PAGE 5

BY HARRIS, FEISTER AND METTLER

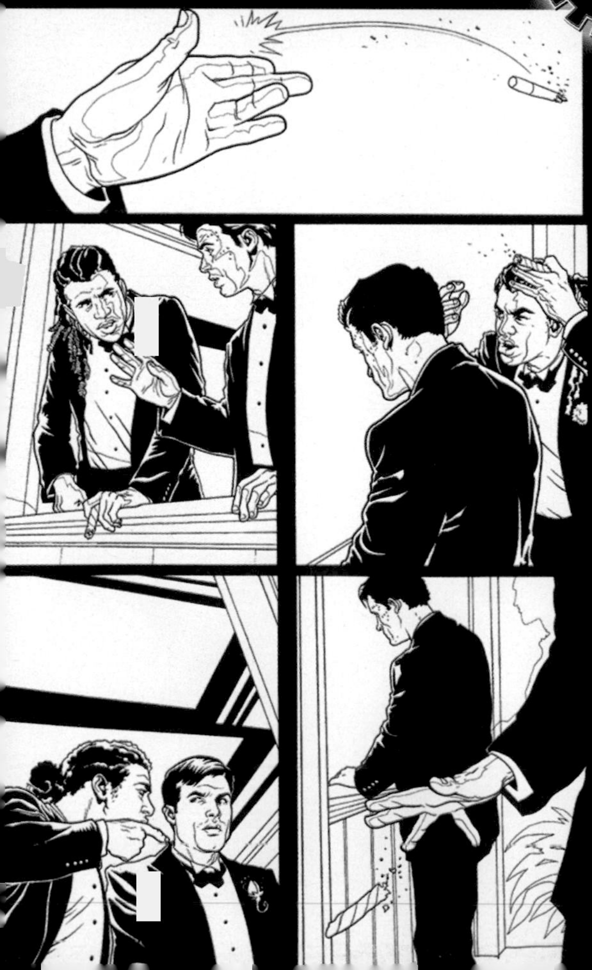

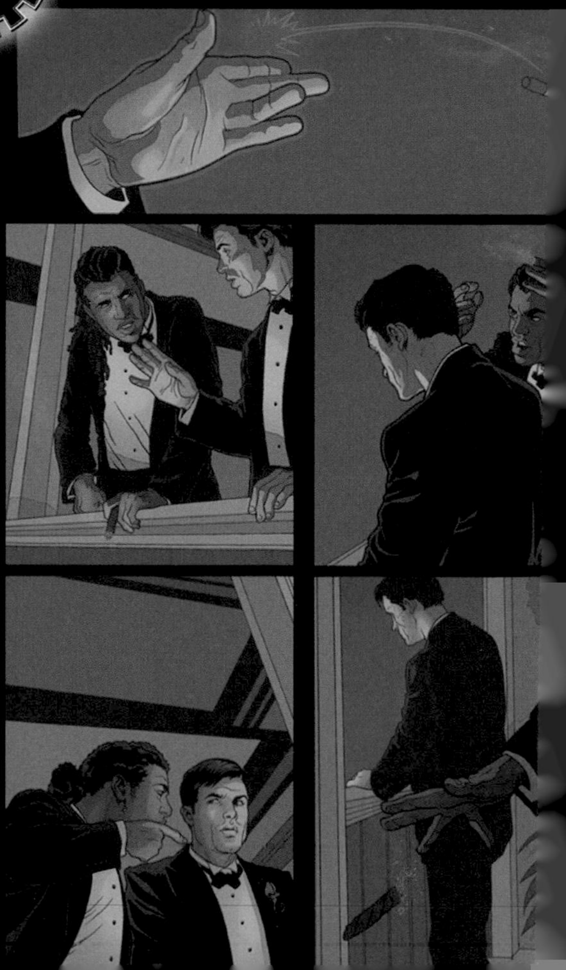

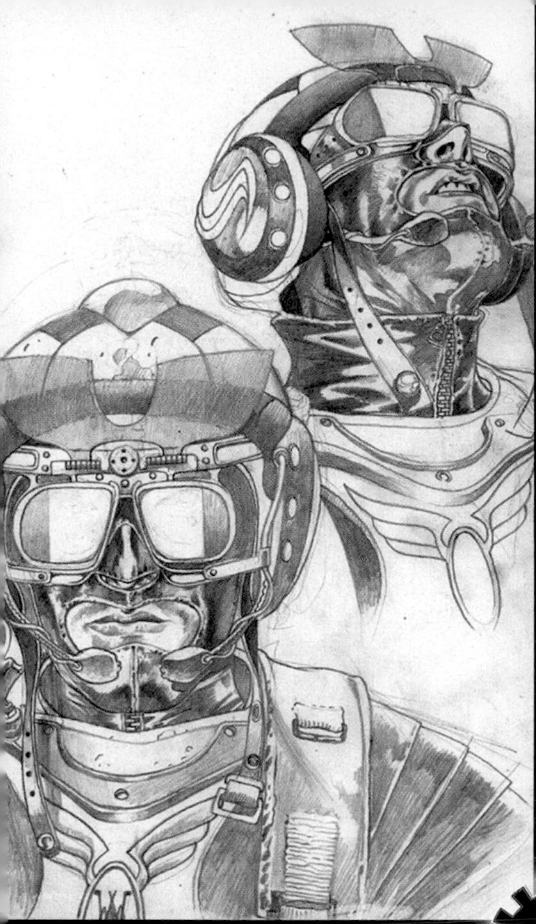

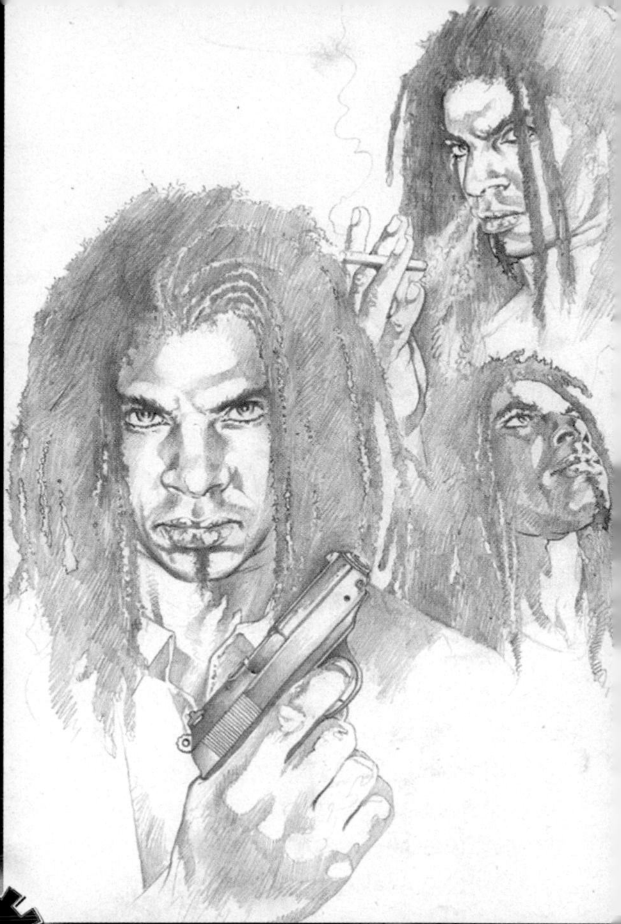

EXTRA SKETCHES

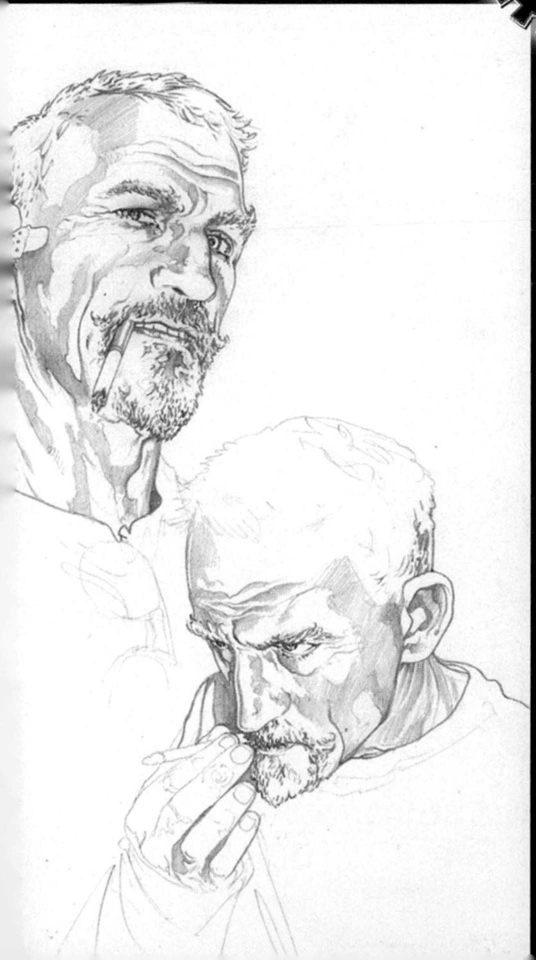

MJOB!!! : Tidy Bowl Killer leaves another Floater!

COLD-SNAP: Winter ain't over till the Fat Lady sings!

NEW ★ ★ ★ ★ YORK

DAILY WIRE

New York's Most Respected Newspaper

★ EXCLUSIVE ★

CRAZED WINGMAN

Shuts Down Subways for Eleven Hours!

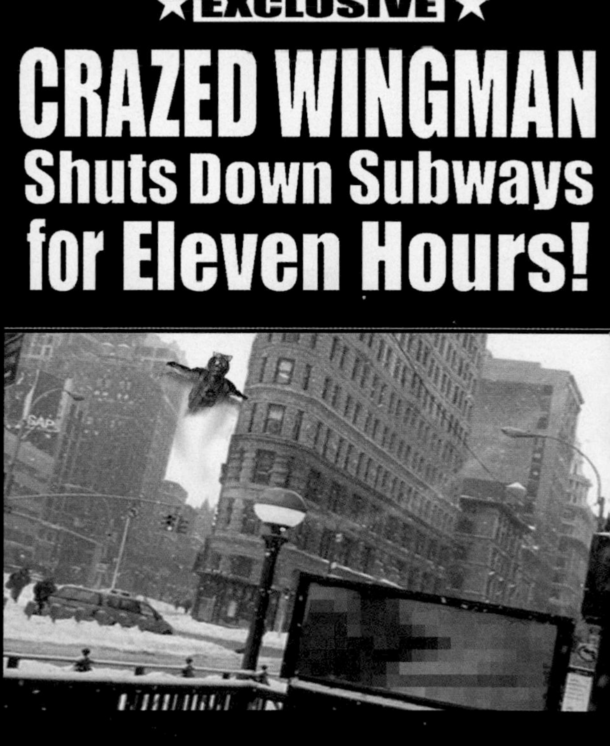

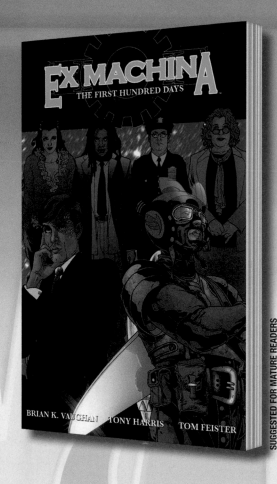
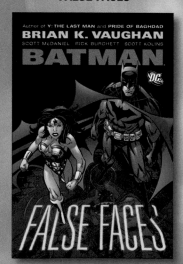